The Other Side of Grief

A volume in the series

CULTURE, POLITICS, AND THE COLD WAR

Edited by Christian G. Appy

The Other Side of Grief

*The Home Front and the Aftermath in
American Narratives of the Vietnam War*

Maureen Ryan

University of Massachusetts Press
Amherst

LC 2008031444
ISBN 978-1-55849-686-6 (paper); 685-9 (library cloth)

Designed by Dean Bornstein
Set in Adobe Minion Pro by BookComp, Inc.
Printed and bounded by The Maple-Vail Book Manufacturing Group

Library of Congress Cataloging-in-Publication Data

Ryan, Maureen, 1953–
    The other side of grief : the home front and the aftermath in American
narratives of the Vietnam War / Maureen Ryan.
        p. cm.
    Includes bibliographical references and index.
    ISBN 978-1-55849-686-6 (pbk. : alk. paper) — ISBN 978-1-55849-685-9
(library cloth : alk. paper)
    1. American literature—20th century—History and criticism.
2. Vietnam War, 1961–1975—Literature and the war. 3. Vietnam War,
1961–1975—Personal narratives, American. 4. Vietnam War, 1961–1975
—Influence. 5. Soldiers' writings, American—History and criticism.
6. Exiles—Vietnam—Biography—History and criticism. 7. War in
literature. 8. Soldiers in literature. 9. Peace movements in literature.
10. Prisoners of war in literature. I. Title.
    PS228.V5084 2008
    810.9'358597043—dc22   2008031444

British Library Cataloguing in Publication data are available.

for
Emily Bishop Ryan
Jack McDevitt Stone
and
Katherine Stone

It's the simple truth that many strange and inexplicable things happen in wartime. Ask any soldier.

—Ward Just, *Echo House*

War could, with art, be transformed into something deeper and more meaningful than its surface violence. . . .

—Ralph Ellison, Introduction to the 1982 Anniversary Edition of *Invisible Man*

Zoe was a doctor in her normal life, but now it didn't matter as she stood on the other side of grief.

—Mary Morris, *The Waiting Room*

Contents

Acknowledgments

The cultural narratives that I engage in this book affirm that the Vietnam War was the defining experience of an American generation. I am a member of that generation, and because I came of age against the backdrop of that vertiginous era, I was formed by its changes and challenges. Yet a subject and a project as expansive as this one inevitably—happily—inspires new interests and preoccupations; working on this book has, for instance, deepened my understanding of the military as an institution and my interest in contemporary Vietnam (a visit to which was one of the more satisfying adventures in this intellectual journey). In short, such an all-consuming venture has, of course, spilled over into the rest of my life—and has brought with it indebtedness to many friends and colleagues.

Over the years I have shared parts of this book with the Vietnam scholars of the Popular Culture Association—a group as varied and resolute as any combat platoon or counterculture commune. PCA colleagues such as Paul and Elizabeth Daum, Catherine Calloway, Tim Blackmore, John Baky, Ann Kelsey, Marilyn Knapp Litt, Renata Prescott, and our redoubtable leader, Mary Sue Ply—most of whom were in the business of making cultural sense of the Vietnam War before I was—have offered their support and feedback and shared their sincere commitment to academic study of the war and its era. Their contribution to this book is considerable.

I thank the University of Southern Mississippi for the support of the Charles W. Moorman Distinguished Alumni Professorship of the Humanities, an honor and a benison that facilitated the final stages of this project; in its early years, G. David Huffman and Myron S. Henry, the two provosts for whom I worked as a dean, supported my commitment to continuing my scholarly work while toiling as a full-time administrator. I offer my thanks, too, to my long-time colleagues, especially Peggy Prenshaw, David Wheeler, Noel Polk, Tom Richardson, Frederick Barthelme, Gary Stringer, and Stanley Hauer, who have been friends and offered academic inspiration throughout my career.

I am grateful to my students who have explored with me the texts and themes in this book. And to Paula Mathis, for being such a fine, daily friend.

My thanks to Clark Dougan and Carol Betsch at the University of Massachusetts Press, and to Philip Beidler and Christian Appy for their insightful, thoughtful responses to the manuscript.

I thank Deborah Ford, with whom I share an interest in this subject and so much more, for her friendship and support. And my family, who have always loved and nurtured me.

Earlier versions of some material in this book appeared in the following publications:

"Outsiders with Inside Information: The Vietnamese in the Fiction of the Contemporary American South." Reprinted by permission of Louisiana State University Press from *South to a New Place*, edited by Suzanne W. Jones and Sharon Monteith. Copyright © 2002 by Louisiana State University Press.

"Woodstock Nation: The Antiwar Movement in Postwar American Fiction," *War, Literature & the Arts* 14, nos. 1–2, Special Double Edition, 2002. http://wlajournal .com/14_1-2/260-279ryan.pdf.

"Pentagon Princesses and Wayward Sisters: Vietnam POW Wives in American Literature," *War, Literature & the Arts* 10, no. 2 (Fall/Winter 1998). www.usafa.af.mil/ dfeng/wla/wlafall/maureen_ryan.htm.

"Breakdown Territory: Aftermath Novels by Vietnam Veterans, 1976–1995," *Studies in the Humanities* 24, nos. 1–2 (June–December 1997).

"Robert Olen Butler's Vietnam Veterans: Strangers in an Alien Home," *The Midwest Quarterly* 38, no. 3 (Spring 1997): 274–294. By permission of the editors.

"The Other Side of Grief: American Women Writers and the Vietnam War," *Critique* 26, no. 1 (Fall 1994): 41–57. Reprinted with permission of the Helen Dwight Reid Educational Foundation. Published by Heldref Publications, 1319 18th Street, NW, Washington, DC 20036-1802. http://www.heldref.org/. Copyright © 1994.

Introduction

The Vietnam War and Modern Memory

The soldiers we sent to Vietnam were not the only ones who went. We were all there. And we all had a long journey to make together to get back home.

—Bobbie Ann Mason, *Clear Springs*

Looking back on it is something we'll do for a very long time. . . . It'll become an industry. There are so many of us who've been there.

—Ward Just, *The American Blues*

T HE cover story of the October 5, 2003, *New York Times Book Review*, a review of *American Woman*, Susan Choi's novel based on the Patty Hearst kidnapping, begins with author Sven Birkerts's assertion that "right now . . . we are awash in accounts of American radicals in the high season of the counterculture" (9). When he acknowledged early-twenty-first-century literary interest in the Vietnam era, Birkerts would not have known that that week's *Book Review* (a generic issue with no planned thematic coherence) would cogently confirm—and amplify—his observation about the counterculture and its motley compatriots in their electrifying moment of history. Elsewhere in the *Book Review*, the reader would encounter a lengthy review of Jessica Hagedorn's *Dream Jungle*, a novel about the filming of a Vietnam War movie in the Philippines. An ad for a book that purports to prove that "LBJ Killed JFK" counterpointed short notes on Maxine Hong Kingston's *The Fifth Book of Peace*, about a poet who flees to Hawaii to evade the Vietnam draft; Nell Freudenberger's short story collection *Lucky Girls*, which includes a tale about a teenaged girl's correspondence with a Vietnam veteran whose well-known fiction is about the war; and *July, July*, the new novel about the class reunion of a "large cast of baby boomers . . . and their long, strange trip from the glory days of the 1960s" by just such a famous writer, Tim O'Brien. The issue also featured a review of David Maraniss's *They Marched into Sunlight: War and Peace, Vietnam and America*, in which Vietnam veteran-author Philip Caputo confesses that "before I read this book, I thought everything humanly possible had been said about the Vietnam war and the 1960s—in fiction and nonfiction, in high culture and low, in film and on television" (10). Caputo's point is well taken. "Vietnam Vietnam Vietnam, we've all been there," plaintively proclaims the journalist Michael Herr at the end of his audacious 1977 book *Dispatches*, one of the earliest and most important literary treatments of American combatants' experience in Vietnam (260).

We've all been there, and a generation and more later we show no signs of forgetting—or fully apprehending—the (mis)adventure.

The national amnesia that followed the momentous decade that bracketed America's divisive military engagement in Southeast Asia was brief and without closure, and since the 1980s American society and culture have been awash indeed in the Vietnam War, its era, and its aftermath. Arguably, America's political life has been determined for the past half century by the debacle of the lost war. As Newt Gingrich, Karl Rove, and Rush Limbaugh might happily affirm, the disgraced Nixon-era attorney general John Mitchell evinced eerie prescience when he predicted in 1970 that, as a result of the excesses of the 1960s, "this country is going so far to the right, you are not even going to recognize it." For a generation or more after the Vietnam War, American foreign policy was largely dictated by our humiliating loss in Southeast Asia, as the country eschewed involvement in international imbroglios. Domestic politics are similarly influenced by the equivocal legacy of the Vietnam War. The presidential aspirant Senator John McCain's reputation as a forthright, independent national leader derives from his endurance of the horrors of the "Hanoi Hilton" as a Vietnam prisoner of war. The 2004 presidential election campaign witnessed partisans of incumbent president George W. Bush (who again successfully deflected the allegations of evasion of Vietnam duty that had not alarmed America's voters in 2000) torpedoing the candidacy of his Democratic opponent John Kerry by attacking both the legitimacy of Kerry's heroic performance as a navy Swift boat commander *and* his public opposition to the war after his return from Vietnam. As the election approached, the satirist Christopher Buckley concluded a *New Yorker* parody of campaign debate regulations with the proviso that "neither candidate shall mention the word 'Vietnam.' In the event that either candidate utters said word in the course of a debate, the debate shall be concluded immediately and declared forfeit to the third-party candidate" (51).

Vietburgers at Hedgestock

Satire aside, America's presence in Vietnam forty years ago resonates throughout everyday life in twenty-first-century America. The composer Tom Cipullo's 2006 opera "Glory Denied" is based on Tom Philpott's book about Jim Thompson, one of the longest-held American prisoners of the Vietnam War, who returned home after nine years to discover that his wife had moved on with her life because she assumed Thompson was dead. The *New York Times* tells us how to cook "Vietburgers," seasoned with lemon grass and *nuoc mam*, and served on a French baguette. John Lahr's *New Yorker* review of director Ang Lee's 2003 movie *Hulk* reminds us that the superhero "came of age in the mid-sixties, when the idea of protean trans-formation fuelled the drug culture and rock-and-roll revolution—a fantasy of escape from the oppressiveness of the Vietnam War" (72). Lahr notes, similarly, that in *Broadway Babies*, his book on "The People Who Made the American Musical," Ethan Mordden suggests that by 1970 Vietnam had wrought the demise of the "good-time musical" because "the culture had lost faith in both its goodness and its gladness" ("Sour Ball," 108).

The examples are legion. The question is why?

Why does the Vietnam War remain for Americans a prevailing influence, touchstone, and metaphor now, thirty-five years after its ignominious end? A simple explanation looks to the cultural hegemony of baby boomers—the generation that came of age in the Vietnam era and that manifests such a fond nostalgia for its eventful youth. In the summer of 2007, fortieth-anniversary celebrations of the Summer of Love that had introduced Amer-ica to hippies and Haight-Ashbury ranged from a Starbucks double CD commemorating the Monterey Pop music festival to the Whitney Museum of American Art's exhibit Summer of Love: Art of the Psychedelic Era. As-saying the remembrances of that 1967 San Francisco happening, which is generally regarded as the birth of the counterculture, John Leland notes in the *New York Times* the nostalgic, revisionist, and "narcissistic" impulse of today's cultural observances of it and suggests that "the past point[ed] to a more utopian future than the one it actually became." In acknowledging that current memories of the early counterculture present "now generic im-ages of gentle hippies and a swirl of pretty colors," while omitting the more ominous reality that, for instance, "by late summer LSD gave way to speed and utopian seekers to ill-prepared teenage runaways, children who could not take care of themselves," Leland recognizes that the influence of the Vietnam War and its era on American society is more complicated than baby boomers' simple nostalgia for their past. Much as John Lahr recognizes the loss of innocence that the era wrought, Leland articulates the dueling impulses of the social revolution that paralleled the prolonged, painful war. Our lingering fascination with the Vietnam War and the 1960s in America can be attributed, in part, to our inability to fully comprehend or agree about the varied meanings of that tumultuous era; and, I suggest, the ambiguity and complexity of the war's legacy both result from and contribute to the expansiveness of today's varied claims on its cultural memory. In *Newsweek* magazine's November 19, 2007, special issue, "1968: The Year That Made Us Who We Are," Jonathan Darman suggests that "all of us, young and old, are stuck in the '60s, hostages to a decade we define ourselves as for or against" (43). Or, as Bobbie Ann Mason acknowledges, culturally, psychically, emotionally . . . we were all there.

And yet, simplistic iterations of the era's "brandedness" (to use Leland's term) abound, and in realms that would discomfit those gentle hippies of forty years ago. In the summer of 2006, thousands of hedge fund managers and financial subalterns gathered at Hedgestock, an "alternative festival" in England that promised "Peace, Love and Higher Returns" and "aimed to marry the ideals, music and fashion of the 1960s with a networking event for the hedge fund world." Hedgestock, a *New York Times* account reports, featured music by The Who, who played at Woodstock in the summer of 1969, and "a painted Volkswagen bus and clean-cut guys wearing strings of love beads, floppy hats, tie-dyed shirts and bell-bottom jeans." Indeed, the entire financial services industry apparently believes that middle-aged baby boomers nearing retirement will conflate their desire for financial security with affection for their youth, now as faded as well-worn Levis. The recent national advertising campaign of the Ameriprise Financial division of American Express superimposes over photographs of a peace sign, long-haired hippies, and a disco ball the proclamation that "a generation as unique as this one needs a new generation of financial planning." GEICO automobile insurance magazine ads feature that ubiquitous Volkswagen hippie bus and the slogan "Survive the '60s? . . . You deserve special treatment." Allstate insurance company proclaims that "the generation that wouldn't trust anyone over 30 never planned on a 30-year retirement." Clever marketing appeals to affluent survivors of the Summer of Love are, of course, among the more superficial manifestations of, and explanations for, our society's

4

ongoing fascination with the Vietnam War era. In reality, cultural incarnations of the war in contemporary American society are not only inevitable but appropriate, for the impact on American society of that war and of the era's concomitant social movements was—and remains—fundamental and profound.

The Myth of the 1950s

Born in the immediate aftermath of their parents' "good war," the post–World War II generation grew up in the financially comfortable, socially complacent America of the 1950s and early 1960s. Or so the myth of the fifties would have it. In the modern suburban homes enabled by the new interstate highway system and paid for by GI bill–educated middle-class Americans, those babies of the boom years encountered the postwar world on new, magical television sets. Yet, much as current stereotypes about the 1960s are simplistic and inaccurate, the reality of the fifties is more complicated than the Ozzie-and-Harriet image allows, for the decade's iniquitous undercurrents were a harbinger of the unrest of the Sixties.

The Supreme Court officially desegregated American public schools in 1954, but Rosa Park's defiant "no, in thunder" the next year augured the racial conflict that lay just over that bloody bridge in Selma, Alabama. The era's scientific and technological advances brought an end to polio and a birth-control pill that would redefine sexual behavior in the years to come, but they developed from the anxiety that a new atomic era, fostered by a prevailing Cold War, introduced. A similarly menacing legacy of the new postwar world order was demagogic Senator Joseph McCarthy and a red scare that egregiously compromised the democratic values that had seemed so ascendant a decade before. In *The 1950s*, David Halberstam confirms that the social protests of the 1960s were nurtured in the earlier decade with his assertion that in the fifties, "as younger people and segments of society who did not believe they had a fair share became empowered, pressure inevitably began to build against the entrenched political and social hierarchy" (xi). But the celebrated antiwar activist Tom Hayden, at the beginning of his 1988 memoir *Reunion*, adopts the more simplistic representation of the 1950s: "The fifties were indeed the best of times for the pursuit of the American dream. After the trauma of two decades—Depression and Holocaust, two wars, the atomic bomb—came a dawn of stability and peace, along with a rising living standard, low inflation and unemployment rates. . . . it was a time of respite, when one could finally sit back and enjoy the good things in life, and raise one's children well. . . . It was in this atmosphere of affluence and affirmation," Hayden continues, "that we who were the future radicals of the sixties grew up" (3–4).

. . . And of the Sixties

Indeed, the youth of the sixties arrived at young adulthood amid a perfect storm of pervasive, transformative social movements that they had fomented. Early in the decade, inspired by the fight for racial equality, future antiwar activists journeyed to Mississippi and Alabama, where they networked and learned the social organizing skills that would, several years later, effect a large-scale domestic movement against the Vietnam War. As Christian Appy asserts, "the experience and example of challenging legal, political, economic, and cultural institutions that sustained racial inequality and division provided valuable political training for many who would later oppose America's actions in Vietnam" (142). Radicalized by their disaffection with a complacent American society, the nascent activists—before Vietnam became the exigent preoccupation of a generation of radicals, as Tom Hayden notes—affiliated to form Students for a Democratic Society (SDS) and to call, in the 1962 Port Huron Statement, for a new left that would foster a true participatory democracy that would emanate from "the independence of the ordinary people" (83). In the 1960s American society was transformed by the conflagration of assassinations and racial warfare, the movement against the widening war in Vietnam, internecine conflicts among family members as they took sides (often children against parents in the newly branded "generation gap") in the increasingly acrimonious national debate about the war, and a dramatic social realignment (or, as many would say, "erosion") in fashion, popular culture, behavior, and attitudes toward authority that accompanied the rise throughout the decade of the youth culture and the influential counterculture. By the early 1970s, the end of the draft and the long, painful trajectory of the U.S. withdrawal from Vietnam only intensified the virulence of the campaign to end the war, as the radical left of the antiwar movement lurched toward increasingly dramatic and violent actions, propelling the antiwar campaign, famously, "from protest to resistance."

Those docile hippies, the other children of Aquarius, seemed to grow out of flower power and folk music and into a manic embrace of psychedelic drugs and acid rock—and a willful repudiation of mainstream American culture. The separatist rhetoric of the Black Panther party, the hermetic anti-establishment violence of the Symbionese Liberation Army, and the senseless carnage of the Manson family fermented a witches' brew that bubbled ominously in a society that seemed perilously out of control. In 1962, the SDS had concluded its manifesto for participatory democracy with the idealistic avowal that "if we appear to seek the unattainable . . . then let it be known that we do so to avoid the unimaginable." A decade later it seemed that the unimaginable had arrived with audacious, frightening fanfare. America, Philip Roth and other cultural commentators have suggested, had gone berserk. Or, as Holland Cotter writes in the *New York Times*, "America was losing its mind to save . . . its soul."

And yet, again, the reality belies the widely documented, disparate myths that suggest that the era was a harmless if raucous saturnalia *or* the dissolution of polite society. In fact, those harrowing, exhilarating years brought an end to the war, demonstrable advances in civil rights, a modern women's movement that would radically redefine American women's lives in the decades to come, as well as a new sensitivity to threats to the environment and to the individual rights of previously silenced, invisible groups such as homosexuals, Native Americans, and other minorities. The period evoked both cynicism about government and broadly based movements for individual rights, at once an abrasion of respect for civility and civic life and a new tolerance for difference and individual expression. Such a profound and contradictory bequest promises a spirited, unfinished reckoning.

The varied commentary on the war only underscores America's persistent campaign to make sense of the cultural inheritance of the conflicted era. On the most literal level, ambiguity about even the facts continues to interest us. As recently as May 2007, for example, a man wounded during the May 1970 Kent State University shootings produced a newly discovered audiotape of the events on which, he asserted, there is an audible order to National Guard soldiers to fire on unarmed students—an allegation that contradicts the assertion of the post–Kent State tragedy's President's Commission on Campus Unrest that it could not determine whether officials had commanded troops to shoot. Of course, the more resonant—and unsettling—questions are interpretive and often, even now, politicized. An August 14, 2006, *New York Times* editorial, for instance, excoriates a proposed new Visitors' Center to be built underground near the Vietnam Veterans Memorial because it will "damage the clarity" of "what is perhaps the finest single memorial ever built in this country."

America's Wailing Wall

In fact, the Vietnam Veterans Memorial on the mall in Washington, D.C., surely the most visible national icon of the war and its aftermath, is an ideal illustration of the country's ongoing negotiation of the war's meaning. Launched by the Vietnam veteran Jan Scruggs in 1979, the campaign for a national memorial to Vietnam veterans coincided with the first wave of cultural narratives about the war and Ronald Reagan's optimistic call for a new morning for America. Competing claims on the monument (and, thereby, on the war) emerged when the competition for its design yielded, from more than a thousand proposals, Maya Lin's conceptualization of a dramatic abstract structure that was promptly and loudly dismissed as a harsh black gash that manifested the war's schismatic effect on American society and therefore dishonored its veterans. The fact that the designer was a woman, a student, and an Asian American only fueled the controversy. The disgruntled successfully advocated for the addition of a representational statue of three American soldiers and an American flag to make the memorial more traditional and more clearly heroic. Less than a year after the 1982 dedication of the Wall, Vietnam army nurse Diane Carlson initiated the also-controversial ten-year campaign to acknowledge the contributions to the Vietnam War of women veterans, which culminated in the 1993 dedication of a large sculpture of three female nurses and a wounded soldier that stands near—but decidedly separate from—the main memorial. Carlson and supporters of the Vietnam Women's Memorial Project boldly contested the narrow definition of "Vietnam veteran" implied in the original monument; their brochures and website remind us that Glenna Goodacre's statue acknowledges the "quiet heroes" of the Vietnam War, and that "women are veterans too."

In 1994, Gustav Niebuhr, acknowledging in the *New York Times* that "for years [the Vietnam Veterans Memorial] has drawn more visitors than either the Washington Monument or the Lincoln Memorial," anointed it as an American Lourdes, "a sacred shrine, where pilgrims come and devotions are paid." That the Wall would become a "hallowed site" was not, Niebuhr notes, "what the monument's creators envisioned." He quotes Jan Scruggs's bemused wonderment that "'here's essentially what is designed to be a military memorial commemorating people who took part in a military effort, and it's been transformed into a national shrine where all these feelings come alive.'"

Affirming this expansive, inclusive connotation of the Vietnam Veterans Memorial, countless American narratives of the Vietnam War conclude with a powerful, if sometimes sentimental, healing pilgrimage to the Wall. The veterans—like *Missing in America*'s Jake, *In Country*'s Emmett, *The Names of the Dead*'s Larry—pay a final call on long-dead combat buddies whose memories continue to haunt the guilty survivors. In *Let Their Spirits Dance*, Stella Pope Duarte offers consolation to an entire family grieving for its lost son during their visit to the "wailing wall" years after the war, and Wayne Karlin's Amerasian Kiet, in *Prisoners*, sees "Daddy daddy daddy daddy daddy 58,108 times" in the names on the granite wall, though she will never find her American father (99). On her excursion to D.C., when she finds, in what Karlin calls the "phone book of the dead," not only her father's name, but her own, Bobbie Ann Mason's Sam Hughes, in *In Country*, recognizes that it is as though "all the names in America have been used to decorate [that] wall" (*Prisoners*, 93; *In Country*, 245).

The Soul's Experience of War

The cultural texts about the myriad experiences of ordinary Americans in the Vietnam era, which both express and create the panoptic significance of the war and its aftermath that Sam Hughes's epiphany suggests, comprise a sizable and growing omnibus of narratives that, individually and collectively, negotiate the contested cultural space of the Vietnam War. Acolytes of the modern women's movement that arose out of the civil rights and antiwar movements famously insisted that "the personal is political"—a truism underscored by the literary artifacts of America's longest war, which, given its scope and the broad home front war against the war, directly touched many Americans (and, of course, the too often overlooked Vietnamese) and yielded powerful personal testimonies that present the impact of the war—on the battlefield, on the home front, and in the war's aftermath.

LaSalle University's special collection of Imaginative Representations of the Vietnam War currently includes some ten thousand short stories, plays, film scripts, works of graphic art, paintings, videos, TV productions, and sound recordings, including nine thousand novels and books of poetry. Much of this fictive writing, as LaSalle labels it, is, unsurprisingly, about Americans serving in Vietnam, particularly in combat situations. Scholarly commentary on these cultural texts about the combatants of the Vietnam War is, of course, plentiful as well. The important full-length critical cultural studies include Philip Beidler's *American Literature and the Experience of Vietnam* (1982) and *Re-Writing America: Vietnam Authors in Their Generation* (1991), Thomas Myers's *Walking Point* (1988), Jeffrey Walsh's *American War Literature 1914 to Vietnam* (1982), Susan Jeffords's *The Remasculinization of America* (1989), Philip Melling's *Vietnam in American Literature* (1990), Tobey C. Herzog's *Vietnam War Stories* (1992), Andrew Martin's *Receptions of War: Vietnam in American Culture* (1993), Donald Ringnalda's *Fighting and Writing the Vietnam War* (1994), Jim Neilson's *Warring Fictions: Cultural Politics and the Vietnam War Narrative* (1998), and Katherine Kinney's *Friendly Fire: American Images of the Vietnam War* (2000). Yet each of these books, each one insightful and salient, is limited by its almost exclusive concentration on literature written about and usually by the men who fought in Vietnam. As Lynne Hanley notes in *Writing War: Fiction, Gender and Memory*, the "premise that war literature is by and about men at the front remains the operative premise in our identification of what poems, memoirs, and fictions constitute our literature on war" (6). Like so many real and fictional veterans, who insist that "you had to be there" in order to understand the war experience, (mostly) male scholars and critics have neglected women's role in the Vietnam experience, as well as the antiwar movement, the aftermath of the war, the Vietnamese diaspora, and the larger relationship between the conflict in Vietnam and the social upheavals on the 1960s and '70s home front; that is, they have underestimated everything but the combat experience.

My interest here is in the "other sides" of the stories of the war: the side that lobbed its grenades across the dinner table rather than the foxhole; the side that waited and worried and had the oil changed in the car while the warriors "humped the boonies" on the other side of the world; the side that screamed that it all had to stop and dodged some home front artillery of its own on the streets of Chicago and idyllic university campuses; the side for which the domestic conflagration was only another chapter in its thousand years of war, and that, when it was finished—not finished, but finally ended—fled their homes to begin life anew in the most foreign of lands; the other side of the fighting for combatants who returned physically or psychically damaged to an America that they could no longer recognize—and that seemed not to want to recognize them. The Vietnam War stories that acknowledge the experiences and perspectives of the millions of Americans and Vietnamese who were—and are—directly touched by the war explain why this country remains fascinated with that long-ago event. There are so many of us who've been there.

Acknowledging both the variety of "sides" in the war and the confrontational implications of Mary Morris's metaphor—and this book's title—the phrase reverberates throughout the voluminous assortment of narratives that I consider in this book. Donna Moreau offers the nonfictional story of military wives and "this other, hidden side of the Vietnam War" (xv). The Australian journalist Kate Webb titled her autobiographical account of her brief imprisonment *On the Other Side: 23 Days with the Viet Cong*. Sigrid Nunez's novelist-narrator in *For Rouenna* recalls her friendship with a British journalist who had covered Vietnam in the 1950s and who shared with her his love of the food, the people, "the land of great green beauty . . . the other Vietnam." Several POWs dismiss antiwar activists who visited Vietnam as "on the other side." Author Jason Aaron's and illustrator Cameron Stewart's 2007 graphic novel *The Other Side* recounts the nightmarish combat experiences of two young soldiers, American and Vietnamese, as they approach each other for an inevitable confrontation. In an experience as protracted, controversial, and pervasive as the Vietnam War, and in its era's turmoil, there are many sides to the story—and, as these cultural narratives demonstrate, combat is only one of them.

In her 2003 novel *Grass Roof, Tin Roof*, Vietnamese American author Dao Strom introduces a narrator, Thuy, who was among the refugees who fled the "American War" for a new life in the United States. Thuy acknowledges that she did not suffer the violence and "damage" that characterize the "first form of war." But Thuy understands that there are other kinds of war that are "less talked about." It is the "soul's experience of war" and the "ongoing" third form, which has "more to do with what remains for those who survive," that, Dao Strom suggests, comprise the other sides of the traditional war narrative (162–163). The cultural narratives (novels, memoirs, films) that present the other sides of the Vietnam combat story—the stories of wives and children, Vietnamese émigrés and antiwar activists, soldiers who negotiate "what remains" for the rest of their troubled lives—dramatically expand and document the dominant narrative of the war.

Although I do not claim to offer an exhaustive survey of these creative narratives, my commentary is wide ranging and representative. I consider well known, canonized Vietnam texts such as Larry Heinemann's *Paco's Story*, Robert Olen Butler's *A Good Scent from a Strange Mountain*, and Philip Roth's *American Pastoral*, as well as little-known narratives (Mary Morris's *The Waiting Room*, for example, and Robert Bausch's *On the Way Home*) and more recent offerings. I analyze works by professional, noted authors (Tim O'Brien, Russell Banks) and by one-time or amateur writers (Sydney Blair, Sandie Frazier). I move freely among novels, short stories, movies, and memoirs or personal histories—texts that are rich, complex, well-written interpretations of the Vietnam War and its aftermath—and, frankly, simplistic, forgettable chronicles interesting more for their thematic insights than for their aesthetic merits (Patti Davis's *Home Front* comes to mind, but there are many).

Most of these authors came of age in the Vietnam era and are, apparently, writing from personal experience. Several, however (Norman Mailer, for instance, and Elizabeth Spencer), are older than the more common now middle-aged authors. A new generation of younger writers—Christopher Sorrentino, Dao Strom, Tim Farrington, Dana Spiotta, Nell Freudenberger, Stewart O'Nan, and lê thi diem thúy—promises that narrative interest in the Vietnam War will not retire with the baby boomers.

More than thirty years of cultural documents about the Vietnam War offer us compelling and complex insights into American life and American culture, now into a new century. Ward Just's Vietnam novel *The American Blues* introduces the plea that could well be the preamble to American culture for the past thirty-five years:

> This is not a story of the war, except insofar as everything in my unsettled middle age seems to wind back to it. I know how much you dislike reading about it, all dissolution, failure, hackneyed ironies, and guilt, not to mention the facts themselves, regiments of them, *armies*. But I must risk being the bore at dinner for these few opening pages, for the life of the war is essential to the story I have to tell. And that is not about the war at all but about the peace that followed the war.

Chapter One

MIA in America: Vietnam Aftermath Narratives

You made it back to the World. You have to be Missing in Action in America for the rest of your life.

—W. D. Ehrhart, *Busted*

Isolatoes *too, I call such, not acknowledging the common continent of men, but each* Isolato *living on a separate continent of his own.*

—Herman Melville, *Moby-Dick*

The men do go on about the war, don't they?

—Veteran's wife in Robert Olen Butler's "The American Couple"

J OHN Rambo has killed nine men and a couple of hunting dogs by the time that Special Forces colonel Sam Trautman arrives to rescue his "boy" from a small Kentucky town, two-thirds of the way through David Morrell's 1972 novel *First Blood*. Trautman is surprised that Sheriff Will Teasle, himself a medaled hero of the Korean War, has failed to recognize the hirsute Rambo as a veteran of the more recent Vietnam War. "We forced him into it over there," Trautman explains in defense of the unemployed, itinerant Green Beret, "and now he's bringing it all back home" (194).

In "Rambo and Me," his introduction to the 2000 reissue of *First Blood*, Morell recounts his decision in 1968 to write an adventure novel "in which the Vietnam War literally came home to America . . . that showed the philosophical division in our society, that shoved the brutality of the war right under our noses" (viii). Morrell's discussion of the ten-year effort to produce the 1982 film of the novel that launched the popular Sylvester Stallone Rambo movies echoes numerous accounts of early Vietnam War authors' difficulties in finding an audience for their subjects in a postwar America that wanted only to forget the disastrous recent war.[1] And his acknowledgment of the increasing "militarization" of the 1985 and 1988 Rambo movies (as well as the most recent iteration of the franchise, titled, simply *Rambo*: "Heroes never die . . . they just reload") reinforces Susan Jeffords's 1989 analysis, in *The Remasculinization of America*, of salient developments in the presentation of the Vietnam veteran between the 1982 movie *First Blood* and the 1985 *Rambo: First Blood, Part II*. Jeffords presents the transformation of the victimized Rambo in the earlier movie into the triumphant leader in the later as a representation of a late 1980s alteration in the image of the Vietnam veteran "in which the victimized soldier/veteran/American male [was] regenerated into an image of strength and revived masculinity" (130).

In the extensive postwar cultural evaluations, revisionist history, and scholarly commentary about the Vietnam War, the paramount subject is, understandably enough, the postwar plight of the Vietnam veteran. Over and over again, in early popular texts arising from the war, the veteran returns from Vietnam, not as a welcomed hero, feted with the parades and celebrations that greeted his father after his war—the "good" war—but as a scorned "baby killer," harassed by antiwar activists, misunderstood by embarrassed families, neglected by a government and a military distracted by the unpopular and increasingly disastrous war and by a home front riven by internal conflict. As John Wheeler stated in *Touched with Fire* (1984), "the Vietnam veteran was the nigger of the 1970s" (16). The transformation of the presentation of the Vietnam veteran between so-called first wave aftermath films like *First Blood*, *Cease Fire* (1985), and *Taxi Driver* (1976) and the more recent *Missing in America* (2005) and *Ulee's Gold* (1997)—and the degree to which these movies and a large group of novels and memoirs paradoxically manifest little change in perceptions about veterans' aftermath experience in the thirty years and more since the end of the war—document one of the more pervasive, important demonstrations of America's apprehension of the Vietnam conflict in the years after the war.

In his foreword to the 1980 book *Strangers at Home: Vietnam Veterans since the War*, Frank Freidel writes of the "suffering" of the "numerous veterans who have felt forgotten, unappreciated, and even discriminated against," the "shattered" men who "have been truly 'strangers at home'" (xiii). Yet exactly a decade later, in the revised edition of the book—citing the Veterans Administration's 1980 recognition of post-traumatic stress disorder, later federal laws ensuring Vietnam veterans' rights, the election of increasing numbers of veterans to political office throughout the eighties, and the large number of Vietnam books and films with veterans as protagonists—Charles R. Figley notes that "Vietnam veterans are emerging from being strangers at home to returning heroes, recognized for their sacrifices and unique strengths as well as problems" (vii).

What remains most intriguing about America's obsession with its Vietnam experience is the obsession itself. A fascinating component of the theme is the evolution of the dimensions of that fixation throughout the decades since the end of the war. Examples are numerous: the 1982 creation and continued popularity of the Vietnam Veterans Memorial, the plethora of television series and popular Hollywood movies—from *China Beach* and *Platoon* in the 1980s to *We Were Soldiers* in 2002—that continue to explore the Vietnam War, most from the perspective of the combat soldier; and the political significance of Vietnam-era activities for baby boomer politicians that surfaced first with Dan Quayle's vice-presidential candidacy in 1988, followed by Bill Clinton's problems with credibility due, in large part, to his resistance to and lack of service in the Vietnam War. The fixation culminated, for now, in the 2004 presidential campaign, in which old questions about George W. Bush's National Guard service yielded to virulent Republican objections to Democratic candidate John F. Kerry's role as an antiwar veteran after his valorous service as a navy lieutenant and Swift boat officer. More recently, the misguided policies of the government and the military in the Vietnam era are evoked as a foreboding parallel to the increasingly vexing and unpopular war in Iraq.

Most critics of the literature of the Vietnam War have recognized the changes in themes and attitudes toward the war and its participants in the cultural texts that chronicled the war's aftermath. In his 1988 *Walking Point: American Narratives of Vietnam*, Thomas Myers notes, as virtually all scholars have, that in literature, as in life, the Vietnam veteran "often became the despised and feared Other, the scapegoat for a variety of ills, the greatest of which was the failure to secure the familiar, unambiguous historical closure that is called victory" (189). Myers criticizes both the injustice of blaming the war's soldiers for America's collective failure *and* later attempts "to reinscribe the war as an American moral crusade" through cultural presentations of the veteran as "historical avenger" (191). Susan Jeffords in *The Remasculinization of America* presents one of the most cogent analyses of developments in America's attitude toward the war as they are depicted in cultural texts. Jeffords perceives that the representation of Vietnam veterans as victims—of the war, of the Vietnamese, of the U.S. government, of an inequitable draft, of American antiwar protestors, of the women's movement, of Agent Orange—underscored a broader problematization of masculinity; and that in the 1980s the Reagan-era "regeneration" of ill-treated veterans was an attempt to restore "their 'rights' and a return of their identity" and that of the patriarchy as well (127).

15

Jeffords's convincing appraisal of popular Vietnam movies reinforces the innumerable examples throughout American society of the gradual rehabilitation of the Vietnam veteran and the Vietnam War. As Arthur Egendorf asserted in 1985, "sympathy for the Vietnam veteran has now joined motherhood and apple pie as a hallmark of true Americanism" (29). And yet, the cultural artifacts that might seem the most likely to reflect this progressively positive perspective on veterans and the war—fiction, memoirs, and movies, most written by veterans themselves, about the "aftermath," the soldier's return to the "world"—demonstrate surprisingly little awareness of any evolution in social attitudes toward Vietnam vets or of the veterans' attitudes toward their own situation. Despite interesting variations in technique (and considerable inconsistency in quality) and with only a few exceptions, the creative narratives written throughout the years since the war about a veteran-protagonist's attempts to re-assimilate into American society immediately or long after his Vietnam combat experience—a group that begins with David Morrell's novel *First Blood* (1972) and Ron Kovic's well-known memoir *Born on the Fourth of July* (1976) and ends, for now, with Dave King's novel *The Ha-Ha* (2005) and Tracy Kidder's aptly titled 2005 memoir *My Detachment*—present remarkably similar themes and concerns and astonishingly little recognition that anything has changed for the Vietnam veteran over the past thirty-five years.

The great aftermath text of World War II was William Wyler's 1946 Academy Award–winning film *The Best Years of Our Lives*. Even immediately after America's triumphant mid–twentieth-century war, the title was ironic. Veterans were welcomed heroes after World War II, yet one of the protagonists of the movie returns to a family grown comfortably accustomed to his absence; another comes back to an unfaithful wife and no job; and the third embraces his loved ones with hooks instead of hands. But since it is a Hollywood movie, a happy ending is only a few hours away. The plot lines—if not the dénouements—are much the same in the imaginative narratives that present the homecoming of the American soldiers of the Vietnam conflict. Michael, in Robert Bausch's 1982 novel *On the Way Home*, who was mistakenly declared killed in combat, was instead captured and tortured by the Vietcong, from whom he escapes and returns to parents who have moved from his childhood home in Chicago to sunny Florida—parents who now must accommodate an emotionally fragile son whom they'd once thought dead. Tim Mahoney's Hollaran (*Hollaran's World War*, 1985) comes back to a wife who demands a divorce and a new boss who demotes the once-prized

16

employee. Bobby Wapinski's welcome home in John Del Vecchio's *Carry Me Home* (1995) is a girlfriend who didn't wait and a mother who has spent his combat pay as payment for his old bedroom (29). Tracy Kidder begins *My Detachment* with memories of his late 1980s interviews with veterans who, unlike him, spent their Vietnam tours in harm's way and his observation that "a lot of strange and violent experience had been transported back into the United States, into jails and treatment centers, and much more often into houses on quiet, tree-lined streets" (7). The future for Ron Kovic and *Fortunate Son*'s Lewis Puller, Jr., is as paraplegics; Braiden Chaney (in Larry Brown's 1989 *Dirty Work*) faces a pitiable existence propped up in a hospital bed as a torso that has lost all of its limbs; they make Harold Russell's missing hands in *The Best Years of Our Lives* seem like a minor inconvenience. Nineteen seventy-six, 1996 . . . these are the *worst* years of their lives. In the world beyond the Hollywood hills, there *are* no happy endings. And the reasons for and vicissitudes of modern veterans' postwar problems recur in book after book with notable similarity.

You Had to Be There

You had to be there. If there is a single theme that echoes most loudly throughout the Vietnam "aftermath" texts and combat novels of the past generation, it is the notion that only the soldiers who directly engaged this singular, complex war can ever understand it. It is this concept that privileges firsthand accounts of the grunts who survived the jungles of Vietnam, and, paradoxically, that accounts for the massive and endless testimony that they offer us. You had to be there. Most of you weren't, so you can't understand. But we'll try nonetheless—over and over—to explain it.[2]

There are, of course, thematic similarities among virtually all war literature. As Tobey C. Herzog notes, "literary war stories, across time, war, continents, and cultures, have common elements" (4). And those literary war stories have always privileged the exhilaration and horrors of the combat experience and the gripping testimony of combat's participants. In *Walking Point*, Thomas Myers discusses how the Vietnam War demanded a rewriting of the historical combat experience. Yet, he acknowledges, the authors of "the finest Vietnam prose narratives . . . as they enter new American terrain, pass a line of ghostly short-timers that includes Cooper and Melville, Crane and Hemingway, Jones and Mailer, Heller and Pynchon" (32, 33). It is the combatant, Myers asserts, "the foot soldier whose testimony, imaginatively and symbolically rendered by the literary point man, would be the most telling historical text" (30).

Yet Vietnam, it is now widely accepted, was unique. It was a war without a front line, where progress was measured by often illusory body counts, and the only movement seemed to be endless, circuitous marches through the hot, unfamiliar bush; a war in which American soldiers were never certain which of the odd-looking natives around them were enemies, which friends; a war fought in the dark of night. It was a war about which Tim O'Brien writes, "the old rules are no longer binding, the old truths no longer true" ("How to Tell a True War Story," 88). It was *not* your father's war.

But you had to be there to really understand that. Ron Kovic is hauled to a local Memorial Day parade and parked on the stage, to sit awkwardly in his wheelchair while the World War II American Legion vets preach about victory for America. Kovic wonders why he hasn't been asked to speak: "These people had never been to his war, and they had been talking like they knew everything." He senses that his war experience and wound mean that there is "something wrong" with him now, so that others have to "define for [him] with their lovely words what they didn't know anything about" (107–108). Ten years later, in his memoir *Passing Time*,[3] W. D. Ehrhart, back from Vietnam and now in college, defends William Calley and his men at My Lai to his girlfriend: "'Look, you don't understand what it's like. You got people trying to kill you every minute of every day and night. . . . You can't even begin to imagine what that does to your head after a while'" (54, 51–52). John Del Vecchio's *Carry Me Home* was published in 1995, but its setting is the period from its two protagonists' return from Vietnam in 1969 to Bobby's interminable Agent Orange–induced death in 1984. Twenty years bring no new insights to Del Vecchio; in fact, the central theme of his 850-page novel is precisely that no one back home understands his characters' Vietnam experience—or wants to: "'It's like nobody here has the vaguest idea what's happening over there. They don't know. They don't want to know. They don't want to know about our soldiers'" (84). Recovering from his medal-winning wounds in Tim Farrington's 2005 novel *Lizzie's War*, marine captain Mike O'Reilly notes that the warrior's slow acceptance of ignoble killing is "not something you wanted to wave a flag about, not even something you wanted to talk about. Just something so deep it changed you completely inside. And then you came home and everyone thought they knew something, everyone had their glorious opinion on war and why and the price of tea, and you just wanted to tell them to shut the fuck up. No one would ever know who wasn't there" (250–251). In short, as the seasoned grunt tells the FNG[4] in Stewart O'Nan's *The Names of the Dead* (1996), if "you haven't *seen* shit . . . you don't *know* shit" (117).

The power and authenticity of the boots-on-the-ground combat experience is the central theme of Michael Herr's 1977 personal journal, *Dispatches*—still widely acknowledged as one of the best books about the Vietnam War. *Dispatches* was perhaps the earliest narrative to suggest, in its fragmented, asymmetrical structure and prose style, that the ambiguous, absurdist undertaking in Vietnam could be captured only through a new kind of writing. As Herr suggests, "conventional journalism could no more reveal this war than conventional firepower could win it" (218). Thomas Myers maintains that "as a model of how the successful union of form and function may transmute private vision into public understanding, *Dispatches* remains the war's most distinctive and eloquent voice, its most abundant and demanding compensatory history" (*Walking Point*, 169). Like Norman Mailer's *The Armies of the Night*, *Dispatches* is a compelling example of the New Journalism, whose technical complexity mirrors the thematic ambiguities of the Vietnam War. Herr's structure (six discrete sections) and prose style (described best by the title of one of those sections, "Illumination Rounds") only underscore his thematic preoccupation with the complexities and ambiguities of the American experience in Vietnam, which he evocatively captures through the image of the outdated, humidity-damaged map of ancient Vietnam that opens the book and the "one-pointed and resonant" *non*-war story that introduces his account of his time in-country. Yet, for all his technical and thematic insistence on the uniqueness and elusiveness of the Vietnam War, Herr, too, endorses the familiar axiom that "you had to be there." The grunts "all had a story, and in the war they were all driven to tell it," Herr suggests in proud defense of his and his fellow *real* journalists' dangerous, difficult missions with the troops (29). And, indeed, Herr tells the stories of ordinary enlisted men: marines Mayhew and Day Tripper and their friend Orrin, whose wife's letter confesses her infidelity and who thereafter becomes "the crazy fucking grunt who was going to get through the war so he could go home and kill his old lady" (127); and the much-wounded Special Forces sergeant who is on his third tour of duty but refuses to go home to his wife and children because "as far as he was concerned, there was no place in the world as fine as Vietnam" (172); and the African American who won't shoot his gun for fear that he might kill one of "th' Brothers, you dig it?" (180).

Herr captures the true stories of the war, he suggests, because he is one of that elite brotherhood of journalists who eschew the official military briefings in Saigon known as the Five O'Clock Follies. "You had to leave the Dial Soapers in Saigon and a hundred headquarters who spoke goodworks and killed nobody themselves, and go out to the grungy men in the jungle who . . . killed people all the time," Herr asserts (42). Despite the famously inclusive conclusion of *Dispatches*—"Vietnam Vietnam Vietnam, we've all been there"—Herr, in fact, accedes to the veteran-author's insistence that you can comprehend the unique horrors of the Vietnam War only if you actually were there.

For these authors, indeed, America's failure to understand is often willful indifference. Larry Heinemann's ghostly narrator announces on page 1 of *Paco's Story* (1986) that "this ain't no war story" because "the people with the purse strings and apron strings gripped in their hot and soft little hands denounce war stories . . . as a geek-monster species of evil-ugly rumor" (3). Stewart O'Nan's Vicki, the unhappy wife of army medic Larry Markham in *The Names of the Dead*, cannot appreciate why her husband, thirteen years after his tour in Vietnam, still treasures his Vietnam photographs and spends his spare time leading a disabled vets' support group. "'You've got to stop wallowing in it,'" Vicki admonishes Larry; "'it's like a religion with you. . . . You torture yourself with it. That's what your group at the hospital's all about— keeping it fresh. God forbid you should talk to me.'" Larry replies: "'You don't want to hear it. . . . You think if you pretend it doesn't exist I'll forget about it,'" though later he wonders if Vicki makes a valid point about his inability to move beyond his Vietnam memories (367). Hollaran's war with the world at home begins when he returns from Vietnam to the recognition that no one "back here" cares about his Southeast Asian war. He wants to talk about Vietnam with his veteran buddy because "the bozos want . . . us to shut up," and he angrily claims the right to "fuck them, talk about it, shout it out, holler it in the goddam streets, don't let them ever forget it" (88, 103). But Hollaran and his friend never do discuss Vietnam, in part because of Hollaran's unusual recognition that he and Eddie have had very different wartime experiences, but more because these veterans' standard response to the "world's" apathy about the war is an unspoken commitment to silence (70).

Unspeakable Things Unspoken

For a few characters, the old Hemingway skepticism about abstract notions and language applies. "I was always embarrassed by the words sacred, glorious, and sacrifice and the expression in vain," notes Frederic Henry in the 1929 World War I novel *A Farewell to Arms*. "I had seen nothing sacred, and the things that were glorious had no glory. . . . There were many words that you could not stand to hear" (184–185).[5] "True war stories do not generalize," echoes Tim O'Brien in "How to Tell a True War Story"; "they do not indulge in abstraction or analysis" (84). Griffin, Stephen Wright's heroin-addicted protagonist in the unconventional 1983 novel *Meditations in Green*, declares that "the Bush was a professional secret. You didn't talk about it. Words were bars. What was important roamed free" (71). Others, like Brown's Braiden Chaney, recognize that the Vietnam experience must be like the issue of race in traditional American literature, "unspeakable things unspoken": "some things people just don't talk about" according to Toni Morrison (28). Chaney's new roommate, Walter James, admits to himself that "I don't like to think about . . . honor and duty and all that shit. . . . You either serve or you don't" (10). Acknowledging, as Mitchell Sanders wryly notes in O'Brien's "How to Tell a True War Story," that "'certain stories you don't ever tell,'" most of these alienated characters simply retreat—without explanation—to a silent, stoic renunciation of the world that has rejected them (83).

The first-person narrator of Richard Currey's 1988 novel *Fatal Light* tries to explain to a typically clueless woman why "nobody talks about it":

We're your basic silent types. We don't mingle.
Oh, right. A legion of Gary Coopers?
High noon. High noon in the rice paddies. (100)

If movie star–tough guy John Wayne is the recurrent metaphor for the fatally romantic macho-heroic myth that sent young American males to Vietnam (and that they haplessly took with them), the image of always-laconic midcentury film actor Gary Cooper is both a feature of that myth and their response to the betrayal of it.[6] The protagonists of Robert Olen Butler's 1981 novel *The Alleys of Eden* and the 1985 *On Distant Ground* are virtual twins; each a remarkably self-absorbed loner whose isolation from the world around him is the defining characteristic of the man—before, but especially after, Vietnam. Bausch's Michael is a boy who has always been a shy loner, and who is so debilitated by his horrific experience as a POW in Vietnam that he cannot discuss it, not even with the frustrated therapist who gives his patient a tape recorder on which to confide his secret anxieties. Michael loses the tape recorder and cannot revisit his trauma, even in his own mind.

Howie Kaposhat, the middle-aged veteran-protagonist of Dave King's *The Ha-Ha*, sustains a serious brain injury several weeks into his tour of duty in Vietnam, and although the small business card that he presents to strangers announces that he is "of normal intelligence," he literally cannot speak (61). And what we know of Paco's story we learn from Heinemann's ghost-narrator, for Paco keeps the terrors of his combat experience to himself. The unnamed first-person narrator of Ward Just's compelling 1984 novel *The American Blues*, is, like Just and Herr, not a combatant but a former Vietnam journalist who struggles to end his history of the Vietnam War. His wife, like O'Nan's Larry's, wonders why he can't forget about the war, and the frustrated author knows that, immured in the "penitentiary" of his obsession with the war, he is driving her away. But, he notes, "how could I explain that on a personal level the experience of the war was inalienable. You could not share it or transfer it or communicate it in any recognizable form. It was yours alone, your own shadow, a doppelgänger present night and day" (18). You don't talk about it—but you never forget it.

Chris Starkmann, the main character in Philip Caputo's *Indian Country* (1987), is, twelve years after his tour in Vietnam, a paranoid loner whose retreat to a virtual bunker in the forest cannot stave off his encroaching post-traumatic stress. Despite a supportive wife and a worthwhile job, Starkmann, who is proud of his macho stoicism, refuses all attempts to help him with his delayed post-Vietnam nightmares. His wife June observes that "he wasn't much for talking. [Her friend] Sandy . . . called him the reincarnation of Gary Cooper. *Yup. Nope.* He was a strange one, all right . . . quiet and self-contained, as though he were living inside an invisible phone booth" (117). Chris Starkmann keeps secret even from himself his debilitating sense of responsibility for the accidental death in Vietnam of his boyhood blood brother, Bonny George. Forced by the lunatic circumstances of a meaningless war to commit unspeakable acts, these men share their secrets with no one—not even themselves.

In one of the most interesting aftermath novels, Tim O'Brien's *In the Lake of the Woods* (1994), John Wade, twenty years after his Vietnam service, breaks the mold. Wade is less Gary Cooper than Harry Houdini, with a little Richard Nixon blended in as well. He is an amateur magician and a professional politician, a "sorcerer" whose manipulations of his life and his world succeed brilliantly until his Vietnam secret comes out in his campaign for the U.S. Senate. John Wade, as voters learn just one fatal month before the disastrous primary election, was a soldier under Calley at My Lai. And more: he falsified his military records to hide his service in that ill-fated, notorious company. Wade's secret is not, like Starkmann's, the unconscious repression of a memory too horrible to bear. His silence is not the skeptical withdrawal of Larry Heinemann's ghostly narrator in *Paco's Story*, who knows that no one back home wants to hear the tale. John Wade buries his war story because he knows that people *will* want to hear it. And yet, finally, John Wade is not very different from his fictional brothers. Like so many of these characters, John Wade is a Melvillean *isolato*, a loner from childhood, well before Vietnam. He offers an accounting of his past and his Vietnam atrocity to no one. O'Brien's narrator explains his protagonist's actions, both in My Lai and in his ensuing public life: "It *was* the spirit world. Vietnam. Ghosts and graveyards. . . . I know what happened that day. I know how it happened. I know why. . . . It was the wickedness that soaks into your blood and slowly heats up and begins to boil. Frustration, partly. Rage, partly. The enemy was invisible. They were ghosts. . . . But it went beyond that. Something more mysterious. . . . The unknown, the unknowable. The blank faces. The overwhelming otherness. This is not to justify what occurred on March 16, 1968. . . . Rather it's to bear witness to the mystery of evil" (203).

Finally, like the other veteran-protagonists, John Wade is a victim, unable to find forgiveness or understanding for predictable crimes in an insane war. A generation after W. D. Ehrhart's and Ron Kovic's surprise that their homecoming evokes no celebration "like in the movies, when the boys had come home from the other wars and everyone went crazy," returning veteran protagonists continue to express resentment at the home front's apparent indifference to their plight and react with a withdrawal into silence, just as they always have (Kovic, 104). The withholding of the sacrosanct combat experience only reinforces the truism that you had to be there.

A Great Division

In his 1984 memoir *Aftermath*, Frederick Downs, Jr., echoes Kovic's incredulity at the veteran's indifferent reception back home. After months of rehabilitation for his serious war wounds, amputee Downs, as he returns to the United States, looks forward to the "band and welcoming committee [that] . . . would be waiting for us—just like the movies and books had always portrayed" (95). That there is no welcoming celebration is the first and least of the unpleasant surprises that await the naïve army lieutenant, whose simplistic book recounts a divorce, outrage at antiwar sentiments, disappointment at the military's failure to provide psychological assistance for disabled veterans, and resentment that "the soldiers of Vietnam entered a limbo for years. Caused by a misperception of their role, they would be miscast as the villains in the historical morality play of America versus Vietnam" (234). Yet Downs prefaces his account of the lingering problems confronting Vietnam veterans, and his hope that his memoir will "explain why there are Vietnam soldiers who have lost their way," with the unexplored assertion that "most of us who went to Vietnam are stronger than our contemporaries who didn't" (xi).

This often-repeated claim about veterans' superiority is a predictable development from the assumption of ownership and the claim of the exclusivity of the war experience, and it is one that occurs most insistently in the inspirational memoirs of the most well-known POWs (see Chapter 3). In the 1984 frame that opens and punctuates the plot of Del Vecchio's *Carry Me Home*, Tony Pisano recounts now dead Bobby Wapinski's implicit rejection of Hemingway's skepticism about abstractions through Bob's declaration that service in Vietnam, whatever its torments, is an ennobling experience: "He'd say, 'I don't think I'd like the person I'd be if I hadn't gone.' Then he'd say, 'And if living with this pain . . . is the price, then I'll take it. I've seen the best. And the worst. But seeing the best . . . that makes it worth it. That inspiration. That awareness. . . . [Y]ou know the price. You know it applies here, in the World, not just in Viet Nam. You know honesty and honor and vigilance'" (3). Ward Just's journalist suggests that "it was a great division, those who attended the war and those who didn't. . . . I thought that the only thing worse than going to the war was avoiding it; those who were not there had no claim on those who were" (*American Blues*, 120). Paul Perry, the placid protagonist of Tim O'Brien's *Northern Lights* (1975), is the older brother of the returning veteran Harvey, who has always been the more adventuresome sibling, his father's favorite, "the brave balled bullock"; yet the novel subtly suggests that Paul assumes that his brother's combat experience is only more evidence of his dominance (9). Michael's parents in Bausch's *On the Way Home* struggle throughout the novel to understand their damaged, difficult son. Though (as in most of these texts) the father-son relationship is the primary theme of the novel, it is Anne, Michael's mother, who recognizes and explains to her husband that, as a result of his war experience, her son "knows more about people now than you or I will probably ever know" (187). In his elegant 1994 memoir *In Pharoah's Army: Memories of the Lost War*, Tobias Wolff, quoting a missionary doctor, notes, simply, that "war [is] God's own university" (99).

Even young Vietnam-era men who failed to serve accept the exception-ality of the combat experience.[7] When the veteran Emmett Wheeler, pro-tagonist of Wayne Karlin's 1988 novel *Lost Armies*, in his search for the truth about mysterious dead deer that plague his rural Maryland community, vis-its his local congressman, an acquaintance, he rankles at the politician's cam-paign photograph of himself proudly sporting a flight suit, "looking every inch the high-tech warrior . . . climbing out of the cockpit of a jet fighter and giving the thumbs-up salute with the hand . . . that had kept him out of the Vietnam War because of . . . 'a slight deformity of the wrist bone,' not quite bad enough to hurt his tennis game" (39). And the congressman, Mundy, admits to Wheeler that he "regrets not going" to Vietnam: "'It was our gen-eration's war, and given who I am, what I stand for in this country, I should have gone. : . . Sometimes I think I'm as haunted by that as any vet is by the war itself.'" Wheeler's disdain for the remorseful civilian's arrogant attempt to share the veteran's "testing in fire" is, understandably, palpable (43).

In Scott Ely's "The Child Soldier," the protagonist, Sam Knightley, middle-aged son of a World War II veteran, is caring for Dallas, the adopted Cam-bodian son of his own son who was killed in an automobile accident. Before his adoption, Dallas had been a boy soldier, and now, contemplating the adolescent's life in Cambodia, Sam—whom a childhood accident left unfit for military service and who had "remained at home when his friends were drafted during the Vietnam War"—observes that he "always felt that he had missed out on something. He realized Dallas was like his father. They knew things he did not know." (142). And middle-aged Wyoming rancher Gilbert Wolfscale, in Annie Proulx's 2003 story "What Kind of Furniture Would Jesus Pick?," who evades the draft because of a growth in his nose, hangs out at the VFW listening to his contemporaries' war stories. "He wanted to understand what he had missed," Proulx writes. "It had been the great experience of his young manhood and he had been absent. It was as though the veterans had learned a different language. . . . The veterans did not seem so much tragic victims as eccentric members of a select club. He felt himself an outsider. They had got the edge on him" (131).

It's Las Vegas

The non-veterans recognize, implicitly at least, what the veterans know: war can be exciting, exhilarating, and sometimes plain ol' fun. In his well-known 1984 *Esquire* article, "Why Men Love War," journalist and Vietnam veteran William Broyles, Jr., acknowledged that "most men who have been to war would have to admit, if they are honest, that somewhere inside themselves they loved it too, loved it as much as anything that had happened to them before or since" (55). F. Scott Fitzgerald acknowledges as much when he writes of his World War I–veteran-protagonist Dexter Green, in the 1922 story "Winter Dreams," that "he was one of those young thousands who greeted the war with a certain amount of relief, welcoming the liberation from webs of tangled emotion" (133). Ward Just—many of whose works explore the old canard that "men go to war because the women are watching"—reiterates throughout his work Fitzgerald's suggestion that Vietnam offered men a temporary evasion of daily life: "Some fled from boredom, some from problems of money or family or health. Most from women" (*To What End*, 73). "In war," Just writes, "all bets are off. It's the frontier beyond the last settlement, it's Las Vegas" (58). O'Nan's Larry Markham knows that, despite his wife's importunate insistence that he put Vietnam behind him, he wants to keep his Vietnam memories. Larry and his rap group vets "did not wish to get rid of it, even if that were possible. It was not a choice. The war lived within them like an extra organ, pumping out love and terror and pity for the world—a necessary, sometimes unwelcome wisdom" (175). Larry thinks that his one year in Vietnam somehow equals the rest of his life, and "occasionally he thought he wanted to go back" (5).[8] If, as Ward Just suggests, men love war because it's an escape from the mundane quotidian of life—Huck Finn slipping the cuffs of civilization by "lighting out for the territory ahead of the rest"—the vets here know that part of its appeal is, even so, another intense experience: a different kind of community.

A Kind of Family

Predictably, if you had to be there to "get" it about Vietnam, and if those who participate in the Vietnam combat experience are fortified by the crucible of combat, inevitably those who endure the unique terrors of the war in Southeast Asia share a special bond. *Lizzie's War*'s Mike O'Reilly is "oddly moved" by the marines he commands; and noting, again, that "it wasn't something you could explain [or] talk about," admits that "combat made a kind of family as real and deep as anything he had ever known" (195). The respected marine captain Mac Clare, protagonist of Donald Pfarrer's *The Fearless Man*, bestowing a Shakespearean "little touch of Harry in the night," inspects his troops as they prepare to engage the enemy and observes, with satisfaction, that "they and Delta Company were a single imperishable world unto themselves" (73). In 1982, in *The Names of the Dead*, Larry Markham escapes his fractured marriage and his strained relationship with his father in his rap group for disabled vets: "It was here, among the other men, that Larry felt most himself. He felt welcome and understood without having to explain" (28). And it is the loss of that combat brotherhood that the movie John Rambo most powerfully mourns at the end of *First Blood*. Michael Herr mythologizes a similarly sacrosanct brotherhood among the "beautiful lunatics" who are his fellow journalists—that special group that excludes the hack reporters who accept the military spin, the Italian fashion photographers, the Frenchmen still dining out on Dien Bien Phu—and consists of a small, special coterie of correspondents who live and breathe the war: "the war gave it urgency and made it a deep thing, so deep that we didn't even have to like one another to belong. . . . [J]ust because it was seldom spoken didn't mean that we weren't . . . in that terrible, shelterless place . . . grateful for each other" (224).

For wounded veterans, such as Meredith in Clyde Edgerton's *The Floatplane Notebooks* (1988) and *Coming Home*'s (1978) Luke Martin, camaraderie with members of one's fighting group is often subtly superseded by a subsequent and more compelling bond with other injured soldiers. During his long stateside rehabilitation, Lewis Puller, Jr., and his amputee roommate in *Fortunate Son* (1991) "host" a "diverse assortment of young marine and naval officers who entered our room in wheelchairs, on crutches, or using the unfamiliar prostheses that for many were to become lifelong companions." These damaged men, Puller notes, "bore the scars of a war that, whatever its devastation, produced a bonding among them far more powerful in some ways than the ties of family kinship" (202). And when Walter James, with his scarred face and problematic memory, is wheeled into multiple amputee Braiden Chaney's hospital room, in *Dirty Work*, Chaney recognizes that the reticent veteran is his savior, that James will come to understand why Chaney can no longer subsist in the VA "junk pile" for "leftover guys," and why he thus will agree to mercifully kill his tormented comrade (12, 49).

Back to the Raft

Many critics have explored literary narratives' evocation of this distinctive bond that combat evokes among warriors, which complicates the protagonist-combatant as *isolato* theme that *Paco's Story*, Robert Olen Butler's protagonists, and self-reliant movie hero John Rambo exemplify. A few authors daringly imply a more audaciously unconventional, thus obliquely rendered, emotional attachment between paired combatants. While the relationship between Mac Clare and his spirited wife Sarah is Pfarrer's primary subject in *The Fearless Man*, for example, the novel intimates (as the opening chapter, "Mac and Paul," implies) the close, almost loving friendship that develops in Vietnam between Clare and navy reserve chaplain Paul Adrano, before the latter is killed late in the novel. Andrew Martin, Susan Jeffords, Robin Wood, and other scholars have noted the vaguely homosexual relationship of Michael (Robert De Niro) and Nick (Christopher Walken), two of the three lifelong friends who go together to Vietnam from their Pennsylvania hometown in Michael Cimino's Academy Award–winning 1978 film *The Deer Hunter*. Close friendships, such as those of Chris Starkmann and Bonny George in *Indian Country* and Megs (Robert De Niro) and David (Ed Harris) in the 1989 movie *Jacknife*, reveal in Vietnam aftermath texts the implied homosexual bond that critic Leslie Fiedler famously recognized in American literature in his 1948 *Partisan Review* essay, "Come Back to the Raft Ag'in, Huck Honey!"

Veteran Wayne Karlin's slight but tortuous novel *Lost Armies* presents the postwar life of failed journalist Emmett Wheeler, who has returned to his boyhood home in coastal Maryland, where he teaches English to the local Vietnamese immigrants. Wheeler begins a love relationship with a young Vietnamese woman, Xuan, but the unfolding of the plot reveals his lifelong preoccupation with his boyhood friend, fellow Vietnam veteran Dennis Slagel, Xuan's former boyfriend and notorious local troublemaker. Orphaned outcasts in their adolescence, Wheeler and Dennis embrace each other as "found brothers," obdurate residents, the adult Wheeler remembers, of "a world where only he and Dennis lived" in an "almost unnaturally deep friendship" (38, 55, 38). The renegade war-obsessed Dennis's Vietnam atrocities have alienated Wheeler, but Wheeler, who wants only to forget the war, returns to their shared home "as if Dennis had a wire hooked to his heart" when he hears from Dennis several years after the war (93). Wheeler ignores, as the reader cannot, the homoerotic undertones of his relationship with the mercurial Dennis, yet he fondly recalls his adolescence trotlining with Dennis, his friend's "skin and slabs of muscle gleaming wet"; and when, on weekend leave in Okinawa, he and Dennis share two bar girls, "the divisions between them melted away—watching the undulating thrust of Dennis' body into his girl's was to Wheeler like watching himself; he felt what Dennis felt" (42, 65). Karlin presents Wheeler's quest to discover Dennis and the meaning of his ostensible, mysterious deer-killings as an exorcism of the madness of Vietnam, but it is no surprise to Wheeler, or to readers of *Lost Armies*, that Wheeler's former lover, Karen, thought of Dennis as her "main rival" (33).

In aftermath texts by and about Vietnam veterans, the familiar representation of the combat veteran as a stoic, heroic, independent loner intersects with the apparently contradictory truism that war forges irrevocable bonds of blood-brotherhood. Alone, or with his combat brethren, the Vietnam veteran testifies always to the exclusivity of war.

America Gone Berserk

And, these texts proclaim, for many veterans the privileged inimitability of the combat experience is only reinforced by the alienating home front once the soldier returns to The World—a society not only inimical to veterans of an abhorrent war, but transformed by the manic excesses chronicled by Philip Roth in *American Pastoral* and by countless other accounts of the antiwar movement and the counterculture. Variantly, the thoughtful memoirists Tracy Kidder and Tobias Wolff qualify the claim to veterans' superiority while internalizing the essential and profound otherness of the Vietnam veteran. Discharged after four years in the army and a tour of duty in Vietnam, Wolff knows, at the end of *In Pharoah's Army*, that though he will be welcomed home by his mother and brother, and despite no other plans, he cannot go to his family: "I thought of my friends and family as a circle, and . . . it didn't seem possible to stand in the center of that circle. I did not feel equal to it. I felt morally embarrassed. . . . a sense of deficiency, even blight, had taken hold of me. In Vietnam I'd barely noticed it, but here, among people who did not take corruption and brutality for granted, I came to understand that I did, and that this set me apart" (195). In *My Detachment*, noncombatant Kidder, who dismisses the myth of the returning vet spit upon by antiwar protestors as a fantasy that speaks to veterans' "disappointed expectations,"[9] echoes Wolff's sense of dishonor at his return to The World: "I felt ashamed, of the uniform itself, of almost everything I could remember doing in it, and of everything people would think I had done in it but, sad to say, I hadn't done" (182). But for far more of the veterans and veteran-protagonists, the painful homecoming attests more to an "America gone berserk" than to a soldier transformed by the Vietnam experience (*In Country*, 106).

At the end of *Vietnam-Perkasie*, marine sergeant W. D. Ehrhart returns to his Pennsylvania home town after his thirteen months in country, increasingly infuriated by his recognition that he's still too young to buy a drink or a car, his community's indifference to his return, his girlfriend's casual dismissal of their relationship, and a "whole [country] gone crazy. . . . bass-ackwards . . . *worse* than Nam" (409). "Everything's . . . different," Ehrhart haltingly explains to his mother as the book ends. "It's not the same anymore. . . . It feels like I finally managed to escape from Jupiter—and I've ended up on Mars" (416). In *Indian Country*, Chris Starkmann withdraws from society to "a marginal life" when he returns from Vietnam because "there seemed to be turmoil everywhere he went. . . . His country . . . was pulling itself apart. . . . He could find no common ground with those who had not shared his experiences, and avoided those who had" (106). In Pfarrer's *The Fearless Man*, Mac Clare returns from service in Vietnam to a country in which "something . . . was broken. He did not recognize it as his country now. Arriving at home, that is to say, in a split nation occupying the same ground as that once occupied by America" (535).

Earlier in *The Fearless Man*, a nurse called The Destroyer (a rare in-country American woman in a male-authored Vietnam text) explains to chaplain Paul Adrano that she has just returned for a second tour of duty in Vietnam because "I never knew how it was changing at home. There's still a country on the map called the U. S. of A., but America, as far as I'm concerned, has ceased to exist." (371). Returning to (or remaining in) Vietnam is indeed an option for some estranged veterans, like The Destroyer and Snake, the gung-ho soldier in James Webb's combat novel *Fields of Fire*. For John Del Vecchio, the logical reaction to the "guts and balls and courage [and a]udacity" that Bobby Wapinski discovers in Vietnam, and his aftermath recognition that "this world is going nuts," is High Meadow, a "contrast community [of veterans]—set apart but not isolated—apart from the callous, chaotic, and corrupt world which I see about me" (3, 364, 405). The nascent High Meadow, a utopian "gathering, a cause, an evolution of thought about energy, about veterans, about the self" is to be founded on a nebulous code "tempered in the ovens of alienation, estrangement, self-imposed exile, expatriation" (551, 184). (Del Vecchio, it seems, has not read Hemingway.) But in 1984, when Bobby dies, High Meadow remains an unrealized dream. Travis Bickle (Robert DeNiro), the vaguely alienated veteran-antihero of Martin Scorsese's acclaimed 1976 film, *Taxi Driver*, acts alone—and violently—to "wash" the "scum" from the mean streets of 1973 New York City. As a mirrored Travis admires his armed self (in the famous "you talkin' to me?" scene), the narrator warns that "fuckers, . . . here is a man who would not take it anymore. A man who stood up against the scum."

That Heavy Heart-of-Darkness Trip

The various responses of the postwar veteran to his experiences in Vietnam and, thereafter, his estrangement from an unsettled and unsettling America metamorphose into another theme that recurs throughout aftermath prose, with subtle variations, regardless of the time of publication: the protagonist's prolonged battle with his own private Vietnam horror—a single epiphanic experience that defines his postwar readjustment; what Tobey C. Herzog (quoting Michael Herr) calls "a heavy heart-of-darkness trip" (24). Related to the notion that the Vietnam experience was too bizarre and horrific to be understood or shared is the literary commonplace that each man's personal journey within our national misadventure left him with a private legacy of secret pain. Invariably, literary veterans grapple with a debilitating physical or emotional trauma, the often-suppressed memory of committing an atrocity, or both.

Robert Bausch's 1982 *On the Way Home* offers, in Michael, a young man who returns from Vietnam physically unharmed but psychologically devastated. Bausch's novel is perhaps the first to present the ruinous effects on his immediate family of the veteran's maladjustment. Neither his psychiatrist nor his patient, if bewildered, parents can assuage the overwhelming fear that is Michael's bequest from the horrible torture that he survived in Vietnam. The novel ends with Michael's breakdown and his mother's reluctant acknowledgment that her son will have to be re-hospitalized. Bausch offers hope that his protagonist will eventually heal, but the novel ends with a young veteran whose emotional wounds remain raw and deep.

The array of fictional and autobiographical representations of emotional and psychological war-induced trauma is, of course, broad and varied. The stereotypically pathological veteran behavior offered in early texts like *Taxi Driver* and *Cease Fire* yielded, after the diagnosis and public acceptance of PTSD (post-traumatic stress disorder), to more sympathetic explorations of the postwar aphorism that "not all wounds are visible." Director Emilio Estevez's 1996 movie *The War at Home* (based on James Duff's play *Home Front*) offers a family drama about the drafted veteran Jeremy Collier's (Estevez) 1972 "final battle . . . waged along an unrecognized front." Jeremy's upper-middle-class parents (played by Martin Sheen and Kathy Bates) blithely advise their obviously troubled son to "forget about" Vietnam and, with Jeremy's increasingly estranged and erratic behavior, even his sympathetic sister eventually dismisses him as "disgusting . . . weirdo . . . crazy." Suffering from flashbacks to combat in Vietnam, Jeremy confides to his sister, just before his father throws him out of the house, that "I died" in Vietnam.

There can be no callous advice to "get over it" for veterans whose injuries are visible, physical, and unquestionably debilitating and whose stories present what amputee-autobiographer Frederick Downs, Jr., calls "a different kind of conflict—what a wounded soldier must endure while he travels the long road home" (xi). Multiple amputee Lewis Puller, Jr.'s "long road home," which he partially chronicles in the Pulitzer Prize–winning memoir *Fortunate Son*, meandered through alcoholism, professional success, clinical depression, and divorce before ending in his 1994 suicide. Dave King's Howie is a compassionate, lonely, intelligent man trapped in a mute, isolated body. Steven (John Savage), *The Deer Hunter*'s amputee, refuses to leave the hospital until Michael forcibly takes him home before embarking on his unsuccessful return to Vietnam to rescue Nick.

Larry Brown's protagonists are, like their injured brothers, unadulterated victims of the vagaries of war, and unlike Michael, Jeremy, and Steven, Braiden Chaney and Walter James have coped with their respective injuries for twenty years. Chaney exists literally and barely propped in a hospital bed, virtually helpless without legs and arms, and determined to convince James, his new roommate, to help him end his intolerable and hopeless existence. Walter James's life is only slightly better; he ventures out only after dark from his room in his mother's house, to which he banishes himself to spare the world the sight of his ruined face. These characters suffer lasting, debilitating injuries from their Vietnam service; and yet, in some ways they are no worse off than their brothers who return home apparently, though misleadingly, unscathed. In fact, their physical and psychological victimization seems to innoculate them against a more complex, and more common, guilt.

Robert Olen Butler's characters Cliff Wilkes (*The Alleys of Eden*) and David Fleming (*On Distant Ground*) inhabit different novels and lead unconnected lives after Vietnam, but they served together, and they shared the torture and subsequent death of a Vietcong prisoner—an act that Fleming commits, but in which Wilkes feels complicit (*Alleys*, 38). Wilkes deserted from the army, in part because of his guilt over this incident, and *The Alleys of Eden* begins with the fall of Saigon, when the cerebral former soldier must decide how to extricate himself from his hiding place in the city. Wilkes's desertion has reinforced his separateness from everyone in his life. His Vietnam atrocity thus effects and represents this character's inability to commit to the army, to his Vietnamese lover Lanh, or, on his return home in the second half of the novel, to his country. "I am . . . the hated stranger. I am the amputated leg," Wilkes understands late in the novel, before his final desertion to Canada, which, he knows, will not "be a home" for him (197, 256).

Ironically, *On Distant Ground*'s Fleming has been indicted and found guilty by the army of letting an enemy prisoner escape; he is absorbed and pleased by this "softening of his heart," and neither he nor the army is much interested in the other prisoner's death. His only remorse for the death of the "bland and inaccessible" Viet Cong soldier is "over the fact that he felt no remorse" (26–27). Fleming's lawyer explains to him why the army finds him guilty, not of killing a prisoner, but of freeing one: "The Army had a gutful of self-condemnation in the Calley trial. Your mystifying bit of compassion is far more provocative to them. . . . That's what they can't tolerate" (27). The military expects and forgives atrocities; it does not allow for kindness. Like O'Brien, indeed most veteran-authors, Butler perceives wartime atrocities as understandable (therefore forgivable) actions in an irrational war.

Most Americans came face to dark face with American atrocities in Vietnam with journalist Seymour Hersh's late 1969 exposé of the 11th Brigade Charlie Company's massacre of several hundred civilians in the village of My Lai the previous March. In early 1971, the Vietnam Veterans Against the War's Winter Soldier Investigation into alleged American war crimes, followed several months later by the Senate Committee on Foreign Relations hearings at which a young John Kerry testified that American soldiers committed torture and other atrocities against Vietnamese prisoners and civilians "on a day-to-day basis and with the full awareness of officers at all levels of command," made the questionable conduct of American combatants a newly troubling aspect of the war and offered fresh support for antiwar activists' insistence that the United States withdraw its troops from Vietnam.[10]

Vindictive, violent actions against combatants and civilians have, of course, always been a component of war, as ancient war stories like the *Iliad* and the mid-nineteenth-century adoption of the first of the Geneva Conventions that regulate wartime activities indicate. But it has been suggested that the commonly accepted peculiarities of the Vietnam War created a battlefield experience particularly conducive to deviant, horrific actions. As early as 1971, at the Winter Soldier hearings, the psychiatrist Robert Jay

33

Lifton asserted that "there's a quality of atrocity in this war that goes beyond that of other wars in that the war itself is fought as a series of atrocities. There is no distinction between an enemy whom one can justifiably fire at and people whom one murders in less than military situations. It's all thrown together so that every day the distinction between every day activities and atrocities is almost nil. Now if one carries this sense of atrocity with one, one carries the sense of descent into evil."[11]

The atrocity is a powerful convention of the Vietnam combat narrative, and for most combatant-authors the "the descent into evil" inspires a meditation on the distinction between guilt and responsibility that John Kerry espoused in his April 1971 Senate committee testimony. When committee member Senator Claiborne Pell asked him to comment on the prosecution of Lt. William Calley for the My Lai massacre, Kerry affirmed that Calley's actions were "a horrible thing," but insisted that responsibility for My Lai lay with "the men who designed free fire zones [and] encouraged body counts" and a country that "glorifies the John Wayne Syndrome." James Webb, in his 1978 pro-war combat novel, *Fields of Fire*, brooks little sympathy for his college-boy marine protagonist Goodrich's quibbling moral qualms about his fellow soldiers' in-country "tragedies": "Every day, some new horror inflicted in the name of winning Hearts and Minds," Goodrich notes. "He tried to count the tragedies. The villages they had assaulted. . . . Shot dogs and chickens and hogs. Accidental wounds and deaths of civilians. . . . It had become a familiar sight, from some black-humored theatre of the absurd" that inspires "no outrage" from his compatriots (199–200). When sanctimonious Goodrich reports his comrades' retributive murder of two Vietnamese civilians, Webb's irony is obvious and damning: Goodrich's betrayal of his fellow soldiers denies sympathetic protagonist Snake the posthumous medal that he earns for saving Goodrich's life. Yet Goodrich's reluctant trials on the fields of fire transform him; the befuddled, hesitant college boy who joins the squad at the beginning of the novel is, by its end, an eloquent apologist for the corrupting influence of the war: "You drop someone in hell and give him a gun and tell him to kill for some goddamned, amorphous reason he can't even articulate. Then suddenly he feels an emotion that makes utter sense and he has a gun in his hand and he's seen dead people for months and the reasons are irrelevant anyway, so *pow*. And it's utterly logical, because the emotion was right. That isn't murder. It isn't even atrocious. It's just a sad fact of life" (407).

A more sympathetic marine, Lt. Philip Caputo, in his 1977 memoir *A Rumor of War*, offers a more serious examination of guilt and responsibility for battlefield atrocities. Late in his rotation, with his C Company enduring high casualties and a low kill ratio, Caputo reflects on his commanding officer's incentive of an extra beer ration for any marine who kills a Vietcong: "So we went along with the captain's policy, without reflecting on its moral implications. That is the level to which we had sunk from the lofty idealism of a year before. We were going to kill people for a few cans of beer and the time to drink them" (294). Soon enough, with his platoon decimated, Caputo indulges the temptation to retaliate against the resourceful enemy, and, because he and his men share an "unspoken understanding," he knows—and accepts—that his order to capture two alleged Vietcong will result in their execution. And like Tim O'Brien's John Wade, Caputo covers up his men's murder of an innocent man—an act that results in a court martial and Caputo's careful defense of his actions. Caputo acknowledges his own guilt and reflects that "the war had awakened something evil in us, some dark, malicious power that allowed us to kill without feeling," but he decides that the murder is "a direct result of the war. The thing we had done was a result of what the war had done to us" (309). And because Caputo and his men are good soldiers, because their conviction "would prove no one was guaranteed immunity against the moral bacteria spawned by the war," because "no one wanted to confront his devil" (as Butler's lawyer recognizes), the charges are dropped, and Caputo, the "moral casualty," is absolved of his crimes in the morally ambiguous war (309, 313–314).

The aftermath narratives of course take a longer view of the ramifications of exposure to, and complicity with, atrocities in Vietnam. *Indian Country*'s Chris Starkmann, as obsessed with his experiences in Vietnam and as self-involved as Butler's veterans, suppresses his heart-of-darkness encounter, which he cannot remember, let alone consciously engage or overcome. Like Chris Taylor in Oliver Stone's *Platoon* and Goodrich in *Fields of Fire*, Starkmann went to Vietnam voluntarily, inspired by his boyhood friend's willingness to fight and the injustice of a system that would draft an Indian boy while he, the privileged young white man, hid in college. Years after his return from Vietnam, having created a tenuous life in a world that seems, after Vietnam, "as alien and hostile as the one he had left," Chris is haunted by combat dreams and the fear that he will break down, as he did after his mysterious horrific experience in Vietnam (97).

As Chris's precarious life—his marriage, his job—begins to unravel, his response to the return of the nightmares and daytime blackouts that catapult him back to Vietnam is to withdraw even further into himself, until his wife forces him to talk to a clinical psychologist who works with "war veterans with emotional problems" (215). Eventually, the psychologist helps a reluctant Starkmann remember the war experience that he has suppressed for a dozen years—that, with his commander and radioman dead in a firefight, a panicked Chris, calling in an air strike on the enemy, misread the coordinates and inadvertently summoned friendly fire on his own company, a company that included his boyhood friend, Bonny George. Long after the doctor explains "survivor guilt" and convinces Starkmann that "chance"—not Chris—killed his friend, the troubled vet ventures, quite literally, into Indian country, to seek forgiveness from Bonny George's grandfather, Wawiekumig, and finally from himself. At the end of the novel, absolved, reborn, a new Starkmann, now "returned to himself," can finally leave Vietnam behind and return "home, the place he had not seen or been these many years" (433).

It takes Chris Starkmann twelve years to come to terms with a wartime horror that is not an atrocity but a mistake. Eight years later, Del Vecchio's Tony reconciles his wartime atrocity when the Veterans Administration learns to treat traumatized veterans. By 1972, Tony Pisano has been in and out of the hospital—misdiagnosed, over-medicated, and ill-treated—several times. Unable to maintain his marriage or a job, Tony drifts in and out of his family's life until he is assigned to a doctor who is "experimenting" with therapy instead of drugs for Vietnam veterans. Leading Tony through his anger about America's failure to win in Vietnam and its "devaluation of [its soldiers'] sacrifice," the therapist helps him to remember that he shot a Vietnamese woman and children (469). But, the doctor tells Tony, he shot the unarmed civilians because "you were afraid the enemy soldier was going to shoot you and you needed to lay suppressive fire even if the woman and children were in the way" (471). Tony must admit to his guilt, which is the cause of his self-destructive behavior, then forgive himself for his understandable and inevitable wartime actions: "You're not alone, Tony. Many men err under the stress of combat. You're not perfect. None of us are. You don't have to hold yourself up against some impossible John Wayne standard. It's okay, Tony. It's okay" (471).

And it *is* okay. The war crime is unearthed, then forgotten—in the novel and in Tony's life. While it would be interesting to observe an evolution in attitudes toward wartime atrocities between Caputo's 1987 novel and Del Vecchio's 1995 text, the latter's relatively cavalier presentation and dismissal of Tony's "mistake" is more likely the result of his more limited talents as a novelist and his more simplistic pro-war sentiments. Though Caputo presents, in *Indian Country*, a serious portrait of a complex man psychologically devastated by his experience in Vietnam, Del Vecchio's aftermath novel is a superficial if ambitious pro-war indictment of America's behavior in Vietnam and its treatment of its veterans. In its tendentious didacticism and its attempt to examine every conceivable aspect of every veteran's postwar experience, it glibly offers and dismisses, but does not explore, Tony's atrocity. So willing is Del Vecchio to attribute all such actions to the vicissitudes of an ill-fated war that he cannot consider Tony's possible culpability in the murder of civilians. Del Vecchio implies that because such events happened in Vietnam (though not—as O'Brien and Caputo suggest—because of any evil inherent in the individual soldiers or in the war itself), they appear in *Carry Me Home*; but his dismissal of Tony's action implies nothing more than his inability to integrate the experience into the character and the novel. For Del Vecchio, the atrocity is a simple convention of Vietnam literature.

Like Butler and Caputo, other authors offer more sophisticated treatments of the theme. In Tim Mahoney's satiric *Hollaran's World War*, it is perhaps the lighter tone that accounts for the approach to the ubiquitous atrocity. Hollaran's central Vietnam memory involves the day that his platoon sergeant, Hoover, "a lifer . . . with his head stuffed full of army crap and regulations," on a sweep of a peasant village, orders the protagonist to search a tunnel (84). Instructed to kill whoever may be hiding in the tunnel, Hollaran almost shoots a small Vietnamese girl (87). The near-atrocity is more traumatic for Hollaran than Tony's actual murder is to him: "I felt something change inside me. Because . . . if I had pulled that trigger, the stain would have been black on my soul forever. But just on mine, do you understand? Because nobody in America would have known or cared. . . . I knew I was on my own. And I realized the Viet Cong weren't my only enemy" (88). The real enemy, Hollaran now recognizes, is "everybody who was back here" (88). Once again, if you weren't there, not only don't you care, you are actively hostile to the defeated warriors. Later Hollaran tries to understand a subsequent incident, when, during a nighttime firefight, he turns on and nearly shoots Hoover: "I actually saw bullets from my rifle ripping through his chest. But the last shred of sanity or whatever kept me from twitching my finger. But it was hard . . . I had to strain to keep my finger still, because . . . it was like I had been taken over by some force. I mean, I wasn't myself anymore" (111).

Hollaran begins to forsake the residue of his Vietnam ordeal, finds a decent job and a sympathetic girlfriend, and by the end of the novel declares an end to his world war. But Mahoney demonstrates that even the *possibility* of culpability that Vietnam forced upon its participants is an incapacitating postwar memory. Compare Wheeler, the veteran-protagonist of Wayne Karlin's *Lost Armies*. It is years after the war ("We're suddenly out of the closet—they build a memorial, and the vets give themselves a parade, and all the movies they couldn't make before come out" [9]), and Wheeler, another loner with a failed career, is nonetheless anything but obsessed with his Vietnam experience. In fact, Wheeler rejects the image of the stereotypical veteran, "the deliberate reduction of complexity to fit an image. The vet. It wasn't him. He was too many other things" (52). Wheeler resists wallowing in his Vietnam experience. He fears "using the war as his own excuse, playing the reclusive vet or the man with a quest as if he were hanging his life on some TV movie dealing with last week's burning social issue" (40). But the Vietnam War returns to Wheeler with a vengeance when mutilated deer begin turning up in his hometown. Recognizing the mutilations as identical to ones committed on the Vietnamese during the war by his boyhood friend, Wheeler, in searching for Dennis, must mentally revisit the scene of Dennis's madness. Wheeler takes some pride in the memory of his tenuous ability to resist the opportunities for atrocities in Vietnam. Flying above the ground as a helicopter gunner, Wheeler "cultivated the detachment of a bird": "When he heard pilots and crewmen talk casually about the villages they'd strafed, he didn't blame them—they took fire from those villages, lost helicopters, men. They shot at their own terror. He didn't blame, but he didn't do it either. The people they strafed had faces for him. . . . it was his personal point of honor, the only one he had. But he'd remained the detached observer: he'd bought his innocence by killing no innocents" (57–58). Wheeler is a good man, and part of the proof is his investigation of the deer killings and subsequent vindication of his friend Dennis. But Wheeler is an intelligent man, and he knows that his virtue is fragile. He recalls that in Vietnam, soon after he learns of Dennis's atrocities, he—like Hollaran—came all too near to his own heart-of-darkness debacle. The chopper pilot, "tired of" taking "fire from an island of thatched huts in the middle of a sea of paddies," tells his crew to "shoot it up." Wheeler "touched the trigger. The village was a village of ants, of lice that crawled over dead bones, and he had the freedom of a god. Wires wound around his insides since birth had eroded to thin rust: they were simply not there. He knew he would fire. . . . In his mind he saw the people he'd known in villages torn to pieces by his rounds. He felt nothing" (58). Just before Wheeler shoots, the helicopter veers away, but "it didn't matter to him. He knew he had eaten the meanness of war" (58). Again, even the atrocity that *didn't* happen consumes and defines the Vietnam veteran.

The common aftermath pattern, then, is that the veteran who survives and endures a serious physical wound is immunized against the atrocity experience and its consequent guilt, while the physically unharmed veteran is invariably deeply damaged by his crimes, near-crimes, or lethal mistakes in Vietnam, all of which attest to his having "eaten the meanness of war," a meal that effects "an alchemist's transformation in him and define[s] him forever" (*Lost Armies*, 59). Michael Cimino's *The Deer Hunter* introduces the pattern in its presentation of a precise trinity of protagonists: the physically wounded combatant (double amputee Steven), the psychologically devastated soldier (Nick), and the apparently well-adjusted veteran who assumes responsibility for his damaged brothers (Michael). Only a few authors proffer protagonists who endure both the lingering pain of perilous physical injuries *and* the shame of committing war crimes—protagonists who are, in short, both victim and agent.

Probably, like Del Vecchio, because of his inability to fashion a well-crafted, complex narrative, Ron Kovic does not explore the moral elements of the relationship between his own misconduct in the war and his devastating injuries, but it is surely there. Kovic drops hints throughout his narrative of the event finally recounted in the final section, when, in the chaos of a firefight, Kovic—like Chris Starkmann and (maybe) O'Brien's John Wade—accidentally shoots his own corporal. Struggling to understand how such a mistake could occur ("It never did in the movies. There were always the good guys and the bad guys. . . . The good guys weren't supposed to kill the good guys" [194–195]), Kovic is proud and delighted when the unconcerned major to whom he has confessed the incident gives him "a second crack at becoming a hero" by sending him into the bush as the leader of a scout team (198). During the next firefight, Kovic and his fellow soldiers—again, by mistake—fire on unarmed children; Kovic tries to bandage the wounded as his lieutenant admonishes the upset men: "You gotta stop crying like babies and start acting like marines! . . . It's a mistake.

It wasn't your fault. They got in the way" (208). Now convinced that his only way out of the war is to be wounded, Kovic begins "taking all sorts of crazy chances" (210). Still trying to "prove to myself that I was a brave man, a good marine" and "to make up for everything that had happened," he—predictably, inevitably—is shot (218–219).

Kovic's account of his injury is illogical and poorly presented. In the last few pages of the memoir, he claims a desire to prove his courage *and*, somewhat contradictorily, to atone for his sins. He asserts that after so much killing he feels nothing; yet after he is wounded he feels "good inside. Finally the war was with me. . . . I was getting out of the war and I was going to be a hero" (221). The book ends with the most confused and incredible claim of all, his revelation that "all I could feel was the worthlessness of dying right here in this place at this moment for nothing" (222). Kovic seems unconcerned about the inconsistency of his claims, both to courageous heroism *and* to a recognition that his wound is "for nothing"; yet this final revelation rings true only years later, after Kovic's conversion to an antiwar position. Ron Kovic only vaguely understands the connections between his wartime murder and his own injury.

But in the National Book Award–winning *Paco's Story*, Larry Heinemann evocatively presents the intersection of Paco Sullivan's wounds and his culpability for his actions in Vietnam. Taciturn Paco Sullivan, the sole survivor[12] of Alpha Company's annihilation at Fire Base Harriette, left for dead for two full days, now is at home, drugged, in pain, peripatetic and alone. Only late in the novel do we learn that Paco, the injured victim, has inflicted some arbitrary damage of his own during his tour of duty. Tormented by the flirtatious games of Cathy, the young "prick tease" who lives in the room next to his in the seedy Geronimo Hotel, Paco fantasizes about wild sex with a perhaps-willing Cathy (186). Suddenly, helplessly, he remembers a Vietnam rape: a "hardcore VC" teenager, captured, gang-raped, "ground . . . into rubble," and finally shot by Paco's angry company to avenge her murder of two of their compatriots (180). Paco's reluctant memory of the incident, in which he participated, is slow and detailed, described in twelve full pages of text in a two-hundred-page novel. The narrator, the ghost, tells us how, after the woman's death, some of the men "lingered with resentful and curious fascination," staring at the body, recognizing "that this was a moment of evil, that we would never live the same" (185). But Paco mentally returns, without comment, to the reality of Cathy having desultory sex with her boyfriend next door. The next (and final) chapter introduces more about Paco and his actions in Vietnam. We learn that Paco is the adept and efficient "company booby trap man," even though such "mechanical ambushes," the narrator notes, "are clearly illegal and expressly forbidden according to the Geneva Convention Rules of War, and to use them is a war crime. . . . However, the zips used booby traps . . . and since what is good for the goose is sauce for the gander, everyone used them (190, 192–193). And once, while setting his illegal traps, Paco has wounded and then (slowly, expertly) killed a "zip" whose cries threatened to expose his position (194). It is Paco's skills with booby traps that facilitate his easy entry into Cathy's room, where he reads her diary and learns of her complex fascination with him, the scarred veteran.[13]

Paco, remember, is a silent, unreflective protagonist. But Heinemann shows the intricate relationship between his veteran's lingering Vietnam wounds and his liability for wartime abominations. At the end of the novel, Paco's participation in the rape and murder of the Vietnamese woman intersects with his desire to rape Cathy, who is both attracted and repulsed by the evidence of his war injuries. Paco has experienced the ultimate wartime horrors—near-deadly combat that literally scars him forever, and clear, willful violations of acceptable combat behavior. His victimization—the evidence of which is visible and irreparable—and his culpability converge in his sudden departure from the rooming house and the small anonymous town where he washes dishes at the local greasy spoon, which is his refusal to confront either. Heinemann's lyrical invocation of the complexities of the atrocity for the Vietnam vet is a more subtle variation on Caputo's investigation of the legacy of shame and guilt. Paco, as far as we know reticent Paco, does not feel guilt about, or even particular interest in, his principal Vietnam action; yet it is clearly inextricable from his Vietnam wound and his inability to undertake a normal human relationship.

Tim O'Brien's *In the Lake of the Woods* varies the pattern. John Wade's atrocity is *the* Vietnam atrocity, the quintessential atrocity for any war—the My Lai massacre.[14] Wade has shot an unarmed Vietnamese civilian; then, in the chaos of the massacre, one of his own men. Later, when another soldier, recognizing the enormity of what happened at My Lai, suggests to Wade that they must report the event, he feels "the inconvenient squeeze of moral choice. . . . There was his future to take into account, all the dreams for himself" (218). John Wade doesn't tell—not anyone, not ever. Just before his tour of duty is up, he gets posted to a desk job in the battalion office. And to compound his crimes—the murders of the Vietnamese civilian and his own

fellow soldier and his unwillingness to come forward to report the atrocities—Wade neatly doctors his records. The Sorcerer Wade weaves his magic,
reassigns himself to Alpha Company, erases from the official account of his
life Lt. Calley and My Lai and a man with a hoe. He gets away with it, too;
for twenty years anyway, until the stakes in a U.S. Senate campaign compel
someone to uncover—and publicize—the truth of John Wade's Vietnam experience. In the wake of his devastating election loss, the first (but career-
ending) setback of his magical public life, Wade's wife disappears from the
remote cabin in the north woods of Minnesota, where they have fled to recover from the humiliation and mend the fabric of their strained marriage.

In the Lake of the Woods is a mystery story. Did Sorcerer kill Kathy in
his despair over his mortifying defeat? Did she—tired of her husband's
machinations, confronting marriage to a man she doesn't know, a man
who could kill at My Lai and keep it a secret, even from his wife—quietly
flee? Did they plan her disappearance and his flight, at the novel's denouement, into the wilds of the northern border, where they will secretly meet
and start life over, together, somewhere new? O'Brien's narrator considers
each of these possibilities, and he explores fully the role of the My Lai
massacre in the story and in his protagonist's life. He cites the experts on
"the psychiatric casualties" of war, the strains of combat under which any
man will break down (27). But he quotes as well Wade's mother and others
who know him well, who describe a man whose fundamental personality, whose values and behavior, were formed well before and beyond his
Vietnam experience. John Wade knows that what happened at My Lai was
"sin . . . not madness" (110). He knows that "at some point he'd caught a
terrible infection. . . . Moral disunity, [that he is] a lost soul" (280–281). But
he considers himself a virtuous man, and he—the Sorcerer, the magician—
believes that he can pretend it didn't happen (68). And now, years later, John
Wade acknowledges, with a bitter irony, that people will think him capable
of killing his wife *because* of his actions in Vietnam (249). Like other veterans, he knows that no one understands: "He couldn't blame them. He'd
tried to pull off a trick that couldn't be done, which was to remake himself, to vanish what was past and replace it with things good and new. He
should have known better. . . . And no one gave a shit about the pressure of
it all" (238). O'Brien's narrator understands how John Wade can erase that
day at My Lai, and that in "the overwhelming otherness" of Vietnam, such
things could and did happen (203). In short, he explores John Wade's guilt
and his victimization, his concerns very much like Webb's and Caputo's

and Heinemann's and those of the other combat and aftermath narratives discussed here. But for O'Brien, the atrocity, and therefore John Wade's entire Vietnam experience, is the context for examination of a larger theme and a more profound moral issue. It is the lie, the deliberate falsification of his experience, that seals John Wade's fate, morally at least. Thus, Tim O'Brien, twenty years after the Vietnam War, creates a protagonist whose war atrocity becomes rich material for a life and a fictional world more complex and therefore more interesting than those presented by authors who have not moved out of the jungles of Vietnam, whether they write in the 1970s or the twenty-first century.

Because the Women Are Watching

In the Lake of the Woods provides an expedient transition to another common theme/convention of the Vietnam aftermath novel: the protagonist's usually troubled relationship with the woman in his life. Kathy, John Wade's wife and the character whose disappearance launches the plot of the novel, is problematic in *In the Lake of the Woods*. In a novel whose major theme is the mystery and uncertainty of life ("Nothing is fixed, nothing is solved. . . . Our whereabouts are uncertain. All secrets lead to the dark, and beyond the dark there is only maybe" [304]), Kathy is a particularly ineffable (and finally unsatisfying) character; certainly less complex and less important in the book than Wade the Sorcerer, the master of mystery. And yet she is infinitely more successful as a character and more significant in the text and in the protagonist's life than the wan women who hover in the shadows of many of these aftermath narratives.

The mystery about Kathy Wade and her whereabouts after her disappearance is crucial to O'Brien's novel. After twenty years as the perfect political wife, falsely smiling and gazing adoringly as her husband shines in the spotlight, she is liberated by Wade's devastating defeat from the political arena that she loathes. But Kathy is more complex than she appears: a brief, unsatisfactory affair some years earlier, for instance, offers a hint of her unhappiness. We learn, too, of her grief over the pregnancy that John has convinced her to end because a child does not fit into his career plans. And though Kathy does not know until the world does about her husband's Vietnam secrets, she does know that for years he has spied on her. In fact, after her disappearance, a friend conjectures that Kathy is complicit in Wade's sorcery: "Kathy *knew* he had these secrets, things he wouldn't talk about.

43

She *knew* about the spying. Maybe I'm wrong but it was like she needed to be part of it. That whole sick act of his" (97).

We don't know much about Kathy—in part because the novel demands that she be elusive and mysterious; in part because O'Brien (whether from lack of ability to create her as a fully developed character or because his interest is so much more obviously in John Wade) fails somewhat in his presentation of her; though we *do* know that her husband, who claims to and seems to love her, almost certainly either kills her or drives her away from him and their marriage. And yet, despite Wade's criminal, or at least deceitful, treatment of his wife, this is one of only several novels of the group considered here that offers a fully developed and narratively satisfying female partner and male-female relationship.

The other male-authored texts that feature "round," complex female protagonists are fictional (two novels and a movie) and, though the novels are quite recent publications, set during rather than after the war, they share a narrative interest in the wartime lives of loyal military wives struggling to cope alone at home while their officer husbands are in harm's way.[15] And, like novels such as Mary Morris's *The Waiting Room*, Susan Dodd's *No Earthly Notion*, and Marge Piercy's *Vida*, as well as several of the memoirs by female activists, military wives and daughters, and POW wives, they include at least an implicit recognition that the strains of wartime for women at home were exacerbated and complicated by the burgeoning women's movement and inchoate but looming dramatic changes in modern American women's lives.

Lizzie's War, post-Vietnam-generation author Tim Farrington's 2005 well-made family drama, recounts, in alternating chapters, career marine officer Mike O'Reilly's 1967 to 1968 tour of duty in besieged Khe Sanh and his whiny wife Lizzie's struggle to (as the *New Yorker* review of the novel notes) "dodg[e] domestic schrapnel" as she copes, stateside, with a difficult and unwanted pregnancy and four young children; including a daughter whose Girl Scout–like group resists accepting a black member and two war-obsessed sons who (as Lizzie and the novel tell us over and over) are clones of their warrior father. Though she is not meant to be, Lizzie is a remarkably unlikable protagonist—disorganized, self-pitying, and shallow. Her opposition to the war ("'A glorious death in a stupid, ugly war is still just a stupid, ugly way to die'") is more resentment of her husband's absence than a thoughtful response to an objectionable war (41). And her dissatisfaction with her own life is less regret that she has traded in her nascent acting career for single motherhood than . . . well . . . resentment at her husband's absence:

> "My husband's off fighting a noble war I really couldn't care less if we won or lost. He's been training his whole adult life for this, and he's happy as a pig in shit. And I could just kill him. I'm in there praying for him to just dodge the bullet of history and get himself back here in one piece . . . and I'm thinking, Honey, you idiot, what are you *doing*? Come home, for Christ's sake. Be a father to your children. Fight the goddamned North Vietnamese when they land in North Carolina. And meanwhile . . . I'm nothing. I'm a cipher. I can't even fight racism in the local Bluebird troop. As least Mike's willing to die for something. I can't even *live* for something." (156)

Though a devoted father and husband, Mike is preoccupied with his beloved Marine Corps and the distractions of war. His letters to Lizzie offer glib, sardonic commentary ("I'm sitting here . . . in my [new] . . . subterranean dwelling. . . . The only real drawbacks are the lousy climate and noisy neighbors. However, be it ever so humble, etc. Let's face it, you can't beat the price") rather than meaningful sentiments or information about the war and his well-being, and when he suffers what the novel misleadingly presents as life-threatening wounds, he doesn't even call home to tell Lizzie that he's been hurt (266). Yet, the novel suggests, vaguely, Lizzie matures and the O'Reilly marriage is strengthened as a result of Lizzie's own war wound— the death of her infant daughter. Mike returns home, scarred but safe, and . . . eventually . . . asks about his dead daughter. Lizzie auditions for a play at the local theater. And so this sentimental novel promises a Hollywood happy ending: "It only seemed like everything had been on fire for a while; it only seemed that the world should be charred and ruined" (367).

Vietnam veteran Donald Pfarrer's more accomplished 2004 novel *The Fearless Man* presents in Sarah Clare a more nuanced and complex character than Lizzie O'Reilly, though the novel concentrates much more than *Lizzie's War* on co-protagonist Mac Clare and his combat experience in Vietnam, and on a 1968 America that continues to smolder. Like Lizzie, Sarah has given up a career as an actor for marriage and eventual motherhood. Though avowedly devoted to Mac and their marriage, twenty-six-year-old Sarah—like her husband, a considerably more introspective character than Farrington's protagonists—struggles to discover her life: "Not just a wife, she was now in the process of defining herself, as a human being. . . . She saw it as her duty, her life process, to wait watchfully for a clearly defined role. She was alive to possibilities, or strove to be" (34). Though Mac, as he confides to his friend, chaplain Paul Adrano, is excited about his postwar plans for "Sarah, babies, home, peace, love, and good cooking," Sarah is reluctant to become pregnant and expedite their planned quiet, modest life until Mac is safely home. And Sarah's stern, widower father—who dislikes Mac because of his rejection of law school for an uncertain postwar future and disapproves of Sarah's dalliance with playwriting—reminds his daughter that she must not count on her husband's return or on his protection. "The world is changing in a way that could transform your life," Sarah's father notes farsightedly, as he attempts to persuade her to go to law school. "The new women will paint their names on the door" (310). Though Sarah rejects her father's careerist advice, she accepts that "you can't make a living out of loving somebody, you've got to do something," that devoting one's life to marriage and motherhood is the outmoded model of "an earlier generation" (177).

Set in 1968, Hal Ashby's Academy Award–winning 1978 film *Coming Home* more manifestly juxtaposes the insanity of the Tet-era Vietnam War, home front unrest, and protagonist Sally Hyde's sexual and emotional awakening. When marine captain Bob Hyde (Bruce Dern) happily heads to "Combat City," his wife Sally (Jane Fonda), ousted from their officers' quarters, finds her own house instead of living, as Bob instructs, with his parents. A volunteer job at the local military hospital introduces Sally to the seriously injured veterans whom her fellow military wives willfully ignore and to former high school classmate Luke Martin (Jon Voight), a paraplegic veteran who offers her emotional and sexual satisfactions of which her healthy husband is incapable. Sally, newly orgasmic, with her liberated curly hair, her new convertible, and her house on the beach, knows that Bob "is not going to like the fact that I've changed. I've never been on my own before." When Bob returns from Vietnam, angry and alienated, with his embarrassment at his self-inflicted wound exacerbated by his discovery that he is a cuckolded husband, his dramatic suicidal baptism liberates Sally to—if not her own life as a feminist heroine—at least a loving relationship with her wounded antiwar veteran.

Coming Home, The Fearless Man, and *Lizzie's War* are aberrations in the canon of home front or aftermath narratives by men, most of which offer as their female characters familiar stereotypes, such as the unfaithful wife or girlfriend who cheats on her man while he risks his life in Vietnam (the "Dear John" letter is indeed a commonplace throughout Vietnam narratives). Ehrhart's, in *Passing Time*, is the almost-universal experience: "We were going to be married as soon as I got home. And then one day amid the heat and boredom and loneliness, . . . the Dear John. Suckers like me in every war, I thought" (19). Memoirist Frederick Downs and fictional protagonists Cliff Wilkes (*Alleys of Eden*), Bobby Wapinski (*Carry Me Home*), and Hollaran (*Hollaran's World War*) are all betrayed by the stereotypical unfaithful woman. And, of course, sexually frustrated Sally Hyde's infidelity, the principal theme of *Coming Home*, contributes to the suicide of Bob, the thwarted war hero, at the end of the movie.

Then there is what the narrator of *Paco's Story* calls the "prick tease," the young, sexy, ruthless woman whose fascination with the protagonist's wartime experiences—but whose lack of serious interest in him—leads her to torment him for her own amusement. Paco's Cathy is the definitive example of the type. Lucy, in *On the Way Home*, casually befriends and flirts with Michael, aware of but blithely unconcerned about his emotional instability. When she disappears briefly toward the end of the novel, everyone believes (mistakenly) that Michael is responsible. Larry's neighbor Donna begins an affair with him when each of their spouses leaves in *The Names of the Dead*; but though she loves Larry, at the end of the novel she returns to her husband. Tony Pisano fantasizes about his cousin Annalisa in *Carry Me Home*, but the late-1960s reality of Annalisa's audacious behavior—too much dope, group sex—is more than even Tony can handle.

Like John Wade, the older protagonists whose lives are somewhat more stable than, say, Michael's and Hollaran's often attempt serious relationships with women. But, again, one-dimensional female characters who embody yet another stereotype—the long-suffering wife—are the rule. Memoirist Lewis Puller's wife Toddy stoically sustains her wheelchair-bound husband through punishing physical rehabilitation, an unsuccessful political campaign, alcoholism, and depression (though the couple separated after the 1991 publication of *Fortunate Son* and just before Puller's 1994 suicide). Jennifer, David Fleming's wife in Robert Olen Butler's *On Distant Ground*, is a patient, loving woman who supports her husband during his military trial and later, when he becomes obsessed with the search for his half-Vietnamese son. Fleming's sole emotion about his wife is his frequent, calm recognition that his lifelong habit of detachment makes him "unable to give Jennifer what she needed" (69–70). Like the novel itself, Fleming is not to the slightest degree interested in his wife or in their relationship. Del Vecchio's Tony's wife Linda is an endlessly forbearing woman who waits literally years for Tony to come to terms with his Vietnam experience and be ready to live a stable life with her and their children. Bobby Wapinski survives his girlfriend's infidelity and his first wife's callow materialism and eventually finds a kind, loving woman in Sara, who stands by Bobby throughout his prolonged death. She is a devoted mother, a right-minded community activist, a supportive wife, but she is no more central to the novel or to Bobby's life—or more credible—than the secondary female characters in the book, who are always (*always*) dismissed as either "bimbo" or "psychobitch." In fact, Bobby's relationship with his dog is more sustained and more meaningful than that with his wife (or his children).

Philip Caputo gives us (and Chris Starkmann) a real, fully developed woman in *Indian Country*. Indeed, the character of June, and Caputo's concomitant recognition that the Vietnam War didn't happen only to the men who fought it, is the most interesting aspect of his 1987 novel. June is a sensual woman with a troubled past, a complicated job, and a surly teenaged daughter; she is, in short, a credible, interesting character who, in her haunting if unlikely experience shooting a bear, takes a heart-of-darkness trip all her own—much like Lizzie's ill-fated pregnancy. June understands that Chris is battling silent demons from Vietnam, that "his wounding, like the war itself, had been an experience too intimate to be shared with her, or with anyone" (you had to be there), that Chris has "another sort of mistress: the war" (125). And she is unwilling to wait, passively, while her husband loses his battle. She intervenes, contacts the psychiatrist, and forces Chris to seek the treatment that promises, at the end of the novel, to bring him back to her and a normal life. But, finally, June, for all her spirit, is not much different from Linda and Sara and Jennifer (and the wives in Beverly Gologorksy's *The Things We Do to Make It Home* and other fiction and memoirs by women), the long-suffering Penelopes who wait endlessly while their men find their convoluted way home from that long postwar war. She tolerates Chris's removal of her and their children to the isolated bunker that shields him from human interaction. She even forgives his brutal rape, when he takes her violently in his most unrestrained moment. June is a fascinating character, but she—like Caputo's narrator and, presumably, his readers—is interested finally and only in Chris.

Sometimes even the loving, loyal wives rankle under the pressures of postwar life with a distracted or damaged Vietnam veteran, demonstrating that, as Patience H. C. Mason writes in *Recovering from the War*, her 1990 "Woman's Guide to Helping Your Vietnam Vet, Your Family, and Yourself": "his problems can become your biggest problem, and it can wear you out" (268). O'Nan's Vicki has left Larry, her husband of thirteen years, many times before, and though the hapless Larry vaguely pleads guilty to a compilation of domestic crimes ("not touching her enough. Spending too much time on the [veterans' hospital] ward. Bolting one too many Genesees before dinner at her mother's"), Vicki—who, the novel suggests, will stay away this time—withholds forgiveness for only one: Larry's inability, or unwillingness, to stop returning, emotionally and mentally, to his dead Vietnam brothers. "You never saw me," Vicki insists to Larry. "The littlest thing and you go into that shell of yours. . . . I don't want to live that way anymore" (166). Vicki admits that it's "her fault" for letting Larry wallow in his Vietnam memories, much as Paula, the wife of Cease Fire's Tim Murphy, blames herself for ignoring her husband's PTSD symptoms immediately after the war. Paula, like June Starkmann, learns about the counseling group for struggling veterans that helps Tim recover from his Vietnam trauma. In the wives' group, Paula explains that she loves her husband, but that "I get tired of watching him destroy himself. I am so tired of Vietnam." Early in their marriage, Mary Schulman didn't mind comforting veteran Brian, the protagonist of Wayne Karlin's 1998 novel Prisoners, during his Vietnam nightmares—"the constant unearthing of the dead in his mind"—but twenty years later, Mary is frustrated at her recognition that "nothing went away," that "she and her husband [are] entwined in a curse whose elaborate intricacies wearied her" (6). In the same novel Louise, the counselor wife of veteran Alex Hallam, has had enough of runaway Vietnamese teenagers and faux veterans and seminars with "awful titles, like Connecting with Your Vet, or Writing After War." The aftermath of the Vietnam War is "everywhere," Louise suggests. "It's leaked into the matrix. . . . Massive seepage has occurred. We are all at the party. We're all in our places with vacant, dull faces" (104). The women understand, as the men do not, that the Vietnam War happened to an entire generation and lingered long after the last bullet was fired.

A number of these books offer notable variations on the stereotypical pattern of male-female relationships. Several present as minor characters the protagonists' mothers—Michael's in Bausch's On the Way Home as loving as Bobby's in Del Vecchio's Carry Me Home is evil—but most are simply naïve and either oblivious or in denial, like Jeremy's mother in The War at Home or Larry Markham's mother in The Names of the Dead, who writes to him in Vietnam "asking him to write about nice things, to be cheerier"

49

(158). Butler in *The Alleys of Eden* and Karlin in *Lost Armies* create Vietnamese women who are in many ways more individual and more interesting than most of the American women (see Chapter 6). But the stereotypes prevail, and, as with the other conventions common to virtually all of these books, they recur with no indication that the sensibility of these authors and their texts evolves throughout the years since the war nor—unlike the women-authored texts—with significant narrative interest in the dramatic changes in American women's lives during the Vietnam era.

Of course, the consistency of these themes can be attributed primarily to the postwar authors' unwillingness (or inability) to move beyond the immediate postwar years, to treat the veteran-protagonist's Vietnam experience in a broader fictional context (as *In the Lake of the Woods*, *Missing in America*, and *Ulee's Gold* do). Neither can most of the authors' protagonists get beyond their privileged and sacred Vietnam experience to undertake any kind of "normal" postwar life. In these narratives, which present a variety of dramatic situations in which the protagonist tries, and usually fails, to come to terms with children, wives, friends, another theme prevails: throughout the aftermath texts, as though to underscore these veterans' inability to attain a mature, healthy adulthood, the silence and the preoccupation with the atrocity episode are underscored and articulated through the almost-universal obsession with the father.

All My Sons

Although in several of these narratives (*Paco's Story*, *Meditations in Green*, Ehrhart's memoirs, for example) the protagonist has no significant relationship with his birth family, in most the protagonist's fixation on his Vietnam experience is very much intertwined with his always unresolved relationship with his own personal (and often absent) symbol of the patriarchy; which is in turn inextricable from the traditional American notions of courage, patriotism, and masculinity that sent so many innocently willing young men to fight in the jungles of Southeast Asia.

Robert Olen Butler's protagonists' memories of their dead fathers are characteristic. In Butler's first novel, *The Alleys of Eden*, protagonist Cliff Wilkes is a deserter, a determined loner whose life is defined by his inability to commit to or connect with anyone. Cliff, even now, years after his father's death, feels abandoned by his father, whose premature death sentences his disengaged son to a solitary existence. *On Distant Ground's* David Fleming's father abandoned him when David was twelve, and David knows that his "aloofness" is his father's legacy to him (15). When he returns to Vietnam years later and finds his Vietnamese son, but at first feels nothing for the boy because he does not look like David, David for the first time feels "an odd little prickle of sympathy" for his own indifferent father: "For whatever reason, the father felt estranged from this child, this David, and the man had no way to pretend the feeling was anything but what it was. . . . David laughed aloud. 'I'm your son after all,' he said. 'We both feel nothing for a child'" (223–224). David's is a sad inheritance.

In *Lost Armies*, Emmett Wheeler's father (like his childhood friend Dennis's) dies when Wheeler is young, leaving Wheeler and Dennis to form the fraternal, vaguely homosexual bond that delineates their relationship. Bobby Wapinski's only important, lifelong human relationship is with his grandfather, the only father he knows since his own father left when Bobby was a child. Bobby thinks often about his father and wishes that "when I came home, you know, maybe I could bring you home too" (174). The lack of closure in Bobby's relationship with his father parallels his inability to close the door on his experience in Vietnam.[16]

Tim O'Brien explores most powerfully the lasting deleterious effects on the son of the father's abandonment or premature death. If the massacre at My Lai is the salient event that John Wade manages to forget, the early loss of his father is the heart-of-darkness experience that affects him throughout his adult life. Wade is truly obsessed with his father, an alcoholic who commits suicide when John is fourteen. As a boy, the Sorcerer, true to his nature, tries to pretend that his father is not dead. "And . . . when things got especially bad, John would invent elaborate stories about how he could've saved his father" (15). John reacts to his father's death with anger. "Kill Jesus," he mutters with rage at his father's death. And "Kill Jesus," he echoes on the night of Kathy's disappearance, as he inexplicably pours boiling water on the houseplants and maybe—just maybe—on his sleeping wife. Wade's complicated feelings about his father converge with his debilitating humiliation and frustration over his political defeat and culminate in the ambiguous climactic action that results in Kathy's disappearance.

Like John Wade, the adult Chris Starkmann continues to grapple with his complicated and unresolved relationship with his father. Unusually, Chris's father is an antiwar activist, a pacifist minister who strongly opposes his son's service in an immoral war. Now, years after his return from Vietnam, estranged from his stern, stoic father, Chris reluctantly returns to his boyhood home when he learns that the older man is dying. By this point in the novel, Chris's Vietnam demons are haunting him more and more, and when Lucius dies without regaining consciousness, without making peace with his son, Chris's behavior becomes even more volatile and erratic. His pilgrimage to Wawiekumig at the end of the novel brings the revelation— followed by forgiveness and healing—that his Vietnam experience was motivated by "hatred for his father":

> His enlistment had been more than a liberating apostasy; it had been an act of vengeance as well, a form of bridge-burning. He'd gone to war seeking an experience so awful there could be no coming back from it, one that would . cut him off completely from Lucius. He'd wanted to return, a creature incapable of loving him or being loved by him, a creature beyond forgiving and forgiveness, scorched and scarred by war. And so he had, in his own mind. He'd came [*sic*] back a stranger and an exile, but his banishment had been largely self-imposed. (432)

Emilio Estevez's Jeremy, unlike these protagonists, still has the chance to reach a rapprochement with his father, but the disastrous yet essentially unexplored relationship between Jeremy and the blustering patriarch is central to Jeremy's inability to reassimilate into his family after the war. In 1972 Texas, Maurine and Bob Collier carry on with their comfortable lives, unable and unwilling to engage their traumatized son and his combat flashbacks, and concerned mostly that their daughter not tell her friends about Jeremy's readjustment problems. "Can't you just forget about [Vietnam] and go on with your life?" an impatient Bob asks Jeremy in one of their frequent, escalating altercations, later clarifying that "it's hard on me . . . on all of us. I know you've been through an awful lot. I just miss you, that's all. I just miss talking to you." As Thanksgiving dinner with the extended family approaches, tensions mount, and even Jeremy's sympathetic teenaged sister Karen (Kimberly Williams) eventually turns on her taciturn brother: "I won't ever be able to understand what happened to you over there. I wasn't there and I didn't go through it. . . . Please don't hold me responsible for that." You had to be there.

In the inevitable, climactic confrontation between father and son, Jeremy—pointing a gun at his father in a stereotypical crazed-vet moment— reminds Bob that when he was drafted and asked his father for money to flee to Canada, Bob insisted to Jeremy that it was his duty to serve his country. "You sent me someplace where we didn't fight for anything but to stay alive," Jeremy angrily taunts his father. "Well, fuck you and that crap about honor, mister; it was your honor and you know it." A final flashback reveals Jeremy's quintessential combat horror; his lieutenant silently orders Jeremy to execute a prisoner, and when a reluctant Jeremy pulls the trigger, he now tells his father, "[the prisoner] was you. . . . Your fucking duty. Your fucking honor. . . . I killed you everywhere I could find you. I come home and you're still here. I killed those people for nothing. It was you I wanted." An emotionally drained Jeremy drops his gun and apologizes to his father, but it is too late for a reconciliation. Bob orders Jeremy out of the house, and the movie ends with Jeremy, at the bus station, another Paco apparently prepared to move on—literally and psychologically—but alone.

A similarly traumatized Michael, in Robert Bausch's *On the Way Home*, returns to his parents' new home after his escape from imprisonment. Dale, the former policeman, enjoys his retirement in Florida, and he is troubled by his puzzling son and the strain that Michael's odd postwar behavior places on the family. Michael's mother, Anne, struggles too to understand and help her emotionally fragile son, but the dramatic focus in the novel is, as always, the relationship between father and son. Bausch's third-person narration alternates sections from the perspective of Anne, Michael, Michael's tapes, and Dale, so here we get the perplexed father's point of view. Like Bob Collier, Dale misses his lost son—his innocent pre-Vietnam son—and Michael's unsettling presence in the house belies the fact that, as Dale insists to his wife, "he's not Michael" (160). Dale begrudges his supposedly dead son's unexpected resurrection and return to disrupt his father's long-awaited retirement. He is convinced that Michael will "explode and assassinate somebody," and he resents Anne's insistence that, for Michael's sake, they should move back to Chicago, to Michael's childhood home (77). "It is as if the boy's return, the coming of this stranger, has caused a plug to be pulled somewhere in the center of all the chemical processes which make Dale a living man—and everything important to him has leaked out" (15). Dale does not know, as we do, that during his imprisonment Michael has imagined his father coming to rescue him, but he does discover (by listening to Michael's tapes) that Michael has dreamed that his father is one of his captors. And when Dale—like Bob Collier—confronts his tremulous son ("What did they do to you? . . . You haven't got a mark on you!"), a cornered Michael blurts out, "I'm afraid of *you*!" (194, 196). Michael's memories of his capture and torture in Vietnam invariably evoke images of his father—the authority figure—and late in the novel, Dale realizes that Michael's fear of him is really his fear of power. Michael's captors "controlled his life the way a parent does," he somewhat pleadingly explains to Anne. "You see? It wasn't me. . . . He isn't afraid of me" (222). Of course, Michael, like Jeremy and Starkmann, *does* fear and blame his father, who is inevitably and by definition a symbol of power.

The country musician Sapper Reeves, the first-person narrator of Richard Currey's 1997 *Lost Highways*, is a more sympathetic, and less culpable, Vietnam father. Sapper's marine son Bob is wounded in 1968 and returns home missing an eye, a hand, and the ability to adjust to life as a damaged man. The doctor warns Sapper and his wife about the "debilitating long-term effects" of "mutilating injuries," and his father struggles to comprehend his typically silent, brooding son, who, when Sapper pressures him to talk, snarls with such "florid hate" that he seems to his father "to be no one I knew, had ever known" (244). The 1997 ending of the novel offers Sapper's belated acceptance of Bob's solitary life, but Sapper's earlier 1968 epiphany affirms the distance between father and son: "We did not speak then, and in that abandoned minute between us we seemed nothing more than casualties of love and random circumstance, sad and isolated men on the hinge of a vacant world" (248).[17]

"We did not speak then." The undisputed maxim that "you had to be there," which mitigates against any attempt to examine, share, or even acknowledge the submerged horrors of combat, is all the more inviolable in the father-son relationship, for it is the father—the fathers—who, as Jeremy and Michael and so many of these young veterans come to understand, have sent their healthy young sons into the line of fire. Trying to understand the secret demons that attack her husband, Caputo's June visits the town's war memorial and notices that "most of the surnames of the men who'd been to Vietnam matched those who'd fought in the other wars. Grandfathers, fathers, and sons—it was as if fighting in distant conflicts were a kind of legacy, passed from one generation to the next" (343–344). For the sons of military fathers—Lewis Puller, James Carroll, John McCain, and others—that legacy is a source of pride and, often, a terrible burden.

For the Vietnam prisoner of war John McCain the pride prevails. McCain subtitles his 1999 personal history/campaign autobiography *Faith of My Fathers* "A Family Memoir," and indeed the first half of the book is a paean to his father and grandfather, both successful World War II naval officers and his "first heroes" (though McCain can—and does—trace his military lineage back to the Revolutionary War) (vii). It is his family's military tradition that sends a young John McCain to the Naval Academy and soon enough to his generation's war and perilous duty flying over North Vietnam. And, when he is shot down and captured, that legacy of "honor and courage . . . that my father and grandfather had passed on to me" sustains the injured pilot. "A filthy, crippled, broken man, all I had left of my dignity was the faith of my fathers. It was enough" (257).

The successful McCain, U.S. senator and potential American president, can only praise and honor his fathers, but the permanently injured, psychologically damaged Lewis B. Puller, Jr., another son of a famous military father, offers a slightly more nuanced response to his military heritage and the man who embodies it. Marine Corps Lieutenant General Lewis (Chesty) Puller, whose grandfather was killed in the Civil War, was the corps' most decorated soldier. In later years, retired and ill, the Korean War hero mandates his only son's life and career by explaining that "he was counting on me to carry on when he was gone and how proud he was to have a son to continue the Puller name. We did not talk about the military or my attempting to follow in his footsteps, but even then there were some unstated assumptions about the course my life would take," and Lew Jr. dutifully accepts, from his youngest years, his "commitment to a calling over which I would be powerless" (33–34, 6). After completing officers candidate school, proud of (and resigned to) his fate, Puller fleetingly recognizes his unsuitability for his father's chosen career: "I felt as if I were on the verge of fulfilling a destiny that had had its origins many generations back in our family history. It was fitting that time and circumstance had so conspired as to make me an officer in the Marine Corps during a period of war, and if *I was by temperament not suited to assuming the mantle of leadership*, I certainly was by birth" (50; italics mine). After three months as a platoon lieutenant in 1969, serving just south of Khe Sanh, Puller is seriously wounded. The bulk of *Fortunate Son* recounts his long, challenging rehabilitation and adaptation to his injuries in civilian life, his gradual conversion to opposition to the war, and his understanding, when his father dies, that they will never have the relationship that the junior Puller desires. Sitting by the legend's deathbed, his son weeps "for a lifetime of missed opportunities to get to know him more fully" and recognizes that he hopes that now "I could stop feeling as though I were living in his immense shadow. . . . I missed the man who had nurtured me though my youth and early manhood, not the legend against whom I had measured myself for so long" (318, 319). Puller eventually understands that he has been "used by [his] country," but—unlike fictional characters Michael and Jeremy—he neither discusses their shared combat experience with his father nor blames him for sending his only son to "the hell of Vietnam" (253, 185).

Larry Brown's Walter James cannot find his father culpable for his Vietnam injuries, for the older man, a World War II veteran, like Chris Starkmann's father, disapproves of his eighteen-year-old son's enlistment in the marines, insisting, James tells us, that "I didn't have any idea what I was getting into" (61). Walter James barely survives Vietnam, and even after his own trial by fire, he and his father do not talk about their wars: "We never swapped any war stories. You'd think we would have, but we didn't. . . . He didn't want to talk about his shit, and I didn't want to talk about mine" (197). And by the time that the still-uncommunicative James joins Braiden Chaney in the VA hospital, twenty years after the war, his much-incarcerated father is dead. James talks about his troubled father throughout *Dirty Work*; it is clear that his relationship with his absent father is the most important one in his life. And Larry Brown dedicates *Dirty Work* to "Daddy, who knew what war does to men."

The father of Stewart O'Nan's Larry Markham knows what war does to men, but like Chesty Puller and Walter James's father, he does not share the knowledge—even with his injured veteran-son. And unlike James, Larry longs to connect with his typically taciturn father by discussing their shared experience. Larry's physician father was imprisoned by the Japanese in World War II, and he too does not want his son to go to Vietnam: "You don't want to know . . . what war is," he tells Larry (41). Years later, Larry encourages his father to talk about his war, but the failing older man's only response, while telling, is all too brief:

> "Can you still remember the war?" Larry said, hoping his father would not stop.
> "Every day," his father said.
> "Me too," Larry said. (319–20)

Ironically, while *The War at Home*'s Jeremy and *On the Way Home*'s Michael excoriate their non-veteran fathers for sending them off to war, the military sons—whose fathers, as representatives of the institution, are arguably even more culpable—do not, cannot, hold their fathers responsible for their war injuries. Raised with strict military discipline, these authors and protagonists cannot allow themselves to question the values and the system that have so cavalierly, as Puller notes, used them. But the question of culpability does arise in these narratives. Braiden Chaney knows that he is the victim of a dangerous myth. "I didn't even understand the whole thing. Just went because it was my duty," he says. "Sentiment was strong for God and Country. . . . Everyone's daddy had been in World War II" (23). As Michael Herr notes, "the old men make the war for the young men to go fight in; that's classic, that's eternal" (Schroeder, 38).

In *Born on the Fourth of July*, Ron Kovic explores the falsely heroic American myth that sends gung-ho young men off to fight for questionable reasons. His lengthy description of his all-American male childhood—baseball, Cub Scouts, war movies, and "plastic battery-operated machine guns"— introduces the ubiquitous myth of patriotic American masculinity that persists throughout these books (55). Invariably, the simplistic ethos of macho heroism is embodied in the much-discussed "John Wayne syndrome" present in nearly every Vietnam text. John Wayne, who is still, according to Garry Wills in his 1997 book, *John Wayne's America*, the model of American manhood. John Wayne who, Joan Didion notes, "forever determined the shape of certain of our dreams" ("John Wayne: A Love Song," 30). The "John Wayne thing" is defined by psychiatrist Robert Jay Lifton as a "form of super-maleness" that entails stoic silence, physical strength, and sexual superiority over women (238–239). For Tobey Herzog, it's the romantic myth of the "American warrior-gentleman" that most Vietnam protagonists recognize as fraudulent, as they "confront the horrors of war, self-doubts, guilt, and feelings of helplessness" (19, 24). Larry Heinemann confirms the veteran's understanding of the hollowness of the myth in *Paco's Story*: Jesse, another veteran-drifter, skeptically envisions the planned Vietnam monument, which will feature a statue of a soldier that "will be some dipped-in-shit John Wayne crapola that any grunt worth his grit and spit is going to take one good look at and say, 'Boo-*she-it!* Ah mean *bull*shit!'" (157).

In *All My Sons*, Arthur Miller's first, 1947 Tony Award–winning play, middle-aged Kate Keller cannot abandon hope that her son, Larry, declared missing in action in the recent war, will return to her. Her husband Joe, a munitions manufacturer and "a man among men," has moved on from his grief and from his exoneration from the charge of selling defective equipment to the air force (59). The play reveals, of course, that Joe Keller was guilty—craven and culpable—of the crime of which he was accused, a crime that resulted in the death of many pilots, a crime that, as Kate recognizes, has metaphorically murdered their son: "Your brother's alive," Kate insists to their surviving son, Chris, "because if he's dead, your father killed him. . . . As long as you live, that boy is alive. God does not let a son be

killed by his father" (114). Joe's defense—he did it for Chris; he was a businessman, doing business; everyone made money in the war; many others
are guilty too—does not convince his idealistic son, the moral center of the
play. "I know you're no worse that most men but I thought you were better. I
never saw you as a man. I saw you as my father," a distraught Chris exclaims
to his father (125). Late in the play, Larry's fiancée produces his last letter,
which reveals his disgust and shame at the allegations against his father and
his intention to kill himself. Finally, belatedly, Joe understands his culpability: "I think to him they were all my sons. And I guess they were, I guess
they were." (126).

The narratives—novels, films, memoirs—written by and about the sons,
veterans of the Vietnam War, over the past thirty-five years present problematic relationships between father and son, but they generally do not offer an
indictment of the military, the patriarchy, the American government . . . the
fathers.[18] With a few exceptions, their protagonists—angry (Bill Ehrhart),
damaged (Lewis Puller, Ron Kovic, Bausch's Michael, Heinemann's Paco),
disengaged (Kidder), hapless (O'Nan's Larry), rootless and restless (Paco,
John A. Miller's protagonists in *Jackson Street and Other Soldier Stories*)—remain too close to the Vietnam experience, too personally involved in their
own postwar problems to consider the larger implications of the war.

Like John Rambo, these men cannot move beyond the horrors of Vietnam. While Susan Jeffords's analysis of the Rambo movies offers trenchant
commentary on the Reagan-era reclamation of the Vietnam veteran, variations between David Morrell's 1972 novel and the 1982 film adaptation of the
book reveal similarly significant, if more subtle, revisions of Morrell's self-
described "allegory . . . [of the] disaffected" (ix). In Morrell's novel, Rambo,
who carries no identification and who declines to identify himself to Teasle's
deputies when he is arrested, escapes the local jail as a naked and anonymous Everyman when the deputy's attempt to shave him evokes flashbacks
to his Vietnam torture. For the novel's account of Rambo's capture, torture
by, and eventual escape from the North Vietnamese enemy, the movie substitutes Teasle's discovery much earlier that Rambo is a Vietnam veteran—a
Green Beret and Congressional Medal of Honor winner. The film subse-
quently presents a John Rambo whose superior survival and killing profi-
ciency, which the novel foregrounds, is triggered by his postwar demons,
and who resents antiwar activist "maggots" and the vague "someone" who
"wouldn't let us win." *First Blood* the novel's John Rambo is a vaguely alienated young man who demonstrates his warrior skills when a sympathetic

but ignorant small-town Kentucky sheriff harasses and eventually kills him. *First Blood* the movie's John Rambo, who discovers at the beginning of the film that his last surviving Vietnam buddy has died (ostensibly of the effects of Agent Orange), is primed to wreak much more lethal damage on a one-dimensional Sheriff Teasle's town, now in the Northwest. The movie Rambo must, of course, live to fight another day, but the movie captures his victimization in his final, nearly incoherent speech to Trautman, in which he sobs his despair at finding himself, seven years after the war, bereft of his wartime buddies and their camaraderie, unable to forget the war, and alone in a world that has nothing to offer him. As Jeffords and others have noted, the image of the Vietnam veteran has been transformed dramatically in the years since the war, but John Rambo speaks for the authors of these aftermath novels and memoirs, and for their protagonists: "Nothing is over. You just don't turn it off."

The Vietnam War continues to fascinate and perplex American society. The country's unwillingness to confront the experience in the years just after the end of the war soon enough melted into a veritable cacophony of voices offering commentary about every conceivable aspect of the war. Jean Bethke Elshtain's 1987 assertion that "Vietnam is even now in the process of being reconstructed as a story of universal victimization—of Vietnamese by us; of our soldiers by the war—and by us when we didn't welcome them home; of our nation by the war at home and *the* war; of wives and girlfriends by disturbed veterans; of nurses by the war and later non-recognition of *their* victimization," remains true today (218). These perspectives are articulated in myriad cultural texts about the war. But in aftermath novels written (usually) by veterans about veterans, there is really only one story—the country's ongoing betrayal of its soldiers who returned to an alien home.

Chapter Two

The Other Side of Grief: American Women Writers and the Vietnam War

Women who stepped up were measured as citizens of the nation, not as women. . . . This was a people's war, and everyone was in it.
> —Col. Oveta Culp Hobby, Director of the Women's Army
> Auxiliary Corp, 1942 to 1945. Inscribed on the World
> War II Memorial in Washington, D.C.

She loved her brother I remember back when
He was fixin' up a '49 Indian
He told her "Little sister, gonna ride the wind
Up around the moon and back again."
He never got farther than Vietnam
I was standin' there with her when the telegram come
For Lillian
Now he's lyin' somewhere about a million miles from Meridian
. . . .
Nobody knows when she started her skid
She was only 27 and she had 5 kids
Coulda been the whiskey, coulda been the pills
Coulda been the dream she was tryin' to kill
> —Emmylou Harris, "Red Dirt Girl"

"EVERY book should have the opportunity to be published," proclaims a disquieting *New York Times Book Review* advertisement for the online self-publishing company iUniverse that features Patti Massman and Susan Rosser's 1999 Vietnam War–era novel *A Matter of Betrayal*. Massman and Rosser published their romance with iUniverse, the ad explains, when "conventional publishers said women wouldn't read a serious love story about war, social upheaval, and its aftermath." Amazon.com's description of *The Things We Do to Make It Home* introduces Beverly Gologorsky's 1999 novel about the troubled relationships of "three returned [Vietnam] veterans and the women who love them" with the similar suggestion that "there's nary a woman among" the "American writers of all stripes [who] have staked out that cataclysmic conflict as a subject for literature." The popular misperception that the substantial and growing body of creative material about the Vietnam War largely eschews the perspectives of women arises, no doubt, from the historical reality that war is paradigmatic of the male experience, the activity that arguably most cogently presents the manifestations and negotiations of power as it works in society, as the early nineteenth-century Prussian military philosopher Carl von Clausewitz confirms when he avows that "war is the natural extension of politics." And if, as feminist critics maintain, woman has traditionally been "other" in our culture, few experiences have been—at least until military women's recent integration into hazardous positions in the combat theater—more alien and alienating to American women. As Jean Bethke Elshtain writes in her philosophical and political inquiry into the myths about women and war, "we in the West are the heirs of a tradition that assumes an affinity between women and peace, between men and war, a tradition that consists of culturally constructed and transmitted myths and memories" (4). Virginia Woolf puts it more succinctly: "To fight has always been the man's habit, not the woman's" (6).

Yet, as Gologorsky's Amazon reviewer notes, "men weren't the only ones affected by Vietnam—for every soldier in a rice paddy, there was a mother, a sister, a lover back home; when their men came back changed by the experience of war, life changed for the women, as well." The complicating insight that the Vietnam War necessarily included and affected home front women is, of course, hardly startling. As Nancy Huston asserts, women's roles in war are diverse—pretext (remember Helen of Troy), entertainment, reward, nurse, spy. And, Huston concludes, "if women were not 'present in their absence' on the battlefield, *nothing would happen there worth writing home about*" (275).[1] Further, if the female role on the front has traditionally been passive or secondary, the removal of men to the battlefield has invoked a paradoxical empowerment of the women who are left at home to sustain the culture. Marginalized by the quintessential male experience of war, women have been simultaneously enfranchised by their appropriation of the roles of earner, sole parent, active citizen. In the twentieth century, and especially in the years during and after the war in Vietnam, as women rebelled against traditional parameters of female behavior and moved (undoubtedly in part because of the war that validated them) into more active social roles—roles reinforced by the Vietnam-era women's movement—the position of women in wartime became increasingly complex and interesting.

Though Gologorsky's and Massman and Rosser's marketers underestimate the substantial canon of creative texts by women about their varied roles in the Vietnam era, they of course accurately note the overwhelming assemblage of men's voices on the subject. And the complementary scholarly commentary on Vietnam War representation is, not surprisingly, largely the work of male commentators, each of whom, however cogent his analysis, concentrates almost exclusively on literature written by and about men—specifically, men who fought in Vietnam. Early on, many of these scholars, seeking to legitimate Vietnam War literature, installed it within the traditional canon of American war writing, anointing Philip Caputo and Tim O'Brien and Larry Heinemann the battle-scarred sons of Stephen Crane, Ernest Hemingway, and Norman Mailer; and thereby (as Susan Jeffords has demonstrated) maintaining "a tacit policy of exclusion—most obviously, of women, men from racial or ethnic minorities, and the Vietnamese—that remains largely unexamined throughout these studies" (Jeffords, "Whose Point Is It Anyway?," 163). Indeed, as Jeffords maintains, it is possible to argue that the Vietnam War remains such a provocative, engaging subject precisely *because* it is one of the last experiences in American life that can be perceived as exclusively male, though the myriad narratives that this book addresses suggest that such a perception is reductive. Indeed, the mainstream Vietnam War scholars' privileging of the experience and voices of the combat veteran, however understandable, in fact ignores a significant component of the creative analysis of the war and the Vietnam era, for, like those combat veteran–authors, women began offering interpretations of the Vietnam experience in the early 1980s, and more and more female authors continue to add harmony to the rich polyphony. Indeed, except for male writers' accounts of the in-country combat experience, the almost three hundred Vietnam War–themed literary texts by women constitute "the largest natural grouping of related texts in existence among writings about the war," asserts John Baky, founder and curator of La Salle University's Collection of Imaginative Literature of the Viet Nam War. Baky's accounting of female authors' diverse recreations of the Vietnam War includes serious literary fiction, romance novels, adolescent stories, science fiction, and mystery-thrillers. These popular fictional offerings complement cogent, influential critical interpretations of the Vietnam experience such as journalists Gloria Emerson's *Winners and Losers* (1975), Myra MacPherson's *Long Time Passing* (1984), and Frances Fitzgerald's *Fire in the Lake* (1972), and

powerful memoirs, poetry, and fiction by and about military women and Red
Cross volunteers who served in Vietnam.

In-Country Women

Because during the Vietnam era the Pentagon did not maintain separate
statistics on military women, no one knows precisely how many American
women were in Vietnam during the years of America's presence in Southeast Asia, and current estimates vary widely. Olga Gruhzit-Hoyt, in *A Time
Remembered: American Women in the Vietnam War*, asserts that more
than 10,000 women worked in military and support positions in Vietnam,
a number that includes nurses and assistance staff, as well as Red Cross,
USO, Peace Corps, and religious- and NGO-affiliated civilians. The Vietnam Women's Memorial Foundation estimates that 10,000 military women
served in Vietnam; Keith Walker, in *A Piece of My Heart*, states that 7,500
military women and 7,500 female civilians were in country; Barthy Byrd's
total number, in *Home Front: Women and Vietnam*, is 33,000.[2]

Home Before Morning, Lynda Van Devanter's 1983 memoir about her
year as an army nurse and the first important book about women's service
in Vietnam, complemented the early-eighties male-authored films, novels,
and memoirs that initially countered America's willful amnesia about the
Vietnam experience in the decade after the end of the war. It announced
that women had served in Vietnam and returned home to the same indifference, hostility, and post-traumatic stress that greeted their military brothers;
and it inspired other women veterans to tell their own stories. Memoirs like
Winnie Smith's *American Daughter Gone to War* (1992) and oral histories
such as Kathryn Marshall's *In the Combat Zone: An Oral History of American
Women in Vietnam, 1966–1975* (1987) and Keith Walker's *A Piece of My Heart*
(1985) all acknowledge the influence of Van Devanter's ground-breaking
personal story.[3] In the 1980s and '90s, women veterans found each other and
heightened public awareness about their roles in the Vietnam War through
the ten-year effort to create the Vietnam Women's Memorial in Washington,
D.C., which was dedicated in 1993, and through organizations for women
veterans (facilitated by websites and discussion groups) such as Vietnam
Women Veterans, the Vietnam Women's Memorial Foundation, A Circle of
Sisters / A Circle of Friends, and Women in Vietnam.

Other creative representations of American women's in-country experience—testimonials to the Vietnam Women's Memorial Foundation t-shirt

that boasts that "Not All Women Wore Love Beads"—include army nurse Susan O'Neill's 2001 short story collection *It Don't Mean Nothing*; *The Healer's War*, Elizabeth Ann Scarborough's 1988 fantasy novel about a military nurse; Red Cross volunteer Terry Farish's 1992 novel, *Flower Shadows*; Diana J. Dell's short story collection *A Saigon Party* (1998); *Visions of War, Dreams of Peace*, a 1991 collection of poetry by women veterans edited by Lynda Van Devanter; army nurse Mary Reynolds Powell's autobiographical *Worlds of Hurt* (2000); and, of course, the popular late-1980s award-winning ABC television series *China Beach*, as well as Susan Fromberg Schaeffer's sui generis 1989 combat novel *Buffalo Afternoon*.

More prevalent—and more relevant to this study—are fiction and memoirs by women that frame the female in-country experience with the stateside preamble to and, more commonly, the aftermath of the Vietnam encounter. Romance novelists Massman and Rosser (who pointedly subtitle *A Matter of Betrayal* "A Novel Inspired by True Events") are interested less in Jenny McKay's intoxicating, execrable year as a Donut Dolly in Vietnam than in their protagonist's mysterious, peripatetic postwar life as country songwriter Justice Dakota. Sigrid Nunez's haunting 2001 novel *For Rouenna* sounds the usual themes in its presentation of Rouenna Zycinski's long-sublimated year as a Vietnam combat nurse: nurses' treatment in-country as second-class citizens; the twin perceptions that no one back home cares and that only the people who were there can truly apprehend the experience; postwar trauma; the ironic recognition that the grotesqueries of Vietnam are nonetheless the most stimulating and important event of one's life. But *For Rouenna* is really the story of the unnamed narrator, the unhappy writer who at first rejects her long-forgotten childhood friend Rouenna's request that she write about Rouenna's interlude in Vietnam, "the only time . . . in her life . . . that she had done something out of the ordinary," and of the oddly diffident relationship between the two lonely middle-aged women (62). Only after Rouenna's inexplicable suicide does her reluctant friend imaginatively re-create the veteran nurse's "one, incredible sleepless year that would mark her forever and that nothing else in her life would ever live up to" (63). Even Lynda Van Devanter acknowledges, at the beginning of *Home Before Morning*, her recognition that, with her return to "the world" from Vietnam, her real war is "just beginning" (4).

The collective chronicle of American women's experience in Vietnam during the war years is important and undervalued. And yet, ambiguous numbers notwithstanding, by anyone's reckoning the number of American women who engaged the Vietnam War directly is relatively small. If the story of America's tragic experience of the Vietnam War is as much about the American home front during the Vietnam War and the war's lingering aftereffects on American society as it is the saga of combat veterans, the expansive consideration of the Vietnam War as a broad and resonating social and cultural phenomenon is a tale told forcefully by women who came of age in the war years and never went to Vietnam. Susanne Carter's 1992 assertion remains cogent in the early years of the twenty-first century:

> Women's war writings of this century, especially the novels and short stories published by contemporary women during the past two decades, have started to erase the boundaries of traditional war fiction prescribed by male writers who once dominated the canon and expand the definition of war far beyond the combat experience to also include the homefront experience of those who do not see combat as well as the homecoming experience of war veterans and its effect on the significant others in their lives. The Vietnam War experience is still being recast by writers of both genders as a "story of universal victimhood" with cross-cultural impact on soldiers and civilians, male and female alike, who have become its victims (Elshtain, 218). (290)

Thomas Myers has noted that "there is no Vietnam War within history books or private memory. There are only Vietnams" ("Dispatches," 411). The books and movies and TV shows are, as scholars suggest, "the necessary personalizing of [Vietnam], the inventing of new aesthetic equipment through which the overlooked historical data may be sifted and understood," and a post-Vietnam generation of women writers has for thirty-some years been offering its own unofficial history of the war, demonstrating, in sometimes poignant, often painful narratives, that for women who did not endure the dueling trials of the front line or the antiwar picket line, the real war begins after the soldiers return home (*Walking Point*, 143). Another side of the Vietnam War is the one that emerges in the stories of the women left behind, the ones who didn't go to China Beach; stories told by contemporary American women writers of the lingering legacy of this profound cultural experience.

The Waiting Room

Sandra Crockett Moore dedicates her 1988 novel *Private Woods* to "every man and woman whose life was touched by the Vietnam War: to those who went and never came back; to those who came back forever changed; and to all of us at home who waited." The epigraph to Mary Morris's 1989 novel *The Waiting Room* is from Marguerite Duras's *The War*: "We are the only ones who are still waiting, in a suspense as old as time, that of women, everywhere, waiting for the men to come home from the war." The tense is significant, for Zoe Coleman, the protagonist of *The Waiting Room*, and a sizable group of recent and contemporary fictional heroines continue to wait long after the fall of Saigon for their men truly to come home from the war and for the declaration of a cease-fire in their own Vietnams. Zoe tells her brother's doctor, Gabe, about her own path to medical school and a summer job reading to comatose patients. "Did anyone ever come out of a coma while you were reading to him?" Gabe asks. "Zoe laughed . . . 'One guy actually did. I was reading *War and Peace* and he came out of his coma and told me to skip the war chapters'" (110). Most women have skipped the war chapters, and their struggle to comprehend an apparently senseless conflict is a search for a kind of knowledge that the veteran does not share.[4]

Again, the prevailing ethos of war insists upon the exclusion of women. Her high school commencement speaker's message about sacrifice for a strong America launches seventeen-year-old Sam Hughes on a summer-long quest to understand the war that claimed her father before her birth and wounded her still-suffering uncle. Bobbie Ann Mason's 1985 novel *In Country* presents in Sam a protagonist who is too young to remember anything about Vietnam, and whose effort to learn is undermined both by her society's indifference and male veterans' exclusivity; despite Sam's persistent questions, her Uncle Emmett refuses to discuss his experience in Vietnam: "'Women weren't over there,' Emmett snapped. 'So they can't really understand'" (107).

Emmett's protestation that the Vietnam War did not happen to (and therefore cannot belong to) women and other noncombatants is, as male authors demonstrate, a recurring theme in literature about the war. Philip Beidler writes of the returning veterans who "found that save for other Americans who had been there or had some other direct communication . . . the actuality of the experience, even for all its years of floating up across the face of the six o'clock news, could not have been harder for most of their countrymen to comprehend" (7). And Thomas Myers notes that "a prime theme in the works that deal even partially with the postwar experience is the radical difference in sensibility between those who have experienced the war and those who have not" (195). If veterans insist that men who didn't fight cannot understand the war, imagine their dismissal of the attempts by women—even *more* different, *more* "other"—who would try to share their apprehension of the experience. Susan Jeffords, remember, demonstrates convincingly that "the defining feature of American war narratives is that they are a 'man's story' from which women are generally excluded" (*Remasculinization*, 49). And women authors champion the "you had to be there" claim as consistently as their brother-authors do.

Although it is seventeen years after the war when veteran Sonny Woods discusses Vietnam with Sarah, the narrator of *Private Woods*, for him the experience remains exclusory: "People who were there share a common memory," he contends. "Maybe it shouldn't, but it makes a difference" (165). In Jayne Anne Phillips's 1984 novel *Machine Dreams*, Billy Hampson's insistence upon his sister's preclusion from his experience of war begins before he even leaves home. Danner wants Billy to flee the draft, and she has the car, the money, and the escape plan to get him to Canada. But Billy, adamantly fatalistic, rejects his sister's help. "'Don't be a pain,' he said gently. 'You're not the one with the number. It's not your show'" (267).

For many of the men in these stories, as in the male authors' aftermath narratives, the refusal to allow their women to share their war experience is less conscious ostracism than a genuine inability to articulate their pain. When Zoe Coleman's father comes home from his war, World War II, in *The Waiting Room*, her mother June believes that her long vigil is over. Having spent three years making quilts to pass the time, having "refused to change one light or chair or knickknack from their room, because she wanted Cal to return to life as he'd left it," she finds that her husband returns fundamentally transformed and irrevocably isolated (88): "The man who got off the train bore little resemblance to the man who had gotten on it. . . . He would not speak, except to answer in brief monosyllables. He would answer questions, such as if he was hungry, but he would not offer information. Not about the war, not about himself. . . . She was as alone with him as she had been without him" (89). Zoe's brother Badger is a veteran who never went to war. Prompted to flee to Canada by the death in Vietnam of Zoe's lover, Badger nonetheless, under the strain of his reluctant expatriation and too many drugs, returns home deeply wounded. His letters to his sister express his voicelessness: "I grow mute. It is odd. I try to speak but I cannot find my voice. Or I speak and it makes no sense to anyone but me. It is not what I really want to be saying, and yet I understand what it is I am saying. It's just that nobody else does" (199). The Badger whom Zoe finds in the sanitarium when she comes home is a taciturn zombie whose infrequent utterances are

67

unintelligible baseball jargon. In *No Earthly Notion* (1986) by Susan Dodd, Lyman Gene Bill is completely silent when he returns from Vietnam to the anxious ministrations of his sister Murana. For five years, until his death from obesity and a weak heart, his only word, "Mama," is neither a cry to his dead mother nor a plea to the sister who cares for him, but a trick to effect his escape to the kitchen for the food that is his deadly obsession. For these women authors' incommunicative Gary Coopers, silence about their agonizing experiences is not a cynical rejection of old sentimental verities about courage and honor or macho manifestations of stoic heroism; it is, even more candidly than the male authors allow, an acknowledgment that the horrors of war are too often "unspeakable things unspoken."

In "Big Bertha Stories," Jeannette, another Bobbie Ann Mason protagonist, angrily expresses her exasperation with her troubled husband's eccentric postwar behavior: "'I haven't been through what you've been through and maybe I don't have a right to say this, but sometimes I think you act superior because you went to Vietnam, like nobody can ever know what you know'" (211). Although Jeannette's irritation is understandable, most of these excluded female protagonists are more frustrated than angry. Their recognition that they have not shared the combat experiences of their men becomes an acceptance of responsibility for their veterans' postwar welfare that has dramatic implications for their own lives. Rejecting the exclusionary silence of their lovers and brothers, women writers present narrative accounts of their veterans' vexing lives in the years after the war that are, finally, testaments to the profound and enduring impact of the Vietnam War on their own lives. Their narratives, fiction and nonfiction, published over some thirty years by unknown or first-time authors and established writers, articulate a range of post-Vietnam relationships and familiar themes: the troubled veteran suffering from PTSD, the healing pilgrimage to the Vietnam Veterans Memorial, the paradoxical excitement and camaraderie of the combat experience, the belief that the war was a mistake. Yet these are most often coming-of-age stories that seek to write women's lives into the American Vietnam experience.

Scholars and critics of Vietnam literature have demonstrated that in the novels written by men about their experiences at the front, "new forms of imaginative invention . . . seem to challenge traditional modes of mythic understanding" (Beidler, 26). As Beidler, Lomperis, Walsh, and Myers all note, Vietnam-era writers such as Joseph Heller in *Catch-22*, Kurt Vonnegut in *Slaughterhouse-Five*, and David Halberstam in *One Very Hot Day* experiment with a technique that foregrounds the fragmentary, disjunctive nature of war. These books and others (Larry Heinemann's *Paco's Story*, Michael Herr's *Dispatches*, Tim O'Brien's *Going After Cacciato*), critics note, demonstrate that "a new war of discontinuous, competing narratives could not be brought into high relief with old sources of illumination, and the . . . most inventive works of the war . . . assume not only the primacy of the imagination, but also the necessity of inventing new aesthetic strategies for the rendering of new history" (*Walking Point*, 146). The women authors presented here rely on the "old sources of illumination"—the linear, realistic narrative culminating in an epiphanic conclusion—not because they cannot replicate the chaos of the war, but because they and their protagonists will not settle for the platitude that "war is hell," because for women the reality of the war is revealed fundamentally through relationships. With very few exceptions (Joan Didion's spare, oblique 1984 *Democracy*, for instance, and Susan Fromberg Schaeffer's combat novel *Buffalo Afternoon*), the narratives by women are traditional, realistic, domestic fiction that could keep Oprah's Book Club busy for a long time.[5] In Hal Ashby's *Coming Home*, one of the earliest and best-known narratives about the repercussions of the Vietnam War on the home front, Jane Fonda's Sally Hyde joins her marine captain husband on his R & R junket. Bob had gone to Vietnam just after the Tet Offensive excited to finally get his chance to test his mettle in combat. Now, months later, the Bob whom Sally greets in Hong Kong is angry and aloof, and when Sally encourages him to share with her what the war is like, he snarls: "I don't know what it's like. I only know what it is. TV shows what it's like. It sure as hell don't show what it is." Although most of them acknowledge—sometimes directly, sometimes subtly—that they cannot know what war is, these female authors would claim to know and reveal what the war *after* the war is. Denied direct engagement with the war, they grant, resist, and write beyond veterans' unvarying insistence that they can never apprehend it. "Henry has cautioned me against learning history from books," asserts Miss Fish, the epistolary narrator of Nell Freudenberger's accomplished 2003 story "Letter from the Last Bastion," about the acclaimed Vietnam novelist who is, we learn at the end of the story, her father; "but," she continues, "he forgets that books are often the only means available. Once I asked my friend Katie's dad what it was like to be a marine, but Katie's mom told me that the Vietnam War wasn't something for the dinner table. Last year I thought we would finally hear about it in tenth-grade American history, but that unit was right at the end of the year and we didn't get to it" (196).

Soldier Daddy

Indeed, most of the women who write about the Vietnam War and its aftermath in America didn't get to the war, though, much as military and
civilian women who served in Vietnam present a distinctive perspective
on the experience and its aftermath, a small sodality of memoirs by the
wives and daughters of career military men offers intimate and compelling authentication of the observations that war neither happens only to
the soldiers who fight it nor ends when the combatants come home.[6] Jenny
McKay, the spirited heroine of Massman and Rosser's *A Matter of Betrayal*,
is keenly aware of the special restrictions on her behavior because of her
army general father's exalted status in the "fishbowl" life of the U.S. military,
a world in which the Vietnam War is, above all, an opportunity for career
advancement (5). Her steadfast mother harbors no illusions about her husband's—and therefore his family's—priorities; in a rare candid moment, she
reminds teenaged Jenny that "we women are here to serve them. It's their
lives that have meaning, not ours, and we are never allowed to forget it. I'm
only appreciated because I can make the domestic and social parts of your
father's life run as smoothly as one of his tanks or guns. But in the grand
scheme of things, Jenny, we aren't even that important. The army issues a
soldier military weapons; they even issue him his clothes. If they thought
a wife was as necessary to the men as these other items, they'd issue one of
us to each of them, too" (18). Jenny at once resents and accepts her mother's
compliant loyalty and her own certainty that the army is her ambitious, successful father's enduring love: "She knew by now that nothing would come
between him and his army. Forced to choose, she feared he would walk
away from his family in a heartbeat" (19).

As Lynne Hanley notes in *Writing War: Fiction, Gender, and Memory*,
"a willingness to forsake wife and family is painstakingly inculcated in the
soldier under the rubric of 'combat readiness.' All the concerns of wives and
children are ultimately deferred to the necessity of making the soldier ready
to desert them" (135). Jenny's untroubled romance-novel acceptance of the
precedence of military life for a career military man and his family counterposes real-life military daughter Gail Hosking Gilberg's adult struggle to
understand her father's fatal partiality for military over family life in her 1997
memoir, *Snake's Daughter: The Roads In and Out of War*. Special Forces sergeant major and World War II veteran Charles "Snake" Hosking does walk
away from his family, serving three tours in Vietnam before he dies a heroic

combat death in 1967, leaving an alcoholic ex-wife and four young children, including, years later, an author who writes to discover why, although her father "loved his family, . . . at important moments he was always someplace else" (2). Like Jenny's mother, Gilberg grudgingly acknowledges the tacit obligations of military families: "We were to support my father's comings and goings, not distract him in any way, and go along with any regulations or change in orders. We were the silent, unpaid staff in the background, growing accustomed to the military's way of life with every year my father remained a soldier. We knew no other life. Orders were orders" (3). In her serpentine memoir, the adult Gilberg immerses herself in the remnants of her quicksilver father's life and inscribes a double journey, "the journey to find myself and the one to find my father" (13). *Snake's Daughter* is one warrior's daughter's desultory, self-absorbed discovery that "war stories include more than just crazy bayonet charges or courage in a faraway jungle. They include as well the lives of children an ocean away. There are many voices in war" (173). Narratives from several of the estimated twenty thousand children of soldiers killed in Vietnam document an important side of the story.

Like *Snake's Daughter*, Karen Spears Zacharias's 2005 memoir, *Hero Mama: A Daughter Remembers the Father She Lost in Vietnam—and the Mother Who Held Her Family Together*, is a therapeutic exercise, the author's attempt to come to terms with her shiftless "trailer park victim" family's struggles to survive after the 1966 combat death of her career-military, Korean War veteran, staff sergeant father (5). Though Zacharias offers little evidence that her abused aunt, bank-robber uncle, drug-addicted brother, or promiscuous mother would have led less troubled lives had her father survived the Vietnam War, she suggests just that: "It's hard to explain what losing a father does to a family. . . . Before [Daddy's] death, ours was a home filled with intimacy and devotion. After his death, it was filled with chaos and destruction. . . . With him gone, we were headless. It was as if somebody came into our home with a machete and in one swift slice decapitated our entire family" (14, 15). Though Zacharias contemplates the lingering repercussions of her father's death for her maladjusted family, her story is, like Gilberg's and that of Mason's Sam Hughes, a personal tale, a daughter's voyage to rediscover a father whom she barely remembers. Near the end of her literary odyssey, a middle-aged Zacharias makes a pilgrimage to Vietnam with Sons and Daughters in Touch, the organization for children of soldiers killed in Vietnam, and, near Pleiku and the site of her father's death, discovers, "finally . . . what it felt like to come home. This was the place where my father had been waiting for me all these years" (337). Its title notwithstanding, *Hero Mama* is not really about the author's unrepentantly unheroic mother—"the mother," she notes, that "I lost to America's most unpopular war"; it is, rather, a daughter's journey to find a long-absent father and her own voice (355). Tracy Droz Tragos's 2003 documentary *Be Good, Smile Pretty* is another daughter's search for the father who didn't return from the Vietnam War. Tragos's peregrinations begin with her long-remarried mother, who resists unpacking the letters and war memorabilia—and the painful memories—of her long-dead first husband, and a very defensive stepfather, who admits that he feels diminished by the "heroic epic" story of his predecessor's death. Mother and daughter visit navy officer Donald Droz's hometown, mother, and siblings; fellow Swift boat officer John Kerry in his Senate office; and, of course, the Vietnam Veterans Memorial, before Tragos attends the thirty-fifth reunion of her father's Naval Academy graduating class. Tragos dedicates her film to the memory "of all the fathers who were killed in Vietnam."

Daniel Trussoni, an ordinary grunt, completes his year in Vietnam as a tunnel rat before his namesake daughter is born, but because he shares photos and memories of his hazardous year in-country with the author of the 2006 memoir *Falling through the Earth*, Danielle Trussoni grows up convinced that her father's unresolved trauma from Vietnam explains his stoic, abusive behavior. Trussoni's memoir counterposes the story of her dysfunctional family (drinking, infidelity, illegitimate children, divorce, unnecessary poverty) and her own rebellious adolescence with the account of her journey, alone, in her mid-twenties, to contemporary Vietnam, where she—like Karen Spears Zacharias and many Vietnamese American Viet Kieu—goes to come to terms with her father's Vietnam trauma (in a way that he will not) and where (in a subplot that the book leaves frustratingly unresolved) she is stalked by a mysterious, vaguely menacing American Vietnamese "half-breed," or *bui doi*.

Though, like the other real-life fathers in these daughters' memoirs, her father is an unloving, unlovable, thoroughly unsympathetic man (whose combat experience is—though Trussoni does not acknowledge this—in fact considerably less traumatic than many in-country stories), Trussoni abandons her mother and her siblings to live with and support him when her parents divorce in her early adolescence. Trussoni justifies her father's always negligent, often appalling behavior as attributable to a Vietnam War that, Daniel Trussoni insists, he has long ago forgotten. "As a girl," she writes, "I believed that the war had taken him from us. It was an amorphous monster that would grab hold and pull us into it, kicking and screaming. Vietnam claimed Dad's past, his future, his health, his dreams. . . . It came to live in our house . . . It trailed me home from school. . . . It was an elusive yet inescapable thing skulking through my life, a Jack-the-Ripper presence that hid in alleyways and in the sewers, waiting to get me alone. We could ignore it, but it would not go away" (170). At the end of the book Trussoni's father offers a grudging, belated acknowledgment that the effects of his Vietnam experience may, in fact, be more pervasive than the throat cancer he attributes to exposure to Agent Orange (what no one told him at his return from Vietnam, he admits, "is that no matter how hard you try, it doesn't really end"). But age, growing maturity, and the trip to Vietnam teach his daughter a lesson about all the fathers' children: "although twenty thousand American children were orphaned by the war, it was only when I looked at my own life that I saw the hole that Vietnam created for all of us" (240, 239). Trussoni's story—one of the *New York Times*'s Ten Best Books of 2006—suggests that many of the emotionally and psychologically damaged Vietnam veterans inflicted upon their progeny a childhood at least as painful and empty as that endured by the children of the soldiers who never came home.

Waiting Wives

However traumatic the literally or emotionally fatherless, postwar lives of Gilberg, Zacharias, Trussoni, and Tragos, their memoirs testify to their ultimate survival. They are young children when their fathers die in or return from Vietnam, and their lives await them. In *Lonely Girls with Burning Eyes: A Wife Recalls Her Husband's Journey Home from Vietnam* (1991), the marine-wife memoirist Marian Faye Novak, echoing Jenny McKay's mother, writes to give voice to the "wives who waited, who in some sense are still waiting," wives who were "quietly condemned to silence" because "we weren't 'there,' we did not see [the Vietnam War's] horrors or feel its terrors in the field" (3, 4). In pointed contrast to Trussoni's and Gilberg's ruminative, self-conscious chronicles, Novak's memoir is bitter and singularly unreflective. Her inability to offer useful insights into her lonely circumstances or to claim her own story and her own voice, as other memoirists here do, is ironically underscored by Novak's misleading subtitle, since her sad story is not about her husband's return from Vietnam but about her lonely vigil for her in-country warrior. Shunned by her antiwar parents, alienated from college acquaintances and others of her generation who, in 1967's Summer of Love, espouse "a strange kind of love . . . that did not include the young men in the armed services," separated from a new husband whose letters from Vietnam (like Mike O'Reilly's of *Lizzie's War*) carefully and patronizingly omit the reality of combat, Novak finds solace only with other military wives (166).

Donna Moreau emphasizes this special bond among the wives of professional soldiers in *Waiting Wives: The Story of Schilling Manor, Home Front to the Vietnam War*, her 2005 memoir-history of the Salinas, Kansas, air force base that became "the only base in the history of the United States set aside for the wives and children of soldiers assigned to Vietnam" (xiii). Moreau, who lived at Schilling Manor with her mother and sisters in 1971 while her army lieutenant colonel father served in Vietnam, tells the story of the military wives who, replicating the unique wartime camaraderie that the male veteran-authors and the antiwar activists present, "forged a sisterhood . . . on the waiting side of war" (112). Though less dramatically, Moreau's account of the women-and-children enclave of Schilling Manor echoes the vivid home front wartime base scenes in the 2002 film *We Were Soldiers*: the tense vigil as the loyal wives of the army's Seventh Cavalry wait at Fort Benning for news of their husbands who were fighting the devastating battle of the Ia Drang Valley and the women's quiet, encircling support each time one of them receives the dreaded telegram. Recounting the history of Schilling Manor through composite characters—Bonnie, who waits for a POW husband who will never come home; Giselle, the unfaithful wife who scandalizes the other women with her casual affair; Beverly, the author's unmemorable mother—Moreau, despite her (inaccurate) claim to have written "the first book to focus on this *other, hidden side* of the Vietnam War," imparts little insight into the lives of "military wives [who] fought on the emotional front of the war [and whose] enemies were fear, loneliness, depression, isolation, destitution, lack of information, and the slow tick of time" (xv; emphasis mine).

These reminiscences by the wives and daughters of professional soldiers offer often intriguing, sometimes tedious testimony about the emotional consequences of a husband's or father's absence during wartime and beyond, but, though written years after the Vietnam War—and therefore ostensibly with the mature insights that time allows—they share a notable lack of interest in moral considerations of the war and the effects of the war on American society. The insulation and restrictiveness of military life that the memoirs present seem implicitly to proscribe engagement with the larger world or acknowledgment of the broader debate about the war and the social upheaval of the era. Much as the sons of career military men—memoirists John McCain and Lewis Puller, Jr., or fictional characters like *Fields of Fire*'s Hodges—understand and unquestioningly accept the patriarchy's expectation that they will follow in their distinguished fathers' courageous footsteps, the daughters and wives of fighting men recognize that putting their lives on hold is the loyal woman's fate in wartime. Like nurses and women volunteers who served in Vietnam, then, the wives and daughters of professional soldiers proffer an essential perspective on the female experience of the Vietnam War. A more sizable and diverse concatenation of stories is those of the mothers, daughters, sisters, and lovers of the two and a half million young men who volunteered for, were drafted into, or even evaded America's imbroglio in Vietnam, fictionalized stories that underscore the military dependents' insistence that the victims of war suffer years and miles away from the fields of fire.

Marrying Vietnam

Sensing, perhaps, the limitations of her ability to create complex, memorable characters, Beverly Gologorsky prefaces *The Things We Do to Make It Home* with a "Cast of Characters," a list that identifies her female protagonists and the Vietnam veterans they love. "Hundreds of thousands of women met, lived with, lost, and/or married the men who fought in Vietnam," begins Gologorsky's dramatis personae. "Their names have never been collected, filed, or written down anywhere." Many of the apparently autobiographical novels by women about the war and its aftermath offer the story of one of these unidentified women and her always complex relationship with a returning Vietnam vet. Gologorsky introduces us to six women and their troubled veterans in a slim novel that begins in 1973, then fast-forwards twenty years to recount the immediate and long-term aftermath of the war and the course of the relationships between these working-class women and their various drug-addicted, post-traumatic stress–afflicted, sexually dysfunctional men. Divorce, homelessness, illness, and premature death ensue, as the long-suffering women attempt to love and support their reticent partners, who, the women decide in 1973, "are all infected with the same weirdness" (25). Twenty years later, Jason is dead, Nick is dying, Rooster is homeless, and Frankie is headed back to Vietnam. And the women have moved on, struggling to support themselves, raising children alone, finally worn out by their men's inability to resume a normal life after Vietnam. "They lived their whole lives in a year or two. Nothing and no one that came after matters," asserts a sullen Sara Jo, Millie and Rooster's daughter, who notes that Millie and her long-suffering friends have at least "taught her what not to do" in a relationship with a man (181, 130). The unsuccessful marriages and love relationships in *The Things We Do to Make It Home* are constructed—and disintegrate—on the tenuous quicksand of the aftermath of the Vietnam War; on the men's refusal to talk and the women's reluctance to ask questions. For these characters, the war is a peacetime minefield, an unbreachable chasm. Sara Jo's critique of her older boyfriend-photographer's exhibit of photos of homeless veterans conveys the central theme of Gologorsky's book: "In none of your pictures is there a child, a wife, a sister, no one but them, only them, selfishly alone" (182). More *isolatoes*.

Nineteen-year-old Deborah Beebe meets the Vietnam veteran and history professor Christy Mahon on April 30, 1975, in Terry Farish's novel *A House in Earnest* (2000), and as Saigon falls and the Vietnam War shrieks to its ignoble end, the two begin their long, unsettled relationship with "the pact between sex and grief" that is one of its defining characteristics (4). Preoccupied at all times with his combat buddy's death in Vietnam from an exploded mine, Christy is withdrawn and uncommunicative—"away from her . . . even when she was there"; their life, with their young son, in a remote, primitive communal enclave in rural New Hampshire made all the more isolated by Christy's aloofness. Like the women in *Waiting Wives* and *The Things We Do to Make It Home*, who understand and support one another to compensate for their unsatisfying love relationships, Deborah and her son move in with her friend Sonia; but Christy lives nearby, and their lives remain very much entangled, in an unconventional marriage from which "there seemed to be no escape" (129).

Samantha, the first-person narrator of Sandie Frazier's *I Married Vietnam* (1992)—interesting only for its presentation of an interracial marriage—struggles to establish a satisfying emotional relationship with her veteran-husband, Jeremy Freeman, who, like Christy, has watched his best friend Doc die horrifically in Vietnam before he himself is wounded. Now Jeremy's wounds are invisible, and Samantha waits patiently for her husband to share the "nightmares" of "his living memories" (180). When he eventually confides his survivor's guilt, Samantha comes to "know Freeman's pain so intensely that it has become my own. When he suffers, I suffer. PTSD, battle fatigue, shell shock, whatever you call it, affects not only Freeman but me as well. We are both products of Vietnam" (201). Unlike Deborah and the women of *The Things We Do to Make It Home*, albeit also without dramatic intensity or narrative interest, Samantha appropriates her veteran-husband's postwar experience: "I," she insists, "married Vietnam" (186). Compare Katie, in Sandra Scofield's 1991 novel *Beyond Deserving*—one of many novels set in the Vietnam era in which the war provides narrative context and texture but is significant neither to plot nor to theme—who similarly mimics the aftermath emotions of her physically abusive veteran-husband, Fisher. Though Fisher refuses to talk to Katie about his Vietnam experience—"Fisher said she would never understand. She hadn't been there"—she starts to have horrific Vietnam dreams of her own: "Was it so strange that, after so long a time, she should start to share his night terror? She didn't ask for the dreams. . . . It was aggressive of her to walk into his secret place and steal from him" (21, 30). Samantha and Katie quietly question their sister-protagonists' acceptance that they can never understand their veteran-husbands' pain, yet *Beyond Deserving* and *I Married Vietnam*, which thereby confront the more common female acquiescence to the men's dismissive "you had to be there," fail to develop their provocative rejection of the exclusivity of their men's in-country experience; they offer instead simplistic relationships and little insight into women's experience of the Vietnam War.

It is doubtful that any woman will encroach on Ray McCreary's Vietnam memories, for the point-of-view character of Sydney Blair's first (and only) novel, *Buffalo* (1991)—unique in its focus on a male protagonist—is the very model of the reticent, self-involved veteran who fails to mature into a fully realized adulthood. Ray is a forty-year-old Peter Pan, terrified, fifteen years after his return from Vietnam, to find himself unexpectedly confronting marriage and fatherhood. Tethered to his volatile Vietnam buddy Bullet— "that they are alive today is based on the single year-long interdependence, and they know it"—Ray abandons his pregnant lover Vivian (who remains a minor, one-dimensional character in the novel) whenever Bullet unexpectedly arrives with another ill-considered, audacious scheme (6). *Buffalo* is the story of Ray's belated, reluctant acknowledgment that a middle-aged man may need more in his life than drugs, sex, and emotional isolation. Initially proud of his austere life of "no flab, no mortgage, no children, no hassles," he comes to understand that the price for such freedom is "no job,

77

no (real) woman, no dough" (89). The novel's improbable denouement is Ray's near fatal confrontation with Bullet over his crazy friend's massacre of his buffalo herd and an acceptance that it's time to jettison his own "perfect insularity" (133). Ray will stand by his bedeviled friend because, he explains to Vivian, "we're soul mates. Some people you're stuck with, for better or worse," but the novel ends with his move away from Bullet and toward his new wife and daughter, whom he will teach that "it doesn't have to be so hard" (145, 197).

Another variation on the familiar scenario of a relationship that founders on the lack of connection between a traumatized, uncommunicative veteran and a frustrated woman is Sandra Crockett Moore's 1988 *Private Woods*, its author's only published text, in which a late-1980s hunting trip reunites narrator Sarah Lannom and guide Sonny Woods, a Vietnam veteran and her first love. Sarah waits for Sonny during his 1967–1968 tour in Vietnam, but when he returns silent and distant, she dismisses him precipitously. Now married, in her late thirties, Sarah belatedly understands Sonny's postwar behavior. "When did we first hear about Vietnam vets having flashbacks," Sarah asks her friend Trudie during the hunting trip, "or about post-traumatic stress disorder?" (77–78). Echoing the many male-authored memoirs and novels that summon up the romantic illusions of John Wayne World War II movies as a misguided motivation for the protagonist's enthusiastic embrace of the war experience, a regretful Sarah reminds Trudie of "the war movies we grew up on," in which "'all the ones who came home, came home winners and swept somebody into their arms.' I'd known wars weren't like in the movies," Sarah ruefully confesses. "All except for that last part" (78). The novel's plot—which turns on the hunting trip; Sonny's and Sarah's happy marriages to other, sympathetic characters; and an unacknowledged near-kidnapping, during which Sarah and Sonny at long last consummate their relationship and she becomes pregnant—underscores the recurrent theme proclaimed by Moore's dedication "to every man and woman whose life was touched by the Vietnam War." At the end of the novel, when a newly mature Sarah decides not to tell Sonny about her pregnancy, and thus not to take him away from his wife, her plaintive plea—"weren't we all victims?"—reiterates the underlying theme of these novels and memoirs by women (287).

Norris Church Mailer agrees that, in Sweet Valley, Arkansas, everyone is a war victim, but—though Mailer's attempt to explore serious themes in a glib, satiric narrative is appealing and promising—her jejune novel *Windchill Summer* (2000) is such a treacly prototype of the popular "Southern, cute, and quirky" genre of contemporary fiction that it is difficult to apprehend the more serious themes of the story. Mailer's Vietnam War–inspired plot—which features the My Lai massacre, PTSD, rape, and murder—tilts decidedly toward the southern gothic, and her immature narrator's sophomoric storytelling undermines the gravity of the novel's subject—though we are meant to find the silly, annoying Cherry endearingly charming. *Windchill Summer* was widely reviewed, surely because its first-time author was married to heavyweight novelist Norman Mailer; in the *New York Times* Jennifer Schuessler suggests that "Mailer's evocation of the war . . . broadens out her story in a way that Cherry's putatively awakening consciousness never does" (30).

Cherry Marshall—gawky, affable, twenty-one-going-on-fifteen—is home from art school for the summer with her Filipino best friend Baby ("a Fillbilly. Get it? A Filipino hillbilly?"), and her final summer of adolescence brings first love with dreamy Vietnam vet Tripp Barlow and a murder mystery, all of which Cherry recounts in her breezy, ingenuous narrative voice (5). Her high school friend Jerry Golden is killed in combat, Cherry announces, "by a booby trap somewhere, I think in Quang something, or someplace that sounds like that. I don't really know a whole lot of details about it, but it was doubly horrible because he was the president of our class and a really great guy" (7).

Mailer limns a small southern town fully yet mindlessly immersed in the Vietnam conflict; with deputy sheriff Ricky Don, her ex-boyfriend, and drug-dealing Bean, Baby's boyfriend, home from Vietnam, two high school classmates killed in action, and cousin G Dub headed to Canada to avoid the increasingly unpopular war, Cherry feels that "the war hung over all our heads like the shadow of a hawk on the chicken yard" (8). Her male friends are "dropping over there left and right," and Cherry, who is becoming depressed "watch[ing] Walter Cronkite every night on TV and star[ing] at all the pictures to see if you recognized somebody you went to school with," is "thankful . . . that I was a girl and didn't have to . . . worry about going to Vietnam" (7, 288).

Cherry opposes the war because, after all, "what does it matter if Vietnam is Communist or not?" (7). Like Freudenberger's Miss Fish, Cherry and her classmates didn't study Vietnam in geography class, and she thinks it's "insane" that "our guys have to go and die for a country they can't even find on a map" (7). Yet, so superficial is this novel's engagement with the Vietnam War that Cherry's coming of age is more about losing her virginity

79

and smoking pot with Tripp than about a deliberate, purposeful response to the war, though Mailer is careful to present an array of combatant motivations and experiences. Pony-tailed, blue-eyed Tripp Barlow, who moves to Sweet Valley from California because his Nam buddy Jerry Golden makes it sound like a nice town, goes to Vietnam "for the excitement. To find out what all the noise was about," but returned vet Tripp supports G Dub's decision to flee to Canada (68). And except to assure Cherry that "you have no idea what it's like," Tripp has little to say about his sojourn in Vietnam, perhaps because, as we learn later, he is present at—but, importantly, not complicit in—the atrocities at My Lai. Baby's musician-boyfriend Bean is drafted, and his postwar drug-enhanced psychosis—which culminates in his murder of Carlene—is a direct result of his combat experiences as a tunnel rat. Jerry Golden, whose letters to Carlene describe the My Lai massacre and his own developing disaffection for the war, volunteers for combat because it is his family's tradition and because "it didn't matter if you believe in the cause or not; you had a duty to fight for your country" (174). Jerry Golden is meant to represent the mature, complex combatant, increasingly alienated by the war and his collusion with it. When, after My Lai, Jerry writes that he is ready to die, in hopes that he can find forgiveness for killing innocent Vietnamese, his death is, narratively speaking, inevitable.

Mailer complements her meticulous litany of combatants with a gratuitous evocation of the cultural ephemera of the summer of 1969. Cherry the Baptist deacon's daughter is nervous about seeing the edgy film *Easy Rider*, and her response to it of "hat[ing] the rednecks and lov[ing] the hippies" is offered as evidence of her growing independence (145). The capricious violence of the Manson murders underscores the inexplicable menace of Carlene's death, but, Cherry chirps, "one good thing that has happened is that concert they had up north at Woodstock," which "looked like so much fun" (155). And though she at first dismisses the moon landing as less interesting than *Star Trek*, Cherry grudgingly concedes that "it was something to tell my kids one day" (35).

Perhaps because of the naiveté of its narrator, *Windchill Summer* omits the introspective angst that characterizes the more serious women's novels and memoirs of the war. Despite Jerry's acknowledgment that Carlene (who kills her father and is sexually abused by the preacher who helps her hide the body) has "been through [her] own war," and Baby's defense of Bean—"he's sick, Cherry. . . . He just lost his mind after what all happened in Vietnam. You can't go from being a killer one day back to being a normal boy the next"—Mailer betrays little real understanding of the effects of the war on anyone other than, arguably, its combatants (263, 388). Toward the end of *Windchill Summer*, Cherry, who feels that "my whole world had done a 180 in the past few weeks," is unnerved anew by just-drafted G Dub's announcement that, after deliberating for two full days, he will flee to Canada to avoid service in Vietnam (287). Cherry reassures her cousin that "it takes a lot of guts to leave your home and take this kind of gamble," but she is, fleetingly, distressed that "the closest thing I had to a brother was being forced to leave his home and family" (287). G Dub is a minor character in *Windchill Summer*, and the novel offers nothing of his relationship with Cherry, but in acknowledging him as a brother, she introduces an emotional bond that is central to another coterie of postwar novels by American women.

"Watch Your Little Brother"

Susan Jeffords notes that "as a rule, when women appear in Vietnam narratives, it is never as part of the 'brotherhood' that is created in battle.[7] They are instead usually trying to stop their husbands, sons, or lovers from going to Vietnam" (64). Many of these women do indeed try—largely unsuccessfully—to keep their men from war, and their exclusion from the brotherhood of that experience is apparent. But their fraternal bonds with the men they love predate Vietnam and endure long after the war is over; they are, in fact, quite literal as well as metaphorical. In this collection of modern novels and short stories by and about American women, though sons and lovers are present, the crucial bond and the principal preoccupation of the protagonists and their creators is that of brother and sister. And for these sisters, it is as though their failure to protect their brothers from war, or to share the experience with them, begets a burden of guilt and responsibility that is more fundamental than the allegiance of marriage and more profound than the relationship between parent and child.

In her introduction to *Shrapnel in the Heart*, which recounts the stories of the war dead's survivors who have left letters and other memorabilia at the Vietnam Veterans Memorial, Laura Palmer suggests that "siblings are the least understood victims of the Vietnam War. . . . for siblings, their own passage through life can be a jarring reminder of just how much their brother missed" (xv). Many of the women in these narratives—like, apparently, Vi, who works at the military hospital that finally cannot keep her drug-addicted, psychotic brother Billy from killing himself in *Coming*

Home—are elder siblings, and, socialized as women, natural caretakers; and their stories document childhood patterns of responsibility for their younger brothers. Each of these women must come to terms with her failure to protect her brother from the ramifications of war. Some, in the course of the narrative, are able to confront their guilt and begin the process of healing; others simply absorb their brothers' damage and pain as they appropriate the scars of the war that the brothers insist they cannot understand.

As a child, Jane, the first-person narrator of Ann Beattie's "A Clever-Kids Story" of the late seventies, idolizes her older brother Joseph, who at seven enthralls her in their shared bed with his clever-kids tales of resourceful, spirited children. Years later, Jane is frustrated by the openendedness of the story that Joseph cannot tell, the story of his death in Vietnam, for the military's version is unsatisfactory: "I don't know if it took him a long while to die, or if he died suddenly. I don't know the name of the place he died in, or if it had a name. Although there were many random facts in the letter, the questions I really wanted answered were not answered" (278). Remembering that her brother dismissed her suggestion that he flee to Canada to evade the draft, Jane recognizes that despite Joseph's confidence in his immortality, she knew better than he the dangers that he faced: "I began to understand the real reason [that Joseph would not go to Canada]: it wasn't a matter of principle, but simply that he thought he wouldn't die; he thought he was indestructible. He really thought that he would always be in control, that he would always be the storyteller. I don't think I said to him in so many words that I knew he was going to die, or that he actually said he knew he was going to live, but that's what our conversation was about. He didn't understand how bad, and how pointless, things were in Vietnam . . . and I couldn't make him understand" (279). Convinced that she has failed her dead brother, Jane cannot assuage her guilt. As the story ends, she again sleeps in her brother's bed, but though she is an adult and shares the bed now with her lover Nick, Jane feels as though time has stopped, as though Joseph is still a child. Childishly mistaking a coat hook for a "demon," she seeks solace from Nick, who tries to comfort her. "It was not what I wanted at all," Jane admits, "but I closed my eyes, not knowing now what to say" (281). Now Jane is the storyteller, but, uncertain of her facts and unable to communicate her grief, she is possessed by the poignant memory of her brother's "pointless" death.

Like Jane, Danner Hampson of *Machine Dreams* does not know her brother's fate, and two years after his disappearance in Vietnam, she has not recovered from her loss. Denial, anger at the government, activism in veterans' organizations, and therapy have offered little consolation, and now Danner is haunted by memories of her childhood with Billy and her futile attempts to protect him from harm: "I covered him, piling on more leaves. . . . The more leaves I gave him, the better chance he had. I wanted him . . . to stay hidden, stay silent. I kept piling leaves, alone in the clearing, hiding him deeper and deeper, the mound of leaves higher than my chest. I kept working until he was secret, buried, warm. Until he was nowhere" (327). Now Billy *is* nowhere for Danner, who refuses to accept his apparent death, and she dreams about her brother with clear visions of his "kid face": "I wake up sweating, scared. Then I tell myself the clarity may be a direct correlative of how alive Billy is, how desperate he feels, how hard he's trying to get through. But in the dreams, Billy isn't desperate. He's just himself. I'm the one who is afraid, who knows something terrible might happen, has happened, will happen. I'm the one who can't stop it from happening" (326–327). Jayne Anne Phillips's novel ends with Danner's recognition of her failure. "*You watch your little brother*, Mom would say to me. . . . She probably didn't take my abilities as Billy's protector all that seriously, since I was only about three myself. But I was very serious. I wouldn't even let him stand up. I kept him entertained with the ball or the block or whatever he was fooling with; if all else failed, I held him down by main force. She'd come back to see why he was crying" (327). Unable to bury her brother safely beneath the leaves, to stop his crying, or to prevent something terrible from happening to him, Danner cannot ignore her liability; though she knows that Billy is almost certainly dead, lacking brother, ghost, or corpse, she cannot declare her own separate peace.

The narrator of Pat Ellis Taylor's 1988 stories "Descent into Brotherland" and "A Call from Brotherland" has welcomed her brother home from Vietnam, and while her solicitude for her wounded vet is very much in the present, it is evident that her commitment to her brother is a lifelong proposition. In "Descent into Brotherland," as she accompanies Okie to the VA Hospital, she is confident about meeting with his doctor because "I've visited Okie in the brig before, I've visited Okie in the psychiatrist wards, and I've visited Okie in the Oklahoma jail, and I've talked to lawyers and jail wardens and policemen and psychiatrist boards and judges" (100). But Okie's sister watches helplessly as the doctor dismisses him, no more able than her brother to explain to the psychiatrist how desperate he is. By the end of the story, Okie is another one of the forgotten "relics of war," and his sister/protector shares his ineffectual silence (100): "My face is burning. She is showing us out. . . . I can't talk. My fist, I am thinking, should go right through this door. . . . Wait, wait, I am thinking and I stop. I've got to stop it. I need to go back and shake her very hard and tell her . . . she's just not listening! . . . We walk on down the hall and I sit down on a chair . . . while Okie swims in a sea of disabled men and disappears by himself through a door" (106). Neither can the narrator rescue her brother in "A Call from Brotherland." Just as Okie, who sees "the devil licking at the wound in his brain that had never healed right," kills his biker nemesis, his sister, miles away, awakens from "a dream of walking up and down streets in a grey foggy dawn in a city unfamiliar to me looking for my brother, thinking something was wrong" (112). Sharing her brother's silent pain, she is at once helpless to heal him and unable to abandon him.

Like Jane and Danner and Okie's sister, Betty Sutton Lusky shares a special relationship with her brother Walter in Laura Kalpakian's 1984 story "Veteran's Day." A Vietnam veteran convinced that the government is "putting Killer Enzymes in our food to turn us into robots and hot dogs," Walter has been declared "a criminal and certified loony" (13, 9). His ex-wife and the rest of his family have rejected the fugitive, but Betty remains supportive. "'We always was a team, Betty,'" Walter declares during a surreptitious visit to her trailer, and Betty assures him, "'That's right and you just tell me if you need any help from me'" (14). Committed to assist her brother, Betty is cooperative when Walter concocts a complicated plan to at once turn himself in and alert America to the government's mind-control scheme. When the plan goes awry and a gas-masked Walter is captured before he can expose the government, Betty insists that somehow Walter will escape from the hospital: "one day he'll turn himself into a kite and fly right out of there, hot wire a hot car and be gone. He'll outsmart them all. He's not crazy. He never was" (30). Betty remains optimistic about her brother's future, but the story's ending can only leave us concerned about hers: "I sit by myself and watch the eleven o'clock News. . . . Sometimes I reach under the couch and I get out the gas mask Walter give me and I hold it. I feel better when I hold it. . . . I feel like I'm holding on to the promise I made Walter, but I don't exactly remember what it was. Can't imagine what I promised him, but it must have been important, otherwise why would I hold that gas mask in my arms when I watch the News? Sometimes I put the gas mask on. . . . It's real quiet inside that gas mask. I can hear myself breathe and I know that if I wear it enough, they'll never get me" (30). Like Okie's sister at the end of "Descent into Brotherland" and the protagonists of *Beyond Deserving* and *I Married Vietnam*, an obviously disturbed Betty believes that she has *become* her brother as she assimilates the pain and paranoia that are his Vietnam legacy.

The sisters of these damaged veterans and lost boys frozen in childhood can neither rescue their brothers nor exorcise the incubus of their accountability; as much as their fraternal casualties, they too are unwitting victims of the Vietnam War. Other narratives proffer protagonists who, while no less loyal to their soldier-siblings, manage to recognize and negotiate through their guilt and, by the end of the story, begin their own recovery.

So intense is Murana Bill's devotion to her brother Lyman Gene in *No Earthly Notion* that when their parents die suddenly and orphan the two teenagers, she wonders guiltily whether "a passing wish" may account for her parents' deaths. Now solely responsible for her fifteen-year-old brother, Murana, three years older, "set[s] out to be a mother to him with a dim, dark uneasiness at the back of her mind. She'd wanted her brother to herself all along" (14). Left financially secure, Murana can devote herself resolutely to caring for Lyman Gene while he is a teenager, and she waits aimlessly during his eighteen-month stint in Vietnam, uncertain how to live without him: "Without Lyman Gene to do for, Murana had no idea just what she was meant to do. Taking care of her brother was the only job she was qualified for" (31). Murana's maternal devotion increases when Lyman Gene returns home, but "not all of him—something seemed to be missing" (38). Repeatedly—and accurately—she insists to military doctors and well-meaning, meddling friends who recommend that she take time for herself, "'He's all I have'" (39). Murana contentedly cares for the incapacitated veteran with the weak heart, bathing, feeding, dressing and talking to and for the silent, child-like man. Like other fictional sisters, Murana essentially becomes her brother: "She felt like a different person. Serving as her brother's tongue seemed to endow her with his eyes and ears, and his heart as well. . . . And as she spoke for him, she began to feel for him so deeply that she no longer knew where she herself ended and he began" (49). But Murana's brother neither appreciates nor shares his sister's dedication. Refusing to speak, though he can, the "traumatized" Lyman Gene endures, and eventually rejects, his sibling's succor. He retreats into sleep and food ("Murana understood that he would fight her, perhaps even kill her, for the block of cheddar cheese concealed in the pie safe, for the roll of Life Savers upstairs in her purse") until, after five long post-Vietnam years, he dies of 423 pounds and "a sickness going deeper even than the heart" (66, 155). Lyman Gene's death occurs halfway into *No Earthly Notion*, and liberated from her role as her brother's mother, her brother's twin, "Murana Bill . . . surprised everybody by becoming an entirely different person. From the day her brother passed on, she seemed to shed her predictability like an old snakeskin" (95). After six months of grieving, Murana sets out for a new beginning in a new city, now, belatedly, able to, forced to launch her own life with the love and slow, healing attention of an ebullient new friend.

Physician Zoe Coleman has dedicated her life to no one, and when she returns home after many years to confront her past, she recalls her early resentment of her mysterious, delicate baby brother, Badger. When they played in the woods, "he was the Indian and she was the cowboy and Zoe captured him" (40). In the winter, "Zoe would take him out and pound him with snowballs or bury him in the snow. . . . She had always been jealous and she tried to get rid of him" (84, 39). But Badger never tells who buried him in the snow, who abandoned him in the woods, tied to a tree; just as later he does not betray Zoe's surreptitious meetings with her forbidden boyfriend Hunt. And when Hunt is killed in Vietnam, it is Badger who sits in another waiting room while Zoe has an abortion. Zoe encourages Badger not to court Hunt's fate in Vietnam and transports him to Canada, but once her brother disappears over the northern border, she goes "about the business of creating as much space as she could between herself and where she came from" (245). She disregards his letters berating her for abandoning him and pleading with her to come rescue him. But years later, when she encounters him, silent and suffering, in the hospital, Zoe can no longer ignore her battered brother: "His eyes told her she had betrayed him. She'd driven him to the border and never looked back. She had made as much space as she could between herself and them. But now Zoe reached down deep inside of herself and found him pulling at her as he'd pulled at her once when he was a little boy" (178–179). Late in the novel, a trip to Florida and a visit to Badger's draft-evader friend, who attributes Badger's condition to his inability to wait for the declaration of amnesty that would have allowed him to return home, help Zoe reconcile herself to Badger's illness and her own guilt: "He would not get better. She knew that now. . . . Something had happened to her brother that would not change. . . . She would find a way to get on with her life. . . . She made her peace with herself. What happened to Badger was not her fault. At the same time perhaps there were things she could have done. Perhaps she could have found him, brought him home.

But in truth, in order to have her own life she had to stay away. Zoe felt the guilt of the survivor. She had made it and her brother had not" (233). Still later, as Zoe contemplates the possibilities of a romantic relationship with Gabe, she wonders, "How can I love someone with my brother the way he is? How can I love someone with everything that has happened to me? But the answer kept coming back: How can I not?" (270).

The Waiting Room ends with the germination of Zoe's liberation from her guilt: "It was as if a child began to grow within her, even though she knew no seed had been planted. But inside her something grew, something she had formed on hope. It would not happen right away, but she knew she would feel it when it did. She felt a tiny round turning inside of her as if her own brother were beginning again" (271–272). The novel's final image—much like the ending of *Machine Dreams*—is a childhood memory. Zoe and Badger are in the woods, and Zoe again tests her brother: "'You must do as I say,' she tells the little boy as she leads him into the deep snow. And then it was, and this was the part Zoe had forgotten, the part that came back to her, that she picked him up in her arms. . . . 'I'm sorry,' she said as she kissed him lightly on the cheek. 'I really am.' And she carried him in her arms all the way home" (273). By the end of the novel, the Zoe who has specialized in dermatology because "surfaces interested her [and] she didn't want to go deeper than that," has moved well beneath the surface, recognizing her lifelong bond with her brother, accepting, as her mother proclaims, that "'he's all you have'" (7, 53). Zoe knows that she is responsible for her brother's pain, and in coming home, in confronting "the other side of grief," she comes to terms with her culpability and moves beyond it; beginning, at the end of the novel, the healing that will allow her to recover from her own postwar trauma (36).

In order to move on with her life, Sarah Lannom in *Private Woods* has had to reconcile herself to her brother's death, though Joe, like Billy Hampson, is officially missing in action: "After four or five years," Sarah admits, "I stopped hoping he was alive. . . . My beautiful blond American brother in a North Vietnamese prison, or worse—I couldn't 'hope' for that any longer. So in my mind, I killed him. . . . It's a terrible thing—not to know" (66). Sarah *has* adjusted to her brother's death, but her coincidental meeting with Sonny, years later, brings back all the pain and uncertainty of the Vietnam era. Sarah and Sonny Woods fell in love just before he and Joe went off to war, but even years later, when Sarah thinks of Sonny, it is more often as a second brother than as a lover; and Sonny confides that when he was a child, the victim of an abusive father, he fantasized that Sarah's parents would adopt him. "When we were kids," he tells her, "I'd pretend that you were my sister" (212). Confronting him again, seventeen years later, she comes to understand that Sonny's remoteness when he came home was not a rejection of their love: "I know that war's over, but I don't think he's ever going to be over it. It's just . . . he's always going to be scarred. . . . Like Joe is always going to be dead" (250). At the end of the novel, pregnant Sarah returns to her husband, who is able to welcome Sonny's baby, which, echoing the conclusion of *The Waiting Game*, grows within her. Forced to confront Sonny and her past, Sarah comes to understand what the war has done to them: "What good did it do, assigning guilt for things past undoing? . . . we'd been young, we'd had no time to learn how to trust each other. I could blame the war for that; Sonny and I, [friends] Lou and Dick—weren't we all victims?" (287).

Although the women left behind know (like Jeremy's sister in *The War at Home*) that they cannot comprehend exactly what happened to their brothers in the war, their experience of those years, though different, is no less profound. They are, after all, the same generation, and they are as dramatically transformed by that distant war as the brothers who go off to fight. As Kalpakian's Betty Lusky recalls:

> When I was in high school, it seemed like every week one of my brother's friends was joining the Army or being drafted. A few of them went to . . . college. . . . I'd come home from school and watch the news and see college kids—kids I might have known—in San Francisco and Washington DC having what looked like peace picnics, protesting the war and singing "Give Peace a Chance" and calling for a halt to the senseless slaughter. I'd watch them being clubbed and gassed and lying limp while they was drug off to jail. Then there'd be a commercial for Anacin or Ex Lax and then I'd see boys in Vietnam—boys I might have known—getting gassed and shot at and scrambling up dirty hills and lying limp and dying in the mud. ("Veteran's Day," 18–19)

Betty, like Mailer's Cherry, absorbs the lessons of Vietnam through daily television coverage. Bobbie Ann Mason's protagonist, Sam Hughes, represents a later generation, and her awareness of war comes not from nightly news reports from Laos or Cambodia, but from reruns of the popular TV sitcom *M*A*S*H*.

Sam Hughes, fatherless and abandoned by her mother, who has moved on to a new family and a better life, lives with her uncle; but, as Sam notes, she and Emmett are more like brother and sister than members of different generations. They share a taste for tacos, television, and popular music—as well as a deep commitment to each other. Emmett's own sister, Sam's mother, has given up on Emmett, whose Vietnam legacy is both physical and psychological. Irene proclaims, in finally rejecting Emmett, that "the war 'messed him up,'" but when she tries to entice Sam to come live with her to attend college in a larger Kentucky city, Sam responds, "I can't leave Emmett" (23, 56). Like Murana, Sam nurtures her veteran, insisting that he visit the doctor for his acne, which she fears may have been caused by exposure to Agent Orange; encouraging him to date, to look for a job, and most important, to come to terms with what happened to him in Vietnam. The first of two climactic scenes in *In Country* is Sam's night at the pond, her own "in-country" experience. Determined to understand the reality of Vietnam, Sam has spent the summer reading her father's diary and books about the war, talking to veterans, and contemplating the war that, despite Emmett's and her mother's advice that she forget it, Sam insists, had "*everything* to do with me" (71). Yet despite her efforts, Sam knows "that whenever she had tried to imagine Vietnam she had had her facts all wrong" (210). So she ventures into the wild and learns to see in the dark, to brave the terrors of the night, to "hump the boonies," as Emmett and his friends have done in the jungles of Vietnam. The experience is instructive for Sam, but it is crucial for Emmett, who finally, when he finds Sam alone in the woods, confides the horrible war experience that he has been unable to share. "There's something wrong with me," he tells Sam. "I'm damaged. It's like something in the center of my heart is gone and I can't get it back" (225). Emmett's confession is cathartic. At the end of the novel, he has found a job and organized a trip with Sam and her paternal grandmother to the Vietnam Veterans Memorial in Washington, D.C. Sam remains confused: "She is just beginning to understand. And she will never really know what happened to all these men in the war" (240). Yet her preoccupation with Vietnam has enabled Emmett finally to transcend his fourteen years of "grieving" (241). *In Country* ends with the sentimental image of Emmett reading his friends' names on the memorial. "He is sitting there cross-legged in front of the wall, and slowly his face bursts into a smile like flames" (245). Because Emmett will heal, Mason leaves us with a teenager who can mature into womanhood without the burden of brother, son, damaged veteran.

Her apparently autobiographical narrator's extended Mexican American family's protracted and very public 1997 cross-country pilgrimage to the Vietnam Veterans Memorial is, similarly, the contrived denouement of

Stella Pope Duarte's 2002 debut novel, *Let Their Spirits Dance*.[8] The memorial is "America's wailing wall [, and] only faith will get us there," proclaims Teresa, the sister of Jesse, who was killed in Vietnam thirty years before. Just before he leaves for Vietnam, Jesse tells Teresa that he is certain that he will die in Vietnam, and Jesse's private confidence still haunts his sister: "I've tried to forget what he said for the last thirty years. I never understood why he told me he'd never come back. . . . My mind battled the truth and a war began inside me. There's nothing worse than a private war going on inside you every day. I should have climbed on the plane with Jesse, I would have been better off in Vietnam, at close range, waiting for the words to come true. I was in my own Vietnam anyway, whether anyone knew it or not" (40). Teresa, newly divorced from her taciturn veteran-husband, is similarly preoccupied with elderly seer Don Florencío's prophecy that Jesse will come back in a new form—a plausible prediction in a novel steeped in contemporary Chicano culture's roots in ancient Aztec mythology. Duarte's casual allusions to parallels between Chicano and Vietnamese culture— altars to honor dead ancestors, physical similarities—underscore her characters' discovery, at the end of the novel, with the visit to the Wall, that Don Florencío's prophecy has come true, that Jesse (like Butler's David Fleming) has a half-Vietnamese son—Joshua Ramirez—who looks just like him.

Let Their Spirits Dance is Duarte's exegesis on young Chicanos' unacknowledged sacrifice in the Vietnam War, in which, she maintains, "Chicano youth were drafted to the war in numbers that were largely out of proportion to their actual population, and . . . once drafted, Chicano youth were most likely to serve on the front lines" (181). It is as well a variation on the prevailing theme that soldiers' families were victims of the war too, "the bodies coming home from Vietnam" mourned by "those left here dying of heartache" (36). Duarte's allusions to parallels between her ancient Aztec culture's values and those of the Vietnamese recur in Judith Ortiz Cofer's 1993 short story "Nada." *Nada*—nothing—is what Doña Ernestina, recently widowed Puerto Rican native and New Jersey resident, is left with when her son is killed in Vietnam. The close-knit female community in the inconsolable woman's apartment building gathers around to comfort her, for her husband's, then son's, deaths have destroyed "the dream of many of the barrio women her age—that of returning with her man to the Island after retirement, of buying a *casita* in the old pueblo, and of being buried on native ground alongside *la familia*"—like the Vietnamese, who must be buried in ancestral ground (26). Distraught with grief, Doña Ernestina begins to give away all her possessions, her behavior so alarming that the women of the building call a meeting: "Only the women attended, since the men were afraid of Doña Ernestina. It isn't unusual for men to be frightened when they see a woman go crazy. . . . When a woman is in trouble, a man calls in her mama, her sisters, or her friends, and then he makes himself scarce until it's all over. . . . men . . . know how much women help each other. Maybe the men even suspect that we know each better than they know their own wives" (31). But the community of women cannot help the heartbroken mother, who has been driven mad with her grief and who, as the story concludes is—not unlike the distraught narrator of Charlotte Perkins Gilman's "The Yellow Wallpaper" and Hai Truong, the ghost-ridden mother in Mary Gardner's *Boat People*—curled up, naked, in the corner of her empty living room.

But more like Sam and Murana and Zoe than Doña Ernestina, Duarte's Teresa, healed by the visit to the Wall and the revelation that Jesse has a son, comes to terms with her thirty-year-old grief and (like memoirists Gilberg and Zacharias) welcomes the therapy of writing: "It's OK that I knew my brother wasn't coming home. I was supposed to," the novel ends. "It got me to write this book, to tell his story to the world" (312).

Storytelling is a central theme of Nancy Peacock's 1996 slight, debut novel *Life without Water* as well. Her mother's stories of her uncle Jimmie's death in Vietnam are ironic lullabies for Peacock's narrator, Cedar, who is a small child when "my mother had told me that if not for her brother Jimmie's death, I might not have ever been born," as Cedar confides on the book's opening page. "She thinks she might not have found my father so fascinating if Jimmie had only lived. She thinks her whole life has pivoted on that moment . . . in 1968, when . . . the doorbell rang" (1–2). Sara's stories of her older brother's death, the totemic souvenir bullet that she wears around her neck as an amulet, and Jimmie's iconic final letter, which Sara saves but cannot bring herself to read, are, Cedar notes, "as close as we ever got to religion. . . . I would hear these stories all my life" (6, 41). Like Mason's Sam, Cedar is discomfited that she gets no answers to her questions about the Vietnam War. "I wanted to know why Jimmie was dead and why my mother was so sad and . . . why we weren't happy when the war was over and . . . who was right. I ended up as confused as anybody" (135–136).

Contrast the relatively insignificant relationship that pregnant Wyoming teenager Sophie Behr has with her combatant brother Clements in Karla Kuban's first novel, *Marchlands* (1998). Sophie is not close to her brother, who, she hopes, will stay away for a long time. But late in the novel, now in

Chicago, though she opposes the war Sophie declines to join an antiwar protest, worrying "what if Clements is one of those baby killers? What if he gets shot in the head? If he dies over there, all the hope I had for being friends with him will be gone. Just when we started" (217). Sophie develops no real relationship with her brother. When he returns from Vietnam, Clements offers the standard response to Sophie's questions about his actions in the war—"You just couldn't understand. You couldn't"—and Sophie recognizes that she must forgive her brother for his unacknowledged crimes: "We only have each other in our growing-up memories. There's no one else" (231).

Marchlands—like *Beyond Deserving*, Lisa Shea's *Hula*, and Thisbe Nissen's *Osprey Island*—offers the war and its aftermath as literary spice, sprinkled lightly to provide dramatic seasoning to the action and characterization, but essentially unintegrated into the text. Similarly, Meg Mowbry, the pregnant college student–protagonist of Elaine Ford's slim 1997 novel *Life Designs*, fleetingly contemplates suicide when her brother Kevin is killed in Vietnam in 1967 at the beginning of the story. But soon enough "her grief for Kevin had shifted from leaded hopelessness to a bittersweet regret for what would never be. Now, she realized, her copious tears flowed for no reason at all" (32). And indeed, Ford's novel and Meg's life progress with hardly another thought for Kevin or the Vietnam War. For most of these sisters, however, the brother-sister bond and their acceptance of their own responsibility for their brothers' varied fates are the defining fact of their lives and of their stories.

Sandwiches in Body Bags

These narratives reinforce the recurrent premise that the war, inevitably, comes home with metaphorical recreations of the war's horrors that underscore their familiar theme. Sam Hughes's archetypal initiation rite, her frightening night at Cawood's Pond is, for example, Bobbie Ann Mason's home-front replication of the Vietnam experience. Sam's C rations are Doritos and granola bars, and the "V.C." who frightens her turns out to be a raccoon. Sam knows that her experiment is only a night in the woods: "She felt so stupid. She couldn't dig a foxhole even if she had to" (212). Yet she does endure the snakes and insects in "the last place in western Kentucky where a person could really face the wild," as she wonders what a rice paddy looks like and how soldiers would negotiate a mined swamp (208). Throughout *In Country*, Mason presents Sam's attempts to imagine the war in vivid imagery. She enters the high school gymnasium for a veterans' reunion dance, and "in the corners it was dark, like a foxhole where an infantryman would lie crouched for the night, under his poncho, spread above" (120). Later, leaving the dance with Tom, Emmett's veteran buddy, "she felt she was doing something intensely daring, like following the soldier on point. A pool of orange light from a mercury lamp was the color of napalm" (124).

Mason's metaphorical evocation of Vietnam foregrounds Sam's summer-long efforts to compensate for her perception that history books don't "say what it was like to be at war over there" (48). While most of the protagonists of these novels and short stories are more sophisticated and less consciously curious than Sam, their authors nonetheless reinforce technically the relevance of the war and their characters' need to understand it. Metaphors illustrate the warlike experiences of everyday life, and violent or stereotypically male settings mirror the war as context and setting for these women's lives. Irene, the protagonist of Jane Bradley's 1989 story "What Happened to Wendell?," understands veteran Wendell Weeks in part because she shares his regular fishing trips and listens to his stories of Vietnam. Because she knows that since the war, for Wendell, hunting and fishing and "looking at the stars just wasn't the same," she is prepared when Wendell starts "acting crazy" and finally commits suicide (15, 20).

For some authors, the stereotypically male, war-surrogate setting demonstrates, not the female protagonist's efforts to understand battle, but her inability to do so. Sarah's reconciliation with Sonny and Vietnam in *Private Woods* develops against the backdrop of a Hemingwayesque hunting trip, which for the men in the novel—as for the male characters in Michael Cimino's *The Deer Hunter*—is a ritualistic rite of passage that rivals that of battle and overtly excludes the women. As her husband anxiously stalks his first deer, Sarah, equally nervously, confronts Sonny: "Talking was like picking my way through a mine field, trying not to hit any explosive topics" (144). Hunting provides the exclusory context for Stephanie Vaughn's 1984 story "Kid MacArthur" as well. Two years after he learns to assemble his father's dove-hunting ammunition (while his sister practices twirling her baton), the narrator Gemma's twelve-year-old brother is a skeet-shooting champion who cannot help but show his disappointment at a bad shot. Only after his battle experience, with his life "defined by negatives—no job, no college, no telephone"—has MacArthur "achieved the gamesman's implacable expression. Even in the long curves of his body," Gemma notes, "there was something which said that nothing could startle or move him"

(127, 129). Now the stoic warrior, MacArthur is impenetrable to his sympathetic sister: "He seemed to have escaped from me in an evaporation of heat. Even in my imagination, I could not go where he had gone" (129).

Pat Ellis Taylor evokes another exclusively male culture that mimics war in "A Call from Brotherland," in which Okie returns from Nam, not to his family, who are scattered and communicate only "with great difficulty," but "to the only family who would really give him a sailor's welcome, the California motorcycle black-leather brotherhood of veterans and dropouts nobody else took care of, so they learned to take care of one another as best they could by manufacturing experiences so intense as to distract themselves from the sorrow of recollection" (108). When Okie sees a "biker brother shot down," he checks himself into a navy psychiatric hospital, which provides the setting for Ellis Taylor's companion piece, "Descent into Brotherland" (108). Another stateside war zone, the VA hospital is a "mausoleum/museum for the relics of war, [a] junkyard of the war machine," populated by "hundreds of would-have-been-beautiful-well-made men come . . . from that place called War," and the only women allowed "are rarely there on their own account, but come instead with their husbands and lovers and brothers" (99–100). Zoe Coleman too finds her brother in "a place for borderlines. For hopefuls" (15). The clinic is not a military facility, but Morris's language emphasizes the postwar atmosphere: "It is a form of triage. You separate the dying from the wounded. You don't do much for the hopeless cases" (15). On the train ride home, Zoe contemplates the sandwiches "wrapped in cellophane body bags" (10). Her reunion with her mother occurs safely in a mall "in the middle of the Midwest in the middle of Nowhere. . . . It was neutral territory" (47).

Maura Stanton situates her story "Oz" in the midst of a tornado. Joe has just left for basic training, and his sister, the unnamed narrator, feels "strange inside when I considered that Joe was a year younger than I was" (26). The tornado approaches, and as the family takes shelter in the basement, another brother asks his mother, who was an army nurse in World War II, "what's worse, tornados or buzz bombs?" (28). Mother distracts the children with a war story, a memory of a fellow nurse who disappears after her fiancé is killed at the end of the war. "'We told each other everything.' My mother's voice shook. 'And then, it was as if she were dead'" (31). Unconsciously recognizing the pathos of her mother's story, the narrator, ostensibly in search of the family cat, flees the basement and ascends to the house for her own in-country experience. Searching the house, the narrator, noticing "with a little shock" Joe's empty bed, "suddenly . . . felt lonely and far away from everyone" (33). As the storm rages, she maneuvers through the house, surveying broken windows, twigs, and branches strewn about. Outside, "the street was impassable. Trees and branches had fallen across it in both directions" (34). Joe's absence, her mother's wartime tale, and the tornado converge into a moment of epiphany: "I felt dizzy, as if I had been spinning and spinning. This must be like the future, I thought. Your past did not blow away. It was you who blew away. You looked out the window and everything was different. I spun around. The living room smelled of mud and greenery. I ran breathlessly toward the basement, telling myself that my family was all down there, all of them, every one" (35).

Perhaps the most sustained metaphorical reverberations of war among these texts are Jayne Anne Phillips's "machine dreams." Danner's father Mitch, a World War II veteran, dreams of horrid smells "full of death" and "a twisted khaki of limbs" as he maneuvers a dozer to "get pits dug and doze this mess" (59). Eleven years later, his son Billy plays with his toy trucks and thinks of his father's new job selling "dozers and cranes and trucks to construction companies" after he sells his concrete company. Like Bobbie Ann Mason's strip-mining machine, "Big Bertha," the obsolete equipment is "giant wound-down toys smelling of aged dust and rock, their separate shapes merged in the twilit far end of the long building. They sat like big, sleeping things" (155). Danner's dream of her lost brother ends the novel: "Danner and Billy are walking in the deep forest. Billy makes airplane sounds. . . . They walk on, and finally it is so dark that Danner can't see Billy at all. She can only hear him, farther and farther behind her, imitating with a careful and private energy the engine sounds of a plane that is going down. War-movie sounds. *Eeee-yoww, ach-ack-ack*. So gentle it sounds like a song, and the song goes on softly as the plane falls, year after year, to earth" (331). Danner cannot let her brother go; for her, his plane will continue to crash "year after year." *Machine Dreams*, with its multiple narrators and often experimental prose, is the only one of the novels and stories here that departs from the traditional form of the bildungsroman. Phillips's world of cars and tanks, airplanes and trucks is the mechanistic, modern setting for her story of a family's dissolution and the shattering of a society wracked by a controversial war.

These narratives by American women, the earliest appearing in the late 1970s and the most recent—undoubtedly—today, offer a variety of quite personal and uniquely female reactions to the reverberating effects of the

Vietnam War on American lives. Arising from the experiences of the millions of women touched by the war and its aftermath, they offer more diverse characters and lives than the aftermath narratives by veterans, the POW memoirs, or the testimonies of Vietnamese Americans. The real and fictional women who found themselves in the midst of the war—Lynda Van Devanter, Nunez's Rouenna, Jenny McKay, Winnie Smith—claim and re-create the terror and exhilaration of the in-country experience. But most of these characters and memoirists live modest lives on the home front; neither warriors nor peace activists, they are private, generally young citizens coming of age in a chaotic era, struggling to cope with absent or damaged husbands and brothers and fathers, to understand the enduring consequences of a long war in their own lives.

As a group, these narratives are uneven. The professional, accomplished fiction writers—Ann Beattie, Bobbie Ann Mason, Jayne Anne Phillips, Susan Dodd—embraced the subject early on, in the late 1970s and early '80s, and their crafted, skillful texts offer the more satisfying interpretations of the material. First-time—often one-time—novelists such as Sandra Crockett Moore, Sydney Blair, and Norris Church Mailer followed with more superficial presentations by less proficient writers, which are nonetheless important for their demonstration of the narrative resonance of the experience and its themes. For memoirists Van Devanter, Gilberg, Novak, and Zacharias, the literary characteristics of the narratives are almost completely eclipsed by the therapeutic purpose of the writing process. "By writing," notes Gail Hosking Gilberg near the convoluted conclusion of *Snake's Daughter*, "I am saying that the survivor cannot be silenced. I am breaking the aloneness and finding language for my father's life in his world, where words meant nothing and only action counted. My father is one of the unanchored dead, restless like an unhealed wound. I see now that I have been one of the unanchored survivors, imprisoned in silence and obstructed grief" (172). In finding her voice, in telling her tale, Gilberg—and all of these women, authors and characters—claim the experience—their unique experience—of the Vietnam era. Though they acknowledge—and both respect and resent—the veteran's requisition of the combat experience, their voices, singly and together, teach us that the Vietnam War was fought, continues to be fought, well beyond the jungles of Southeast Asia. At Jenny McKay / Dakota Justice's funeral, at the end of A *Matter of Betrayal*, the illustrious attorney and Dakota's would-be suitor Drew Richards delivers the eulogy: "he described the life she led in the shadows, maintaining that she was as much a victim of the Vietnam War as any of the names on that black granite memorial wall in Washington, D.C. Hers was another life wasted by that wasteful war, and the damage it inflicted had wounded her so deeply that part of her had already died years before her actual death" (369). Sentimental rhetoric aside, Massman and Rosser capture the consistent, unifying theme of fiction and memoirs by American women about the Vietnam War: we were there too.

The realistic stories of brothers and sisters introduce into the collective Vietnam narrative lifelong relationships of love and dependence that are rooted far deeper than the haunting wounds of combat. These brothers and their sisters are doppelgangers; the men going off to confront—or evade—the perils of the front lines, the women left behind to accommodate their immunity from the war and their responsibility for its aftereffects. Journeying through diaries, photographs, the reminiscences of combat comrades, the Vietnam Veterans Memorial, or even the battlefields of Vietnam, daughters embark on missions to discover the fathers whose sacrifice to the Vietnam War is the denominative event of their own lives. And wives and lovers toil to love and support broken veterans whose traumatic, exhilarating experience in Vietnam all too often leaves them incapable of a life beyond it. Some of these women are able to recognize and survive their guilt and grief; others are infected by their veterans' pain. All suffer the other side of grief: the endless waiting, the lifetime of healing, the protracted struggle to bring the war home.

Chapter Three

Years of Darkness: Narratives by and about American Prisoners of the Vietnam War

. . . a welcome stranger. An enemy to be sure, but a man from out of the sky, a man of great accomplishment and from an advanced society.
—POW Larry Guarino, in *A P.O.W.'s Story*

I used to tell myself, when we were over there, that if I ever got home, I wasn't going to say one word about it. . . . It was going to be like the blue sky behind you—wasted air space. But you know what? . . . I am a sonofabitch if sometimes I don't miss it.
—Unnamed POW, quoted in *Bouncing Back*

REPUBLICAN partisans deployed a savvy strategic weapon against the Democratic candidate John Kerry in the 2004 presidential campaign when they launched a "Swift Boat Veterans and POWs for Truth" media blitz that lethally attacked the decorated Vietnam combat veteran-turned–antiwar activist. In television ads and a documentary film titled *Stolen Honor: Wounds That Never Heal*, Vietnam veterans and prisoners of war—including such prominent POW heroes and memoirists as Robinson Risner and George Day—denounced Kerry's 1971 testimony to the U.S. Senate Foreign Relations Committee and his leadership of Vietnam Veterans Against the War. For these George W. Bush loyalists, the antiwar movement prolonged the war (and therefore the POWs' imprisonment) by emboldening the North Vietnamese—a familiar argument, of course—and the movement was in turn fortified by the support of antiwar veterans, who, the conservatives clearly believe, were particularly culpable quislings. John Kerry, proclaimed George "Bud" Day, a POW and Medal of Honor winner, was "the Benedict Arnold of 1971."[1]

The vitriol directed against John Kerry because of his efforts thirty-odd years ago to expose the horrors and misprision of the Vietnam War demonstrates that the passions and controversies about America's presence in

Vietnam that roiled the United States during the war years have not abated. And the prominence of the former prisoners of the Vietnam War in the successful 2004 effort to deflect the Democrats' challenge to the incumbent president testifies to the iconic stature of the only acknowledged heroes of the Vietnam War more than thirty years after their triumphant repatriation from North Vietnam. The Arizona senator and presidential candidate John McCain—whose *Faith of My Fathers* is one of the most recent additions to a sizable collection of personal testimonies about the Vietnam War, the POW memoir—has, for example, nurtured a reputation as a resolute, ethical, independent national Republican leader based largely on his endurance of five and a half years as a grudging guest at Hanoi's notorious Hoa Lo prison, the turn-of-the-century French-built internment camp, christened the "Hanoi Hilton" by its American residents, that was the primary "home" for Americans captured in the North during the Vietnam War.

Of all the complex, intriguing issues that continually remind us of the persistent relevance of the Vietnam War in our present lives—parallels with the current Iraq War, distrust of government, U.S. economic relations with Vietnam, Vietnamese refugees, and on and on—perhaps none has, in the decades since the end of that lost war, loomed larger in the American psyche than the POW/MIA phenomenon. As Elliott Gruner writes about the American POWs held in Vietnam until 1973, "their plight proved to be one of the few issues that might solidify American sentiment about the Vietnam War. . . . Their plight had a metonymic quality: their suffering stood for the suffering of a nation through an uncertain war guided by unreliable and frustrating forces Americans did not understand. In contrast, the POW problem was simple: get them back!" (13–14). And once the POWs came home, in the spring of 1973, another, more protracted struggle began: the unceasing efforts of the families and advocates of the alleged POWs or Missing in Action to discover the fate of their fathers and sons who did not return from Vietnam. The subtitle of Dorothy McDaniel's 1991 memoir, *After the Hero's Welcome: A POW Wife's Story of the Battle against a New Enemy*, which recounts POW Eugene (Red) McDaniel's efforts "now, as proof has emerged that POWs still languish in Asian prisons," to reveal alleged government subterfuge about the dirty secret of the Vietnam War, illustrates the still current potency of the widespread certainty that all the POWs did not come home (flyleaf).

During the Vietnam War the Pentagon began to conflate counts for prisoners of war with soldiers missing in action, so exact numbers are difficult to determine; but by any account, the number of prisoners in America's longest war was small: 591 American prisoners released during Operation Homecoming in 1973; some 2,200 to 2,500 men unaccounted for—dead or left behind. Compare some 400,000 POWs in the Civil War, 4,500 in World War I, approximately 100,000 in World War II, and 7,000 in the Korean War.[2] The number of still-controversial MIAs is similarly modest: fewer than 2,500 from the Vietnam War, compared with 3,350 from World War I; 79,000 from World War II; and 8,200 from the Korean War (Doyle, 4). How and why this relatively small number of men collectively, and sometimes individually, achieved and retain such mythic status, and how the autobiographical testimonies of those men contribute to that myth, is a highly politicized story that reveals much about America's continuing fascination with the Vietnam War.

We Came Home, Capt. and Mrs. Frederic A. Wyatt's 1977 "yearbook" of photographs and brief biographies of the POWs released in 1973, features an introduction by the comedian and entertainer-to-the-troops Bob Hope, who praises the POWs for their "unprecedented example of patriotism, dedication, dignity, and strength," and by then California governor Ronald Reagan, who salutes the heroes returning to "a Nation where each generation can pass such manhood on to those who follow." This exuberant celebrity welcome for the leading men of the Vietnam War echoed "Operation Homecoming," the official national celebration mounted for the 591 returning POWs in the spring of 1973, and represented an appealing corrective to the indifferent reception to which, according to conventional wisdom and veterans' testimony, most Vietnam veterans returned. Feted by the White House, the Pentagon, and the popular media in what the resentful wounded veteran Lewis B. Puller, Jr., calls "the orgy of renewed patriotism," many of these men went on to enjoy distinguished military, business, and political careers. A sizable number of them (especially the career pilots shot down and imprisoned in Hanoi) have written memoirs of their captivity—memoirs that invariably testify, as Elliot Gruner and others have demonstrated, to their authors' resilience and patriotism and to the fact that they emerged from the crucible of their harrowing experience better men—that is, honorable, even heroic, warriors worthy of the ceremonial welcome-home party, and thus endowed with the moral authority to instruct a discordant American society (329).

Recent critical studies such as Gruner's *Prisoners of Culture: Representing the Vietnam POW* (1993), H. Bruce Franklin's *M.I.A. or Mythmaking in America* (1992), Robert C. Doyle's *Voices from Captivity: Interpreting the American POW Narrative* (1994), and Craig Howes's *Voices of the Vietnam POWs: Witnesses to Their Fight* (1993) examine our preoccupation with the prisoners of the Vietnam War, the numerous personal testimonies offered by the POWs, and the enduring conviction of many Americans that a corrupt North Vietnamese government and a duplicitous American government abandoned thousands of American POWs, who remained languishing in Southeast Asia long after the fall of Saigon. Indeed, to a significant extent, the POW/MIA issue remains popular because of the belief—despite several congressional investigations (including one in 1991 led by senators John Kerry and John McCain) that have proved otherwise—that all POWs were not released in 1973, despite the provisions of the Paris Peace Accords. In the years since the end of the Vietnam War, the National League of Families of American Prisoners and Missing in Southeast Asia (the organization of POW families that was instrumental in effecting the negotiated release of the prisoners in 1973); Ronald Reagan and Ross Perot; reported POW sightings by Vietnamese refugees; mercenary adventurers like Bo Gritz; and Hollywood macho adventure movies such as *Rambo*, the *Missing in Action* series, and *Uncommon Valor* have fueled the determined belief that America's leaders cavalierly abandoned U.S. soldiers in Vietnam.[3] Today, the United States spends hundreds of millions of dollars annually on Department of Defense–sponsored missions to identify and repatriate the remains of American military personnel in Vietnam and around the world, an effort that, to date, has identified 750 long-missing Vietnam War casualties. Each year the Hawaii-based Joint POW/MIA Accounting Command (JPAC) sends eighteen recovery teams to southeast Asia to search for the increasingly elusive remains of the 1,800 Vietnam troops still listed as missing.[4] And contemporary relations between the United States and Vietnam depend, in part, on American perceptions of Vietnam's cooperation with our MIA recovery efforts.

As H. Bruce Franklin and others have argued, the widespread conviction that POWs from the Vietnam War remain captive in Southeast Asia today, or died there in the years since America failed to bring them home, has become so ingrained in our national consciousness that it has become an American myth. Indeed, the insistence that in Vietnam our government betrayed the military's commitment to return all its combatants, dead or alive, "could be regarded," Franklin asserts, "as the closest thing we have to a national religion" (7). The enduring viability of this belief that American

POWs remained in Southeast Asia after 1973 is an immutable element of the power of the entire POW myth and therefore of America's lingering interest in our experience in Vietnam—what the veteran-scholar Walter A. McDougall calls "the Vietnamization of America." More important, the POW/MIA phenomenon presents a variety of cogent perspectives on the lingering cultural power of the Vietnam War. The experience of the POWs offers valuable commentary on the home front during the war and in the years since. Many of the wives of the POWs, who endured their own peculiar imprisonment in their long, lonely vigil, became public activists in their efforts to effect their husbands' release, and their stories proved fertile material for timely and unlikely narratives—both autobiographical and fictional—of female empowerment. And because the Nixon administration politicized the plight of the POWs in the waning years of the war, the POW phenomenon is an important component of an examination of political and military execution of the war. Again, the POWs, whose "years of darkness," in Fred Cherry's phrase, ranged from several months to nine years, returned to an exuberant patriotic welcome quite unlike the indifference or antipathy that awaited the ordinary grunt (Terry, 290). And a substantial number of the officer-heroes, anointed as creator-protagonists of what Craig Howes calls "the official story," embraced the valorous mantle and embarked on a public campaign of speeches, writing, and elected offices in an effort to share the ennobling lessons of imprisonment with a fractured, compromised American society. Narrative interpretations of the unique experience of the Vietnam-era POWs—both the variations of the "official story" and a few conflicting alternate voices—which appeared even before Operation Homecoming in 1973 and have continued in the years after the war, contribute important perspectives on the cultural appropriation of one of the more provocative aspects of America's assimilation of the Vietnam War.

The Official Story

Gruner and Howes delineate the process by which the Pentagon, the White House, the media, and the senior officer POWs themselves, reinforced by John G. Hubbell's 1976 *P.O.W.: A Definitive History of the American Prisoner-of-War Experience in Vietnam, 1964–1973*, collaborated to anoint the largest group of POWs—the male, career military, pilot-officers held in the Hanoi Hilton and nearby North Vietnamese prisons and released in the spring of 1973—as proprietors of the quintessential Vietnam POW experience, willfully indifferent to the testimonies of the variant voices. North Vietnamese–imprisoned antagonists like the antiwar POWs James A. Daly and George Smith, and outlier escape artist John Dramesi, for example, offer interesting variations on the sanctioned saga. Several of the less numerous enlisted men captured and imprisoned in South Vietnamese jungle camps published accounts of their more primitive incarceration—including James N. Rowe, whose *Five Years to Freedom*, published in 1971, is one of the earliest Vietnam POW memoirs and, according to the bibliographer Joe Dunn, one of the best. A handful of memoirs by civilians (the German nurses Monika Schwinn and Bernhard Diehl, the Australian journalist Kate Webb, and the American missionary Carolyn Paine Miller) offer salient variations on the primary narrative—offer, that is, the other side of the prisoner of war story. Yet fundamentally and finally, it was the collective testimony of the stoic pilots that inscribed "the first, dominant, and enduring story of [POWs'] captivity" (Howes, 77). Promotional material for the 1999 documentary *Return with Honor* promised "the powerful, moving story of American pilots shot down over North Vietnam and their challenge to survive with honor as POW's. A tribute to heroism, endurance, and brotherhood under duress, the film recalls the transformation from top-gun aviators to captives." Presenting the pilots' captivity as "a universal story of honor and duty," the film fails even to mention that enlisted men, women, and civilians shared the Southeast Asian POW experience.

As more than one POW memoirist attests, these soon-to-be-prominent prisoners of war released by the North Vietnamese in early 1973 anticipated their liberation from the deprivations of Hanoi's Hoa Lo prison with exhilaration, relief—and some trepidation. For propaganda purposes, most of the POWs had been tortured into writing or taping confessions of their alleged crimes against the Vietnamese, and, gripped with shame for their perceived weakness, they worried that upon their return home they would be castigated as traitors. From daily broadcasts of Voice of Vietnam radio and reports from later shoot-downs, the POWs knew that the war was increasingly unpopular in the United States, the returning veterans often excoriated as criminals. "We had heard about the antiwar activities, the demonstrations and marches," writes the POW Howard Rutledge, in his 1973 *In the Presence of Mine Enemies*, who wonders "how would they feel about me now? Would we be booed in the streets? Would our families be humiliated, our children scorned? We had no idea of what our reception would be" (94). In the summer of 1971, in the 1987 Hollywood film *The Hanoi Hilton*, one of the new, young shoot-downs tells the "old men" that by now most people at home oppose the war, which leads one of the old-timers to wonder whether they will be put on trial as criminals when they return to the United States.

In fact, however, the POWs returned to a White House–choreographed patriotic celebration that embraced them as exceptional American heroes and feted them with ticker-tape parades, free automobiles, and lifetime passes to professional baseball games. Jeremiah Denton remarks in his 1976 memoir, *When Hell Was in Session*, that "from the moment of release, the prisoners received an excess of warm, loving care from their countrymen. Operation Homecoming was planned and executed to the last detail to provide for our needs, and the doctors, nurses, and government people, pilots, and hundreds of citizens who greeted us at the airport all have our everlasting thanks" (180). Or, as Eddie Keller notes in James Kirkwood's irreverent 1975 novel *Some Kind of Hero*: "When we landed at Clark [Air Force Base in the Philippines, the POWs' first stop during Operation Homecoming], it was all lights, camera, action" (103).

The universally accepted myth of the Vietnam POWs as *the* heroes of the Vietnam War—a still-salient parable constructed and codified with the cooperation of the memoirists of the master narrative—demonstrates the power of literary narratives to create and reinforce significant political and social perceptions. Elliott Gruner most cogently examines the confluence of forces that, late in the war, collaborated to employ the previously unknown POWs for political ends—a calculated program that introduced them originally as victims and, upon their 1973 release, as true American heroes who, by their mere survival, vanquished the soon-to-be-victorious enemy. The League of Families appeared on the national stage in 1968, that watershed year that presented the Tet Offensive, a failed presidency, a vibrant antiwar movement, assassinations and racial turmoil, and, soon after, discovery of the My Lai massacre—a perfect, roiling storm of evidence that the war was a misguided disaster. The League introduced a story, a constituency (imprisoned officers, loyal families, evil North Vietnamese) that was sympathetic and morally unambiguous. Confronted with the once silent, now organized POW families, by 1969 the Nixon White House recognized the political advantage of making the fate of the POWs a central negotiating point in the Paris peace talks, and by the time of the POWs' release (which, of course, coincided with the United States' official declaration of its failure in Vietnam), the country was primed to celebrate and mythologize one of the few redeemable themes of the dominant story. When the patriotic officer-POWs returned to tell their consistent story of deprivation and survival—indeed of triumph and redemption—they presented a defeated America with a master narrative of endurance and heroism. "The POW struggle," Gruner notes, "came to represent the whole of the Vietnam war to Americans. The POW experience provided the United States with an ersatz victory, with a face-saving litany that could be read comfortably" (35).

Embraced as American heroes in a jaded era, the acclaimed POWs reveled in their unexpected celebrity, and the senior POWs (those who had been interned the longest and whose military rank—sometimes advanced during their imprisonment—credentialed them as leaders in the strict hierarchy imposed by the military's Code of Conduct for imprisoned combatants) valiantly embarked on lecture tours and documented their courageous endurance in formulaic, inspirational autobiographical narratives (often prepared with professional co-writers) that echo one another with notable consistency. Navy captain Rutledge's *In the Presence of Mine Enemies* and air force colonel Robinson Risner's *The Passing of the Night* appeared before the year was out. The Vietnam War correspondent Stephen A. Rowan interviewed some twenty of the POWs—whom he introduced as "the only heroes Americans are eager to honor in the wake of our longest and most unpopular war"—for his 1973 *They Wouldn't Let Us Die* (11). Reiterations of the acknowledged Vietnam captivity saga, such as navy captain Eugene McDaniel's spiritual memoir, *Before Honor*, in 1975 and Jeremiah Denton's story in 1976, followed. Hubbell's *P.O.W.*—which, its author audaciously suggests, was likely to be the most complete history of the Vietnam POW experience ever written—is based on several hundred interviews and asserts that each offers a tale of "towering courage, self-sacrifice and endurance" (xi). In Ronald Reagan's 1980s, the first wave of novels, memoirs, and films about the Vietnam War included *In Love and War* by Vice Admiral James Stockdale and his wife Sybil (1984) and, in 1989, the first of two memoirs by the longest-held POW, navy officer Everett Alvarez. A handful of offerings from the 1990s culminated in John McCain's *Faith of My Fathers*, which complements his POW saga with his panegyric to his military father's and grandfather's legacy of honor and integrity; and, more recently, George R. Hall's slight *Commitment to Honor*, published in 2005. Stuart I. Rochester and Frederick Kiley in *Honor Bound*, their exhaustive 1998 study of "American Prisoners of War in Southeast Asia, 1961–1973," list thirty-two published personal accounts by POWs held in Vietnam, Laos, and Cambodia—and they miss a few.

Though the POWs—both the authenticated heroes and the dissident fellow-prisoners—indicate no awareness of the tradition from which they write, their chronicles, in fact, emerge from a well-established American literary genre: the captivity narrative. As American historians and cultural critics have documented, Indian captivity stories, and, later, slave narratives, popular from the earliest years of the Republic, "constitute the first coherent myth-literature developed in America for American audiences" (Slotkin, *Regeneration*, 95). For early Puritans, notes Gary L. Ebersole, "captivity narratives were part of a spiritual regimen of self-examination and moral improvement" (9). Robert Doyle concurs: "some prisoners validated their experience as a manifestation of the providence of God and their suffering as acts of redemption" (5). Indeed, most of the arbiters of the official Vietnam POW story (though fewer of the non-military captives) echo in their personal accounts the perception that they are ennobled by their captivity experience. The memoirs of the career officers who adhered to the Code of Conduct and eschewed the special privileges or early release that their captors promised in exchange for confession of war crimes invariably reinforce the mythic vision of American history that, Richard Slotkin claims, "is seen as a narrative of man's regeneration and purification from sin, through the suffering of an ordeal by captivity" ("Dreams and Genocide," 41).

Regeneration through Violence

The Vietnam captivity narratives also share the genre's conventional, repetitive narrative structure. Slotkin notes that in the narratives about slavery in the nineteenth-century American South, whether autobiographical or fictional, "the consistency of the narrative pattern from account to account is remarkable" (*Regeneration*, 441). And Ebersole suggests that Indian captivity narratives, replete with "stereotypical scenes and characters," offer "little or no suspense" and replicate a basic central story: "the author or the protagonist is snatched from his or her home and forcibly carried into an alien culture, into the world of the Other. There the captive undergoes a series of ordeals or adventures while living among the Indians and later escapes or is ransomed and returned to civilization" (11, 10). The plot and structure of the personal accounts of the soldiers and civilians imprisoned in Vietnam during America's military presence there conform to the fundamental pattern of the traditional captivity narrative—what Doyle labels a "highly repetitive common narrative contour" that presents seven consecutive stages

106

(precapture autobiography; capture; the death march or remove; the prison landscape; resistance, survival, or assimilation; release and repatriation; and lament). The important themes and details recounted by the inmates of the Hanoi Hilton—some badly injured, others relatively healthy; some held in solitary confinement for part of their internment, others housed with one or more roommates; some senior ranking officers in their section of the prison, others loyal followers—recur with marked homogeneity.

They begin, these virile, gung-ho pilots, usually with the ill-fated mission. Autobiographical facts—military academy, marriage, advancement through the ranks—and expressions of commitment to the military and to its enterprise in Vietnam generally appear in a subsequent early chapter, but the suspenseful mission that ends with "the kill" invariably sets the pace. The action is rapid, the description replete with realistic, even arcane, details of the plane, the ordnance, the target. Air force lieutenant colonel Robinson Risner assures us, for example, that "for maneuverability, we wanted only two-ship flights because we were looking for SAM sites" (6). Navy squadron commander James Stockdale describes his departure from the flight deck of the USS *Ticonderoga*: "The big A-3 electronic jammer and weather scout launched with the Skyhawk tankers; then came the Crusaders, looking incongruous with those massive bombs on each side; then we [sic] flak suppressors" (96). And the sortie is always dangerous: "I was to lead twelve F-105 Thunderbirds, carrying the maximum load of 750-pound demolition bombs," explains air force major Larry Guarino (call sign "Geronimo") in the opening paragraph of *A P.O.W.'s Story: 2801 Days in Hanoi*. "The target was a control center near the Thanh Hoa Bridge. It was so hotly defended, the air force and the navy had already lost more than a dozen aircraft" (1).

Reconciled to the peril, these men present themselves as experienced fighter pilots, exhilarated by their profession and dedicated to their mission. And yet, a notable number—admittedly from hindsight and perhaps for dramatic effect—confess prescient reservations about the fateful final flight. Guarino confides to a fellow pilot that "there's something awfully wrong about today. I don't like it! I don't like the way the mission was planned or laid on, and the briefing was all screwed up" (2). Risner admits that "for the first time in twenty-two years of flying, I had a strange premonition about leaving that would not go away" (1). On the morning of his last flight, naval commander Eugene "Red" McDaniel is surprised to feel, as he prepares for his eighty-first mission, "the nibbling fear that maybe death was waiting for me today" (15).

The thematic similarities persist. The captured pilots are invariably amazed to find themselves prisoners of war; though they, unlike the enlisted men or, of course, civilians, have had survival training. Though admittedly prepared to die, they unaccountably never anticipated imprisonment. Most eject from their damaged planes calmly confident about imminent rescue and initially stoic about the long, enforced march to Hanoi through the Vietnamese jungle, with stops at small villages populated with angry, often abusive locals. Several—Jim Stockdale, John McCain, George Day, for instance—were badly injured, and all eventually resign themselves to imprisonment with the expectation that, under the 1949 Geneva Convention regarding prisoners of war, they will be treated humanely. Each describes his discovery, at his initial interrogation by the North Vietnamese, that, because the United States has not declared war, his captors consider him not a prisoner of war but a war criminal, and therefore unprotected by the Geneva agreements that stipulate no torture, decent food and conditions, mail privileges, and release according to physical condition and length of incarceration.

Once forcibly settled into Hoa Lo (in areas familiar to American prisoners as Heartbreak, Little Vegas, and New Guy) or nearby Hanoi prisons such as "Alcatraz" or "the Plantation," most of the pilot-memoirists describe more or less consistent conditions: two meals a day of unappetizing and meager stodge, which varies only depending on the season and the captors' provisions—rice, pumpkin soup, perhaps a little stale bread; on a good day "animal hooves, chicken heads . . . unidentifiable chunks of meat covered with hair" (Rochester and Kiley, 90). Three daily cigarettes. Six-feet-square cells (insufferably hot in summer, frigid in winter) with sleeping platforms or straw mats and antediluvian leg irons that were painfully tight on sturdy American ankles. A tedious, punitory ritual of early rising, limited exercise, forbidden communication, and irregular but predictable torture.

Torture, a commonplace of the Hanoi experience, is a prevalent theme in these texts. Generally reserved for prisoners held in the North, it was particularly harsh for officers, who, the Vietnamese correctly assumed, were responsible for organizing and leading the other POWs. Though senior officers endured the most sustained physical torture, all of the Hanoi captives who arrived before the cessation of extreme punishment in late 1969 vividly describe beatings with rubber "fan belts" and the notorious rope regimen, inflicted either for violations of the Camp Authority's rules or to elicit confessions of crimes against the people of Vietnam. And each writes at length and painfully about the inevitable culmination of such horrors—the point at which he "breaks" and writes or tapes the confession that was an essential component of the North Vietnamese propaganda campaign. Air force pilot Thomas Kirk notes that "the toughest thing was the battle within myself as to how long I could hold out. . . . Physical torture will achieve the desired effect in a *short* period of time. I don't care who you are. . . . At some point, you just don't care anymore, and then you will give them something" (Rowan, 41). In *Bouncing Back: How a Heroic Band of POWs Survived Vietnam*, Geoffrey Norman recounts navy pilot Al Stafford's humiliation and despair at his torture-induced capitulation to his captors' interrogation. Ashamed that he has broken, even though he provides only inaccurate information to his inquisitors, Stafford confesses his collapse to his cellmates: "Finally one of them spoke. 'You too?' he said. 'Well, then, join the fucking club'" (51). The vicissitudes of torture—how adamantly to resist it; what to do when you fail; how to respond to a fellow prisoner who breaks—is a recurring theme in the Hanoi memoirs and an introduction to another fundamental preoccupation of the Hoa Lo inmates throughout their testimonies: the sanctity of the military structure, the inviolability of rank, the insistence on camp unity, and the Code of Conduct.

The Code of Conduct

When Tim O'Brien's grunts trudge into the jungle in the title story from *The Things They Carried*, they haul comic books and razor blades, malaria and M&Ms, mine detectors and the ambiguities of Vietnam. And, among the necessities and burdens for O'Brien's combatants, "plastic cards imprinted with the Code of Conduct" (15). Formulated in 1955 after the ostensibly ignominious behavior of American POWs in the Korean War, the Code of Conduct for Members of the Armed Forces of the United States was the POWs' Ten Commandments, their Pledge of Allegiance, the landing lights that would guide them home. As Howes notes, their duty was "clear. Hold tight to traditional American values, maintain a command hierarchy, and follow the Code" (19). The code mandated resistance to captors, efforts to escape, rejection of special privileges or parole, refusal to harm comrades or make compromising statements, acceptance of leadership for senior officers, acquiescence to officers for lower-ranking prisoners, and "trust in God and in the United States of America." Yet, virtually every memoirist acknowledges, adherence to the code under the conditions of North Vietnamese imprisonment—with its unpredictable torture, the improbability of escape, an interdict against communication that compromised identification of senior officers and complicated mutual support—was often difficult. "Our fidelity to the Code was almost constantly challenged. Yet its principles remained the most important allegiance of our lives," recalls John McCain, who, like many of the pilots, reproduces the complete document in his memoir (241). Or, as the Peace Committee member Frank Anton more cynically suggests, "the vast majority of POWs were guilty of violating the Code of Conduct. The ones who refused to give the North Vietnamese anything but name, rank, and serial number didn't come home" (Grant, 341).

For interpretation of and assurance of adherence to the code, the POWs relied on the leadership system of rank and hierarchy to which, as career military men, they were accustomed and committed. And since it was predominantly the senior officers—Stockdale, Risner, Denton, Richard Stratton—who, anointed as the official heroes of the POW experience, tell the noble tale, the importance of the leadership system mandated by the code is emphasized throughout the autobiographical accounts of imprisonment in the North. With frequent moves—especially of senior officers—around different areas of the camp, and into and out of solitary confinement, plus the vagaries of surreptitious and limited communication, identifying the senior officer in a particular camp was difficult. Although the senior men agreed to determine seniority by rank at the time of shoot down, as later officer "kills" arrived, occasionally with news of a long-term inmate's promotion, the situation was complicated even further. But for the men giving the orders, their command was inviolable. Indeed, they were eager for the responsibility, for these American heroes, with their "fly-boy ego[s]," are not humble men (Blakey, 9).

In the second chapter—the officer-memoirist's standard litany of factual personal information—of *When Hell Was in Session*, Jeremiah Denton assures us that at his capture, at age forty-one, he was "physically and mentally . . . in my prime" (12). He is, Denton matter-of-factly declares, "widely [read] in philosophy, history, and religion. . . . thoroughly grounded in the military sciences . . . an expert in airborne electronics as well as a recognized expert in antisubmarine warfare and air defense. In fact, I had devised fleet tactics that were regarded in the Navy as revolutionary. In other words, the North Vietnamese had made a good catch" (12). When Jim Stockdale, who, he proudly suggests, "had taken my upbringing a lot more seriously than most," takes off on the 1964 mission that immediately follows the alleged Gulf of Tonkin incident, he knows that "this flight was a history maker and I felt like the load of the world was on my shoulders" (60, 28). A month later, shot down and captured, Stockdale trusts that "word was out that I was somebody who should be kept alive," and he is delighted when he arrives later at the Zoo and learns that he is the senior ranking officer (SRO): "I'd be the senior man in the system, the boss. This was where I was supposed to be. This was my life" (107, 239). Rochester and Kiley romantically concur:

> The Navy and Air Force aviators who comprised the bulk of prisoners in the Northern camps were career servicemen for whom discipline and motivation were natural. But this solid corps of professionals would become greatly emasculated and debilitated from imprisonment. Their "fighting" capability had somehow to be restored. The job of leadership was to institute and maintain a semblance of organization, even as the leaders were continually being segregated, and to nourish hope and a will to resist even as the leaders themselves bore the brunt of punishment and were being tested to the limits of their endurance. Fortunately, they were senior officers up to the assignment, a coterie of exceptional individuals who managed to devise a resistance organization with cleverness and skill and who, when singled out for abuse by the Vietnamese for their efforts, and sometimes removed from direct contact or communication with their troops for extended spells, continued to lead by courage and example. (129–130)

Although a few of the officers' memoirs briefly and obliquely mention several (unnamed) sequestered senior officers who shirked the demands of leadership, the SRO-memoirists who would become the celebrities of Operation Homecoming enthusiastically embraced their responsibilities, with particular attention to interpretation of the code. "Bounce Back," their Denton-defined policy in the early years, mandated that once a POW could no longer resist torture, he must confess his capitulation, recover from it, and renew his resistance. Subsequent disagreements about the value of resisting to physical extremes, which led to dissension between so-called hardliners and others, such as Richard Stratton, who advocated "accommodation and a more pragmatic, flexible approach to resistance," resulted in SRO Stockdale's refinement of camp policy in 1967 (Rochester and Kiley, 350). His BACK US, an acronym, defined what POWs were expected to accept torture for; BACK prohibited bowing to captors in the presence of reporters or foreign officials, taping confessions for broadcast, admitting crimes, and "kissing [captors] goodbye." US mandated the most essential principle: Unity over Self. In the later years of imprisonment, treatment and conditions ameliorated as the war waned and with developments such as the death of Ho Chi Minh in the fall of 1969 and the November 1970 Son Tay Raid (which failed in its mission to rescue the POWs, who had been moved to other camps, but dramatically improved the prisoners' morale and frightened the Vietnamese into centralizing the POWs' location). With more sustained contact among a larger group of POWs, the leaders established a complex organization with committees for communication, education, and escape plans, and refined BACK US into long, complex policy statements code-named "Plums." Some of the contrarian POWs objected to the authority and rigidity of the senior officers' policies. With the likelihood of imminent release, the antiwar Hanoi POWs—called "the Peace Committee" and repudiated as traitors by the budding heroes—considered the possibility that they would be prosecuted for treason if they returned to the United States. James A. Daly, in his *Black Prisoner of War: A Conscientious Objector's Memoir*,[5] notes that "most of the guys agreed that they could always claim, if they had to, that they'd been forced to write letters, or tortured into it. After all, the Code of Conduct was written by men who had never had to have these decisions or had never had any understanding of them" (186). You had to be there. Yet, these memoirs affirm, for most of the Hanoi POWs, the Code of Conduct and its interpretation by the SROs were a lifeline. As Howes notes, "their growth as a community paralleled the growth of their laws" (31–32).

Indeed, community is the sacrosanct tenet for the Hanoi prisoners. "My whole concept of proper prisoner-of-war behavior was based on sticking together," Stockdale writes in his metaphor-challenged explanation of his BACK US injunction. "One interested only in keeping his own nose clean could score lots of points by remaining a loner. I asked everybody to give up this edge of individual flexibility and get in the swim and communicate, level with your American neighbors on just what-all you compromised, what information you had to give up in the torture room, to freely enter into collusions with Americans, to take your lumps together and, if necessary, all go down the tubes together" (252). Testimonies to the strength and integrity of the group, and to bonds between cellmates, are prominent throughout these personal accounts. In a post-release speech, Stockdale surprisingly— and apparently without irony—appropriates another familiar metaphor of the era: "We built a successful military organization and in doing so created a counterculture. It was a society of intense loyalty—loyalty of men to one another; of rigid military authoritarianism" (*A Vietnam Experience*, 9). His arrogation of the term "counterculture" unconsciously acknowledges that the POWs' sense of community and camaraderie approximates the activists' more licentious coterie. Red McDaniel, recalling his memories of imprisonment, "saw men who cared for each other, nursed each other, took risks for each other, gave up their food for each other, and devised ways to keep hope alive for each other" (168). Some men (nebulously hinting at the homoerotic relationships occasionally apparent in the male aftermath novels) insist that their relationship with their POW cellmate was more precious, more sustaining than the one with their wife. And no punishment was more dreaded than solitary confinement. Memoir after memoir documents that its author's darkest hours occur in isolation from other prisoners. Solitary, John McCain notes, "crushes your spirit and weakens your resistance more effectively than any other form of mistreatment" (206). Howard Rutledge, in *In the Presence of Mine Enemies*, concurs: "Isolation is a terrible weapon. . . . there is still no torture worse than years of solitary confinement" (70). As every memoir attests, then, the group's salvation and the validation for the military structure was community, camaraderie—and communication.

Joan Baez Succs

Recognizing that fidelity to the Code of Conduct and general morale depended on the POWs' ability to maintain contact with one another, the North Vietnamese strictly proscribed communication among their prisoners and went to considerable lengths to ensure that the POWs were unable to support and instruct each other. They would not allow the Americans to learn Vietnamese words (or even their captors' names, which inspired clever and persistent nicknaming); they remodeled areas of the old Hanoi Hilton to prevent audible wall-tapping or signaling through windows and doorways. And still, communicate the POWs did—indefatigably and creatively. Each new arrival was quickly initiated into the tap code, a venerable wartime system based on a five-by-five matrix in which each letter of the alphabet is assigned two numerical values. As the twenty-sixth letter, "c" substitutes for "k," which several of the autobiographers illustrate with the epigrammatic proclamation (and movement dismissal) that "Joan Baez Succs." Other communication methods included hand signals, coughing and sneezing signals, note passing, and, for adjoining cells, speaking through an inverted porcelain drinking mug wrapped in a towel and heard through one placed between the listener's ear and the wall. Surreptitious communication, Stockdale notes, allowed the POWs to "set up a chain of command, encourage the doubtful, console the depressed, comfort the hurt" (*A Vietnam Experience*, 89). Camp policies; information from new guys about families, the war, and life at home; updates on the condition of a tortured or injured compatriot; jokes, life histories, intra-cell games—all flew through the primitive communication systems when the guards disappeared. Punishment for prisoners caught communicating was severe, but only the apostate Daly—who grouses that "it seemed crazy to risk punishment for asking questions of new POWs like who won big sports events, or what were the new cars like?"—demurs (182). His fellow POWs insist that continuous communication was the Americans' life preserver. As POW Bob Shumaker suggests, "communication [was] the key to sanity" in the Hilton (Rowan, 84). In *Return with Honor*, air force captain George McKnight calls communication "our one major victory."

Mental Golf on the Dark Side of the Moon

Assuredly, their postwar satisfaction with their individual behavior during imprisonment and the prisons' social organization do not obviate the chroniclers' testimony to the deprivations and despair of prolonged incarceration. They write convincingly—sometimes powerfully—about hunger and malnutrition; debilitating, often untreated and chronic injuries; mind-numbing boredom. The solaces of camaraderie and interaction with fellow prisoners notwithstanding, the authors reiterate their understanding that they are, finally, alone. As Ben Purcell notes, "I was lost in the wilderness . . . on the dark side of the moon . . . on a deserted island . . . at the South Pole. Robinson Crusoe had his Friday. The man without a country had his shipmates. I was alone" (179; ellipses in original).

Sequestered, often in solitary confinement, (until late in their imprisonment) without reading material (except an occasional propaganda pamphlet), and generally forbidden to write or receive letters or to exercise, the prisoners struggled to stave off boredom and maintain physical health and mental acuity. A physical fitness regimen meant push-ups or endless circumlocutions of a tiny cell. To pass the time, to distract themselves from hunger, pain, and emotional despair, to combat sensory deprivation, they devised complex, clever diversions. Larry Guarino mentally calculated storage space for canned peaches, and George Hall played eighteen carefully choreographed holes of "mental golf" every day (50). Ben Purcell re-ran his favorite movies in his mind and fashioned a wedding band from an empty toothpaste tube to replace the one that the Vietnamese had, typi-cally, seized. Several POWs, including Monika Schwinn, designed dream houses. For his, Howard Rutledge selected the site, negotiated the purchase, constructed and furnished the house, sold it ... and began again. Later, when restrictions against communication eased somewhat, men within the same area of the camp shared the narration of a recalled movie or tutored each other in math or engineering. By early 1971, after the Son Tay Raid, when most of the Hanoi POWs were moved together to the communal compound that they named Camp Unity, they had formed a toastmasters society, choirs, and "Hanoi University," which offered classes in astronomy, biology, wine appreciation, meat cutting, and more. Alone, then together, the survivors endured.

Throughout the Hanoi memoirs, then, the trajectory of the official story is consistent: shoot down; biographical backstory; early torture and the privations of imprisonment; eventual reconciliation to a long, spartan in-carceration; commentary on individual POWs, daily conditions, and the author's particular vulnerabilities and coping strategies. And almost without exception, the recital of the slow unfolding of the grim years is underscored by a recurrent declaration of the author's faith in God. The Christian God who sustained Puritan captives of Native Americans and African American slaves in earlier centuries was summoned to Hoa Lo prison in the middle of the twentieth.

Surely, in contrast, John Dramesi's spiritual despair is understandable. In late 1969, after thirty-one months of imprisonment and a failed escape at-tempt, and with his fellow POWs resistant to his plans for another escape (because of their conviction that one could not successfully escape from the Hanoi prisons—as, indeed, no one did—and their legitimate fear of the in-evitable Vietnamese reprisals against the other prisoners after an escape at-tempt), Dramesi, yearning for solace and strength, reflects that "there was no God in that cubicle. The only people who could help me were myself and those attempting to defeat the North Vietnamese" (163). Dramesi's denial of spiritual solace is reasonable, but it is virtually unprecedented in these texts. Similarly uncharacteristic is his oblique confession of his antiwar sen-timents and reference to those of people "back home in the United States who were working to getting us out of this place" (163). Only the German nurse Monika Schwinn, whose expressions of a creeping lack of faith in God recur throughout *We Came to Help*, shares Dramesi's spiritual skepticism. The other Hanoi POWs, in fact, attribute their survival to the immanent presence of God in their cells.

God Is My Roommate

Indeed, most of the POWs attest not only to the sustaining power of their faith, but to its intensification during—and because of—their years of hardship. Near the end of *The Passing of the Night*, Robinson Risner (casually acknowledging the construction of an "official story"), explains the "unified stance" presented by the returning POWs, suggesting that surviving imprisonment meant adhering to "very basic, clear positions" and clinging to "something that would give us strength on a minute-by-minute basis" (169). Risner enumerates the "four essentials" that sustained him and his compatriots: first, understanding that they were the NLF's "prime war weapon," and that to deny their enemy "propaganda resources" was to continue their battle against Communist aggression[6]; second, commitment to patriotism and duty to country, reclaiming their American heritage from "the nuts and the kooks" who had made "patriotism a dirty word"; third, maintaining faith in the American people; and fourth—and most important—faith in God (170). "Before imprisonment," Risner suggests, "many of us had been too busy to put God in our lives. A North Vietnamese prison cell changed that" (172). Ben Purcell asserts that his years as a POW were "an investment in [my] relationship with the Lord" and suggests that "few people are blessed to meet Him on the intimate terms" that he did (flyleaf). During imprisonment, Howard Rutledge comes to regret his pre-capture indifference about God and religion, proclaiming that "it took prison to show me how empty life is without God" (34). After he watches yet another prisoner-comrade die, Green Beret lieutenant James N. (Nick) Rowe, who was captured in 1963 and escaped from his southern Vietcong captors on New Year's Eve, 1968 (and whose memoir is, as Dunn notes, the most introspective of the group) "turn[s] to the one positive force our captors could never challenge, God." Admitting that he has never met a life challenge serious enough to force him to depend on "a Supreme Being," he acknowledges that now, if he is to survive, "I could only turn to faith in the Power I believed to be so far greater than that which imprisoned me" (231, 232).

More dogmatically spiritual memoirs, such as Red McDaniel's *Before Honor*, Norman McDaniel's *Yet Another Voice*, and dissident James A.

Daly's *Black Prisoner of War*, vehemently declaim throughout the sustaining power of faith. Even the more secular Jim Stockdale, who in 1982 suggested that although religious faith was a "positive force for the great majority of us . . . some *good prisoners* did not rely on it" (my emphasis), assures his wife Sybil in rare letters from Hanoi that "God has become my roommate and he's taking care of me," and that "this experience has taught me to love Him completely, and hopefully to better serve Him (and to better serve you all), when I get home" (*A Vietnam Experience*, 126; *In Love and War*, 137, 128). As Howes notes, faith in a Christian God was the POWs' most exigent value: "These POWs were grateful for their military training, their fellow prisoners, and their national heritage. Having rendered to America what was America's, however, they then declared that God had been their greatest support" (174). Rochester and Kiley concur that "there is virtually no personal account in the Vietnam PW literature that does not contain some reference to a transforming spiritual episode" (413). As Larry Guarino exclaims, "Do I pray? You're damned right I pray! What else have we got in here?" (57).

The testimonials to the sustenance of religious faith as a "positive force" for the POWs underscore the implied apprehension that, after all, the POW experience was salutary. Many of the memoirs and interviews, unwittingly confirming Slotkin's concept of regeneration through violence, affirm the POWs' belief, much like that displayed by novels and memoirs by and about combat veterans, that they became better men as a result of the trials of imprisonment. Ev Alvarez, in his aftermath memoir, *Code of Conduct*, explains that by the mid-1980s what Stockdale calls "the good prisoners" shared an "emerging consensus that keeping honor intact throughout the POW experience had actually strengthened us in spite of some lingering pain and disability" (194). James Stockdale, writing at the same time, professes that "there were many of us who were able to use the fire that was meant to destroy us as a saving fire, as a cauterizing agent, as a temperer of what became our steel" (*A Vietnam Experience*, viii). The theme recurs throughout the memoirs of the hero-POWs, those brave men whom Stockdale anoints as "persistent practitioners of endurance" (126). "Faith in God, faith in country, and faith in your fellow prisoners," as John McCain asserts, made these men the Vietnam War's only heroes and superior human beings (252). Compare the veteran-protagonists' suggestion that the horrors of combat have earned them superiority over noncombatants.

The memoirs of the pilot heroes, to reiterate, in their replication of the structural and thematic conventions of the captivity narrative, present their authors as the ombudsmen of the inspiring story of America's imprisoned patriots. So congruent are their features that their manufacture of an official story is undeniable. Indeed, most critics have recognized the characteristics that the Hanoi memoirs share; less addressed, if no less significant, however, is what this group of texts fails—or refuses—to acknowledge.

Taking Captivity Captive

In stark contrast to other memoirists of the Vietnam era—Tom Hayden, Bill Ayers, and other movement activists, for example—none of the POW memoirists, whether purveyors of the sanctioned POW-as-hero myth or the dissident or variant voices, notes the possibility that his or her memories are unreliable or limited. This is perhaps understandable for those protagonists who penned their tales immediately upon release—Risner, Rutledge, and Rowan's and Hubbell's subjects, for instance—but more problematic in the later offerings from, say, Hall and McCain. None muses about the genre of memoir or autobiography, or about the formal demands or inexorable subjectivity of what James Olney calls "life-writing"; none refers to, or even appears familiar with, the canonical personal writing of earlier possible models—Augustine, for instance, or Benjamin Franklin. Also, although by the later years of imprisonment at least some of the POWs were allowed paper and writing implements, apparently none of the military POWs anticipated the composition of an autobiographical account by making notes while incarcerated. Monika Schwinn, in contrast, successfully hides her "letters, notes, the addresses of American friends" in the lining of her departure bag in 1973, and her colleague Bernhard Diehl is so distressed by his captors' confiscation of his papers that he threatens to refuse to leave Hanoi (249–250). Rochester and Kiley preface their historical account of the American POW experience with the qualification that "memoirs, which comprise the bulk of the published literature, must be viewed with caution, not only because of their discretionary nature but also owing to the lack of overall perspective beyond the prisoner's own small cell or circle and inevitable memory lapses in the time between living and recording one's experience" (xiii). Yet other commentators on the POWs' testimonies and, most important, the autobiographers themselves, fail to engage the issue of reliability.

These are high ranking, successful military officers; they do not doubt their abilities, their moral rectitude, or their version of events. They were fighter pilots, men of action, and years of forced inactivity apparently did not foster introspection. Like Risner, most of the Hanoi POWs believed that, even incarcerated, they remained combatants in their country's war. They knew that the NLF would use their torture-induced confessions—however factually fallacious—as propaganda. In *A Country Such as This*, the 1983 novel by Vietnam veteran, former secretary of the navy, now U.S. senator James Webb—one of very few fictional representations of the POW experience to aspire to a more serious exploration of the theme than the exemplars of the *Rambo*-clone, violent, let's-go-get-them-out-of-there, pulp adventure genre—navy pilot Red Lesczynski endures a long Hanoi Hilton imprisonment that is faithful to the autobiographical accounts in every detail. Lesczynski understands that, unlike in previous wars in which POWs are merely held for the duration, in the "political . . . rather than military" Vietnam War, he and his compatriots are "political pawns. Far from being put on ice, they were in many ways the centerpiece" (421).

And the POWs discovered, as the war progressed, that their status was politically powerful back home, beyond the Pentagon and the White House. New shoot downs, dreaded visiting movement dignitaries, and, in the waning years of imprisonment as treatment improved, letters from home all affirmed both the increasing virulence of antiwar sentiment in the United States and the rising visibility of the POWs' predicament. After years of official government silence on the POW issue, in 1969—in part responding to pressure from the newly organized and vocal League of Families—the Nixon White House (initiating the PR campaign that would consecrate the POWs upon their release in early 1973) featured the fate of the POWs as an issue to rally support for its escalation of the war and to defuse the protest movement. "Support for the POWs was now one of the central issues of the Vietnam War," suggests Elliot Gruner. "Their cause became a source of agreement for a divided America" (19). Yet despite their claim that they remain active warriors (and despite limitless time for introspection and reflection about the war, not to mention a daily diet of anti-American propaganda from Voice of Vietnam radio), the pilot annalists, like military wives and daughters, offer virtually no commentary about the war—and even less about their role in it. Air force colonel Fred V. Cherry (like Norm McDaniel one of eighteen African American POWs immured in Hanoi) articulates the popular Pentagon "one hand tied behind our backs" theory, asserting that "the war just went the way it did because the military was not allowed to win it. That's all." But even this tepid critique of the official conduct of the war is undermined by his declaration that "I had no problems with the orders to go to Vietnam. It was just like the people in South Vietnam wanna be free to make their own decisions, to have a democratic government. And the Commies were trying to take over. And being a serviceman, when the commander in chief says time to go, we head out" (Terry, 290, 269). Late in the war, Webb's Red Lesczynski (who is, as a fictional character, arguably better positioned for candor in his assessment of his superiors) wonders bitterly, "*If there was to be a war, and if I was to be sacrificed on its altar, could it not at least have been carried out with a clearness of purpose that matched the commitment of the men being sent to fight it?*" (508).

It is, of course, not surprising that career military officers would question a perceived government hesitancy to pursue the war assiduously or to trust in-country officers and soldiers to make day-to-day decisions. Other POW officer memoirs betray their authors' reservations about the conduct of the war, but the critique is directed, similarly, at government policy and strategy rather than at ethical considerations. James Stockdale, who begins his memoir (co-authored with his wife) with an account of the August 1964 Gulf of Tonkin debacle,[7] punctuates it and the rest of his memoir with a critique of government control of the war. As an on-site participant, Stockdale knows that the second Gulf of Tonkin attack was mythical, that the United States was about to "launch a war under false pretenses," but his reservations about the "fiasco" arise not from the moral enormity of the mistake or official mendacity but from the "bad portent that we seemed to be under the control of a mindless Washington bureaucracy, vain enough to pick their own legitimacies regardless of evidence" (*In Love and War*, 23, 19, 23). In a 1982 postmortem on the war, Stockdale declares that "the tragedy of Vietnam" was that "Defense Secretary Robert Strange McNamara and his Whiz Kids took over the Department of Defense and tried to run the Vietnam conflict as if it were the Ford Motor Company with a knock in the engine and an unfavorable balance sheet" (*A Vietnam Experience*, 109, 111). Alvarez concurs, suggesting in his 1991 memoir that "militarily, the war was fought from Washington rather than in the field" (176). Compare John McCain's 1999 assessment (which, perhaps, elucidates his intractable support for the Iraq War) that "it was a shameful waste to ask men to suffer and die . . . for a cause that half of the country didn't believe in and our leaders weren't committed to winning. They committed us to it, badly misjudged the enemy's resolve, and left us to manage the thing on our own without authority to fight it to the extent necessary to finish it" (334). Adding the important codicil acknowledging the lack of popular support for the war, Mc-

Cain echoes his fellow prisoners' indictment of a government that lacked faith in its military and the will to win the fight by any means necessary. He, like his comrades, proffers no discussion of the ethical implications of his own participation in the war.

With remarkable congruity, the Hanoi prisoners' personal accounts imprison the POW experience, as it were; their focus is on the conditions of incarceration and the POWs' struggles, individually and collectively, to resist "breaking." Pre-capture life—education, family, career—is described cursorily; and during imprisonment, concerns about home, family, or the progress of the war are as much about negotiating with the NLF for mail privileges as they are a demonstrable interest in life beyond the walls of the Hanoi Hilton. Several of the narratives indicate that thoughts of home and family are so painful that they must be dismissed, and indeed the daily battle to remain alive and psychologically sound would understandably trump all other preoccupations. Yet the construction of the official narrative so privileges the noble campaign to return with honor that it obviates introspection, experiences, or perceptions about anything that would complicate the gallant story.

Similarly off limits in these pilots' narratives is attention to prison behavior that compromised the dominant myth (though the "assimilationist" memoirs I discuss later in this chapter present many examples of it). Although encomiums to fellow survivors and brave prisoners who didn't make it—Lance Sijan and Ed Atterberry, for example—are standard, we learn little from the hero-authors about POWs who violated the Code of Conduct out of defiance or weakness. The NLF courted vulnerable or particularly visible POWs (John McCain because his father was an admiral; Risner because he had been featured in *Time* magazine), offering them special treatment or early release in exchange for propaganda statements. Acceptance of such favors mocked the "Unity over Self" maxim and violated the Code of Conduct, and the now-obscure POWs who succumbed to such temptations undermined the goal of return with honor and were treated with scorn. Fred Cherry dismissively asserts that "not more than a dozen guys ever did anything that was aid to the enemy," but his disdain for those traitors is palpable. Though he echoes the assessment of Rochester and Kiley and other scholars who suggest that the problematic POWs were likely to be younger, enlisted men and South-held captives who were usually isolated and moved frequently, and therefore ignorant of the Code of Conduct, Cherry notes that "there were two senior officers who refused to take orders from us, made tapes for them to play on Radio Hanoi, and met with the antiwar people, the Jane Fonda and Ramsey Clark types" (Terry, 285). Noting that those "assimilators," as Doyle characterizes them, received special treatment, Cherry insists that for their own protection they had to be housed separately from the other prisoners. "I had less respect for those two than I did for our captors," Cherry concludes. "Most of us did. We considered them traitors then. And I feel the same way today" (Terry, 285). Most of the Hanoi POWs are similarly, if fleetingly, judgmental about colleagues who embraced what Stockdale called the "Fink Release Program," and immediately after Operation Homecoming, Stockdale and Ted Guy brought charges against allegedly treasonous POWs. But the official government policy was to declare amnesty for all returning POWs, and with the POWs' 1973 release—either because America was so relieved to be at long last free of the burden of the Vietnam War or because the official story was so widely embraced that the public hesitated to question its universality—there was little home-front interest in prosecuting collaborators. By 1978 the always-philosophical Stockdale was stoic about the shortcomings of the Hanoi minority, whose violation of "a gentleman's code" he presents as more tragic flaw than actionable crime. Years later, John McCain (who declined the North Vietnamese offer to release him early) comments on the decision of Norris Overly, his cellmate who tended to his serious injuries and who, McCain says, saved his life, to accept early release. "I thought him a good man then, as I do today," writes McCain. "I feared he had made a mistake, but I couldn't stand in judgment of him" (204). John Dramesi records Dick Stratton's prescient prediction that "when we get out of this place . . . [e]verybody's going to be a good soldier. And everybody will be so tired of this Vietnam war and the P.O.W. issue that the question of resistance won't even be brought up. We'll all be part of one big group" (258). For the senior, long-interned men who had endured so much to be able to return with dignity, such a leveling of the POW reputation was understandably unthinkable. Craig Howes suggests, in fact, that it was the senior POWs' frustration with the government's unwillingness to sanction the Code of Conduct by punishing its violators that accounted for the formal composition of the official story:

> many Vietnam POWs remained worried that their time in captivity had been whitewashed or ignored. These POWs had prepared for official scrutiny, and many were disappointed when they didn't get it. This dissatisfaction was one

of the most compelling reasons why so many POWs set to work on recording their stories. Within months of Operation Homecoming, biographies,
histories, interview collections, and memoirs began pouring from presses
small and large—a flood which continues. Public interest in POW narratives
and stories of torture undeniably helped to create the market, but the POWs'
own agenda was to defend the Code and its followers—to see in short that
justice was done. Slighted by their government, the POWs therefore turned
to the American people, confessing their weaknesses and crimes, but also
proudly describing their individual triumphs and many successes as men
fighting adversity together. (39)

Yet the personal writing of the longtime officer-tenants of the Hanoi Hilton,
whether they write immediately or long after their release, and whatever
their motives for calling attention to their own heroism, pays little heed to
the prisoners whose actions challenged the code.

Back in the World

Further, if the exemplary memoir offers only perfunctory allusions to life
before capture, it similarly circumvents any sustained examination of the
author's personal readjustment to the United States. Howes notes that
"though POW memoirs usually mention the welcome at Clark, they move
quickly to that moment when the father, husband, or son embraces his family, and his story ends. Few POWs describe the following months, when
corporations, private citizens, and federal and local governments practi-
cally fought with each other to supply the POWs the biggest welcome or
most impressive gifts" (159). Howes thus mentions, but fails to examine,
the memoirists' relative silence about the often-vexatious accommodation
to freedom and family. Rochester and Kiley conclude *Honor Bound* with a
brief account of the May 1973 White House celebration for the POWs and
an even more cursory coda on the post-POW career of some of the more
well known POWs; they note only that "as with coping with prison, some
would make the transition more easily than others. Some picked up their
lives as normally as if they had merely served overseas for the better part of
a decade, and some never recovered from dissolved marriages, missed career opportunities, or the awful memories" (591). Alvarez's second memoir,
Code of Conduct, concentrates on the aftermath of his imprisonment; he recounts his discovery, upon his return home, that his wife has not waited for

him (a situation that replicates countless combat veterans' experiences) and that his sister has been actively protesting the war in an effort to secure his release; his quick remarriage; his unexpected celebrity; and his post-release career. But the more conventional memoirs—by Purcell, Dramesi, Guarino, Red McDaniel, Purcell, and Stockdale—either end with the departure from Vietnam or present a few scant pages on Operation Homecoming.

Only Norm McDaniel, who concludes *Yet Another Voice* with a protracted jeremiad about a post-Vietnam America in spiritual decline, recounts the difficulties that he and his family had readjusting to each other. Because he thought that "she'd be completely lost without me," McDaniel did not tell his wife Carol that he was flying combat missions, and she did not learn that he was alive until 1969, several years after his capture (16). At his return, because he thinks Carol has spoiled his son and daughter, McDaniel must discipline his children, and, he tells us, Carol, though initially disapproving of his harshness, "now agrees that proper parental discipline is very necessary" (93). Carol, with whom McDaniel renews his marriage vows on the very day of his return from Vietnam, eventually re-learns her proper role as a dependent wife, but, McDaniel admits, "comparing the situation that I left in early 1966—with no divergence of views between Carol and me on religion, the war, women's liberation, and attitudes toward other people—to *my return situation, in which I had not substantially changed, but in which Carol had changed significantly and had cultivated rigidity in her views as a source of strength*, it is evident that she and I had a serious problem of readaptation to each other" (96; emphasis mine). Although he is the only male memoirist to acknowledge that the changes wrought by the POW experience are more substantive for his wife than for him, Norm McDaniel does not elaborate on this extraordinary perception.

That the majority of the POW memoirists exclude from their triumphant tale the vicissitudes of "readaptation" to an inevitably changed family and to a society that was virtually transformed during the years of their absence perhaps accounts for the autobiographical and fictional representations of life during the POWs' absence by and about the wives who were so unexpectedly left behind. The wives of the POWs understand, if the men do not, that their families' years of waiting were a consequential component of the POW experience. Their testimonies, and a small group of popular novels based on the wives' own stateside imprisonment, offer an interesting counterpoint to their husbands' accounts of life in the prison camps of North Vietnam. As Fred Cherry's son observes about the POWs' families in *Two*

Souls Indivisible, James S. Hirsch's account of the interracial friendship of Fred Cherry and cellmate Porter Halyburton, "we were all POWs." (9).

Women in Limbo

The handful of memoirs written by POW wives (occasionally in collaboration with their returned POW husband) and a quartet of novels written by, and obviously for, women offer "the other side" of the POW experience. Joan Silver and Linda Gottlieb's 1972 novel (and subsequent film) *Limbo* immediately follows Sybil Stockdale's late-1968 incorporation of the League of Families and precedes the Paris Peace Accords and Operation Homecoming. Phyllis Rutledge's story, which, interestingly, is only a quarter as long as the accompanying narrative by her POW husband Howard in their collaboration *In the Presence of Mine Enemies, 1965–1973: A Prisoner of War*, appeared in 1973. Throughout the 1970s, '80's, and '90's, women's voices sounded an important counterpoint to the dominant male narrative of bravery, patriotism, and self-determination. From the 1980s, Sybil and James Stockdale's *In Love and War* and Barbara Mullen Keenan's *Every Effort* offer personal testimony of the daily lives of the women left behind by husbands incarcerated for many years, while popular novels like Jonellen Heckler's *Safekeeping* and Laura Taylor's *Honorbound* provide interesting variant fictional presentations of life for the POW wife. Fern Michaels's 1994 *To Have and to Hold* revisits the themes explored by the 1980s romance novels. Later memoirs, like Dorothy McDaniel's *After the Hero's Welcome* (1991), Ben and Anne Purcell's 1992 *Love and Duty*, and George and Pat Hall's *Commitment to Honor* (2005), testify to the lasting interest in these women's stories and to the lingering significance to the authors of their experience as POW wives long after their husbands' return home. More important, as a group, these texts yield profound insights into the intersection of the war and changing roles for women in late-twentieth-century America. The experience and testimony of the wives of the men who were captured and incarcerated in prisons by the North Vietnamese complement and complicate the official story by relating the home front parallel of the POW experience; they are as well a synecdoche for the roles and responses of countless American women throughout our long imbroglio in Southeast Asia.

The women most of the Hanoi-held career officers left behind were, as Donna Moreau notes, "the last generation of hat-and-glove military wives": young or middle-aged; usually mothers of young children; white, educated, and committed to a peripatetic life devoted to the career of their own gung-ho military officer[8] (back cover). They were company women who voted Republican, doted on their husband and children, and believed in the U.S. government, the military, and the Vietnam War. And their stories of their multiyear vigil offer intriguing commentary about the home front during the Vietnam experience—and in its aftermath.

In mid-1965, just before her husband Jim becomes a prisoner of war in North Vietnam, Sybil Stockdale, a middle-aged navy wife with four young sons, listens to a naval commander at a wives' meeting inform the women "how to conduct yourself if your husband was shot down and taken prisoner in Vietnam." The family is instructed to tell no one—including the news media and anyone outside the immediate family—that their military man has been captured; nor are they to "intercede on behalf of the prisoner in any way," lest civilian interference jeopardize "State Department negotiations" or compromise the captors' treatment of the prisoner (76). In 1965, Sybil Stockdale is, and essentially remains, a loyal, unquestioning military wife. From the time of her marriage in 1947, her job, she tells us, is to be "a Navy wife" and therefore "to make the best of my situation. I didn't want to fail [Jim] in any way" (46). When the young officer's career requires frequent moves, Sybil reluctantly but dutifully relocates. When her husband is off on deployment with his fighter squadron when she gives birth, Sybil gamely handles the arrangements herself. And when her second pregnancy ends in a miscarriage, she cries disconsolately and guiltily, until her absent husband returns and "reassured me over and over again that he did not consider me a failure in any way" (48).

So Sybil Stockdale, perfect navy wife, when she becomes a POW wife calmly accedes to the navy's "keep quiet" policy for POW families, acknowledging, indeed, that she "was impressed that the government seemed so well informed and so well prepared" (77). And so do the other POW wives, at least for a while, accept that, as another navy officer tells Dorothy McDaniel, their husbands "would want you to be quiet, to stay home and take care of the kids. That's your role and that's what [your husband] expects you to do. For God's sake, do what the Navy says!" (50). These women—real and fictional—remained isolated from each other and ignored by the military for years, until—slowly, gradually—recognizing that their silence was not helping their husbands, in the late 1960s they began to come together and speak out. Mary Kaye Bell, one of the three air force–wife-protagonists of *Limbo*, the 1972 novel first serialized in *McCall's* magazine and clearly written to serve as a primer on the POW situation, welcomes her liberation from enforced silence:

> Though this was only the third meeting of the Tampa group, Mary Kaye felt its formation marked the beginning of the end of the POW wives' long adolescence under the government's paternal hand. For five years, since the first flier was downed in 1964, the government had urged POW and MIA next of kin to avoid publicity, keep a low profile, and let Washington handle everything, and for five years the women had played by the government's rules. In return, they had received only a trickle of mail and almost no information about their men. . . . She . . . had been gratified to discover that next-of-kin groups were springing up in other parts of the country. . . . There . . . was even talk of forming a national organization. (46)

This group, Sybil Stockdale's National League of Families of American Prisoners and Missing in Southeast Asia, and its public efforts to publicize the POWs' situation, catapulted the long-invisible POW issue to the forefront of public awareness in the final years of the war. Traditional wives, unexpectedly and reluctantly transformed into single mothers, came together initially out of isolation and frustration with the military's apparent inaction on the POW situation. They had been steadfast military wives who doted on their children and left the politics and the warfare to their dominant husbands. Navy lieutenant commander Richard Stratton's wife Alice admits, in the biography of her pilot-husband, that at her first POW/MIA wives' group meeting, when the discussion turned to the war, she didn't know who Ho Chi Minh was (Blakey, 221). Soon enough, however, these women and other POW family members educated themselves, found strength in one another, and began the campaign to bring their husbands and sons and brothers home. The wives wrote letters about their husbands to congressmen notably ignorant of the POWs and of dubious official efforts to gain their release, and (in the most blatant violation of official policy) gave interviews to the press and appeared on talk shows to spread their message; "Are we wives or widows?" was their plaintive mantra. Joined in time by other groups, such as the Victory in Vietnam Association, they sold bumper stickers and the POW bracelets that became chic fashion accessories in the early 1970s; they met with White House and State Department officials, and even, in 1969, flew to Paris to discuss their husbands' incarceration directly with the North Vietnamese. Bruce Franklin outlines the stages of, and reasons for, the late-war increasing visibility of the POW/MIA phenomenon, which became a cause célèbre for the White House, the protest movement, pro-military conservatives, and Hollywood. But originally (and only after considerable hesitation about violating military policy), it was POW families who told America that there were hundreds of men being held captive in North Vietnam.

Of course, not all of the POW wives subscribed to the goals of the League of Families. The fictional Eden Benedict, though she "chafes at the lack of information" about the POWs, keeps "her personal apprehensions . . . to herself" in the novel *Honorbound* (52). She is aware of the collective efforts of the League of Families but reluctant to go public with her frustrations. Barbara Mullen Keenan, whose memoir *Every Effort* recounts her futile attempts to learn the fate of her pilot husband, who was captured in Laos and who never returned from Vietnam, and Delia Alvarez, the sister of the longest-held flyer, reject the League of Families loyalists as "Statue of Liberty women . . . who will let the war go on and on as long as they don't have to cross the President." A more radical splinter group, the Families for Immediate Release, rejected the insistence of the "Pentagon princesses" of the League of Families that their efforts and the POW issue were not political; these "wayward sisters" were eager to politicize the incarceration of their husbands and brothers as the only way to effect their men's release (Keenan, 140, 158, 170).

Ignored by the military, lied to by the government, and politically antagonistic to the antiwar movement, these POW wives—"the forgotten of forgotten"—broke their imposed silence and came together to form their own public organizations (Moreau, 243). But each would deny the feminist implications of her difficult decision to claim her own voice. Their cause, after all, was the survival of their men. And none of them professes lasting independence as a result of her unusual public activism. Dorothy McDaniel dedicates her book to her husband Red, "my most admired man and the love of my life" (viii). Just before Red returns home, McDaniel burns the materials that testify to her activism in the League of Families, thus happily relegating "Mom's public life" to the ash heap (87). And indeed, McDaniel's most admired man shows no interest in his wife's indefatigable efforts to extricate him from North Vietnam. When, a decade after his return, Red McDaniel credits Richard Nixon with his release, Dorothy's retort is predictably silent: "*We made you so important to the American people that the politicians had to bring you home,* I wanted to say. But I didn't say it. He didn't want to hear it" (140). As Elliott Gruner notes, "[McDaniel] defined her efforts only in terms of what they might mean for her husband" (94). Anne Purcell expresses her enthusiasm for the nascent efforts of the League of Families: "Until this time the government policy had been, 'Keep quiet' . . . and this we had done for many years. But when we . . . saw the war continuing and saw very little being done to get our men better treatment or to get them home, we could keep quiet no longer. It was out of this frustration that the National League of Families was born." Yet Purcell undercuts the import of the enterprise with her flippant conclusion that "the government should have known that you could keep women quiet for just so long" (115–116).

Perhaps it is not surprising that these texts claim no feminist liberation for their heroines, for not only were these women conservative, military wives; they were as well busy mothers forced by circumstances beyond their control to raise their children alone, and women themselves imprisoned by uncertainty (when will he come home?), fear (*will* he come home?), and isolation. Over and over, each of these protagonists and memoirists articulates her recognition that she, like her husband, is a prisoner of war.

Neither Wife nor Widow

When Anne Purcell learns that her army colonel husband Ben has been shot down (and maybe—or maybe not—captured) in North Vietnam during the 1968 Tet Offensive, she is overwhelmed by the responsibility of being a "woman alone" with five children, a house, and a car to tend to (38). And the stresses of her life are reinforced by the uncertainty of her situation: "MIA wife. What a horrible category! It's like being in limbo—maybe a wife, maybe a widow; nothing definite to put my mind at rest" (40). Phyllis Rutledge acknowledges her dependence on her husband, who throughout their marriage "made almost all the decisions." When navy pilot Howard is captured in 1965, she accepts that "now that he couldn't tell me what to do," she must maintain the house and family, acting as both mother and father to their four young children. What she cannot bear is the perception that, neither wife nor widow, she is "nothing" (109). Barbara Mullen Keenan knows too that she is "a wife without a husband . . . wait[ing] (like her husband) to be rescued" (60). She recognizes the marginal status of women like her. Waiting to appear on a television show to publicize her husband's plight, Keenan sits between "a black . . . dancer who described the difficulties faced by black people in the arts" and "an advocate of gay rights." "Maybe," she observes, "we have more in common than is immediately apparent" (245). Although the memoirs by the male POWs demonstrate that their ability to survive the prison experience increases their sense of dignity and self-worth, the testimony of their wives gives us their perception—despite the contradictory reality of their lives—that women without their men are "nothing."

The novelists explore more fully the debilitating stasis and emotional imprisonment endured by POW wives. Sandy Lawton, one of the protagonists of *Limbo*, has been married only two weeks before her young husband goes off to Vietnam. It is two years before Sandy even knows whether Roy is alive, and four years longer before he returns home, a "stranger" to his waiting wife. "Statusless" in military circles, "anonymous" at the college she decides to attend, Sandy belongs nowhere. "The lack of definition is what bothered her most, more even than the loneliness. She was neither wife nor widow; she could not plan her life with Roy, or without him. Her days seemed devoid of the usual markers of grief or hope: there was nothing to look forward to, nor anything to mourn the passing of. And no end to this emotional wasteland was in sight" (44). Judy Greer, in *Safekeeping*, also rankles under the restraints of her "captive existence": "she was neither wife nor widow. She was entombed" (1, 36). With the help of her marine corp casualty assistance officer, *Honorbound*'s Eden Benedict gradually pulls herself out of her despair when her infant son dies (a female crucible like Lizzie's in *Lizzie's War*) soon after her marine captain husband is declared missing in action. But, once she eschews the solace of alcohol, Eden feels as though she is in "some kind of permanent emotional traction" (95). While Matt is tortured by the North Vietnamese, Eden is tormented by the death of her baby. When Matt returns home, their eventual happily-ever-after marriage is preceded by a period of difficult adjustment. As the reunited couple (who, like Sandy and Roy Lawton, had been married only a short time before Matt's departure for Vietnam) struggle through Matt's efforts to reassimilate into American society, Eden reminds him that he was not the only prisoner in the family: "You don't get it, do you? I was in prison, too. We both were. I grant you mine was prettier, the food better, but it was a jail cell nonetheless. Do you think for one minute I haven't suffered? I buried our son, and that nearly destroyed me. And then I held on to my sanity with my fingernails once I sobered up enough to recognize what was going on around me. After that, I learned how to wait, how to mark the days, one by one, off the calendar without ever knowing the extent of my sentence" (306).

Fern Michaels's 1994 protagonist Kate waits an improbable twenty years, long after the end of America's involvement in Vietnam, for her air force pilot husband Patrick to be released from a Russian prison. Patrick is declared neither prisoner nor killed in action, and though after a dozen years Kate has staged a mock funeral and moved on with her life, she is steadfast and supportive when he inexplicably (and secretly) returns home two decades later. "I have a life too," Kate cries, when she learns that Patrick will return to intrude on her long-awaited, newfound love. "What about me?" (265). Predictably, the Patrick who returns to his wife and now grown daughters is weak, confused, and dissatisfied that the world has gone on without him. "We're different people now, both of us," a now strong and independent Kate admonishes him. She and her daughters have "lived in our own hell for a lot of years" (290, 291).

In *A Country Such as This*, which counterpoints its presentation of Red Lesczynski's imprisonment with his wife Sophie's long vigil, fictitious Sophie—unlike the memoirist military wives—can express her resentment of her fate as the wife of a military officer and a prisoner: "sometimes I get *mad* at Red!" she confides to Joe, Red's fellow naval academy graduate and one of the three protagonists of the novel: "Can you believe it? . . . I say, 'Red Lesczynski, you wanted to fly and I said okay. I left my family and my home for you and I followed you all over creation. I wrote you letters when you were gone. I learned to be alone and to raise a family by myself. I learned how to do plumbing and to fix a car. I did all these things for you and I guess for me, and I wouldn't do it any other way, but I've spent more than half my adult life *waiting!*' I feel so useless, sometimes" (401–402). Similarly, Kate and Eden and the fictional POW wives of *Limbo* and *Safekeeping* share their real-life counterparts' frustration with their lives in "limbo," yet their fictional lives are at once complicated and eased by their exploration of their neglected sexuality—an aspect of their suspended lives that Sybil Stockdale, Dorothy McDaniel, Anne Purcell, and the other memoirists cannot even allow themselves to acknowledge.

As he and Kate make love just before he departs for Vietnam, to "serve his country, get his ticket punched, and come home a fucking hero," Fern Michaels's Patrick, another self-satisfied fly-boy, marvels at "the power he had over his wife. . . . Without a word or a look, rarely an explanation, she would do or say whatever he wanted. She was perfect, a shining example of himself" (2). Neither Patrick nor Kate recognizes—and he would surely not care—that their sex life, while satisfying for him, is for Kate a perfunctorily performed marital responsibility. Only after nearly twenty years of fidelity to a husband she must admit is surely long dead does Kate—slowly, guiltily—begin an affair with Gus, a young *New York Times* reporter more than ten years her junior; and only after all those years does Kate, like *Coming Home*'s Sally, discover fulfilling, satisfying sex. For Kate, sex is inextricable from love. For the other fictional protagonists, it is therapy. *Honorbound*, like *To Have and to Hold*, opens with its protagonists having sex just before he leaves for Vietnam. Sex, we are to understand, is (in standard romance-novel tradition) an essential component of Matt and Eden's relationship. Throughout the novel, which alternates chapters detailing Eden's experiences with chapters that present Matt's life as a POW, both characters happily relive their shared sexual memories. Halfway through the novel, David, Eden's military assistance officer, introduces her to Jim, a fellow marine whose "wife divorced him while he was overseas," and whose interest in Eden is immediate and obvious (133). Reluctantly, Eden admits her attraction to the handsome marine, which she resists only until her supervisor at the naval hospital where Eden works as a volunteer assures her that sexual release will be therapeutic and ethically acceptable:

> "This is more a human issue than a moral one. You're a loving, giving woman, a woman with passion and laughter and love that needs to be shared. Those qualities aid you in your work with the patients, but like any asset or skill that's being used, it must be refurbished and revitalized periodically. You can't just give, Eden. You've got to be on the receiving end once in a while. . . . [H]owever you get through this separation from your husband, the only person you owe an explanation is yourself. No one else, other than God, has the right to make moral judgments about how you conduct your personal life." (144, 145)

Eden has her affair, which she enjoys, then ends efficiently, without emotional complications and without guilt. Like childbirth, her job at the naval hospital, and her new house, Eden's sexual interlude is simply one of the experiences that make her—not a nothing, like the POW wives who put their lives on hold until their men return—but, by the end of the novel, a sensual, strong, independent woman.

Limbo's Sandy Lawton drifts into an affair with her hippie-like graduate-student college instructor; but though sex with Alan is better than it was with the boyish Roy, her adulterous relationship arises more from loneliness than physical need or love. Similarly, Sandy's older friend, fellow POW-wife Mary Kaye, whose husband has been imprisoned for four years, misses companionship more than sex. But it is clear that her extramarital relationship with Alan helps Sandy survive her six-year ordeal in limbo;

however bleak the post-imprisonment prospects for Sandy and Roy, she is waiting for him at the end of the novel, in part because of the emotional and physical diversion that her relationship with Alan has provided.

In *Safekeeping*, Jonellen Heckler suggests that there is a formal military plan to keep POW wives from divorcing or abandoning their imprisoned husbands. Early in the novel, a frustrated Judy Greer, after "five years as society's misfit," has decided to divorce her POW husband Ron. Her friend and fellow army wife Susan, knowing that the army will disapprove of such disloyalty, suggests that Judy instead partake of an "unofficial . . . very private" army tradition: "While all the good husbands are away, doing their duty for the entire world, the good husbands whose turn it is to stay home at old Fort Whatever take care of all the wives. . . . They're all good—all the husbands and the wives. But they get lonely. And, when it's their turn to be lonely, there's always someone . . . whose turn it is to be a helper" (32). Judy rejects Susan's clandestine tradition as a "crazy rumor" (though soon enough a young, blond major does offer "to do anything to help" her "difficult situation"), because she knows that her husband will not forgive her if she is unfaithful (33, 55, 36). But she falls hard for handsome Lt. Joe Campbell, who is kind to her son and loving and attentive to her. Like Jim in *Honorbound*, Joe is a good military man whose wife didn't wait; and, demonstrating his ultimate loyalty to the military and to his imprisoned army comrade, he assures Judy that an affair with him will not break up her marriage. Now sexually and emotionally fulfilled, Judy drops her plan to divorce Ron; Joe convinces her to abandon her antiwar activities, helps her son Kevin come to terms with his own fears and anxieties, and quietly retreats when the POWs are released.

In the world of the romance novel, satisfying sex is the answer to any problem. In the world of real military wives it is obedience: "Suppose . . . the military [is] . . . the ultimate machine in which all items—from paper to people—were deliberately and completely controlled. . . . What if she *had* been manipulated—but for the good of Ron Greer? And for the convenience of the Army. What if they had placed her in a kind of protective custody in which her life was made happier and her attacks against the government were curtailed?" (272–273). The fictional POW wives enjoy healthy, emotionally uncomplicated sexual relationships that help them survive their own imprisonment and happily welcome home their husbands. The real-life POW wives—at least the long-suffering ones who wait around to write the memoirs—are hardly sexual beings at all.[9]

Close to breaking down from the stress of her family responsibilities, her husband's incarceration, and her public activism, Barbara Mullen Keenan in early 1972 seeks help from a psychiatrist. As she awkwardly tries to explain her conflicted feelings to the therapist, Keenan talks about her frustration that she is "not allowed to be a woman," and insists that she doesn't really exist (282–283). She hesitantly accepts a few unsuccessful dates before learning that her husband, because he was shot down in Laos, will not be released during Operation Homecoming, news that essentially ends Keenan's story and her book. Barbara Mullen Keenan's veiled reference to her frustrations at her inability to "be a woman" is the closest any of the women memoirists comes to acknowledging her sexuality. Phyllis Rutledge and Anne Purcell mention nothing about their physical needs or their sexual relationship with their husbands, either before their imprisonment or upon the men's return home. Neither do Sybil Stockdale or Dorothy McDaniel acknowledge any sexual frustrations or temptations during their long years of waiting; when each tells us that she enjoyed sex at her first reunion with her released husband, she does so to contradict the military's warning that the POWs may experience sexual impotence as a result of their long incarceration and to proudly testify to her husband's virility. As Gruner notes, Sybil Stockdale's sole reference to her sexual life is particularly informative:

> In Love and War concludes with Admiral Stockdale's physical absence and figural impotence resolved in the hospital where the POWs are convalescing. Sybil Stockdale is eager to point out "how completely wrong they had been about the sexual impotence." Jim Stockdale echoes Sybil Stockdale's jubilation by replying in a telephone call from a high-ranking naval officer with "yes, sir, everything is just fine here at the hospital and Sybil is right here in bed with me." . . . Admiral Stockdale reasserts his dominance by speaking for a silent Sybil in a situation serving as emblem for his returned sexual potency and natural male dominance. (95)

The loyal, faithful authors of the women's memoirs and the more resourceful adulterous but emotionally steadfast fictional POW wives are contrasted throughout the genre with the female betrayers of the POWs—women who didn't wait and Jane Fonda–like antiwar activists. Each of the real and fictional protagonists of these texts rejects—or comes to repudiate—the peace activists' role in the POW drama. Although the North Vietnamese allowed antiwar organizations like the New Mobilization Committee, Women Strike for Peace, and the Committee of Liaison with Families of Servicemen Detained in North Vietnam to observe, speak with, and deliver mail to and from the POWs, the wives in these novels and memoirs consistently spurn the efforts of what one of Matt Benedict's cellmates calls the "antiwar pukes" (*Honorbound*, 180). Anne Purcell parrots the familiar rejection of the peace movement as un-American and responsible for "prolong[ing] the war by strengthening the will of the enemy not to negotiate" (116). Army wife Judy Greer, the protagonist of *Safekeeping*, is, when the novel begins, active in the antiwar movement; encouraged by her activist friend Connie and Connie's confused, antiwar veteran husband—and particularly valuable to the movement because of her POW wife status—Judy believes that peace activists are the only ones trying to help the POWs. But, predictably in this fundamentally conservative novel, Judy is convinced by army lieutenant–turned-lover Joe Campbell that her antiwar efforts cause her to neglect her adolescent son. By the end of the novel, when her POW husband returns home to his sexually refreshed wife, Judy has abandoned her injudicious activism for motherhood and the private role that the military and her husband expect her to stoically play. Barbara Mullen Keenan begins to question U.S. involvement in Vietnam and, almost guiltily, works for antiwar presidential candidate Eugene McCarthy in 1968; but she is as critical of the movement, whose leaders "seemed to believe anything the North Vietnamese or Viet Cong told them," as she is of the League of Families (117).

Significantly, throughout these texts particular venom is directed toward peace activists who are women. Sybil Stockdale wonders why "the U.S. government [doesn't] say something about" the "Women's [*sic*] Strike for Peace crowd" who, she believes, "were giving aid and comfort to the enemy" (203). McCarthy-supporter Barbara Mullen Keenan sees the controversial actor-activist Jane Fonda discussing her visits to North Vietnam on the Dick Cavett Show and notes that "most of the POW families resented Fonda's willingness to believe the North Vietnamese, and I sometimes wondered if she'd have accepted their word so easily if her brother or husband were hidden behind those barricaded walls" (139). Sharon Dornbeck, the third and most pro-military protagonist of *Limbo*, desperate to determine whether her POW husband is alive, reluctantly turns to a local antiwar group for help. As the affluent female director of the group accepts Sharon's package for her husband, she fairly drips with her disdain for the poor, misguided POW wife: "Another one, Emily Brunner thought, another Bible-belt, bouffant-haired wife expected sympathy while she lived on her husband's paycheck, with only the dimmest notion of the geography of Vietnam and probably less notion of the war's politics" (104).[10] For the POWs and their wives, antiwar protesters—especially female movement activists—are traitors to the American cause.

As in the veterans' aftermath texts, in the numerous male POW narratives, a special misogyny is reserved for the POW wives who cheated on or divorced their imprisoned husbands. Several of the POWs, including Charlie Plumb, Fred Cherry, and Everett Alvarez, learned during their incarceration, or at their return, that their wives had not waited for them. Red McDaniel reports that late in the war, in his "love and marriage seminar" offered through Hanoi University, he and twenty-five "students" discussed "how we could adjust when we got home, if for example we found our wives . . . had remarried? Or supposing they had been unfaithful? These possibilities," McDaniel asserts, "were real ones, which lurked in the back of every man's mind" (141). Ev Alvarez admits that discovering his wife's "desertion was the hardest blow dealt to me in an imprisonment that included periods of physical torture" (13). Yet the real POWs' avoidance of thoughts of home precluded extensive commentary on their fears of female betrayal.

The fictional representations of the POW experience are more candid. As Elliott Gruner notes, "Even though . . . less than one percent of POW wives were unfaithful [this a Pentagon statistic whose origins are unclear], few movies would do without highlighting a woman's betrayal. Few autobiographies could keep from mentioning the adulterous wife. The adulterous female betrayer would become a stock character in POW films" (97). In *Charlie and the Children*, Joanna Scott's 1997 novel about a grunt captured, imprisoned, but later inexplicably released by the Vietcong, Charlie's squad is decimated after its once-skillful point man Lou receives a letter from his mother-in-law informing him that his wife is sleeping around: "She put a knife in his heart and turned it slowly, slowly. A mad lover who fucked and killed. A preying mantis. She killed him, God curse her soul. She killed them all. . . . they'd gone through the jungle with a deadly wound at point. A wound that killed them all" (156, 162). Eddie Keller, the unconventional army corporal protagonist of Kirkwood's *Some Kind of Hero*, survives his five-year incarceration by thinking of his wife and daughter (well, that and having passionate sex with his cellmate Vin, who dies just before Operation Homecoming); when he returns to the states, he fantasizes about satisfying Lisa sexually—about "recaptur[ing] her"—until she reluctantly admits that, unsure whether Eddie was even alive, she has returned to an old boyfriend (129). Eddie, a most atypical POW in this most unusual novel, belatedly recognizes the invalidity of his expectations: "Because my life had stopped for five years I'd assumed hers had. I'd suspended her in limbo, put her in a gold locket, snapped her shut and held her close to my idiotic romantic-assed heart, only to be released when I was released" (133–134). Eddie claims to accept Lisa's infidelity, but the discovery that his wife did not wait propels Eddie onto the path of robbery and Mafia money laundering that provides the plot of the second half of this satiric novel.

The female novelists and memoirists also reject the wives who didn't wait, but they do so with an apparent understanding of the adulterous women that undermines the force of their condemnation. Given their own ambiguous fidelity, it is probably to be expected that the fictional wives do not altogether share their husbands' disdain for their more blatantly unfaithful sisters. In *Limbo*, Sandy and Mary Kaye discuss some "juicy" news about "that gal from Milwaukee" who "went to court and said he's been missing for three years and to the best of her knowledge, he's dead"; yet their reaction to the woman's remarriage is curiosity rather than censure (136). When Matt Benedict returns to Eden, unaware of her affair during his absence, he expresses his gratitude to her for waiting and his scorn for the wives who didn't. But Eden, understandably, defends the impetuous wives and hints at her own infidelity: "'Don't judge them too harshly. Those who survive all this will be the ones who made a conscious decision to get through it any way they could.' She knew it wasn't her place to judge the other women" (292–293). And yet, these women reserve their real sympathies for their men. Jim Clayton in *Honorbound* and Joe Campbell in *Safekeeping* are credentialed as unthreatening sexual surrogates for their imprisoned military brothers because they are cuckolds: decent, brave men betrayed by selfish, adulterous wives.

More interesting is the reaction of the always-faithful memoirists to the defection of some of the arguably weaker wives. A fellow POW wife calls Barbara Mullen Keenan with news about the wife of one of the men shot down with her husband, explaining that the other woman "decided she had had it with the whole bit. She divorced her husband for desertion or something and remarried—against the advice of the Navy and everybody else." Barbara's friend's response to this development—"It's like . . . this woman has put it behind her, and . . . I'm the only person who even remembers"— is more plaintive than censorious (239). And Anne Purcell mentions, but does not comment upon, the tragedy of a POW wife who commits suicide a year and a half after her husband's capture (204).

Maybe the apparent, if unenthusiastic, acceptance of the actions of unfaithful wives—even by the long-suffering real-life POW wives who waited patiently—is the result of the theme that echoes most loudly throughout these female texts. Each of these narrators, however conservative, recognizes and articulates that one of the consequences of her ordeal is significant personal growth and empowerment—a sense of self-worth often inspired and reinforced by her solidarity with other women like her, and a theme that undermines her stated perception that, neither wife nor widow, she does not exist.

Each, that is, except one. *Safekeeping* is the most conservative of the novels, and Judy's movement is from antiwar activist contemplating divorce to devoted mother, daughter-in-law, and wife. Even her ostensibly risky affair is, apparently, a carefully controlled military plot to keep her in line. Not until the final pages of the novel does she recognize the radicalism of her now-repudiated antiwar activities, as she considers, belatedly, whether her returning husband will not admire but will, in fact, "condemn . . . the role she had taken against the war" (288). Judy's concern about her husband's judgment on her actions echoes the consternation of every one of the real-life POWs wives, who wonder, when they have to make a decision about the children, the house, or money, "what would my husband want?" Heckler's failure to create a well-developed and complex protagonist is the most obvious weakness of her limited novel. Even the similarly one-dimensional heroines of *Limbo* change as a result of their experiences as POW wives.

Limbo's Mary Kaye learns early on that "a husband is not indispensable. I bought our house myself," she proudly asserts. "I furnished it, I finished my degree, I got a job" (129). Her education, her job as a schoolteacher, and her ability to raise her family alone are not particularly significant in her life or in the novel, but they certainly threaten the male school colleague who is her one date before she learns that her husband has died in captivity: "You don't need a man," he snarls. "You're so busy being Wonder Woman, mother, father, and breadwinner all in one, that you aren't going to be good for a goddamned thing when your husband comes home" (133). Young, newly married Sandy grows up while her husband is imprisoned overseas. "A girl who would have been a traditional wife and mother, except for an accident over the skies of North Vietnam, had become liberated in spite of herself" (147). She knows that, with her education and her new sexual experience, she cannot follow the military's advice for wives of returning POWs: "Don't spring too many changes on him. . . . Just be yourself, the

138

way you were when he left you. That's what he married, and that's what he's been dreaming of returning to" (177).

The Club Nobody Wants to Join

Like movement activists and Vietnamese refugees, Sandy and Mary Kaye and many of the POW and career military wives find support for their new independence in each other and in the other POW wives who come together in the founding days of the League of Families. Women alone, they are members of "the club nobody wants to join" (*Limbo*, 47). Because of frequent moves, these military wives were usually separated from their families. Neither were they assisted by military officials, who only reluctantly "handled" the POW families, who were an embarrassment and a distraction. Dorothy McDaniel includes as an appendix to *After the Hero's Welcome* disquieting, now declassified 1971 White House memos that discuss plans to keep the POW wives "in line" and "on the reservation" (205, 207). Even pro-government Sybil Stockdale expresses frustration with the red tape and runaround that she received when trying to get assistance or information from the State Department and the Pentagon (119, 141, 215). With a public ignorant of the existence of POWs and a government and military anxious to keep them a non-issue, these women had only one another. Their mutual dependence and unexpected pleasure in female camaraderie—which reinforces the familiar Vietnam War theme, "you had to be there"—parallels their husbands' testimonials to the importance of the POWs' fraternal bonds.

The POW wives of *Limbo* support each other throughout the novel. "It was understood, without any words being exchanged between them, that just as Sandy had helped Mary Kaye through [her husband's] death, Mary Kaye would be with Sandy through Roy's rather more protracted return to life" (176). Mary Kaye recognizes the parallels between the lives of the POWs and their wives, and the important fact that led to the League of Families and to the unacknowledged role of the new women's movement in these women's lives: "Just as war bound together the men under fire . . . it united the women left behind back home" (34). Sybil Stockdale suggests that the shared purpose and conviviality of league meetings gave the wives freedom "to do and say whatever we want. Being together gave us all strength"; solidarity, she adds, also instilled in the women "a newfound spirit of assertiveness" (225). Again, this theme of community in adversity resonates, with interesting variations, throughout these war-inspired narratives.

The fictional Eden Benedict is, however, as indifferent to the solace of other POW wives as she is to the public activism to which so many of them eventually turned. She is a rare female *isolato*, a woman defiantly independent and self-sufficient. In fact, her close relationship with her only female friend, Tracy, is compromised by the many changes that Eden embraces in her new, solitary life. Yet, though *Honorbound* proclaims no solidarity among women, its enthusiasm for Eden's evolution as a woman is unadulterated. With Tracy and casualty officer David's help, Eden drags herself out of her depression after the death of her child and consciously embraces the development of a new, stronger self. After a move across the country, a new job, a new home, and a brief love affair, Eden proudly—and repeatedly—proclaims that she is "not the frightened rabbit Matthew married four and a half years ago" (220). Unlike Judy Greer, Eden recognizes that, upon his return, neither she nor Matt will be the same people who parted years before. She worries, in fact, that their reunion will be complicated by her new independence: "When he left for Vietnam, all she'd wanted was to be his wife and the mother of his children. Now she had a career, professional commitments, people who depended on her. She'd become a decision maker, a leader, a woman who contributed and made a difference in the lives of others. Would one role have to be sacrificed for the other? Or would he understand that she'd changed and grown, that she needed both?" (241). And, as the romance novel genre promises, Eden gets both. Matt's return is complicated by his resentment of the new, self-possessed Eden and his own unresolved conflicts with his Native American heritage. Eventually, of course, the loving couple move beyond the horrors of their mutual imprisonment and difficult reunion, but Eden will keep her job and her new friends, and motherhood will be on her terms. In this sentimental novel, the POW husband is lucky—and content—to return to a more sensual and resilient wife.

For Patrick and Kate, the separation is too long. Kate, at the beginning of *To Have and to Hold* a contented "little Miss Homemaker, who didn't have the faintest idea how to be strong and tough," who knows only how to be a "wife and mother," is forced by her sudden circumstances to get a job and an education (8). Two-and-a-half years later, Kate nervously welcomes "the new, improved, better version of Kate Starr" who is "making a life for herself, one step at a time" (75, 83). A decade into Patrick's absence, Kate (echoing Sally Hyde) sadly acknowledges that her husband would not "like the new person I am," and Patrick returns to a professionally successful, sexually liberated woman who is the exact opposite of the "shining example of himself" that he'd left a lifetime earlier (127). Faithful Kate stands by Patrick when he comes home, cares for him, helps him to recover; but eventually they both recognize that each of them has changed and that they no longer belong together. "You grew wings, Kate, and you need to fly," Patrick concedes as they amicably part at the end of the novel. Neither Kate nor the reader questions that she is a better woman because of the "extraordinary situation" of her husband's long captivity (341, 304).

The real-life POWs were not all like the tall, dark, handsome, fictional Matt Benedict or the reluctantly pragmatic Patrick Starr. As Dorothy McDaniel's immolation of the relics of her public life indicates, their wives do not loudly and proudly declaim their new independence. But their recognition that they were changed—and often for the better—by their ordeal and by their unity with other women is nonetheless a theme of their autobiographical texts. Dorothy McDaniel chronicles her frustration at her isolation and at the early lack of information about the POWs; for her, the imperative to come forward and speak publicly about her husband's fate is reinforced by the fact that the POW wives will speak out together. Anne Purcell, too, finds strength and validation in the communal actions of the League of Families. And Barbara Mullen Keenan is thrilled at her first meeting with another POW wife because "no one else, no one can understand what it's been like—except another woman who's been through it" (43). (You had to be there.) Keenan is like the other real POW wives, underplaying the developments in their own lives much as they ignore the vicissitudes of their sexuality. But after she and her sons celebrate her new graduate degree, she feels "more in control and wanting to use my new independence," and, long before she knows that her husband will never return from Laos, like so many of the POW wives she wonders whether he "would . . . like the changed me?" (134, 233).

Elliott Gruner is one of the few critics of the American literature of the Vietnam War to note and discuss any of the panoply of voices that offer commentary on the women's perspective of the experience. Though he does not engage the novels discussed here, his analysis of the memoirs of Sybil Stockdale, Dorothy McDaniel, and others is often trenchant. "Their narratives," Gruner writes, "are amazing accounts of how women's roles could expand beyond the claustrophobia of tradition and domesticity. Their narratives identify gender boundaries as they describe the struggle for POW repatriation. What is perhaps more remarkable is how these hard-won, expanded roles snap back into traditional domestic structures once the POWs return" (93). Given the pro-military, conservative beliefs of the flesh-and-blood military wives and the inherent conservatism of American society's appropriation of the POW phenomenon, what is remarkable is not that these women "snap back into traditional domestic structures" (an assertion undermined by bringing the POW-wife novels into the analysis), but that they push gender boundaries even in the tentative, sometimes temporary, ways that they do. As Gruner acknowledges, "the roles were reversing. Imprisonment feminized the POWs by making them silent objects of sentiment, subjects of rescue, and pawns of public attention. The active, masculine role vacated by the POWs was assumed, to a degree, by their families. POW wives inherited traditionally male roles with political and media muscle that politicians had to reckon with. While their husbands languished in . . . North Vietnamese prisons, the POW families struggled with newfound freedoms to activate stagnant political and media powers back in the United States" (89–90). But then the men—the resilient heroes—came home. Much like women who worked outside the home for the first time during World War II, the POW wives dutifully returned to their traditional, domestic roles once their men came back to reclaim their masculine identities. Yet, like those Rosie the Riveters whose exile from the larger world of work and commerce was only temporary, the POW wives were surely dramatically transformed by their unbidden experience. Some remained active in the League of Families; for others, undoubtedly the changes were more subtle, less public.

Edna J. Hunter's 1978 study of the physical and psychological effects of captivity on the released POWs attests to the relevance of these narratives as commentaries on the real-life experience of these husbands and wives. As she notes, "when the men returned, the wives expected much change and found little. The husbands, on the other hand, expected little change in their wives and families, and found much. It is little wonder that a substantial part of the post-repatriation reintegration adjustment was staged within the family arena" (194–195). Remember Norm McDaniel's churlish acknowledgment that their shared POW experience had a more demonstrable effect on his wife than it did on him. The women writers, directly or subtly acknowledging the era's dramatic social changes for women, at least address the challenges of the POWs' readjustment to home and family; McDaniel notwithstanding, the POWs themselves do not.

Though very different genres written for quite different audiences, the women's memoirs and novels by and about POW wives share a unique perspective on one of the more sustained and singular experiences of the Vietnam War. The real-life POW wives tell the most powerful tales. At once defined by their conservative, middle-class, military backgrounds and empowered by the blazing women's movement, these women struggled with the vicissitudes of their unique circumstances. As Gruner and others have demonstrated, the stories of female POWs and POW wives have been underestimated. With no publishers and readers clamoring to hear their stories, these loyal wives had little reason to speak out except to claim their own voices, and to a degree to which many of the authors are unaware, their texts articulate the tensions within their own lives and a changing society. They offer as well a collective story whose parallels to the Hanoi imprisonment of their real and fictional husbands are fascinating. Their gradual discovery of other POW wives and the consolations and empowerment of the group identity and sense of common purpose fostered by the League of Families echo the strength that the Hanoi POWs discovered in one another. Similar, too, to their husbands' insistence that they are enriched by their tribulation is the wives' more reluctant and complex perception that enduring and surviving the POW crucible was for them, however briefly, a liberating experience. Their stories are a fascinating demonstration of the Vietnam War's haunting presence on the home front during the war years—and beyond.

Off the Record

The voices and perceptions of the real and fictitious wives who waited back home indeed present an important amplification of the consistent, even repetitive, versions of the official story offered by the Hanoi POWs. But, with the exception of the novels, which allow for some failure to adhere without deviation to the standards of stoicism and devotion set by the memoirist POWs and their wives, the official story of courage and fidelity to family, country, and God stands largely unadulterated and unassailable in accounts by the wives. The saga of the American prisoners of the Vietnam War is, however, complicated and embellished by the more distinctive voices of female and civilian POWs (German nurses Monika Schwinn and Bernhard Diehl, UPI reporter Kate Webb, missionary Carolyn Paine Miller, for instance); POWs like John (Nick) Rowe, who was held in jungle cages in South Vietnam; deviant Hanoi POWs such as escape-prone John Dramesi and members of the repudiated Peace Committee; and one audacious POW novel, James Kirkwood's 1975 *Some Kind of Hero*. If the published memories of the career-officer patriots shot down over and imprisoned in North Vietnam relate the sanctioned, gratifying version of the Vietnam POW experience, this assorted and uneven collection offers the entangled and overlooked "*un*official story"—another side of the POW story—and codicils, conditions, and contradictions even to that version of events. Although most of these autobiographical accounts and Kirkwood's novel reiterate some of the themes and details of the more acclaimed memoirs, the variations on the tale present a more nuanced and more problematic account of the Vietnam POW experience than the mainstream texts allow. Civilians and enlisted men captured in the South (therefore moved frequently and often held in isolation), such as Schwinn and Diehl, and Nick Rowe, illustrate the vicissitudes of imprisonment without the security or rigidity of the Code of Conduct and the command structure that the pilot-officers mandated. Prisoners who were reluctant warriors (such as conscientious objector James A. Daly) or for whom exposure to the relentless indoctrination of the Vietnamese provoked uncertainty about the validity of the war (for example, the "assimilationist" POWs interviewed by Zalin Grant) inevitably demonstrate attitudes and behaviors quite unlike those of the return-with-honor-at-all-costs pilots held at the Hanoi Hilton. Even John Dramesi, a pilot and officer but one whose intransigent adherence to the code's injunction to escape made him an unpopular renegade among his Hanoi prisonmates, provides a divagation from the common story. And female POWs demonstrate, usually unconsciously, that women prisoners were an unusual and unwelcome presence in the camps.

The Australian journalist Kate Webb (the subtitle of whose early, slight memoir, *On the Other Side: 23 Days with the Viet Cong*, announces the relative brevity of her Cambodian imprisonment) had reason to believe that she, like other foreign journalists, would be killed by her captors—and indeed, until her release her friends and colleagues believed that she was dead.[11] Suspected of being a spy by her Vietcong captors, who were incredulous that she would court danger "just looking for the truth," Webb endures repeated interrogations (108). Yet, as she recounts them, her three weeks of peripatetic imprisonment are most memorably characterized by exhaustion, hunger, illness, and a "daily routine ... of boredom, punctuated by two meals" (75). As vacuous as the pilots' memoirs, Webb's account avoids engagement with the ideological or ethical implications of her experience. As Gruner notes, "by effacing her gendered role, politics, and distinctions between combatants and journalists, Webb struggles to find a space for her narrative in the context of a war that thrived on such distinctions. The attempt to erase such boundaries eventually keeps Webb from sorting out the assumptions that fuel the conflict she seeks to describe" (115). The missionary Carolyn Paine Miller, who was seized with her husband and daughter in 1975 as the North Vietnamese marched ineluctably toward Saigon and held for eight months, is similarly unreflective in her 1977 fatalistic account, *Captured!* Monika Schwinn, interned for four years and the only female survivor from her apprehended group of three women and two men, offers a more introspective response to her unexpected and prolonged immersion in a political situation about which, after eight pre-capture months of "dawn till dusk" nursing in a Da Nang hospital, she, by her own account, understood very little (3). When she is captured, Schwinn (whose German father was taken prisoner by the Russians during World War II and never returned) learns immediately that her incarceration is to be defined by her second-class status: "I was only a woman. A woman was nothing; a woman was even less than a prisoner" (66). She is both detailed and philosophical about the treatment that results from her peculiar position:

> The Vietnamese attitude toward women profoundly affected my life for the next four years. A woman, and a prisoner to boot, possessed no rights whatever. Female prisoners were assigned the worst clothing and lodging, and their needs were always ignored. . . . When the Americans bombed the region around Hanoi, all the male prisoners were removed from their cells and taken to the dugouts. The guards never bothered to take me along, for, after all, I was only a woman; it would make no difference if I was killed. . . .
>
> In the prison camps, a woman had only two advantages. Women were considered nonentities; therefore, female prisoners were assigned the most thick-witted interrogators, who could easily be gulled into believing anything. . . . The second advantage lay in the fact that the Vietnamese would never lay hands on a woman prisoner . . . in four years, no one physically molested me. To have touched a female prisoner, a creature without rights or honor, would have been an unpardonable crime. . . . (66; final ellipsis in original)[12]

Like many of the soldiers captured in South Vietnam, Schwinn and Diehl were held originally in various jungle camps in the South, then marched to Hanoi; thus, they experienced and describe both the deprivations and primitive conditions of the South—where a much larger proportion of the prisoners died—and the structured, comparatively endurable life in the Hanoi Hilton. They met, but offer no commentary on the differences between, obedient officers like Ben Purcell (who wrote the foreword to *We Came to Help*) and collaborators such as John Young and the notorious Bobby Garwood.[13] To Schwinn and Diehl, the Americans are simply those "inveterate optimists" who "were always decent and treated us kindly" (245, 126). Publishing their commentary in 1973, before the dissemination of the official story, the German survivors could not appreciate the antipodean relationship between the Stockdale-Denton-McCain "return with honor" contingent and the more accommodationist prisoners such as Young, Daly, and army captain and physician Lloyd Kushner, who told the newly captured Bernhard Diehl that "one day you'll think only about yourself. . . . In the end, the only thing that matters is staying alive" (114). Advice, to be sure, that the Unity-over-Self crowd would have repudiated as treasonous.

Though she does not acknowledge—or, undoubtedly, recognize—the similarity, Monika Schwinn (though not Diehl) shares the assimilationists' protean attitude toward their captors: an ideological complication that distinguishes most of the sui generis accounts from the official story. Although she is inevitably hostile to her captors, Schwinn reluctantly comes to concede the human complexity of the Vietnamese. "During our years in the camps," Schwinn notes, "we were always torn by conflicting emotions. For a little while we would feel uncomplicated hatred for the Vietnamese and their callous, cruel behavior. Then something would happen to make us forget our hatred. Often I wished that I could feel nothing but hate. It might have been easier that way" (170). By the end of her four years with the North Vietnamese, having interacted with occasionally compassionate captors and locals, Schwinn understands how the Vietnamese, after ceaseless battles with the vagaries of nature and, for a thousand years, varied political enemies, "could learn to be enemies themselves" (244).

Too Late, Too Junior, or Too Minor

In 1975 the Vietnam veteran–journalist Zalin Grant interviewed POWs—including the conscientious objector James A. Daly and Lt. Col. Ted Guy (who later brought charges against some of his subordinates)—who, like Schwinn and Diehl, were imprisoned in the South and later moved to Hanoi. The dust jacket of his *Survivors* promises "the story you *haven't* read told in the words of nine American prisoners of war," and, indeed, the captivity story that Grant's subjects tell is not the familiar tale. For these captives, for example, a more ambiguous POW experience, like Schwinn's, results in—and arises from—a complicated, ambivalent attitude about the Vietnamese. At his capture south of Da Nang just before the Tet Offensive, army warrant officer Frank Anton is relieved to observe armed Vietnamese women, because "I had sometimes thought that what we helicopter pilots were doing was maybe terrible. Were we killing women and children? Who could tell?" (6). Army PFC David Harker expresses "hurt" to see the Vietnamese "caught in the middle of a war they didn't want" (13). James Daly, describing the privileged POWs' final dinner before their Operation Homecoming release, admits that "we had reached the point where everyone felt . . . like the Vietnamese were brothers and sisters to us" (327). In his autobiography, published originally the same year as *Survivors*, Daly again embraces the Vietnamese as his siblings and claims that he can no longer think of them as enemies.

Some Kind of Hero's Eddie Keller awkwardly expresses condolences to his enemy camp commander (nicknamed "Mine Fury" after *Mein Führer*) when he learns that the man's mother and sister have been injured in an American bombing raid. Much as Tracy Kidder's and Tobias Wolff's shame about their apparently innocuous Vietnam activities differentiates them from other veteran-memoirists, the civilians', fictional protagonist's, and antiwar POWs' humanization of the Vietnamese, which is one of the distinguishing characteristics of their texts, complicates the consistently antipathetic attitude of the Hanoi POWs toward their captors; the few officer-memoirists who betray any understanding of the Vietnamese (Ben Purcell, Red McDaniel) do so only to attest to the power of God's love. Their ability to forgive the enemy is a statement about their humanity, not that of their captors.

The divergent POWs' ability to empathize with the Vietnamese (and to admit doing so) is but one illustration of their marginal status—much like that of women prisoners—within the internment experience. The scholars demonstrate, and the memoirists support, the official story's insistence that younger and later-captured POWs as well as enlisted men held in the South were less disciplined, less committed to the Code of Conduct, (and therefore, the exemplars would insist, less worthy) than the pilot-heroes; they were, as Howes notes, "too late, too junior, or too minor"[14] (193). But the aberrants' testimonies are more complex than that dismissal allows. As Grant's oral histories illustrate, by the time that the Southern-held enlisted POWs—Anton, Harker, Daly, Young, and others—were moved to Hanoi and met other disaffected enlisted POWs like Robert Chenoweth and Abel Kavanaugh (who committed suicide upon his return to the United States, ostensibly because of the pressure of the charges filed by Stockdale and Guy against the dissident POWs) and formed the group of malcontents dismissively labeled "the Peace Committee," they had already demonstrated the antiwar sentiments and the internecine group conflicts that would make their testimonies a powerful rejection of the official story. The *Survivors* and Daly in *Black Prisoner of War* recount a convoluted tale of petty grievances: sometimes race-related dissension over power grabs; unstable health, which led to some prisoners' inability to contribute to the group's daily work and thus to others' resentful charges of laziness; and disagreements about how much to cooperate with their captors' attempts to extricate antiwar statements. An almost-comically botched escape attempt and a relentless undertow of deaths from the deprivations of jungle internment—not to mention the erratic presence of the "rifle-toting turncoat" Bobby Garwood—reinforced the disorder (Anton, *Survivors*, 110). Personal animosities were direct and sometimes rancorous: Daly hated Kushner, whom he thought racist and elitist; Anton disliked Willie Watkins, a strong African American who emerged for a time as camp leader; everyone loathed the apparently manipulative marine corporal Russ Grissett (whom Daly calls Grisson), who died in late 1968.

Without the military hierarchy and clarity of expectations imposed by the Code of Conduct, without the survival training and military discipline of the officer-pilots, without the structure and (torture aside) better conditions of the Hanoi camps, the Southern enlisted POWS were a disorganized, protean assemblage of young, sick, frightened—and, like the pilots, incredulous—prisoners: "So at first we fell victim of a lack of self-discipline," explains David Harker. "No, perhaps it was a failure to understand what we were up against. . . . And there was the shock factor. None of us could actually believe we were prisoners of war. Arriving in Viet Nam we had subconsciously anticipated being wounded or killed—but never captured. It wasn't a war in which people were captured in the south. That was for pilots flying over the north" (*Survivors*, 92). According to Daly and some members of the Grant group, they countered the northern POWs' commitment to the group with desperate, every-man-for-himself survival efforts. "Nobody much cared about anyone else," the always-defensive Daly insists. "We were just a bunch of guys living from day to day in our own ungiving world" (*Black Prisoner of War*, 128). Anton concurs: "Compassion," he admits, "like food, was in short supply" (112).

148

Given their complication of the heroic official story, the "deviationists" (as memoirist Jim Mulligan termed them) are unsurprisingly omitted from most of the Hanoi pilots' accounts. The northern POWs who do acknowledge the deviants are much more concerned with allegedly disloyal officers like navy captain Walter (Gene) Wilber and marine colonel Edison (Ed) Miller than with the Peace Committee and the enlisted men moved up from the South. McCain forgives Overly. Stockdale, writing about Garwood in 1981, reiterates his SRO-mandated prison policy that "it is neither American nor Christian to nag a repentant sinner to his grave," and acknowledges that some of his fellow prisoners objected to his "overgenerous offers of reinstatement and absolution of the very few 'losers' . . . who would not conform to the minimum standards of our military organization" (*A Vietnam Experience*, 102). Alvarez is less magnanimous; angry at Secretary of Defense Melvin Laird's declaration of amnesty for all POW offenses, he acknowledges that "not surprisingly" most of the disloyal POWs have been left out of the "postwar bonding." "I don't understand how they can live with themselves," Alvarez snarls (174). John Dramesi, himself excoriated by some of his prison mates because his dubious escape attempts inevitably yielded harsh treatment for other prisoners, is critical of all the accommodationists, but he finally blames weak leaders for the substandard performance of their followers. As Howes notes, "the official story's judgment is . . . clear. The PCs [Peace Committee members] lacked the intelligence, discipline, and integrity necessary to avoid betraying their country" (109). Yet Rochester and Kiley's suggestion about the problematic POWs, whose number, they state, "was greater than postwar memoirists remember or care to admit"—that "whether they were turncoats who willfully disobeyed orders, ratted on comrades, and bartered antiwar messages for special privileges, or were simply confused youngsters who sincerely opposed the war and saw no downside to expressing their feelings, depends on the perspective of the participants"—allows for at least some rehabilitation of the image of the dissident POWs (592, 562).

Daly and Grant's *Survivors'* testimonies attempt to explain their apparently sincere opposition to the war and growing sympathies for the Vietnamese and their cause. Several express loyalty to other POWs, complicating Anton's and Daly's statements about the disunity of the group. Tom Davis, for instance, insists that when someone was ill, "personal differences were forgotten," and fellow army mortarman Isaiah (Ike) McMillan, encouraged by the camp commander to "cross over" like the always controversial Garwood, proclaims that "there's no way I could ever cross over, no way. How could Garwood do a thing like that? How could he turn his back on his family? That's what the guys in that camp were to me. Family. I mean, we got into arguments and fights all the time. But it was the sort of thing that comes into the natural relationship between man and wife" (*Survivors*, 170, 117).

Obviously, all defend their concessions to Vietnamese pressure to provide antiwar statements; they recognize the significance of their actions and statements, acknowledging, once in Hanoi, the antipathy of the other POWs, expecting to be imprisoned upon their return and even, in some cases, seriously considering not going home to the United States in 1973. Predictably, the divergent POWs present themselves not as weak or disloyal, but as ignorant of the officers' expectations, enervated by the volatile conditions of their jungle imprisonment ("disease and malnutrition were our constant companions," testifies Nick Rowe), and genuinely skeptical about America's motives in the Vietnam War (218). Their variations on the official story in fact support many of the recurring themes of the mainstream memoirs—most clearly, the commitment to fellow prisoners and group solidarity. But, like the wives' testimonies, their acknowledgment that the American experience of imprisonment in Southeast Asia was more complicated than the consistent representation of endurance, camaraderie, and honor presented by the Hanoi officers recognizes "the other side" of the POW myth.

"We Won the War"

John McCain concludes *Faith of My Fathers* with his determination that his imprisonment will not be "the leitmotif of my life," but his resolution leads directly to a lengthy litany of the lessons of the experience: enhanced self-confidence, seriousness of purpose, a recognition of dependence on others. "Vietnam changed me in significant ways," McCain concludes, "for the better" (346, 347). McCain's declaration that the rigors of his imprisonment made him a better man today echoes the Hanoi prisoners' consistent claim that the POW experience was an ennobling one. In 1974, Jim Stockdale boldly concluded that the Hanoi POWs "were able to establish communication, organization, a chain of command and an effective combat unit. We lost some battles, but I believe we won the war" (*A Vietnam Experience*, 9). This unchallenged claim illustrates America's compulsion to salvage some uplifting consolation from the debacle of the Vietnam War. The vendors of the official story did, after all, nothing heroic. Most confessed under torture to war crimes; none successfully escaped—though instructed to by the sacrosanct Code of Conduct—and few even attempted to. Yet that their collective survival and postwar embrace of a consistent, patriotic narrative remains heralded as unqualified heroism is underscored by John McCain's contemporary reputation as a war hero—while his Senate colleague John Kerry is branded by many as a turncoat.

Like McCain, Stockdale unwittingly embraces the captivity narratives' requisition of redemption as he dramatically suggests that the courageous, unified American prisoners' triumphant repatriation to a polarized American society was *the* victory of the disastrous Vietnam War. In the early 1970s, the POWs were a rallying point for disparate, even antithetical participants in the Vietnam experience. Antiwar activists visited Hanoi to certify that the North Vietnamese treated American prisoners humanely and, sometimes, to accompany home the prisoners released to their custody. POW families finally defied the Pentagon's "keep silent" policy and advocated broadly for the return of their men. The Nixon administration, recognizing that the plight of the POWs was arguably the only aspect of the increasingly contentious, unmanageable debacle on which its disparate constituencies could agree, made the fate of the POWs integral to the Paris Peace Accords and orchestrated, in Operation Homecoming, "a mass media morality play, something joyous salvaged out of the Indochina disaster, something unifying and relatively clean in a nation divided by war and about to be sullied by its greatest political scandal" (Blakey, 327).

In the years since the war, the still familiar black-and-white silhouette flag designed by the League of Families, which promises "our Nation's concern and commitment to resolving as fully as possible the fates of Americans still prisoner, missing and unaccounted for in Southeast Asia," continues to proclaim that "You Are Not Forgotten." The powerful combination of the campaign to "never forget" the unrecovered MIAs and the national endorsement of the POW heroes makes America's Vietnam POW experience one of the more resonant aspects of our cultural appropriation of the Vietnam War.

Chapter Four

The Fugitive's Hour: The Counterculture and the Vietnam Antiwar Movement in American Fiction

Out on the street I couldn't tell the Vietnam veterans from the rock and roll veterans. The Sixties had made so many casualties, its war and its music had run power off the same circuit for so long they didn't even have to fuse. . . . What I'd thought of as two obsessions were really only one.

—Michael Herr, *Dispatches*

That was just a dream some of us had.

—Joni Mitchell, "California"

The best time was dusk, she realized. . . . That was the fugitive's hour, when the darkening air felt like shelter, yet you still had your eyes.

—Jenny Shimada, *American Woman*

I N 1998, in one of the many celebrations of the coming millennium, the U.S. Postal Service invited American citizens to vote for representative American events and images of each decade of the twentieth century. Millions of ballots were cast, on the Postal Service website and at 40,000 post offices and 300,000 public school classrooms around the country. The resulting issues were colorful sheets of first-class stamps—fifteen for each decade—commemorating what average American citizens selected as "the most significant people, events, and accomplishments of the 20th century." For the stamps of the "rebellious Sixties," as the accompanying narrative labeled the decade, nearly a million citizens voted to acknowledge such icons as the Barbie doll, the Ford Mustang, the Superbowl—*and* Martin Luther King, Jr., the Beatles' yellow submarine, a large black-and-yellow peace symbol pinned to a denim shirt, a helicopter dropping American soldiers into the jungle of Vietnam, and the memorable image from Arnold Skolnick's colorful 1969 Woodstock music festival poster of a dove perched on the neck of a guitar.

Surely we are not surprised that five of the fifteen unforgettable images of the tumultuous 1960s are representations of the civil rights movement, the antiwar movement, the Vietnam War, and the counterculture—in short, of canonized contemporary memories of the turbulent 1960s. And we can probably assume that the predominately young Americans who selected those icons—even baby boomers who came of age in that decade—would be hard pressed to explain intelligently the intersections and relationships among those powerful metaphors of that complex period in American history. Is it fading memory or lack of understanding, even at the time, of the complexities of that era that accounts for the simplistic representation of the 1960s in contemporary American culture?

In Marylouise Oates's 1991 *Making Peace: A Novel of the Sixties*, the protagonist, Annie, is a middle-aged television journalist preparing a documentary on the 1960s for a 1980s Democratic National Convention. Though Annie welcomes the documentary assignment as an opportunity to "indulge in the luxury of her own past," she is surprised that the "vibrant colors" of the news film of the era belie her black-and-white memories (3). She has struggled to find "some original film, some footage that hadn't appeared on the air in the nostalgia trips the network loved to take: a speech by Dr. King that didn't say he had a dream; a clip of Bobby Kennedy in which he wasn't walking on the beach; JFK without his daughter and not saying, '*Ich bin ein Berliner*'; black students before Afros, hair all slicked down with pomade; antiwar protesters who weren't from Berkeley or Columbia" (5–6). Are our inaccuracies and stereotypes due to protean memory or cultural simplification?

The sixties activist and, now, sixties scholar Todd Gitlin, in his preface to the 1993 revision of his hybrid memoir–critical analysis *The Sixties: Years of Hope, Days of Rage* (1987), asserts that "perhaps no decade has suffered" the inevitable and unfortunate reductionism that simplistically labels all historical periods "more than 'the Sixties,' which in popular parlance has come to stand for a single seamless whole" (xiii). And, as Van Gosse suggests, "the poor decade cannot bear the weight" (*Rethinking*, ix). The cultural critic H. Bruce Franklin, in *Vietnam and Other American Fantasies* (2000), more specifically decries the simplification, demonization, and denial of the Vietnam antiwar movement, which he calls "the . . . movement we are supposed to forget" (47). The turn of the new century brought a spate of new books (not to mention websites) about the 1960s, including work by a new, younger generation of academic commentators who offered a revisionist, often conservative, assessment of that long-ago era.[1] The best of the recent reevaluations of the New Left and the Vietnam antiwar move-ment—scholarly reconsiderations by historians such as Maurice Isserman, Richard Moser, and Van Gosse—offer a more expansive analysis that chal-lenges the neatly artificial parameters of the decanal definition of "the Six-ties," a demarcation that, they assert, obscures the origins of the Vietnam era protest movement in the Old Left; the "constant efflorescence of sub-movements, temporary coalitions, breakaway factions, and organizational proliferation" that characterized the Left in the sixties; and the profound influence of the New Left and its multifarious social issues well after the end of the Vietnam War (Gosse, "A Movement of Movements," 279). Though their appraisals present a more balanced and sophisticated interpretation of the decade than Franklin's overstated thesis implies, he does have a point. If the years since the Vietnam War have brought an evolution in the popular conception of the Vietnam veteran, who is now a more apologetically em-braced hero than psycho baby-killer, the vet's antiwarrior brethren remain, in popular perception, young, spoiled, self-indulgent traitors.[2]

Such revisions and misperceptions matter. Some of us are like Oates's Annie, who recognizes that she, "like many others in her generation . . . [is] a captive of her youth, her personal history," an insight that the memoirs by movement participants underscore (3). Gitlin goes further, claiming in 1992 that the issues raised in the 1960s—"civil rights and antiwar and coun-tercultural and women's and the rest of that decade's movements"—offered fundamental challenges to our culture and values that remain relevant to-day (xiv). Similarly, Tom Brokaw, in his 2007 *Boom!*, asserts that "many of the debates about the Sixties are still as lively and passionate and unresolved as they ever were" (xiv). In *The Greater Generation: In Defense of the Baby Boom Legacy*, Leonard Steinhorn asserts that the baby boomer generation confronted social injustice in ways that its parents—the much heralded "greatest generation"—did not: "Two generations stared at the same short-comings, inequities and hypocrisies of American life, but it was the Baby Boom generation that chose to tackle them, to hold this country to its grand ideals, to agitate for justice when it would have been easier to remain docile and silent, and we are a better nation because of that. It is why this gen-eration's accomplishments eclipse what came before it, and why the Baby Boom must be recognized as the Greater Generation" (13). Oates's Annie, as she witnesses the 1980s convention floor fight over the Democratic plat-form, recognizes that "the controversial planks were the same issues that had caused such violent and widespread reaction in the Sixties—race, war, civil rights" (8). Her documentary film is promoted as "a revealing look at how the problems of the Sixties have become the politics of today" (8).

The Vietnam antiwar movement is the least understood of the important and controversial phenomena of the 1960s in America and the legacy of the Vietnam War in contemporary America. Like the Vietnam combat experience, the movement to end the war, and its complementary social movements, have, since the late 1970s, inspired a steady stream of fictional interpretations and autobiographical assessments of the New Left and its more colorful communicants. Indeed, the cultural texts that have offered commentary on the antiwar movement in the years after the Vietnam War are as numerous and diverse as those that attend to the war itself; they concentrate on unaffiliated radicals and on direct participants of what its partisans called, simply, "the movement," and, most poignantly, on its protagonists' bewildered family members—the collateral damage of the home front war against the war.

The movement (variously known as the antiwar movement, the peace movement, the New Left, and sometimes, less accurately, the counterculture) was a loose affiliation of primarily, though not exclusively, young people who coalesced in the mid- to late 1960s in opposition to the widening American war in Vietnam. Rooted in the University of Michigan–based Students for a Democratic Society, organized in 1960 to advocate for participatory democracy and to fight racism, poverty, and social injustice, and the free speech movement, founded in 1964 at the University of California at Berkeley to advance students' rights, the movement embraced values and tactics that were strongly influenced by the civil rights movement of the early 1960s. It is important to remember that the SDS manifesto, the Port Huron Statement, was written in 1962—three years before Vietnam meant anything to most Americans, and five or six years before it meant everything. Toward the end of the decade, frustrated that massive national antiwar marches and local protests were failing to effect an end to the war, radical activists (most notoriously, the Weather Underground, which took over the SDS in 1969) turned to increasingly violent militancy designed to make continued execution of the war untenable. It has been generally accepted that, despite some fringe activity well into the 1970s, the movement effectively ended with American withdrawal from Vietnam in the early 1970s. Yet recent historiography extends the chronological range, the diversity, and the significance of the broadly defined New Left, insisting that the traditional acceptance of the Vietnam antiwar movement as synonymous with the increasingly radical SDS obfuscates the diversity and minimizes the impact of the larger movement. Privileging the white, student-led SDS (as many of the standard assessments of the era do), Gosse and others argue, marginalizes comparably vibrant and influential movements for the rights of African Americans, women, gays and lesbians, and others. "If one presumes a single, coherent New Left of white youth led by SDS," Gosse writes, "then other movements and struggles . . . are either captured in isolation . . . or pushed to the margins and deprived of agency, portrayed as either precursors (the civil rights movement) or legatees (women's liberation) of the student New Left at the Sixties' center. This makes for a tidy, but profoundly limited, narrative" ("A Movement of Movements," 278).

Many (perhaps most) traditional texts now accepted as the Vietnam War canon—novels such as Winston Groom's *Better Times than These*, Philip Caputo's *Indian Country*, and James Webb's *Fields of Fire*, for example— include some attention to the peace movement: often brief scenes of young, unkempt civilians abusing recently returned veterans. My interest here is in creative fiction (and, in a subsequent chapter, memoirs) that offer a more sustained and often sophisticated commentary on the constituency, goals, and repercussions of the antiwar movement. For most of these novelists, filmmakers, and memoirists, and for their characters, involvement in the movement to end the war in Vietnam is—like participation in the war itself for countless real and literary veterans—an experience that defines one's life forever. In many of these novels and participant histories, the antiwar experience is long past, the protagonist's sympathies for efforts to end the war did not extend to active participation in the organized movement, or the turmoil of the era is merely context for a traditional coming-of-age experience. But the texts in which the movement is more contextual than central proffer the most interesting, if often similar, representations of the antiwar movement and the era. That is, some of the most aesthetically sophisticated and resonant of these narratives present the profound effects of the passions and purposes of the period on their usually young protagonists, who are often only minor players on the crowded, crazed stage of the sixties. The less successful novels offer more expansive, but usually more superficial, portraits of the era and its stakes.

Something Special Happened

Bart Schneider's slight 2001 novel *Secret Love*, set in San Francisco in 1964, offers the parallel stories of the recently widowed, Jewish, middle-aged attorney Jake Roseman's unlikely romantic liaison with a younger, mixed-race actress, and a gay black Muslim's relationship with Peter, a white actor. Jake is famous locally as a civil rights leader, and the movement for racial equality—as well as the Nation of Islam—provide context for the development of the novel's interracial relationships. The inchoate Vietnam antiwar movement—through its precursor, the free speech movement—appears briefly midway through *Secret Love*, when Jake is summoned by the beleaguered chancellor of his alma mater, the University of California at Berkeley, to advise the administration on how to handle growing protests against the institution's prohibition against students' political activism on campus. To the chagrin of the white male administrators in their "tweedy civility," Jake's sympathies are with the students, and he joins the crowd of angry students at Sproul Plaza as Mario Savio delivers his now famous "bodies upon the gears of the machine" speech and announces the administration's concession to the students' demands for free speech (147). Schneider embeds in the turmoil and excitement of 1960s San Francisco *Secret Love*'s presentation of his characters' struggles to find happiness and live decently. The setting offers texture to and commentary on an otherwise conventional contemporary, politically correct love story.

Several of James Carroll's (apparently autobiographical, given his poignant memoir, *An American Requiem*) Irish family sagas are similarly developed against the backdrop of the protest movement. In his 1980 novel *Fault Lines*, protagonist David Dolan, draft dodger and former antiwar leader, returns home from a twelve-year exile in Sweden to try to come to terms with his former life. Though the novel suggests, when David seeks a teaching job, that the price of his antiwar activity will be higher than he thinks, it quickly turns into a love story and eschews narrative interest in David's activist past. Carroll's 1984 *Prince of Peace* more fully integrates the antiwar material throughout the novel. Narrator Frank Durkin relates his lifelong friendship with Father Michael Maguire—Korean War hero, Catholic church liaison in Vietnam in the early years of the Americans' presence there, and ultimately virulent Berriganesque peace activist. Extensive material on the involvement of the American Catholic church with the Diem regime, and later, on the activities of antiwar clergy provide the backdrop for the brother-like bond between Durkin and the glorious celebrity priest, and for the narrator's betrayal of their deep friendship.

The 1983 novel *A Country Such as This* is another popular, historical saga—this one from a much more conservative author, Vietnam marine veteran and Virginia U.S. senator James Webb, best known for his accomplished combat novel *Fields of Fire*. *A Country Such as This* recounts the lives from 1951 to 1976 of three naval academy graduates and their wives: Red, a fighter pilot who is shot down and taken prisoner in Vietnam; Judd, who abandons a career in the FBI to become a minister and, later, a member of the House of Representatives; and Joe, a military, then civilian, missile defense engineer who marries a strident antiwar activist-feminist whose activities explain the novel's grudging interest in the Vietnam antiwar movement. Critically and superficially, Webb recounts the major events of the peace movement and the media's complicity in glamorizing what Judd dismisses as "the Spoiled Baby Brigade" (470). Webb pushes all the usual buttons: the protestors' signs and chants, the major urban marches (which he calls "the Semiannual Temper Tantrum"), the familiar argument that the movement prolonged the war by emboldening the North Vietnamese. Like many of the fictional and actual women in these movement narratives, Joe's wife, Dorothy Dingenfelder, is a singularly unappealing character. She is intelligent, committed, and successful, and she has the last word in the novel; but she is the character who embodies the sins of the era and the central theme of Webb's elegiac novel, which is the title of part four of the book: "We Are Not Ourselves Anymore" (307).

Webb's jeremiad against the youthful movement is, more significantly, a lamentation for a disintegrating America that echoes throughout many of these narratives. It recurs more humorously in T. C. Boyle's lively 2003 counterculture novel *Drop City*, about an early 1970s California commune that relocates to Alaska and struggles to accommodate its individualistic native neighbors, the untamed wilderness, and its own internal frictions. The thirty-some young communards of Drop City, who have eschewed "the plastic world" for "a life of peace and tranquility, of love and meditation and faith in the ordinary, no pretense, no games, no plastic yearning after the almighty dollar," are young, idealistic, and usually stoned (12, 10). And because Drop City South (in California) is an open commune, "weekend hippies,"[3] angry blacks, and assorted trouble makers complicate the lives of the regular residents—"chicks" and "cats" and Reba's children, Che and Sunshine. A rape, sexual jealousy, racial tension, the outside community's fear and hostility, and the struggle to live off the land challenge the group's commitment to an alternative lifestyle. Against the story of Drop City South's demise and its partisans' removal to Alaska (Drop City North), Boyle counterposes trapper Sess Harder's unconventional courtship of and marriage to Pamela, a strong-willed nonconformist who signs on for Sess's isolated, survivalist life in the Alaskan wilderness because "everything they knew, the whole teetering violent war-crazed society, was about to collapse. . . . And the riots in the street were just a prelude to what was to come, because if nobody worked and they all just sat around using drugs and having promiscuous sex all day, then who was going to grow the food? And if nobody grew the food, then what would they eat? To her, the answer was obvious: they'd eat your food, and when they were done with that, they'd eat you" (88).

The war-maddened, precarious society is merely context in *Drop City*, a distant, menacing rumble in the parallel lives of these happy hippies and hard-working trappers, all of whom reject "the nine-to-five life in a little pink house in the suburbs" (301). It's been two years since Drop Citizen Marco has fled Connecticut just ahead of a misdemeanor drug possession charge and a "cold hard incontrovertible black-and-white draft notice" (16). When Norm, Drop City's founder and paternalistic guru, picks him up in a van painted with a crude peace sign and welcomes him to Drop City, where he can "turn on, tune in, drop out and just live there on the land doing your own thing," Marco knows that he is "home" (17, 19).

Home. Family. Camaraderie. For the protagonists of *Drop City*, the commune promises mutual love and support within an alternative lifestyle, much like the loyalty and solidarity that memoirists such as Jane Alpert and Bill Ayers and fictional protagonists like *The Darling*'s Hannah Musgrave and *American Woman*'s Jenny Shimada find in their radical movement cells, and that combat veterans, POWs, and POW wives discovered in their respective wartime cadres. Ronnie/Pan and Star arrive at Drop City together during its last days in California, and Star decides immediately that "this was her family now, this was where she belonged. . . . Until Drop City, she'd never belonged anywhere" (34). And when county health and fire and building inspectors close down the community of "NO MEN, NO WOMEN—ONLY CHILDREN," and Norm leads his own Merry Pranksters to his uncle's land in Alaska, Reba greets the incredulous natives Sess and Pamela with open arms. "We're a family," she reassures them. "Just a family, that's all" (8, 263).

The complicated plot that unravels once the "whole weird Halloween procession" of hippies arrives in Alaska involves Sess's old nemesis, bush pilot Joe Bosky, several guns, a plane crash, a night in the frigid wilderness, and a thriller denouement, but the dramatic conflict that the first two-thirds of *Drop City* promises between Sess and the Drop City North residents never materializes (262). Despite Sess and Pamela's skepticism about the counterculture kids—"they were like children, utterly confident and utterly ignorant," Sess thinks—the novel proposes that the native *isolatoes* and the groovy cats and chicks from California have more in common than not (335). Star befriends a lonely Pamela and quickly recognizes that "Pamela was just like them. She wasn't buying into the plastic society . . . she'd dropped out just as surely as anybody at Drop City had" (301).

Caryl Rivers's simplistic but spirited 1987 novel *Intimate Enemies* is the more traditional story of conventional, thirty-five-year-old, divorced, smart, and ambitious Jessie McGrath and her unlikely but passionate romantic relationship with an army major and Vietnam veteran. Mark Claymore is now, fifteen years after the war, ROTC coordinator at the small Boston college where Jessie serves as provost. Jessie's success in her career is contrasted by her failure in relationships with men, and her determination to avoid the risk and vulnerability of another love relationship (before she meets dashing Mark Claymore) is mitigated by her ticking biological clock. Mark, who despite losing a leg in Vietnam seems remarkably well-adjusted and successful, begins—once his long-controlled emotions are set loose by his love for Jessie—to experience flashbacks and other symptoms of post-traumatic stress disorder.

The novel gives us a fairly one-dimensional portrait of the movement as well, through Jessie's diary from her years at Boston University, and through the contemporary residue of the movement at Jessie's nearby current college, Kinsolving, which in the Vietnam era was, the narrator tells us, "competing with Boston University for the title of the Berkeley of the East" (7). Now, in the late 1980s, Jessie's faculty meetings are enlivened by the hostility between two former New Left leaders—Abbie Hoffman–like Brian, who still sports jeans and a (graying) ponytail and teaches courses called "From Marx to Mao" and "The Counterculture"; and Jerry Rubinesque Jake, who has gone corporate and now runs buttoned-down weekend success seminars that are part business philosophy, part pop psychology, and part est. Through Jessie's memories, Rivers give us a movement that looks more than anything else like a lot of fun. Jake and Brian, the notorious radicals, are famous for pranks like putting a papier mâché head of Ho Chi Minh on Mount Rushmore. And Jessie's college friend remembers that her final exam was canceled when she and Jessie called in a bomb threat to the department office. "I gave peace a chance, and I got an A minus at the same time," Andrea reminisces happily (63).

Yet Jessie's mid-sixties diary entries present—yes, a naïve, self-absorbed college girl whose commitment to the antiwar movement is detached and safe—but also a young woman who believes sincerely that the Vietnam War is morally wrong. Neither pacifist, Marxist, nor Yippie, Jessie remembers that all those years ago "she felt there was a great moral choice to be made by her generation over Vietnam, and she wanted to be part of that choice. She was proud of her role in the movement, always would be, and she made no apologies" (21). Yes, Jessie and Mark have to overcome mutual wariness about the other's role in that war, but the point of *Intimate Enemies* is that the *real* enemies are those who have forgotten the entire experience. One of Jake's young clients sneers at love-beaded Brian—"Nobody told him that the Age of Aquarius dawned twenty years ago"—but Brian, unlike Jake, has not sold out; he's merely frustrated: "'I try to tell them, the kids, what it was like, that we had a dream we could make things better. . . . And we did good things, for a while. We ended a war, and things got better for poor people and Blacks and women. . . . I try to tell them that, about the passion, and they just sit there and stare at me, as if I'm speaking Greek'" (156, 157). Real-life activist Mark Rudd echoes Brian's disillusionment with the younger generation, almost word for word, in the 2003 documentary *The Weather Underground*.

Late in the novel, a traumatized Mark learns of the unexpected, delayed war-related suicide of his best friend. When Jessie tries to comfort him, he spits back the retort directed at the sympathetic wife or girlfriend in virtually every Vietnam combat narrative: "You weren't *there*. Nobody knows who wasn't there. We're the only ones who know. Not you people" (205). But the central thesis of *Intimate Enemies* is that Jessie *does* know. She wasn't *there* in Vietnam, but she was *there* in the Vietnam era. Importantly, it is Mark who utters that greater truth earlier in the book: "It's funny, you and I would have been on opposite sides of the barricades, throwing rocks at each other. But we understand each other better than people who didn't get involved in it" (94). Compare Neil Gordon's acknowledgment, in *The Company You Keep*, that "Good people fell on both sides of the question of Vietnam" (204). That, despite apparent and real antipathies, Vietnam-era warriors and antiwarriors shared a direct, profound engagement with the age's most significant event is a theme that resounds throughout the narratives of the movement. As Christian Appy notes in *Patriots*, "those who fought in the war and those who fought against it shared the struggle of their times, and in that sense they had more in common with each other than they did with the millions of young people who quietly avoided the war" (264). For Rivers, the Vietnam era and the peace movement are long gone. Twenty years later, no one remembers and no one cares. But for those who lived through it—even on opposite sides of the barricades—the strangely shared experience is the defining (if sentimentalized) one of their now busy, complicated lives. "Jessie wondered if her generation would always measure their lives against that time" (60).

William Cowling, the protagonist of veteran-author Tim O'Brien's futuristic 1985 novel *The Nuclear Age*, also suggests that the Vietnam era is over. "It's finished now," he notes as a middle-aged man in 1995, "no more crusades. . . . Times change. . . . Who among us really cares?" (8). Yet like Rivers's characters, William measures his life against that time, though for him "that time" begins well before the Vietnam era. William is a baby boomer, a duck-and-cover kid whose childhood was forged by the Cuban missile crisis, fallout shelters,[4] and what will become a lifelong "conviction that the world wasn't safe for human life" (9). By the mid-1960s, college student William senses "that things were accelerating toward the point of hazard," and in his one-man crusade to alert his fellow students to "the coming fracture," he reluctantly falls in with a motley group of antiwar activist misfits called "the Committee" (66, 74). Throughout the late 1960s, the protestors' activities escalate; teach-ins and pep rallies for peace ("half protest, half party") metamorphose into darker, more mysterious actions, but always William holds back: "what disturbed me was the outlaw mentality. Too reckless, I thought" (99, 113). Graduation precipitates a draft notice, and William's decision to become a draft evader is "not honor, not conscience," but a desire for "safety": "I was running because I couldn't envision any other way, because the dangers exceeded the reach of my imagination. . . . All I wanted for myself was a place to ride out the bad times" (149).

Cheerleader Sarah, William's activist girlfriend, arranges his underground adventure—flight to Key West and a pleasantly indolent beach life; but when the bill comes due, it's basic training in Cuba for the revolution to come. Then, for two years, William skirts commitment and danger by paying his dues as a "network delivery boy," as Sarah (whose enthusiasm for the antiwar cause makes William's reservations seem all the more pronounced) and the others raid Selective Service offices, bomb National Guard armories, and become famous. By the mid-1970s, with the waning of the war and his father's death, William wants out; he returns home to Montana, studies geology, finds uranium, buys its remote location, sells it for twenty-five million dollars, and shares the riches with his antiwar comrades. Years after the end of the war, Sarah dies of cancer, and the rest of the Committee, hoarding a nuclear warhead, die in a Symbionese Liberation Army–like shoot-out, "a TV spectacular" (295). Even later, in 1995—the future—William, convinced since childhood that "when there is nothing, there is nothing worth dying for, and when there is nothing worth dying for, there is only nothing," digs a hole in his yard, determined to retrench from a perilous world (303). Though William's undeniable love for his wife and daughter inspires a conclusion to the novel that grudgingly affirms endurance and engagement, the story that O'Brien tells in *The Nuclear Age* is one of late-twentieth-century madness; the Vietnam War merely the most unnerving evidence of "a general ungluing of things . . . the fundamental process of our age: collapsing valences and universal entropy," the protest movement (like Boyle's Alaskan trappers' survivalist existence) a feeble response to the lunacy of modern times (230).

Published a year after *The Nuclear Age*, Patti Davis's 1986 novel *Home Front* is a co-written autobiographical *bildungsroman*, interesting only because it was written by Ronald Reagan's famously obstreperous daughter at the height of his presidency. In the mid-sixties, Beth, the narrator, is in boarding school and then college while her father serves as governor of California. Beth's sexual awakening and rejection of her parents' (especially her mother's) conventional values are predictable. The antiwar movement is a convenient instrument for Beth's adolescent rebellion, and at the exact midpoint of the novel, at a 1969 campus rally, moved by news of the My Lai massacre, Beth commits herself to the fight to end the war. Her relative celebrity makes Beth a popular speaker in a movement that created and attracted stars, and she is delighted to ignore her parents' admonitions against her participation in the era's glamorous anti-establishment crusade.

What saves Beth's story and Davis's novel from complete banality is Davis's presentation of Beth's relationship with her high school boyfriend Greg, who is serving in Vietnam as Beth protests the war at home (not unlike Margot Adler's correspondence with an in-country soldier in her autobiographical *Heretic's Heart*). Implicitly, Beth's sympathy for the soldiers fighting the war explains her rejection of some of her fellow activists' calls for more dramatic action. "These Weathermen tactics will destroy everything we've been working for. They play right into the hands of the hawks who want the public to see us as mindless lunatics," Beth asserts, echoing a sharp-edged appraisal of the radical Weather Underground that is articulated throughout these antiwar novels and many of the movement memoirs (122–123). Late in the war, against the backdrop of the Vietnam Veterans Against the War Dewey Canyon III protest in Washington, Beth befriends a young antiwar veteran, who introduces her to amputee vets at the local veterans hospital. Sensitized (like Sally, the Jane Fonda character in *Coming Home*) by the grim reality of wounded veterans' lives, Beth now feels "compelled to relate the experience of seeing boys whose lives had been irrevocably changed, who had come home only to be shunned by the country that had sent them off to fight its war" (185). At the end of the novel, Beth reaffirms her commitment to Greg, now home from Vietnam, bitter, and (like Rivers's Mark) just beginning to confront his Vietnam horrors. Davis and Rivers, writing in the 1980s, offer what Susan Jeffords and others identify as a typically Reagan-era appreciation for the Vietnam veteran; and Davis, like Rivers, affirms the importance of the shared bonds of protestors and vets. Davis dedicates her antiwar novel to her husband and "to all Vietnam vets."

Marylouise Oates's *Making Peace* extrapolates on Davis's and many of the historians' and memoirists' glances at the tensions within and the diverse constituencies of the movement. Oates was the deputy national press director for the Vietnam Moratorium,[5] and her novel is a detailed behind-the-scenes fictional presentation of the issues and participants in the more or less "official" peace movement. It is as well a complicated political mystery novel whose stereotyped and simplistic characters cannot sustain her complex plot. But though *Making Peace* is a novel whose potential as a serious exploration of a significant historical and political era is undermined by its author's limitations as a novelist, it is, nonetheless (undoubtedly because of its author's direct engagement with the movement), one more interesting retrospective literary representation of the movement and its participants.

The plot of *Making Peace* turns to an extent on the diversity of constituents and goals of the unwieldy antiwar movement mentioned by Davis, Marge Piercy, and many of the memoirists but that are beyond the more simplistic and revisionary presentations of the movement that most of these novels offer. DeBenedetti, Garfinkle, Gitlin, Terry H. Anderson in *The Movement and the Sixties: Protest in America from Greensboro to Wounded Knee*, Tom Wells in *The War Within: America's Battle Over Vietnam*, and others have explored the tensions within the formal antiwar movement and the often conflicting goals and strategies that, most commentators agree, ultimately compromised its effectiveness as a coherent social force. As an umbrella under which pacifist and religious groups, civil rights activists, disarmament organizations, the Old Left, and varied student groups jostled for space, the antiwar movement was, as Zaroulis and Sullivan state, "a loose, shifting, often uneasy coalition of groups and individuals who often disagreed on every issue except their hatred of the war" (xii). Our failure to appreciate the boisterous heterogeneity of the movement's partisans is, of course, one of the more fundamental oversimplifications about the movement as it is remembered today.

Making Peace proposes that a covert group of CIA affiliates and liberal elder statesmen, all Old Leftists who are committed to incremental change within the system, having successfully attenuated the civil rights movement by sowing the seeds of dissension within it and expediting blacks' ejection of white activists from its ranks, works surreptitiously to undermine a peace movement that is becoming increasingly visible, vocal, radical—and therefore threatening to the liberal establishment. This persuasive and powerful coalition, and Tom Burnett, its representative in the movement leadership, execute the intricate political conspiracy that drives the plot of Oates's novel. Only at the end, some fifteen or twenty years after the fact, do we learn that the union organizer, "red diaper baby" Kapinski—who worries in the sixties about the "balkanization of the peace movement"—is similarly committed, not to the revolution, but to the preservation of the liberal status quo (79).

Like Jay Cantor in *Great Neck*, Oates also adds to the overview of the movement presented by this panoply of texts some treatment of its relationship with the civil rights movement of the earlier 1960s. Annie, Pisano, Burnett, and Kapinski—the major players in the planning for the Offensive Against the War—are veterans of the 1964 Mississippi Freedom Summer. Bitsy Clark, a black upper-middle-class civil rights activist, is the novel's voice for the position that the war and African Americans' involvement in the antiwar movement undermine Lyndon B. Johnson's Great Society programs. Finally, however, though Oates understands the important issues that energized and problematized the antiwar movement, her inability to present a compelling story confines *Making Peace* to the ranks of the more popular and superficial literary treatments of the subject.

Scott Turow's 1996 legal thriller *The Laws of Our Fathers* is, like *Making Peace*, a popular novel that exploits the turmoil and intense interpersonal relationships of the decade to provide dramatic historical context for a convoluted contemporary story. When the forty-something Kindle County (Turow's fictionalized Chicago) Superior Court Judge Sonny (Sonia) Klonsky agrees to hear the state's case against a probation officer accused of arranging the gangland murder of his mother, a former activist, she quickly learns that virtually all of the actors in the drama that unfolds in her courtroom in the winter of 1995 were at college together—with Sonny—at a loosely fictionalized Berkeley in the late sixties. The action alternates between the 1995 trial (and the burgeoning romantic relationship between single-mother Sonny and her old college boyfriend, Seth Weissman, now a syndicated journalist) and Seth's and Sonny's accounts of the then youthful characters' personal uncertainties and political imbroglios at the peak of the counterculture.

The late 1969 to early 1970 back story features all the usual suspects: splenetic Black Panthers, red diaper babies, "students and street freaks, hippies, home runaways, and communards" (107). Turow trots out the threat of the draft, the escalating violence of the Weather Underground, the Kent State massacre, the bizarre story of a barely disguised Patty Hearst; but his real interest, in both narratives, is the generation gap in its most profound sense: the youthful response in "those crazy times" to the lives and values of its parents (135). As Seth Weissman admits, "the rage of that era was not simply about whose prediction of the future of Southeast Asia was accurate, or the issue of an indigenous people's right to control their own nation. . . . the war protest represented an entire generation in combat against the rigid views of our parents. . . . The furious issue was what would happen to all of us, parents and children, if the laws of our fathers were forgotten" (135). Sonny struggles with the psychic legacy of her emotionally distant, politically passionate radical mother, Zora. And only at the novel's conclusion, in his elegy for the irascible Bernhard, does Seth come to terms with his father. Like many of the movement activists, and thus of the protagonists of these narratives, Seth is Jewish, the only surviving child of European immigrants who cannot accept their American son's rejection of the country they embraced. Bernhard Weissman dismisses his son's comparison of Vietnam-era America with Germany in the 1930s: "It was the students at Columbia whom my father compared to the beer-hall *putsch*; the Panthers, in his eyes, were the brownshirts with berets" (191). Like Leo Jacobs in Jay Cantor's *Great Neck*, Seth's father is a Holocaust survivor, intransigently silent about the unspeakable horrors of his early life and the concentration camp murder of his older son. Only the middle-aged Seth can understand, as the twenty-three-year-old Seth could not, his parents' powerful legacy: "I did not see any relationship between my parents' past and my political passions. I didn't recognize the futile deal I'd silently negotiated with myself:

that if the world could be reformed, made right, if I *knew* there could never be another Holocaust, I would be free of the burdens they had placed upon me" (195–196).

In 1996 Seth Weissman is a successful, even renowned, syndicated newspaper columnist, who grapples in his column, The Survivor's Guide, with his father's painful past, his own youthful idealism and evasion of the draft, and his young son's accidental death. He acknowledges that "it's probably useless trying to explain the passions of one era to another," but he (and the novel) believes, however tentatively, that the activities of the antiwar generation were, though sometimes misguided, in the end admirable and successful (134). Don't just tell me to get over my romanticized youth, he writes, "things changed. The war. The cruel formalities that disadvantaged minorities or women. People stopped behaving like they'd all been knocked out of the same stamping plant. . . . something special happened in the sixties. Didn't it? Or is it just because I was at that age, between things, where everything was still possible, that time, which in retrospect, doesn't seem to last long?" (64). Something special did happen, most sixties scholars would suggest, and something lasting as well: "The least-told story of U.S. history in the late twentieth century is how the social movements of the Sixties institutionalized themselves," Gosse avows. "We live in a world the Sixties made" (*The World the Sixties Made*, 25, 5).

Despite its early (1977) publication, Sara Davidson's formulaic novel *Loose Change* (which, like many of these narratives, offers the multiple protagonists that are the movement's variation on what combat novel commentators have called "the melting pot platoon") also recognizes the exhilarating idealism and fatal excesses of the movement and the era. Presenting itself as a "social history of the sixties," *Loose Change* (which became, in 1978, an NBC television miniseries and was reissued by the University of California Press in 1997) follows three Berkeley sorority sisters from 1961 through "that decade that belonged to the young," in which "we were certain we belonged to a generation that was special. We did not need or care about history because we had sprung from nowhere. We said what we thought and demanded what was right and there was no opposition. . . . We had glimpsed a new world where nothing would be the same and we had packed our bags" (3). Hackneyed, simplistic summaries of the vagaries of the times underscore the feminist-era beach blanket–bestseller aspirations of *Loose Change*, which follows the tumultuous fortunes of Tasha, Susie, and Sara as they careen through a decade of failed romantic relationships, feigned orgasms, abortions, careers, and New Age spirituality:

> ... the years from 1965 to 1967 are a jumble of meetings, teach-ins, rallies, marches, and talk, endless talk. Words were changing so fast. Negroes became blacks. Liberals became scum. God was declared dead. There was a New Morality, a New Journalism, a New Music, a new way of looking at everything and out of it all, a New Left!
>
> *Time* magazine selected as its Man of the Year for 1966: "the man—and woman—of 25 and under." Even the establishment agreed: anybody young had more important things to say than anybody old. (107)

Seventy-five pages later it's 1968: "The improbable—the shock—became a daily occurrence, and it all happened in live color in our homes. Two assassinations. A President dumped from office" (181). But by 1971, as twenty-eight-year-old journalist Sara writes incredulously in a *Life* magazine article about high school students, "the next radical generation" has helped elect Richard Nixon over George McGovern and is "swinging back to caution and conservatism" (331, 332). By 1973, as the war ends, Sara wonders—as so many of these fictional protagonists and memoirists do—"what went wrong?" (396). *Loose Change* pushes—or dons—all the sixties buttons in service of its coming-of-age themes. Like many of the popular narrative treatments of the era, it presents the wonder and tumult and disintegration of those "exciting ... scary" times with clichéd, if colorful, simplicity (401).

As Charles DeBenedetti, Nancy Zaroulis and Gerald Sullivan, Van Gosse, and others (including Philip Caputo in *Indian Country* and Russell Banks in *The Darling*, whose protagonists' fathers vehemently oppose the war) have shown, the movement was *not* (as the media would have it, now and at the time) populated primarily by young, upper-middle-class college students intractably rejecting their bourgeois parents and "the stagnation of those who have closed their minds to the future" (Port Huron Statement). Yet the widely accepted image remains of antiwar protestors as carefree college kids or grungy, drugged hippies out for a good time—and prevails in most of the texts considered here, resulting in a pervasive narrative interest in the newly branded "generation gap" and an often moving thematic preoccupation with the protagonists' perplexed and aggrieved parents. The dramatic, glamorous revolutionaries of the Weather Underground are, not surprisingly, particularly likely protagonists. They are, after all, young, passionately ideological, and determined to overthrow a corrupt, capitalist

America "by any means necessary," and they and their high-stakes actions virtually guarantee compelling narratives. Novels like Turow's, Oates's, and Rivers's capture the zealous intensity of their young characters and the energy of the motley movement even as they fail to examine the often tragic collateral damage that results from their characters' passions. A number of thematic and aesthetic features distinguish these popular, mostly flawed fictional treatments of the 1960s and the antiwar movement from more complex, literary, and successful representations of the same subject and themes in such narratives as Marge Piercy's 1979 novel *Vida*; Sidney Lumet's 1988 film *Running on Empty*; Elizabeth Spencer's 1991 novel *The Night Travellers*; Philip Roth's 1997 Pulitzer Prize–winning *American Pastoral*; Jay Cantor's *Great Neck*, Susan Choi's *American Woman*, and Neil Gordon's *The Company You Keep*, all from 2003; and, most recently, Russell Banks's *The Darling* (2004), Christopher Sorrentino's *Trance* (2005), and from 2006, Dana Spiotta's *Eat the Document*, Sigrid Nunez's *The Last of Her Kind*, and Joyce Carol Oates's *Black Girl/White Girl*. Though these narratives also present the stories of young, romantic partisans of the bold new age (many now older and more reflective some years after their youthful activism), they concentrate on characters who do more than flirt with the antiwar movement. In most of these narratives, the characters' dramatic antiwar activities (or inadvertent entanglement with the upheaval of the era) are violent, felonious actions that drive them underground and change their lives—and those of the people they love—abruptly and forever.

Running Before the Wind

Piercy's *Vida* is a long, third-person novel set in the late 1970s, when its mid-thirties protagonist has lived underground for a half dozen years. The story moves back in time to the late sixties and early seventies, describing Vida's resistance activities and the other members of Students Against the War (a fictionalized SDS, whose name demonstrates the narrowed postwar perception of the SDS's purpose), in which Vida is a major player. Piercy, however, is most interested in—and most successful at presenting—Vida's draining, arduous life as a fugitive. Vida disdains her former compatriots who have allowed themselves to be discovered and arrested, or who have turned themselves in. "Every day you defeat them by continuing," she insists (55); and, indeed, Vida—unlike the underground fugitive Louise Barrot in *Eat the Document*—remains faithful to the goals of the revolution and active in the now subterranean network. At the end of the novel she proposes an anti-nuclear platform for her organization, and plans and implements the bombing of a local power plant.

Like Webb's Dorothy Dingenfelder and Roth's Merry Levov, Vida is an unsympathetic protagonist—though undoubtedly Piercy intended her to be attractive and admirable. Piercy, like many of these texts' authors, offers little explanation for her heroine's passionate anti-establishment beliefs, and, indeed, little character development at all. Vida, much like Banks's Hannah Musgrave, emerges as a self-pitying, self-absorbed woman whose choices have earned her a life of nomadic hardship and transitory personal relationships. Her inability to acknowledge the end of her marriage to her husband Leigh, a sympathizer who has remained marginal to the movement and who continues his life above ground, underscores her unwillingness to admit that her movement and her network are crumbling. She is, in short, a remarkably naïve character.

Vida is interesting primarily for its sustained, even wearisome, presentation of the vicissitudes of its resolute protagonist's life on the run. Even more than the memoirs of fugitives like Bill Ayers and Daniel Berrigan or fictional texts about nomadic fugitives such as *Running on Empty* and *Eat the Document*, Piercy's novel captures the labyrinthine machinations and constant vigilance necessary to elude capture. Vida must avoid New York City, her home, because surveillance is greater and more fugitives are caught in large cities. And cities mean other dangers as well; Vida lives with a special fear of being raped, since a visit to a hospital would mean certain arrest. She travels constantly, exhaustingly, staying with strangers and carrying all her possessions; she interacts with Leigh and her mother and sister only through pre-scheduled telephone calls. Like Mimi Laurie, in Gordon's *The Company You Keep*, Vida knows "how to use a disguise, how to clean a room, how to lose a tail, how to deal with the people that, inevitably, one meets in criminal circumstances. Above all . . . how to handle fear, because it is above all fear that makes criminals crash and burn" (Gordon, 130–131). Vida admits to being tired of the constant movement and vigilance, but the novel ends with her assertion that the good war rages on and that she will stay in the battle: "No great problems in this society have been solved, no wounds healed, no promises kept except that the rich shall inherit. What swept through us and cast us forward is a force that will gather and rise again. Two steps forward and a step and a half back. I will waste none of my life" (412).

Like Oates's novel and many of the participant histories, *Vida* also in-cludes a fairly well developed if heavy-handed presentation of the diver-sity of, conflicts within, and tactics and activities of the antiwar movement. At an October 1967 "Smash the State Fair" march-cum-celebration in New York City, Vida notes the carnivalesque countercultural atmosphere: "This year the earnest idealists and organizers of SAW had cross-fertilized with the gypsy hoards, and no one knew yet what the hybrid armies in the parks would turn out to mean. The organizers were smoking dope and growing their hair, and the flower children, weary of being beaten by the police, were beginning to talk about the war, but mistrust between the two tribes remained" (106). Like Tom Hayden and other New Left intellectuals, Vida welcomes the hodgepodge of agendas represented in the movement. "SAW was a fiercely, totally democratic organization open to anyone," she notes. "Every person in SAW had their own politics—anarchist, liberal, commu-nist, democratic-socialist, syndicalist, Catholic-worker, Maoist . . . but what mattered was the politics of the act. Decisions rose from solving problems in struggle. Everyone was accommodated in the vast lumbering movement" (110). The flashback chapters include protracted arguments among SAW members about strategies and priorities for their work.

Compare O'Brien's more cynical commentary in *The Nuclear Age* on the conflicts within the antiwar movement. Activist Ned Rafferty cynically re-cites the litany: "Classic worm can. Slimy creatures, very messy. Panthers here. Weather guys there. Shades of red . . . SDSers and Quakers and . . . the People's Coalition for Peace, Dwarfs for a Non-Violent Solution. You name it. Lots of moral hairs to split. . . . The famous network," all clamor-ing in what Christopher Sorrentino calls "the exhausting encounters, the minuteman keenness, the leery reexamination of old pieties, required of the political radical" (O'Brien, 158; Sorrentino, 226). By 1970, Vida knows, the carnival has become for mainstream America a frightening freak show: "People in the other world viewed them as barbarians . . . [and] called them beasts when they ran in the streets with NLF flags and broke windows" (196). Yet even after years underground, in what she acknowledges is an "off period" for the movement, Vida remains convinced of the sanctity and viability of her cause: "Maybe nobody loves this country as much as fugi-tives running before the wind, back and forth across it," Vida somewhat sentimentally asserts. "Nobody knows this country like those who hide in its folds and crevices. Our land. Our country. That's what the screeching paper won't say" (250, 255, 256).[6]

Vida's defiant nationalism echoes in Dana Spiotta's *Eat the Document* (a finalist for the 2006 National Book Award), which offers in its underground Katherine Anne Power–like protagonist a lonely radical who attempts to accommodate her unexpected life with the self-reassurance that "there is a long history (seldom spoken of in the gloriously amnesiac everyday) in America, and in a democracy, of starting over. It was almost an imperative, wasn't it? America was founded, of course, by people who invented new lives, who wanted nothing more than to jettison the weight of all that history, all that burden and all that memory of Europe. That was one form of freedom. Freedom from memory and history and accounting" (198–199). Spiotta's Mary Whittaker (who is known variously throughout the novel, in other underground identities, as Freya, Caroline Sherman, and Louise Barrot), the self-described plain-jane forgettable fugitive, mimics Vida's perambulant life after she and her boyfriend, radical filmmaker Bobby De Soto (who reappears in the novel as Nash Davis), split up and disappear when their attempt to bomb the summer home of a corporate board member in 1972 inadvertently kills an innocent housekeeper. In Oregon, Mary (now Caroline) befriends the members of a women's consciousness-raising group, which she flees when she is recognized after several months. She heads for rural New York and lands among a community of women living—some in teepees and mud huts, others in "high-tech conceptual houses with recycled industrial waste, pod rooms, pressed plastic and synthetic particleboard construction" (173)—on the site of a Brook Farm–like nineteenth-century Christian socialist commune. Fourteen months after she becomes a fugitive, with the FBI at her heels, Caroline runs again, and when her hitchhiking results in an oddly perfunctory rape (not unlike Georgette's in *The Last of Her Kind*), she declares her separate peace, eschews the roving life, and embraces "her second life." After a short stint as a waitress, she acquires a permanent identity as Louise Barrot and marries, moves to Washington state, suburbia, and the motherhood that she perceives as "a revolutionary act" with "all the same complications of being both selfless and selfish" of her "first act" (195, 233, 232).

Eat the Document, which the *New York Times*'s Michiko Kakutani called a "stunning . . . symphonic portrait of three decades of American life, an era bookended by the radicalism of the Weather Underground and the anarchist protests of the millennium, by the leftist manifestos of the 1960's and the '90's willful commodification of the counterculture," is indeed ambitious. In presenting a continuity between the social activism of the sixties and that of the end of the twentieth century, it satirically suggests the contemporary legacy of the Vietnam-era movement. Using the familiar structure of alternating chapters, spanning 1972 to 2000, Spiotta counterposes the progress of her protagonist's life throughout those years with present-day situations: Louise's teenaged son Jason's gradual discovery of his mother's identity; the relationships of an alternative-bookstore owner, Nash, with Henry, who guiltily did not serve in Vietnam but is suffering from the symptoms of PTSD and exposure to Agent Orange, and Miranda, a young idealist who is attracted to Nash but is in a relationship with Josh, a technological corporate saboteur turned shill for a corporate "radiant posturbia," a closed community to be built, ironically, on the site of the "women-only commune" that sheltered Caroline in 1972 (238). Spiotta offers an often clever, sometimes arch satire of ineffectual late-nineties young antiglobal ecoanarchists and millennial commercial nostalgia for the counterculture—the "New Left series" playing cards (a photo and biography of a movement activist on each card), "a datebook with a cover photo of Bernadine Dohrn in a miniskirt holding a fist in the air," available for purchase at a trendy "postmall" store called Suburban Guerilla (258, 257). The hasty denouement is a suspiciously tidy parcel, as Jason discovers Louise's past just as she decides to turn herself in, and at the same time that Miranda recognizes that Nash is Bobby De Soto.

Bomb Throwers and Uppity Women

Louise's explanation for her war-era radical violent actions is compelling. "I'd had enough of demonstrating against the war," she explains to Berry, her one confidant, not long after the last, botched bombing. "We'd all had our fill of it—years of it. It changed nothing. . . . I had to do something, I had to put myself at risk, personally. I had to meet the enormity of what they were doing with something equal to it" (188–189). Yet thirty years later, a middle-aged Louise, like so many of her comrades, has come to regret her "huge mistake." (274). In the years between, Spiotta creates a Louise whose quiet life as chef, widow, and mother contrasts with the persistently, insistently activist Vida's. Neither does Louise (or Spiotta) share Vida's (or Piercy's) feminist politics. Like *The Last of Her Kind*'s Ann Drayton and such activist-memoirists as Joan Baez and Jane Alpert, Louise is indifferent to the nascent women's movement: "other issues and things she cared about were more important than women's rights. She focused on opposing the war—and what did women's issues mean in the face of the war?"

(100). *Vida*, however, is a novel that wears its politics on its sleeve, and one of Piercy's more politicized concerns in the book is her somewhat oblique indictment of the deep-seated misogyny of the movement.

In *The Wars We Took to Vietnam*, his 1996 study of "cultural conflict and storytelling" in interpretations of the Vietnam experience, Milton J. Bates discusses the sexism of the young male New Leftists in the Vietnam period. Bates interprets many young men's participation in the protest movement as a Freudian rejection of the father (always, throughout these narratives, the father). Further, he asserts, having rejected both military service and a conventional career path as the means of establishing their masculinity, men in the movement adopted a distinctly macho attitude that included a dismissal of women—who were already spurned because they did not have to face evading the draft or risking their lives in combat. The attitude toward women in the civil rights movement—expressed in Stokley Carmichael's infamous 1964 pronouncement that "the only position for women in SNCC is prone"—only reinforced this diminution of the role of women in the movement (136).

In a chapter on "women in the revolution" in *The Sixties*, Todd Gitlin discusses women's second-class status in the organized movement and early feminists' struggle to decide whether their own liberation issues should be considered secondary to the goals of the revolution. Female activists' understanding by the late '60s that "the male-run movement was moving nothing but itself," Gitlin suggests, propelled their subsequent defection to the incipient women's movement, a desertion that accelerated the demise of the antiwar movement (373).

In *Vida*, the mostly male board of Students Against the War convenes in 1974 to try to resurrect a "mass movement" that is, they know, "becoming invisible" (310). Though they are worried about the women's movement, the male leaders demonstrate no understanding of the forces that propelled so many activist women into their own organization as the antiwar movement faded. Similarly, Piercy's exploration in *Vida* of the role of women in the movement is compromised by her peculiarly myopic protagonist. Vida's example of a women's issue is deciding whom she will sleep with that night; she is, in fact, somewhat perplexed by her sister Natalie's heightening feminist consciousness. When a young Vida speaks at an SAW national convention, offering a report from the first SAW women's caucus, she is upset that the men stop listening as soon as they learn her subject—yet Vida admits that she doesn't care much about day-care facilities either.

Several of the novelists considered here similarly present examples of women's lesser status in the antiwar movement. In *The Last of Her Kind*, Georgette George resists her friend Ann's attempts to radicalize her; she finds the movement meetings to which Ann drags her devitalized by "talk interminable and impenetrable"—and almost always uttered by men (52). Jessie McGrath, in *Intimate Enemies*, notes in her college diary not women's roles within the movement but reactions to antiwar women from unsympathetic bystanders at a Boston rally. Roughed up, strip searched, female protestors were, Jessie understands, especially suspect because they were stepping out of their assigned place in society. Fifteen years later, Jessie knows that between "bomb thrower" and "uppity woman . . . the last one is the big sin" (92).

Press liaison Annie O'Conner is the only woman in the inner circle of organizers of the Offensive Against the War—the 1967 Labor Day rally in Washington that is the setting for Oates's *Making Peace*—and she, as a woman, is excluded from the steering committee meetings. Women Strike for Peace activists and a few women who are "saying 'Off our backs,' and wanting part of the action" hover in the background of the offensive and the novel, but Oates's antiwar movement is effectively For Men Only (113). The middle-aged 1980s Annie wryly dismisses a souvenir button from the movement that claims that "Girls Say Yes to Boys Who Say No" as "another ideological failure" (5). In *The Laws of Our Fathers*, Turow's Seth Weissman remembers the "Girls Say Yes" badge and articulates the problematic issue, noted by Bates and implicit, but essentially unexplored, in movement narratives, that "the war had a special gender inequality, since only men were being drafted" (135–136).

Sexual politics complicate the counterculture as well. T. C. Boyle's *Drop City* drop-outs reject the mainstream culture's rigid sexual mores and embrace free love, but sexual freedom usually means "cats" pressuring "chicks" into frequent, emotionally uninvolved sex, and Star begins to suspect that "Free Love was just an invention of some *cat* with pimples and terminally bad hair and maybe crossed eyes who couldn't get laid any other way" (9). As Marco and Alfredo, Reba's husband, work companionably digging a latrine at Drop City South, they discuss the vulnerability of their communal lifestyle, which all too often fails "under the pressure of the little things, the essentials, the cooking and the cleaning and the repairs" (48). His earlier commune disintegrated, Alfredo notes, because "nobody wanted to tend the garden or make the food. The chicks, I mean. Because they're the key to the whole thing. If the chicks don't have any energy and don't want to, you know, wash the dishes, sweep up, cook the meals, then you're in trouble, big time" (52). The chicks are indeed the caretakers at Drop City, cooking, making preserves, cleaning up, while the men play solitaire or huddle in the corner with a book.[7] Mimi Laurie concurs, in *The Company You Keep*: "it was revolutionary girls, using the skills taught to us by our fifties moms in our clean kitchens, who kept the revolutionary boys warm, fed, and at least somewhat clean" (301).

In a 1969 essay titled "The Grand Coolie Damn," Marge Piercy calls for women to recognize and reject their second-class citizenship in the movement. In an argument that presages Bates's thesis, Piercy maintains that the antiwar movement's glamorization of the charismatic male "professional revolutionary" reinforces a system that relegates women to what she calls "shitwork": "Shall the professional revolutionary haul garbage, boil potatoes, change diapers, and lick stamps?" she asks rhetorically (425, 424, 426). Piercy ends with a call for women to repudiate the movement's insistence that "women's liberation is a secondary issue, to be dealt with when the war is won. . . . No more arguments about shutting up for the greater good should make us ashamed of fighting for our freedom," she asserts; ". . . if we wait for the males we know to give up control, our great-grand-daughters will get plenty of practice in waiting, too" (437–438).

Jenny Shimada, the protagonist of Susan Choi's *American Woman*, "hates" the girls in the movement who "emphasiz[e] their traditionalness— these girls who always end up acting as caretakers, the ones who stroke the foreheads of the boys overcome by LSD, who gladly whip up omelettes for twenty at four in the morning, who are always to be found, the next day, gliding easily among the prone, pungent bodies on the living room floor, collecting the glasses and plates and wiping up the spills" (227–228). Yet, Jenny must admit (and the novel affirms), "she is more likely to be a caretaker herself than a prone body on the living room floor" (228).

The Terrorist Princess

Like Vida, Spiotta's Louise, and bona-fide fugitive Jane Alpert, Jenny is— for an activist—a paradoxically passive young woman, drawn to bombing California draft offices less by ideology than by her boyfriend William and focused on her eventual reunion with her imprisoned companion while she hides out, underground, in a small town in upstate New York. It is 1974, and

Jenny has been in New York for a lonely year, contemplating surrender in hopes that the Watergate scandal and disclosures about the Nixon administration's transgressions might mean sympathy, even amnesty, for her own comparatively inconsequential crimes. But much as James Grant's efforts to maintain custody of his daughter are jeopardized by a fellow fugitive's surrender in *The Company You Keep*, Jenny recognizes that her opportunity to turn herself in without facing imprisonment is undermined by the kidnapping of the teenaged daughter of a prominent California family by "a revolutionary cadre that nobody had heard of before" but who claim "kinship with a long list of better-known threats, like the Weather Underground and the Black Panther Party" (75–76). Several weeks later, the heiress (now renamed Pauline), having joined the "comrades" in a bank robbery, is one of only three survivors when the police and the cadre face off in Los Angeles (87). When movement hanger-on Frazer tracks Jenny down in New York, he prevails upon her to help him hide the trio, whose story, he is convinced, can become a successful book. For the next year Jenny (who is based on the real-life activist Wendy Yoshimura, now a California artist) tends to the fractious younger revolutionaries, at first hiding out with them in an isolated farmhouse. Later, after Juan, the sole man of the group and thus the self-styled leader,[8] botches a robbery and kills a man, a dispirited Jenny takes Pauline and flees to California, where they settle in San Francisco together, for what the press calls Pauline's "lost year" (318).

Like the stories of so many of the radical activists—real and fictional— *American Woman* is oblique about Jenny's motivations for the dramatic actions that send her to the peripatetic, solitary life of the underground fugitive. Though clearly, as with many of the real-life and fictional female activists, the close community that the movement promised appeals to Jenny. When she approaches a lawyer about emerging from underground, he tells her that her fate will depend largely on "how much you cooperate. . . . Your only advantage is the stuff that you know" (79). But Jenny—like the actual Weather Underground members, who never turned on each other, and *Eat the Document*'s Louise Barrot—will not "name names," insisting that she "can't betray friends" (79). Pauline (i.e., Patty Hearst) also embraces the revolutionary cadre that kidnaps her as "her family" (87). After her capture, the cadre assigns Pauline to form a cell with Juan and Yvonne, and, in the aftermath of a bungled supply run, the three come together—sexually and spiritually. "They were solemnly bound—by having survived, by being pursued, and by something that might be called blood. They were a family now. It was a feeling that sustained them through the days of crisis—or perhaps crisis had sustained the feeling" (257). The familial sentiment wanes, however, under the quotidian, mundane pressures of life underground, and Pauline bonds with Jenny, in part because "her island existence with Juan and Yvonne had become sharply lonely for her" (258). At his reunion with Jenny early in the novel, Frazer recalls their early days in the movement, "when none of them were in prison, and when they were feeling that unalloyed excitement about being together, about being a group of friends that felt more like a family, like the sort of dream-family nobody had and that doesn't exist" (51).

American Woman devotes only slight attention to Jenny's movement life before she goes underground, alone, and in this novel the dream-family indeed does *not* exist, though Jenny's longing for it is understandable. A motherless only child, Japanese American Jenny Shimada is estranged from her only family, her father, who angrily insists that his daughter's opposition to the Vietnam War is arrogant and naïve (163). When she falls for the more radical William, who becomes "her world, his language her language," though Jenny is thrilled to be "propelled . . . toward a life she had never imagined," her happiness comes at the cost of her increasingly "tenuous" relationship with her father (164, 163). And yet, ironically, it is Jenny's father—Jim Shimada, interned at Manzanar with his Japanese parents in 1942, then imprisoned at the Camp for Incorrigibles for his apparent refusal to sign the loyalty oath, finally convicted of draft evasion—who inspires her political awakening. Like the Holocaust survivor fathers of Scott Turow's Seth Weissman and Jay Cantor's Beth Jacobs, Jenny's father does not speak of his ineffable past, but Jenny's (like Beth's and Seth's) "discovery of what he'd endured was the beginning of her discovery of history and politics, of power and oppression, of brotherhood and racism, and finally, of radicalism" (163).

Not until Choi's clunky denouement, with the belated introduction of journalist Anne Casey, do we learn the details of Jim Shimada's tragic life and its connections to his daughter's own "catastrophic adventure" (321). Eventually captured with and soon betrayed by Pauline, Jenny receives a light two-year sentence and time to evaluate her past. "It had been overwhelming anger that drove her when she set out to protest the war," Jenny recognizes. "She had been enraged at the state of the world, but perhaps even more she'd been enraged by herself, such a ridiculous, small, not-taken-seriously, average American girl" (350). Jenny comes to understand that her years of privation underground and her refusal to "be a stool pigeon" are futile acts in a post-Vietnam world that remains as evil and inequitable as it ever was (357). Two years later, finally out of prison and free to live openly, Jenny, now twenty-nine, returns to Berkeley to a communal but conventional life, with the pleasures of "regular work," buying a car, and anticipating having a child (362). The novel ends with Jenny and her reluctant, still silent father driving into the Sierra Nevada for a Manzanar Reunion. As Sven Birkerts notes in his review, "Choi has no political ax to grind and no revisionist interpretation to offer. . . . Jenny is wised up by the novel's end, but less from any political realization than from facing the fact that what was for a time closest, most real, has dissolved like the residue of a fitful night's dream." "Remember stuff?" Jenny asks her father when he remarks that the desert terrain looks just as it used to. His reply, "Don't ask me to"—which echoes Larry Markham's father's refusal to revisit his own wartime imprisonment in O'Nan's *The Names of the Dead*—is a fitting conclusion to this vaguely inconclusive tale of one American woman (368).

Christopher Sorrentino's *Trance*, a finalist for the 2005 National Book Award, is a long, diffuse fictionalization of the SLA–Patty Hearst story. Wendy Yoshimura (Choi's Jenny Shimada) becomes Joan Shimada, sharing the narrative stage and point of view with Teko and Yolanda and the "terrorist princess" herself, the SLA members who remained underground for some nineteen months after the abduction of the "fugitive heiress"—here called Ann Galton—whose identification of herself as a "POW" two weeks after her kidnapping suggests a bizarre variation on the captivity stories of the then recently released military prisoners of the Vietnam War (247, 151). Sorrentino's wide-ranging account of Tania and her compatriots includes erstwhile scholar–journalist Guy Mock, several FBI agents assigned to the case, and a host of fellow travelers who variously assist and exploit the hapless revolutionaries (who in *Trance* decidedly do not exhibit the camaraderie, or the quest for it, that Choi and other movement authors present). The leftover comrades of the waning antiwar movement are puzzled when the SLA emerges publicly in November 1973 with its murders and bank robberies in support of its esoteric goal of bringing "death to the fascist insect that preys upon the life of the people." *Trance*'s Susan Rorvik (apparently Kathy Soliah in the real SLA story), who joins the irresolute group in their last months after their return to California from New York, initially hates the SLA for resurrecting the excesses of the counterculture, for "allow[ing] millions to put a finger once again on what it was that bugged them, really pissed them off, about Berkeley. Why, it was a drug-saturated cesspool of

free-love and women's lib and black militancy and miscegenation and ho-
mosexuality and Communist thought" (129). Paradoxically, Joan Shimada
comes to sympathize with the SLA out of frustration (more accurately, her
boyfriend Willie's Tom Hayden–like frustration) with the fading New Left
and what he perceives as its single-minded and reductive commitment to
merely ending the war in Vietnam: "OK, Willie would say to them, so we
stop the war. Then what? . . . To his way of thinking, you wanted to end the
war by bringing the society that waged it, that developed and continually
refined its rationale, to an end. You wanted total revolution" (230). Sorrentino's simplistic (and sometimes shapeless) critique of the decline and whimpering fall of Vietnam-era radicalism—"there wasn't one single radical in
the USA who hasn't spent a minute or two wondering who'd play him in the
movie"—includes the familiar investigation of the generation gap, this time
through the heiress's parents (408).

"She Belongs to Them Now"

With Patti Davis's fictionalized parents hovering in the background, Sorrentino introduces the hapless newspaper editor Hank Galton and his
cold, snobbish wife Lydia, whose concern for her daughter Ann's safety
is tangential to her outraged shame and her annoyance at the protracted
media attention to her family. Hank Galton shares his wife's—and Roth's
Lou Levov's—bitter indignation at "the ingratitude, the venality, the envy,
the hypocritical greed, the ineducable recalcitrance, the superficiality, and
above all the cavalier disregard for fact that, as far as he was concerned, distinguished the new generation from the preceding one" (156). But this is his
little girl, and though Ann was a difficult child, he'd believed that their family had escaped the horrors of the preceding decade and "the doomscape of
history": "The story was the same for everyone: There were the sixties, here
were the seventies, and it had seemed so certain that the whole thing was
going to blow over, leaving them untouched" (247, 117). Hank Galton's misguided belief—and relief—that the sixties would "blow over" is a testament
to the myopic perception that the end of the war and of the alarming decade
would be the end of the campaign to undermine the privileged Hank Gal-
tons of American society.

As Tania releases audiotapes that publicly upbraid her parents, her father
month after month feebly assists the FBI, even consorts with unsavory in-
formants, in an effort to rescue his daughter. Lydia (like Michael's mother

in *On the Way Home*) knows by the end of the ordeal that "she belongs to them now. . . . she'll never come back," but Hank can only wonder how it all happened, and how he and all the fathers failed: "So, how is it, Hank thought [about a grocery clerk], that you're here? How did your dad manage to keep you? How come you're ringing up groceries instead of carrying a rifle through your days?" (461, 154). Consistently, these narratives evoke the generation gap and the youth of the movement's participants through sad, befuddled fathers who mourn for their lost children and bemoan the threats to their comfortable, complacent lives.

In his 2004 novel, *The Darling*, Russell Banks reiterates the problematic father-child relationship and introduces us to yet another dour, self-absorbed zealot whose youthful passions result in years of rootless wandering and emotional isolation. Unlike Vida, Louise Barrot, and Jenny Shimada, Hannah Musgrave (aka Dawn Carrington) narrates her own eventful story; Hannah is an ideological criminal—"the last of the Weather Underground to come in from the cold" (224). She is, and remains, a woman with "secrets untold," and her subjective interpretation of her life, her limitations and deceptions as a narrator, are central concerns of Banks's tale (382). "It's easy," Hannah warns us early in the novel, "to construct a believable false story from a miscellany of partial truths" (24).

Like many of these novels, *The Darling* begins and ends in the present when Hannah is the aging owner of a small organic farm in the Adirondacks. The story that Hannah tells—the chronicle of her politicized, emotionally solitary adult life—circles back to the late 1960s and her antiwar activism and subsequent life underground as Dawn Carrington, and through three separate trips to Liberia, where she lives in the late 1970s and '80s with her African husband, a mid-level government official, and their three small sons and to which she returns near the chronological end of the novel.

Hannah Musgrave is the daughter of a Dr. Spock–like pediatrician renowned for his books on childcare and for his liberal antiwar activism. During her years underground and in Africa, where she flees when her underground identity is compromised by a cell member, her only knowledge of her parents is occasional news stories about her famous father—"his arrest at an antiwar protest with a dozen other distinguished citizens, people like William Sloane Coffin and Arthur Miller and the Berrigan brothers, an interview or essay under his byline in *The Nation* or *The New Republic*" (144). Like many of her fellow fictional activists, Hannah shares a complicated but vital relationship with her father and dismisses her vapid, narcissistic

181

mother. Hannah attributes her youthful anger and virulent politics in part to her resentment—and rejection—of her role as her famous father's "test case, the proof in his pudding, exhibit A-to-Z" (109). When she abandons her small, enclosed family "to change the world by any means necessary," she understands that her "desertion" will devastate her parents (109, 153, 154). Hannah lives for years without contact with her mother and father, but when she is exiled from Liberia in 1983, and forced (not unhappily) to leave her husband and children behind, she returns, unannounced, to her New England childhood home, only to discover that her father has suffered a life-threatening massive stroke. Hannah's visit with her sedated, dying father is an odd benison: "I saw him, and at the same time in the same way, he saw me, and in that instant he and I became real to one another and to ourselves. By that means we both came into existence. My father had given life to me, whether by accident or intention, it didn't matter; and I had given it back to him, an exchange begun probably at birth" (269).

Hannah's moment of connectedness with her father is unprecedented in her life. In Liberia Hannah is more political asset than soul mate to her ambitious husband, and she is an indifferent mother to her young boys. In fact, her only friends are chimpanzees (whom she calls her "dreamers"), the caged victims of a complicated, corrupt government scheme to trade animal subjects for medical equipment and personnel from an American university. When Hannah returns to Liberia for the last time, the political chaos in which she unwittingly, naively collaborated ended, she goes initially to the chimp sanctuary before searching for her long-dead sons, participant-victims of the political upheaval. The chimps are dead too, of course, but among their spirits, Hannah understands why she was compelled to make this one final visit to Liberia: to suffer "their strict, final judgment," to be reminded "that the themes of my life were betrayal and abandonment" (43, 44).

Despite her ingenuous and injurious participation in Liberia's political turmoil and her frequent admission that she "alter[s], delete[s], revise[s], and invent[s] whole chapters of my story," Hannah emerges as an emotionally self-aware and honest—if unlikable—purveyor of her own grim tale (101). She acknowledges that she is difficult: ungenerous, "dark and judgmental," "edgy, moody," and cold (8, 9). In her youth, an angry Hannah outgrows her father's tepid liberal politics, and in college she becomes "the girl who, in the interests of justice and equality for all people everywhere, was perfectly willing to break as many laws as seemed necessary. The girl who found moral clarity in the phrase *by any means necessary*" (296). On summer vacation from Brandeis, Hannah goes south to register black voters, "a newly minted rebel, fresh faced and romantic . . . confident that we were about to cleanse our parents' racist, oppressive world by means of idealism and simple hard work" (12). From SDS, she gravitates to the Weather Underground, and though her role in the radical organization was always, she admits, "sordid and lowly," she does not clearly describe the antiwar activities that catapult her to the FBI's Most Wanted List, though she does reveal that she dropped out of medical school and became a full-time activist in Cleveland. She mentions as well the Chicago Democratic Convention, the Days of Rage, "arrest, indictment, and flight . . . bombings . . . robberies . . . the terrorist campaign against the war, against colonialism and U.S. imperialism" (73, 109). For Hannah, more than for Vida, Jenny, Beth Jacobs, and the other fugitives in narratives about the movement, life underground is more an interior drama of multiple identities and emotional isolation than an adventurous saga of roaming and subterfuge.

Yet like other female activists, Hannah finds emotional solace in the movement; SDS and later the Weather Underground become, she writes, "my university, my employer, my church, my family" (48). But after her 1970 federal indictment and "the Greenwich Village townhouse bombing that sent me and the entire Weather cohort permanently underground," Hannah is—and in all meaningful ways remains—alone (211). "There is a crucial transition from radical activist to revolutionary," Hannah explains, "and when you've made that crossing you no longer question why you have no profession, no husband, no children, why you have no contact with your parents, and why you have no true friends—only comrades and people who think they're your true friend but don't know your real name" (53). Compare Caroline's (later Louise's) recognition, soon after her forced disappearance in *Eat the Document*, that she has now become "a movement of one. That most radical separatist of all. You are moved to save the world, and then you are reduced to organizing everything just to save yourself" (102). Years after life in Africa allows her to appropriate another new identity, Hannah admits that "the dream of a truly democratic socialist revolution in America . . . had died shortly after 1969, probably in Chicago at the end of a police club in a cloud of tear gas" (294–295). But like Vida, she scorns her comrades who have surrendered or sold out—women who'd "had their taste of political activism in the sixties" and moved effortlessly on to marriage, women's movement-enabled careers, divorce; women who "were becoming their mothers" (309). And for all the sacrifices that it has demanded, she does not regret "my youthful radicalism and the idealism that drove it" (332).

For Russell Banks and Susan Choi, their protagonists' psychological and emotional motivations for and repercussions of accepting the sacrifices of a life in the movement are more intriguing than the cultural and sociological elements of a troublous era. But Neil Gordon's engaging 2003 novel *The Company You Keep* intricately embroiders an early-twenty-first-century retrospective assessment of the movement that—like *Trance* and *Eat the Document*—captures the moral, political, and literal complexities of that volatile period and offers a convoluted response to the inquiry, "what happens to aged vanguardists of a failed revolution?" (172). Gordon, in effect, reintroduces us to Vida and Jenny twenty years later.

Gordon reveals the details of his multilayered, convoluted story through a series of emails, written in 2006, about events that occurred in 1996, as a result of activities of the Weather Underground in 1974. A 2010 epilogue projects his characters' lives and the legacy of the antiwar movement into a hypothetical future and affirms that "most of the people who lived for and were defined by that history are still alive, and lots of others will bear the scars well into this century" (63).

In early summer 2006, the middle-aged liberal attorney James Grant and a half dozen members of "the Committee" send an elaborate round-robin of emails to Grant's teenaged daughter, Isabel, importuning her to return from England to collaborate in the Committee's campaign to effect Mimi Laurie's parole after ten years in prison. Through the forty-two long messages that constitute *The Company You Keep*, readers learn the intricate events of 1974 and the explanation for the startling developments of 1996—the players, the era, the stakes—as Isabel does. James Grant, we learn, is Jason Sinai, a former Weather Underground member whose long-successful underground identity is threatened when fellow fugitive Sharon Solarz's decision in 1996 to turn herself in jeopardizes his battle to get custody of Isabel, his beloved young daughter. The complicated thriller begins when James/Jason inexplicably abandons his daughter and searches for another former Weather member, Mimi Laurie, who can exonerate him from old, false charges; and it unfolds as the hapless journalist Ben Schulberg pursues the story—which he initially dismisses as "some ancient hippie history"—and hangs on for the daring ride that the emails, ten years later, recount (53).

In June 1996, when he stumbles upon the career-making chronicle of Jason Sinai's involvement in the Weather Underground, Schulberg is in his late twenties. Tailing Grant/Sinai as he returns to Ann Arbor and his college home, Schulberg falls for Rebeccah Osborne, the smart, sassy Michigan senior who learns during the events of that summer that she is directly involved in the lives of the former activists who suddenly surround her. As they puzzle out the byzantine complications of the drama that unfolds around them, Becca and Schulberg—young, intelligent, cynical—offer a mid-nineties perspective on the youthful idealism and misguided activism of their parents' generation. Schulberg may be drunk, but he is not entirely joking when he denigrates "these little sombitches, playing at being revolutionaries with Mommy and Daddy's money" (251). "It's not just that they were turning the boys our president sent to Vietnam into devils, it's that they risked life and limb all over this land," he complains. "Their death trip, their stupid orgies, their glorification of Manson" (251). Granted, Schulberg's understanding of and support for the movement are more complex than his barstool histrionics suggest. In fact, the more he learns about Jason Sinai and the events of 1974, the more sympathetic he becomes to James Grant's plight. The war *over* Vietnam continues to rage, Ben insists, and now, in the mid 1990s, we acknowledge that protesting the war *in* Vietnam was "a patriotic duty" (238). Compare the reluctant understanding of *Eat the Document*'s Louise Barrot's teenaged son Jason, who, after his mother admits—and expresses regret for—her past, acknowledges that "at least you did something. What a world that must have been where ordinary people actually did things. Things that affected, however tangentially, history" (274). But Rebeccah Osborne, raised by an FBI agent father (who was also involved in the 1974 events of the novel) and aspiring to a career with the FBI herself, dismisses the Underground as "a bunch of damn criminals" (239). Further, Becca, who has studied the movement with her former activist American studies professor, knows that "the criticism of the radical edge of the antiwar movement isn't from the right. It's from the left" (257). Original SDS members will attest, Becca maintains, that "Weather . . . put the New Left to death. . . . that they were involved in a movement that could have transformed our entire country and a gang of thugs—shortsighted thugs on an ego trip and a death trip—ruined everything" (257). Becca, it seems, has read Todd Gitlin.

Through the Committee's ruminative emails (which are a Jamesian tour-de-force exercise in point of view), Gordon offers an investigation of the motives and actions of the radical movement by juxtaposing the younger generation's inevitably biased analysis of the movement with the explication, confession, and apologia of his aging activists. Mimi Laurie, who is at the end of the novel revealed to be Rebeccah's mother, acknowledges that the radicals' actions were ill-fated, their contemporary reputation negative, but, Mimi sentimentally writes, "for hundreds of thousands of people the revolution never stopped. . . . in fundamental ways, real ways, and irreversible ways, our lives were transformed, and each one of us and our children feel the benefits of that transformation, every time one of our daughters graduates from medical school, every time one of our sons cooks dinner for his family, every time a public school class studies Martin Luther King and Rosa Parks, every time a black woman marries a white man, every time a court stops a corporation from emitting pollution" (184). Compare Seth Weissman's 1996 evaluation of the movement's successes in *The Laws of Our Fathers*. James Grant/Jason Sinai, who, in his attempt to explain his former life to his daughter, writes most of the emails, presents a more measured assessment of the fearless folly of his antiwar excesses. James Grant feels "regret [and] remorse" for his Weather Underground actions, but he insists that, finally, the radical campaign to redefine American society "was the best dream any of us every had, that it failed," he tells Ben Schulberg, "it didn't have to happen that way. If the country had made the three central ideas of the Port Huron Statement—antiwar, antiracism, and anti-imperialism—the law of the land, today we'd be living in a safe, just, and prosperous society. . . . All we ever asked them to do was practice the fundamental principles of constitutional democracy, like they always said they would. And they wouldn't . . . it's so sad, I can't tell you" (365).

The Lovely New World Children

Though Choi, Piercy, Sorrentino, Banks, and Gordon concentrate directly on the lives of their protagonists (some remorseful, some defiant, all disheartened) and other radical activists who are driven underground by their antiwar actions, the best of these narratives—novels such as Philip Roth's *American Pastoral*, Jay Cantor's *Great Neck*, Elizabeth Spencer's *The Night Travellers*, Joyce Carol Oates's *Black Girl/White Girl*, and Sigrid Nunez's *The Last of Her Kind*, along with Sidney Lumet's elegaic film *Running on Empty*—are more interested in the devastating effects of the activists' behavior on their friends and families than on the erstwhile revolutionaries or the actions themselves. If, for most of the combat veterans and former POWs, the drama and narrative power of the in-country Vietnam experience overwhelm postwar life, for their contemporaries who experienced

186

the Vietnam era stateside, as the narratives of women writers illustrate, the hydra of the Vietnam War and its corollary movements and events casts a longer and more menacing shadow. And like O'Brien's *In the Lake of the Woods* and Mary Morris's *The Waiting Room*, the most satisfying narratives here are those that offer their characters, and their readers, the ruminative perspective that time and distance allow.

The Vietnam War and the protest movement are late-career new territory for Elizabeth Spencer, a southern writer best known for her 1956 novel about race relations in small-town Mississippi, *The Voice at the Back Door*, and for her 1960 innocents-abroad novella, *The Light in the Piazza*. Spencer's protagonist, fragile Mary Kerr Harbison, is a talented dancer who complicates her already difficult relationship with her volatile mother when she meets and falls for Jefferson Blaise, a graduate student whose involvement with the antiwar movement grows increasingly violent. After giving birth to a daughter and a failed suicide attempt, Mary ends up, alone, in Montreal, waiting for her fugitive husband, who floats in and out of the novel and in and out of Mary's life. Her loneliness punctuated by letters and an occasional brief, surreptitious visit from Jeff, who eventually goes to Vietnam to avoid prison, Mary struggles to sustain a life of endless waiting. The novel concludes with the still-separated protagonists' reaffirmation of their commitment to each other.

Issues surrounding the war in Vietnam and resistance to it are central to *The Night Travellers*. Ethan Marbell, Jeff's professor and mentor, must give up his high-level career in a Washington think tank after he discovers a secret plan to use nuclear bombs in Vietnam. Mary's unsympathic mother Kate works in a university laboratory that has a Department of Defense contract to test chemicals for a defoliant. Jeff's antiwar activities include writing articles for alternative newspapers, protesting at the Chicago 1968 Democratic Convention, and bombing a weapons factory outside San Francisco. But all of this is backgrounded to Spencer's real interest, which is the curiously vapid Mary and her relationship with the nomadic Jeff. In this political novel, the protagonist is avowedly, insistently apolitical. As another character says of Mary and Jeff, "his purity was his stand against the war, a stand that Mary, for all he treasured her, was not very much involved in taking. . . . she wasn't like that. She came from somewhere. She knew somewhere else. Her mystery was in that" (213). Finally, Spencer is intrigued more by the effect of Jeff's antiwar activities on Mary's life than on the political and moral motivations for those actions. For Mary, the wages of her great love is a life that is ascetic, unsettled, and isolated; she is, like many of the wives in aftermath novels about veterans, a modern-day Penelope, patiently waiting for her antiwarrior-turned-warrior husband's return; she is "one of those wives and mothers," as Hannah Musgrave describes, "walking mournfully through the wreckage and desolation made by men and boys" (Banks, 33).

In her melancholy novel *The Last of Her Kind*, Sigrid Nunez also offers a protagonist, Georgette (Georgie) George, whose life is profoundly and persistently shaped by her long relationship with a passionate, idealistic, unaffiliated radical, Ann Drayton, whom she meets, in 1968, when they are freshmen roommates at Barnard. Nunez reprises her technique (from *For Rouenna*) of filtering the dramatic actions of a main character through the point of view and first-person narration of the protagonist. Narrator Georgie writes in New York City just after September 11, 2001, with the advantage of hindsight (which—in an affectation that plagues Sorrentino as well—too frequently results in glib asides like Ann's 1968 prediction that "if the revolution fails . . . rich women could pay poor women to incubate their babies for them" [65]) and the burden of uncertainty about the reliability of her memories of the events of the novel, which unfold over the final third of the twentieth century. Privileged, accomplished, and angry Ann Drayton maintains her rigidly idealistic commitment to racial equality and social justice from her earliest childhood. Alienated by the imploding SDS, the "hedonism at the heart of hippie culture," and the "blossoming women's movement (which, like Louise Barrot, she dismisses as "a fatal distraction from the work at hand"), Ann eschews the seductions of the era; her politics are personal and unyielding, and when some years later she shoots a policeman who is harassing her African American partner, she refuses to express remorse for her action or to exploit her white privilege or her parents' resources in order to avoid imprisonment (55, 54). Georgie is intrigued with the fanatical Ann, with "her strictness and her purity, her diamond hardness, her terrifying honesty" and whom she compares, variously, with would-be martyr St. Teresa of Ávila, early-twentieth-century French radical Simone Weil, and, finally, Jay Gatsby ("For hadn't Ann done it—held on to her purity and her dreams and her illusions all those years? Hadn't they both remained faithful to an ideal vision of themselves formed when they were still in their teens? . . . the fierce determination to escape where they were born, the passionate belief in unselfish devotion. The *heart*") (369, 373). But for the public, in 1976, when Ann violently, futilely tries to prevent the murder of her lover, Ann Drayton is the terrorist princess Patty Hearst: "they were both young women from wealthy families who had renounced the privileges to which they'd been born and condemned their own class, their own families. They had both taken up guns; they both had had sexual relations with black men. . . . in some photos [Patty Hearst] bore a resemblance to Ann. They could have been sisters. And that was exactly how a lot of people saw them, as sisters" (205). Ann's partisans—Georgie, her lawyer, her father—confidently spurn the Hearst comparison. The imprisoned Ann has not seen her father for years, but through her lawyer Turner Drayton knows that "'Patty Hearst is everything in the world Ann hates.' Hearst had betrayed people who'd helped her and had proved herself willing to do anything, regardless of the truth or of the consequences to anyone else, to save her own skin" (216, 289).

Georgette knows Ann's father's understanding of his daughter's motivations and behavior because in the late 1970s, after Ann is imprisoned and her aloof mother dies, literally and metaphorically, of a broken heart, Georgie has a loving, passionate, and finally ill-fated relationship with Turner Drayton, "an ordinary, decent man transfigured by grief" (263). Georgie, who has fled an abusive, impoverished mother to go to Barnard, first meets Ann's feckless parents in 1968, and she remains puzzled by her friend's unrelenting rejection of her overindulgent but loving parents. Turner Drayton—here, as in most of these narratives, a more complex and emotionally relevant character than his wife—comes to understand his daughter's "shame at having been born wealthy and white," and he refuses to blame Ann for her mother's death (288). Ann's father, though he recognizes that "it was the times" that explain his daughter's tragedy, does not lash out at the "era that had tipped over into madness," as his fellow fathers here do, but another voice of the patriarchy in *The Last of Her Kind* spouts the bitter indictment of a generation (293, 149): "I do not know who or what is responsible for the behavior of young people like yourself, who start out in life with every promise, cherished by fine, decent parents, given every means to pursue good, productive, happy lives, and who end up throwing it all away," lectures the judge in Ann's trial, "but God knows we've seen enough of you. It would be a blessing to think this sorry chapter in our country's political history is coming to an end" (216). Expressing his wish that Ann will be "the last of her kind" and "an example to others," the irate judge sentences her to twenty-five years to life in prison (216).

The judge's denunciation of Ann is a small irony in this subtle novel, for she, like the mysteriously motivated Merry in Philip Roth's *American*

Pastoral, is not really "of her kind" in the "you ungrateful brats" way that he means it. In fact, Ann, who is the living embodiment of the sixties aphorism that the personal is political, shares the patriarchy's repudiation of the immoderation of the late movement. *The Last of Her Kind* does, however, limn the more social and eventually extreme characteristics of the era's radicals through Georgette's relationship with her unstable runaway sister Solange, through whom Nunez examines "the general madness of the day" (94). For if Ann represents the passionate ideological purity of the times, Solange is the dissolute denizen of the craziness.

Like many disappointed ticket-holding children of Aquarius, Solange does not quite make it to the overcrowded Woodstock festival, from whose fringes she joins a motley group of Iowan gypsies in an old school bus called the Yellow Submarine. But six months later she is front and center at the Rolling Stones' tragic December 1969 Altamont Speedway concert that many people consider the last gasp of the counterculture. And years later, when John Lennon is shot, the mentally ill, often drugged poet Solange has a mental breakdown. If Ann is the independent radical, Solange is the ethereal flower child of the counterculture: "a free spirit, a wild (but gentle) thing, a natural woman, instinctive, unschooled" (152). Each, Nunez's somber novel affirms, is, sadly, the last of her kind.

Like many of the most resonant and haunting of these narratives—those by Russell Banks, Susan Choi, Philip Roth, Neil Gordon, Sigrid Nunez, Jay Cantor, and Sidney Lumet—Joyce Carol Oates's *Black Girl/White Girl* is anchored in the complex, wrenching relationship between eighteen-year-old narrator Generva (Genna) Hewett-Meade and her emotionally and physically elusive father, Mad Max Meade, flamboyant, notorious antiwar lawyer and radical philosopher, whose 1960s grandiloquence about the shame of white privilege and the obsolescence of family and private life "in a time of Revolution" have profoundly and sadly influenced his adoring daughter's life (34).

While Turner Drayton, Swede Levov, and Hank Galton grieve for their radical daughters' inexplicable rejection of their families' values and affections, Max Meade himself is the radical in this novel, set in 1974–1975. Genna is a freshman at an exclusive women's college established by her father's Quaker ancestors; Max is on the road, pursuing his undercover lawyer activities—which are risky but entirely honorable and legal, insists Veronica, ingenuous Genna's drug-addled mother, a "middle-aged hippie-survivor of the psychedelic revolution" (105). Veronica was a loving mother when Genna and her now estranged brother were young, but after a breakdown when Genna is ten, she announces to her daughter that "'love' is an illusion of the ego, no more substantial than vapor," and thereafter—this opaque novel gradually suggests—Genna is an emotional orphan: "For *daughter* is a leash around the neck. *Daughter* is a thorn in the heart. *Daughter* is acid-anguish shaken in a bottle to foam and froth and spill over scalding your hand" (33, 74).

These sentiments about her parents, which a thirty-something Genna writes in the 1990 "text without a title" introduced by the novel's frame, are among very few candid insights by the narrator in the novel's tale (a plot that uncannily parallels Nunez's) of Genna and her defiant black college roommate, Minette Swift. For Genna—like so many of the young female protagonists in these narratives—is a maddeningly, intriguingly passive girl, self-effacing, eager to please, and remarkably naïve about her relationship with Minette, as well as about her inattentive father.

The story that the title *Black Girl/White Girl* promises is Genna's account of her desperate and ill-fated attempts to deny her privilege as a white person and as the great-great-granddaughter and namesake of the feminist-abolitionist founder of her toney women's college by befriending Minette, the dismissive, unpleasant African American scholarship student who becomes her roommate. When haughty Minette begins to perceive—and then become the victim of—racial harassment at the college, Genna defends and supports her resentful roommate; and when Genna—and only, ever Genna—discovers that Minette (from motivations that neither she nor Oates elucidates) is herself concocting the racial slurs and attacks, Genna devises cover stories that conceal the lonely black girl's actions, encourage suspicion of and re-criminations among their student-housemates, and eventually—to Genna's remarkable incredulity—send an irate Minette away from their shared suite to isolation, emotional instability, and an apparently accidental death.

In her account of her frustrating attempt to befriend her increasingly hostile roommate, Genna slowly reveals—generally without comment—her abusive childhood with her activist parents, a childhood that creates the ingratiating, unobtrusive girl who, in her desire to be loved, virtually stalks the dismissive Minette. As a child, Genna quietly watches her parents—"giants . . . deities"—as they engage in group sex with their many young acolytes, even with young girls—"and it was not clear to me if Genna was one of these or only the sly inquisitive lonely child who observed" (113). At eleven, she discovers one of her "charismatic radical theorist" father's devotees disemboweling himself with a paring knife (121). At twelve, she is sexually abused by a female follower who sees "that my parents did not have time for me" (197). And Genna withholds—from the reader, from herself—her response to her parents' neglect and abuse, for, she notes, "I was a sly one long practiced in not-seeing as I was practiced in not-hearing what was not meant for me to overhear" (75). Late in the novel, Genna's "ambitious young investment banker" brother visits to warn her of rumors of their father's latest misadventure: that the young man who bungled his self-evisceration years before and thus lived to participate in the bombing that killed a security guard "has killed himself at last," and that Mad Max has not only provided the .38 but buried the fugitive body as well (217, 214). Typically, Genna rejects this rumor as unfounded, insisting that their father is incapable of any such actions, and her brother Rickie's parting statement is the judgment on their narcissistic parents and their childhood that Genna will not—cannot—make: "I'll never forgive them, Genna. Those 'adults,' our parents. Exposing us to that life. You, at that age" (220). It is the not-seeing, not-hearing Genna who quietly facilitates Minette's sick, racist actions that spiral into her premature death, though Genna knows at eighteen and acknowledges at thirty-four that "I was the one to have saved her, yet I did not" (1).

Joyce Carol Oates, notes the *New York Times* review of *Black Girl/White Girl*, "has never been shy about peering into the darkest corners of American culture," and Genna's tragic obsession with Minette and her "angry dignity" is a subtly menacing story of racial tension and white guilt (75). Yet Oates probes deeper into that dark corner, and the 1990 narrator/author of the "text without a title" is surprised to discover that her narrative continues after Minette's death, that "unwittingly, as I composed my text about Minette Swift, I was composing a shadow-text," an "inquiry into Max Meade and a portrait of the daughter who betrayed him" (262–263). When the stoic and accommodating Genna finally breaks down, after Minette's death, and begins to "confess," she reveals, not the truth of Minette's seditious actions and her own complicity in them, but the story of her father's participation in a 1970 bombing that killed a black guard and her belated acknowledgment that "he has never taken responsibility for the death of the night watchman, no more than his young comrades have taken responsibility" (260). Her confidant "behave[s] as most Americans would behave in such a situation" (and "who," Genna asks, "is to say that she behaved wrongly?"); she turns in Max Meade—who is promptly sentenced to thirty-five years to life in Follette prison—without revealing Genna's confession (264). Only in the novel's frame, fifteen years after Minette's death and Genna's oblique retribution on the father she continues to visit and support, will Max—when he reads Genna's narrative (i.e., *Black Girl/White Girl*)—discover who turned him in. Genna, now a successful historian and lonely woman, wonders whether her failing father will forgive her; these days she is his only visitor, and she in turn has, she tells us as her story ends, "no one but him" (272).

In the touching *Running on Empty*, director Sidney Lumet and writer Naomi Foner (Gyllenhaal) present the late-eighties itinerant lives of more conventional movement radicals Annie and Arthur Pope, who have lived underground since their 1971 bombing of a supposedly empty University of Massachusetts military research lab, in which—neatly echoing Mad Max Meade's crime as well as historical reality—an unexpected janitor was blinded and paralyzed. The Popes, played by Christine Lahti and Judd Hirsch, are complex and sympathetic characters—good, committed people who, like Vida, continue to work for social justice even as they must uproot their family over and over again in order to stay a fleeting, precarious step ahead of the FBI.

The movie poignantly portrays the lingering cost of what was, as far as we know, Annie and Artie's single violent action—and their stolid commitment to it. Artie learns of his mother's death only a month after the fact, and Annie has not seen her bitter, perplexed parents for fourteen years. Their lives—and those of their ten- and seventeen-year-old sons—are, much like those of Piercy's Vida and Spiotta's Louise, a continual rehearsal of dyed hair, fake names, quiet searches for cash-under-the-table jobs, falsified school records, and abrupt departures. Assisted by the underground network, members of which offer necessary medical services and occasional money, the Popes are nonetheless essentially hunted and alone. They are heroic and stoic, as the network dentist plaintively attests when he tells Annie, admiringly, "you're living it." And because they're living it, as Artie insists to his family throughout the movie, they have only each other to depend on.

This dependence is crucial to the subject of the film, the inevitable coming-of-age of Danny, the elder son, played by River Phoenix, a talented musician (like his mother and maternal grandmother) and a boy preternaturally sweet and good, who at seventeen experiences first love and an opportunity to study music at Julliard. Like Faulkner's Ab Snopes in the 1938 story "Barn Burning," who reinforces his son's loyalty by reminding him, "You got to learn to stick to your own blood," Artie insists that his family remain together; and Danny understands of his father that "without us, he can't keep it going. He needs us to hold him up" (503). Isolated, by an underground existence, from their parents and their movement siblings, Annie and Artie cling to their nuclear family. But Annie, who knows, as her husband does not, that "there's nothing to win. It was over as soon as the war ended," plans, like Louise Barrot, to turn herself in when her younger son is grown. Annie recognizes the hardships and injustice of their difficult lives for her sons. "Look what we're doing to these kids," she pleads to Artie. "They've been running their whole lives like criminals, and they didn't do anything. It isn't fair." Annie arranges for her parents to care for Danny, so that he can study at Julliard, and at the end of the movie, as the family prepares to flee once more, Artie reluctantly releases Danny to his own life. "Now go out there and make a difference," he tells his son. "Your mother and I tried, and don't let anyone tell you any different."

Though *Running on Empty* focuses on Danny and his journey toward adulthood, the most powerful scene in the film is another one that portrays the toll the fugitives' actions have taken on family members and another extrapolation of the father-child conceit that so many of these narratives develop. Near the end of the movie, Annie arranges a meeting with her long-estranged father, a successful industrialist played by Steven Hill. As Annie struggles to maintain her composure, her angry and wounded father confronts her with his life of pain as he lives not only without his child but with the knowledge that it is his "child that's pulling the triggers, setting the bombs" and with the fear that she might "be responsible for that death and mutilation." His beautiful, talented daughter has not only "thrown it all away"; she has thrown it in her father's face: "The last thing I remember you saying to me was that I was an imperialist pig, personally responsible for the war, the spread of poverty, racism." Annie's response—"I was young"—is, perhaps, convincing, but it is nonetheless obvious that her father, a man who clearly loves her, will live with his daughter's betrayal for most of his adult life. But Annie reiterates Ann Drayton's indictment of her privileged parents and Katherine Alman (Sissy Spacek)'s insistence, in the artless 1975 TV movie *Katherine* (issued on videotape as *The Radical*) that "my parents are just as responsible for the system's injustice as anyone."

Psychoanalyst Leo Jacobs, whom the *Great Neck* reviewer Adam Begley calls Jay Cantor's "most melancholy creation," is another famous, successful father obliquely complicit in his child's radical activism. Though it is the letters from her friend and teenaged lover Frank Jaffe—which arrive mysteriously and powerfully *after* his murder in Mississippi—that are directly responsible for

Beth Jacobs's commitment to profound social change, Leo worries that Beth's felonious actions are "his fault too . . . all his talk about changing the world" (113). Later in the novel, when a disconsolate Leo (in a scene reminiscent of Annie Pope's brief, heartbreaking rapprochement with her father) surreptitiously meets a fugitive Beth for lunch, he wonders again whether he unconsciously gave "his own beautiful, lost daughter" a "coded message . . . that she must go make the world revolution for him" (422). The power of the father and the complex relationship between Leo Jacobs's survival of the Holocaust and the next generation's political passions are among Jay Cantor's multitudinous concerns in this sprawling novel, a baggy omnium gatherum every bit as loose and problematic as the movement that is its subject.

Great Neck is Cantor's expansive rumination on "the lovely New World children," the generation that came of age in the 1960s, and the effects of the antiwar movement, the civil rights movement, and the social turmoil of the era on their troubled lives (112). The interwoven, sometimes arcane stories—which Cantor himself labels "the most opaque of texts"—begin in 1978, as the childhood friends who are the primary protagonists of the novel enter their thirties: historian Arthur Kaplan, nicknamed Arkey; analyst Laura Jaffe, sister of the murdered Frank; Jeffrey Schell, a homosexual art dealer; attorney Jesse Kelman; diminutive Billy Green, the comic book creator who immortalizes the group as the "Band of Outsiders" in his Billy Books comics; and Beth Jacobs, the passionate fugitive (18). Succeeding sections move the characters through 1982, and circle back to their early 1960s upper-middle-class adolescence in the Jewish community of Great Neck, New York. When Laura's older brother Frank disappears in Mississippi, where he has gone to register black voters during the 1964 Freedom Summer, Billy Green insists to his friends, the "smart misfits," that Frank is dead: "I don't know how I know, I just do. They've murdered him and buried him under tons of earth" (87, 205). Frank, the novel's Michael Schwerner or Andrew Goodman, *is* dead, sacrificed to the noble cause by his civil rights compatriots who know that "if one of the people murdered was a white person, well, *good*, it would focus the country on the horror of Mississippi" (196). Frank's fatal southern misadventure introduces another of *Great Neck*'s plots and cast of characters. Jacob Battle, whose brother Joshua dies with Frank, is sent by Laura's family to the pretentious white school where he befriends Arkey. Jacob is torn, racially, between the assimilationist, nonviolent movement for racial equality embodied by his schoolmate Bobby Brown (nephew of Laura Jaffe's maid) and the more militant politics of the charismatic black leader Sugar Cane. The novel presents the relationship between the Jewish and African American communities and between the civil rights and antiwar movements, as well as the dissension within the civil rights movement between Martin Luther King's nonviolence and the more radical, confrontational methods of Malcolm X and the Black Panther Party.

When Frank's body is discovered, Billy's prescient perception that his friend was dead well before Frank's letters continue to arrive from Mississippi earns Billy his sanctified role as seer of the group, who are, Billy proclaims, "linked souls since the beginning of time" (210). So when Billy announces that the friends must "keep Frank in our hearts and do acts of justice. Or he'll be trapped there forever," each of the juvenescent gang of six embraces the admonition, which ordains each of their lives well into adulthood. Throughout young adulthood, the Band of Outsiders remain interwoven, "linked . . . throughout eternity—chosen to make justice and to rise together," and the linchpin, the daring darling of the sextet, is Beth Jacobs (296). "Was the Book of Beth the story of them all somehow . . . ?" Laura wonders. "And if Beth had gone astray, did that mean she had?" (286).

Beth's story *is* their story; the story of Billy Books's wonder woman, also the tale of that "family of lost boys and girls" who grow up together in Great Neck, and of the larger family, the children of the sixties who, their "parents thought, had lost all restraint, the old folks not seeing that it was probably guilt for not stopping the war, for not healing the world so Auschwitz would never happen again, that had actually driven the kids mad in the first place" (174, 121). Bright, bold Beth, more advanced than her compatriots, has skipped several grades in school, and by the time the others enroll at Harvard, Beth has joined the battle for racial equality and the war against the war in Vietnam. Increasingly radical, Beth understands

> what she needed to do to ease Frank's pain in the grave, what arduous, courageous feats would help justify her life and almost something beyond her life, greater than her life, that still needed her help, still needed to be justified and made whole. . . . Imperialism—the seizure of the fruits of this world from those with darker skin—was racism, like the death camps that had nearly killed her father. . . . Beth swore she would do her small part to help overthrow this racist, imperialist government; to free the black masses, the American working class, and all humanity. (339, 340)

Beth follows the radical Weather Underground in its takeover of the SDS, and, "the comic book star," another daughter of another famous father,

196

is welcomed into the leadership, the Weather Bureau, determined to move her friends and followers "toward the next, the necessary, the violent and irrevocable step that would bind them forever to their black and brown comrades" (370, 372). Beth participates in bombings, goes underground—albeit reluctantly, since it means "not seeing her friends anymore. Or arguing with her father"—and remains faithful to the fight, even after the slow demise of the movement, resentful (like Vida) that the Kent State killings ("the pietà of Ohio") in the spring of 1970, the end of the draft, and "the Paris farce . . . cranked up . . . to buy time so Nixon and Kissinger could carpet-bomb Vietnam, finish the genocide" have let the less radical activists (including her friends) "pretend imperialism had nearly croaked" and abandon the revolution to finish graduate school, embark on careers, return to the establishment (418, 545). During these years, Beth acquires a life partner, Snake, and has a baby; among the radicals in these narratives, she more than anyone battles her fear and self-doubts and has to remind herself continually that she must remain steadfast in her commitment to the revolution: "Would she be one of those cowards who needed God's or the State's permission to do what needed to be done to help the world's black, brown, and yellow peoples?" (443).[9] And, indeed, Beth, who is as unrepentantly ideological as Vida and Ann Drayton, remains resolute. Through Snake, Beth affiliates with Sugar Cane, who has just been released from jail, and—in an impossibly complicated subplot—she signs on for a bank robbery with Snake and Jacob that goes inevitably, fatally wrong and lands Beth in prison, with Jesse defending her and the Band of Outsiders rallying around her for support.

In *Great Neck*, Cantor rehearses most of the themes of the other movement narratives. He recounts the set pieces of the home front revolution: McNamara's petulant upbraiding of the "ungrateful children" at Harvard in 1966 (355); the spring 1968 assassinations and riots and "the Battle of Chicago" (364); the Greenwich Village townhouse explosion ("She and her friends had blown themselves up, that's what they were famous for," Beth acknowledges, bitterly, as she contemplates the movement's mid-1970s demise [550]); the movement's internal squabbles, as the SDS discusses its stance on the Vietnam War ("NOTHING EVER HAPPENS IN SDS UNTIL THERE IS A MEETING ABOUT IT," Laura observes in 1965, so "NOTHING HAPPENS *BUT* MEETINGS") and, later, its terrifying glide toward fury and violence (289).

Among these fictitious narratives, Cantor proffers the most sustained—if sometimes maddeningly convoluted—dramatization of the intricate intersections of the civil rights and antiwar movements, and of the ponderous prominence of race in the social and political interactions of the era. Beth and Laura (who suspects—and fears—that she will follow Beth anywhere) are with Sugar Cane and other civil rights proponents as they debate whether to expand—and risk attenuating—their campaign for racial equality to embrace formal opposition to the war. As always, Beth wields the most forceful rhetoric: "I think we should support people who stand up for their rights when the ruling class tried to massacre them. Here or in Vietnam," she pronounces, dismissing her compatriots' reminder that theirs was to be a nonviolent movement (293). Though Sugar Cane commits himself to racial equality "by any means necessary," Jacob's and Bobby Brown's struggle with their roles in the fight allows Cantor to explore the range of positions within the civil rights movement and its relationship to the antiwar movement (294). Pressured by Mr. Hartman (poet, former teacher to Billy and the gang) to take a moderate position on race and by Sugar Cane to wear his dead brother's activist mantle, Jacob acknowledges that "there were *two wars* going on now, here and in Vietnam, and *both* of them were shooting wars" (317). Sugar Cane sends Jacob a letter from Che Guevara, insisting that "they had to be ready to make another Vietnam in *this* jungle, prepare to be urban guerrilla fighters" (333). Reacting to riots in Newark and Detroit, Bobby notes that "by black alchemy, blocks and blocks of downtown had burst into flames, tanks rolled down the avenues, machine-gun fire sliced up the front of the housing projects like Vietcong villages, and helicopter after helicopter whirred above the urban rice paddies" (324). With Martin Luther King's murder, the riots erupt anew, and the confrontational rhetoric escalates. "Black Power," Beth happily pronounces, "is Tet come home to America" (360).

The Sins of the Fathers

Cantor reinforces and historicizes the parallels between the domestic war against racial segregation and the imperialistic aggression in Vietnam with his investigation of the legacy of the Holocaust, which becomes another important thematic integer in *Great Neck*'s moral equation. After its opening chapter, in which the friends gather at Beth's 1978 trial, the novel moves back to 1960, chronologically its earliest point. Eleven-year-old Billy Green's sixth-grade report on European Jews seems hopelessly simplistic to his teacher, Mr. Hartman, a troubled homosexual and the guilt-ridden sole member of his family to escape the Nazis (sole survivor, like Paco and Bausch's Michael). His termination from his teaching position is the inevitable result of his candor to Billy, Arkey, Laura, and his other students about the Nazis' search for a final solution, but, he resolves, "they had to know there was nowhere safe from the muck and blood and the mean-spirited pettiness of life" (34). Sickly, sensitive Billy is so unnerved by his study of the Holocaust that his parents take him for help to their psycho-analyst neighbor, Leo Jacobs, Beth's father and a Holocaust survivor him-self. Leo, echoing veterans' dismissive refusal in countless Vietnam novels to talk about their inexpressible experiences—"Oh, darling, you don't want to know about that"—will not share his past with his daughter ("more than anything in her life she wanted to have been *there* with him"). But, oddly, he confides in sniveling Billy Green, the doctor becoming the patient, and the jealous daughter slowly liberated from her obsession with pleasing her father (61). As Beth and her confederates—the "dopers&runaways&crazies, rads&working-class kids [of] the Weather Nation"—intensify their efforts to end the war, "camp survivor and media favorite" Leo Jacobs underscores the novel's investigation of the relationship between the Holocaust and the sixties radicalism of these children of Jewish immigrants in his famous *Commentary* essay on guilt, which becomes a critique of his daughter and her "misguided generation[']s" dangerous seduction by "fantasies of escape to a simpler time" (546, 9, 370). In his essay Leo speaks for the "parents worried that their children might follow Che Guevara's or Herbert Marcuse's piping right into the ground" (9). Arkey becomes the historian of the movement, rather than a participant, largely because his beloved immigrant grandfa-ther, Abe, a bastion of the Old Left, the man whom he most admires, insists that Beth and her cohorts are dangerously misguided: "She was never part of the world she supposedly wanted to save, Arthur. She acted without guid-ance from any class organization. No discipline. No solidarity. . . . She and her pals really served their own meshuginah psychologies" (4). Little Billy Green learns to draw because comic books are his father's business, and in "the dream of being linked with his father . . . Billy had felt something good pour into him from the page, something that would make him more like his father, closer to him, and maybe to his father's father, and to all the fathers before who, Billy dreamt, bent over the world" (43).

Laura's liberal father cautions her against joining the demonstrations at the Democratic convention, presciently fearful that her friends will un-dermine Humphrey's chances of beating Nixon and convince the country that the Democrats "can't run the country" (363). Indeed, in *Great Neck*, as in so many of these texts, the recently labeled generation gap between the "spoiled baby brigade" and their often liberal parents (and the effect of the children's actions on the lives of the fathers) is a recurring theme. We see it in Hannah Musgrave's rejection of her father's liberal ideology and her confidence "that we were about to cleanse our parents' oppressive world by means of idealism and simple hard work" (12); in Annie Pope's apology to her heartbroken father for causing him such pain, but her insistence—after everything—that "what I did was an act of conscience to stop the war"; in Scott Turow's suggestion that "the war protest represented an entire generation in combat against the rigid views of our parents" (135). Yet, despite their apparent rejection of the patriarchs, these bright, privileged "New World children" long for the elusive approval of their outdated fathers even as they risk everything to destroy the world that those fathers have created. Late in the novel, Beth meets with her long-estranged father, resentful that she still loves and respects him, that "long ago [she] had swallowed him whole" (428). Leo supports his jailed daughter, sending money, letters, advice. At the end of the novel, Beth opts for a guilty plea rather than a riskier trial, and her twenty-years-to-life sentence leads her aging father to question his lifelong commitment to "tending the whole," the pledge that, he suspects, instilled in his daughter her passion for justice (686). Bereft, defeated, Leo, the guilty survivor, kills himself. But before he dies, Leo visits his granddaughter, who is being raised by Laura and Bobby Brown, and befriends the black lawyer who continues to question his own life. "Their talking each week, it had eased Bobby a little. A father thing, right? Leo Jacobs, the famous analyst, the Holocaust survivor, treated Bobby like a son, or better, like a *fellow sufferer*—and that . . . seemed the most honorable estate the world could offer" (702). Leo's benediction ennobles Bobby, reinforces his commitment to caring for Beth's child, "like doing right by her . . . might briefly quiet the awful sound the world made rushing away from him" (702–703).

In his 1997 Pulitzer Prize–winning *American Pastoral* (the second in the trio of novels that includes *I Married a Communist* and *The Human Stain*), Philip Roth puts the fathers center stage. Like Annie Pope's, Ann Drayton's, and Ann Galton's fathers, Seymour (Swede) Levov is a successful businessman, an assimilated New Jersey Jew who has parlayed his high school athletic prowess and fame, and his golden boy good looks, into a pleasant, if delusory, upper-middle-class life in a beautiful country home in suburban New Jersey. As presented in the first part of the novel by Nathan Zuckerman, Philip Roth's familiar narrator/author (before the narration and point of view shift to Swede) Swede Levov is a tragic hero who has outlived his time. He is a decent man, an idealist, a late-twentieth-century Jay Gatsby who has lived by the values of post–World War II America only to find, in late middle-age, that those precepts of hard work, commitment to family, and confidence in the American dream are spent currency in an America that has gone truly crazy. The novel ends with an acknowledgment that Swede's world "is rapidly going under . . . [that] the rampant disorder" is spreading, and with the plaintive and bitter inquiry, "What on earth is less reprehensible than the life of the Levovs?" (423).

The evidence of the decay of late-twentieth-century America—a theme articulated throughout these narratives—is the detritus that clutters this haunting, rich, deeply conservative novel. Liberal, stubborn Swede refuses to move his glove-making business, built by his immigrant father Lou and lovingly nurtured by the dutiful eldest son, from the downtown Newark, New Jersey, location that is now a post-sixties-riots urban wasteland. His black employees are now willfully sloppy and irresponsible. And what, after all, are the prospects for such a business in a world in which no one even wears fine gloves anymore? Bitter, aging Lou rails against the decay of an America that he loves as only an immigrant could: "where will it end? . . . We grew up in an era when it was a different place, when the feeling for community, home, parents, work . . . well, it was different. The changes are beyond conception. I sometimes think that more has changed since 1945 than in all the years of history there have ever been. I don't know what to make of the end of so many things . . . how did this happen?" (364–365). Lou hates Catholics, Richard Nixon, his younger son Jerry's talent for multiple marriages. By the end of his life, he is both puzzled and repelled by the world around him. Swede's wife Dawn, Miss New Jersey 1948, a woman who has spent her adult life proving that she is more than just a pretty face, has, by the end of the novel, demonstrated that she is, after all, just that, as she resorts to a face lift and an affair with a shallow, ersatz architect to assuage the disappointments of her ruined, now empty life.

Doomed business. Physical deterioration. Raging father. Unfaithful wife. "The outlaws are everywhere," Swede discovers. "They're inside the gates" (366). Swede, like Zuckerman, has many reasons to deplore the betrayal of his life by time, everyone he loves, and "the indigenous American berserk." But the one, true villain in this hate-filled book, the single action and character that bring Swede Levov's perfect American life crashing down into the sordid streets of Newark is his outlaw daughter, the merciless monster

Merry and her inexplicable, brutal statement against the Vietnam War—and against everything her father is and stands for.

The ironically named Merry. Who enters the world screaming, which evolves into stuttering, and an angry sixteen year old who spews a renunciation of "her meaningless manners, her petty social concerns, her family's 'bourgeois' values," and demonstrates her rejection of it all by bombing their small-town post office and inadvertently killing the local doctor who has stopped to mail a letter (101). A bereft brother of *The Last of Her Kind*'s Turner Drayton, Swede is obsessed with his lost, adored daughter and flummoxed by her repudiation of him and the life that he has built: "There wasn't much difference, *and she knew it*, between hating America and hating them. He loved the America she hated and blamed for everything that was imperfect in life and wanted violently to overturn, he loved the 'bourgeois values' she hated and ridiculed and wanted to subvert, he loved the mother she hated and had all but murdered by doing what she did. Ignorant little fucking bitch! The price they had paid!" (213–214). Swede's anger is fleeting, though. While his brother Jerry urges him to spurn his evil, maniacal daughter—"Miss America . . . [of] America amok"—Swede grieves for her, puzzles over her incomprehensible action, and, after five years, in 1973, finds her, living right under his nose in the slums of Newark. The fugitive Merry is a reclusive mystic, unwashed and placid, who has devolved to a near nonexistence after more bombings, more murders, rape. . . . what her father finds a repugnant life. And he finds that she has no interest in returning to her family and her repudiated former life.

Roth's Merry is a despicable child: venomous, unloving, and unlovable. She is notably passive and unappealing, like memoirist Jane Alpert and fictional characters Hannah Musgrove, Mary Kerr Harbison, and Generva Meade. She is, indeed, "one of the most floridly and obscenely ungrateful children in all of literature," as A. O. Scott writes (in his explanation of the novel's ranking fifth in a 2006 *New York Times* competition for the best American fiction of the past twenty-five years). And yet, to Roth, Merry is representative of her generation, which has sent the glorious America of his own boyhood spiraling into madness. Roth—through Zuckerman—is fascinated by the horror of Swede Levov's life and "that mysterious, troubling, extraordinary historical transition" between the "triumphant" postwar years of his childhood and "the disorder occasioned by the Vietnam War" (88). Finally, for Roth, there is nothing wrong with the Levovs' life, and no explanation for Merry's betrayal of it. It is the diseased times that are to blame: "All that public display. The dropping of inhibitions. Authority powerless. The kids going crazy. Intimidating everybody. The adults don't know what to make of it, they don't know what to do. Is this an act? Is the 'revolution' real? . . . What's going on here? Kids turning the country upside down and so the adults start going crazy too" (69). The antiwar movement is merely "angry, infantile egoism thinly disguised as identification with the oppressed" (134). It is the symptom, not the cause; only a part of the ultimate destruction of a once magnificent world: "Three generations. All of them growing. The working. The saving. The success. Three generations in raptures over America. Three generations of becoming one with a people. And now with the fourth it had all come to nothing. The total vandalization of their world." (237). Compare Marylouise Oates's disquisition, in *Making Peace*, on "the American way. One generation in the factories, the next one in the offices, and the third one anxious to get done with college so they could begin tearing down the whole system that got them there in the first place" (126). Merry is a child of her time, and what happens to her is "the sort of thing that *does* happen to the wonderful perfectly normal kids" in a world gone mad (272). As James Webb insists, "we are not ourselves anymore" (307).

Swede's secret and his tragedy, the defining fact of his adult life, is that, through his daughter's incomprehensible, capricious act, "he had learned the worst lesson that life can teach—that it makes no sense. And when that happens the happiness is never spontaneous again. It is artificial and, even then, bought at the price of an obstinate estrangement from oneself and one's history" (81). Philip Roth is, of course, a major American novelist, *American Pastoral* a prize-winning book. Even if it were not as well a powerful novel, it would sound loudly among the turn-of-the-new-century jeremiads that bemoan the decline of American civilization and see the roots of that decay in the excesses of the 1960s. Roth's novel proffers an indelible portrait of a family destroyed by the youthful passions of its youngest child.

Only Children

These fictional narratives about the home front during the Vietnam era explore a variety of responses by their young alienated activists to their "disillusion" with "the hypocrisy of American ideals" (to quote the Port Huron Statement). They capture the salient twin consequences of the youthful rejection of the inequities and complacency of the old world: the young protagonists' slightly desperate quest for love, camaraderie, and family in embryonic communities like the Weather Underground, the Drop City Commune, the "new drifters [and] destitute vagabond youth . . . all those rootless, restless kids who began taking to the road" in search of . . . a meaningful life (Nunez, 138, 137). And their lingering, complicated relationship with the parents— almost always the fathers—themselves gripped by their sad, doomed efforts to understand how it all went so wrong. The wild children blame the complacent parents for failing to fulfill the promise of democracy and reject the materialistic, complacent culture of post–World War II America as racist and imperialistic. The parents are, in turn, appalled by the excesses of the sex, drugs, and rock 'n' roll hedonism of the privileged children and watch in paralyzed horror as the children wreak havoc on a society they struggled to build. Yet because neither can finally give up on the other, the collective story in these narratives is that of the tenuous, awkward embrace of distraught father and angry, lost child. By the middle of the 1970s, these texts affirm, the whole mad era is over (rejecting a recognition of the reverberations of the movement into the coming years for the dramatic closure that a cataclysmic, if whimpering, finale implies)—the Vietnam War has ended, the hopeful quest for a new way to live has been tragically misappropriated by Charles Manson and the Symbionese Liberation Army and more prosaically co-opted by the soulless, mainstream culture that it reviled. In the spring of 1970, *The Last of Her Kind*'s Georgie, on her way with friends to see the new movie about the Woodstock festival, notes that Bloomingdale's has "come out with a line of Woodstock-inspired clothes . . . designer . . . height-of-fashion . . . versions of the very fringed shirts, bell-bottoms . . . and granny dresses we had on, and for which altogether we had paid probably less than fifty bucks. . . . All over the neighborhood, stores . . . were selling merchandise bearing the Woodstock name or the flower-power logo, and a diner . . . had renamed its everyday breakfast offering of pancakes and eggs the Woodstock Breakfast Special. All this made us want to turn around and go home" (71).

Probably we will never fully understand or appreciate the Vietnam antiwar movement. Arguably, it was simplistically presented by the popular press at the time. And despite serious, comprehensive (but often politicized) scholarly studies in recent years, it is today a nearly forgotten, or, more accurately, misunderstood aspect of America's involvement in the war in Vietnam. It has been argued that among the thousands of novels, films, and cultural texts that Americans have produced about the Vietnam War, no title has emerged as the definitive fictional treatment that captures the agonizing complexities of that protracted event. Perhaps it should come as no surprise, then, that the antiwar movement similarly lacks a single compelling narrative voice. There is, and can be, no conclusive creative treatment because there was no definitive experience. The novels and film I have discussed here offer some consistent themes and patterns, certainly. The more superficial, popular treatments by Sara Davidson, Marylouise Oates, and Caryl Rivers came early, among the 1980s and early 1990s texts that parallel the so-called first wave of combat narratives. Reversing the patterns for women's aftermath narratives, more sophisticated variants appeared in the later 1990s and in the early years of this century, when Roth, Nunez, and Joyce Carol Oates, with the leavening of twenty or thirty years of rumination on the era, linger over the painful, personal legacy of that riotous time. Several of the more ambitious narratives acknowledge the intersections of various elements of the era and the New Left: Boyle, for instance, in *Drop City*, concentrates on the counterculture—which Marge Piercy and Sigrid Nunez treat more tangentially; Jay Cantor directly and Joyce Carol Oates obliquely address the bequests of the civil rights movement. As a whole, however, these narratives recount a remarkably consistent story: the avowed movement accomplice or independent ideologue, deeply if vaguely committed to violent, revolutionary action, regretting or defending his or her (most commonly her) invariably youthful felonious activities, immediately or long after the heyday of the antiwar movement. Most find rich narrative material in the naiveté and ingenuous romanticism of their young heroes and in the poignant tensions between the generations that their youthfulness creates. All quietly accept that, by the mid-1970s, the end of the war, the lurching violence of the official movement, and a broader cultural decline have compromised the hopeful promise of the early movement and sealed the unfortunate fate of its disciples.

The protagonists who populate the films and novels that re-create the complex, anarchic movement are, in sum, dour misfits, ingenuous ideologues, and passionate patriots. Peripatetic and rooted, remorseful and defiant, they fight—not unlike their brothers in the jungles of Southeast Asia—for a different, a better, America. Their authentic historical counterparts present, in their own words, a similarly variegated commentary on the bold, mad adventure that extradites them to the margins of mainstream America, where they linger, in the shadows, at the fugitive's hour, with a clear vision of a world that they once—almost—created.

Chapter Five

Something Strange and Extravagant: Personal Histories by Vietnam Antiwar Movement Activists

What you finally decide to think the '60s was is one of the forms in which you affirm or repudiate a whole part of your life.
— *The '60s without Apology*, Sohnya Sayres et al.

When you have chosen your part, abide by it, and do not try to weakly reconcile yourself with the world. . . . Adhere to your own act, and congratulate yourself if you have done something strange and extravagant, and broken the monotony of a decorous age.
—Epigraph from Tom Hayden's *Reunion*: "Emerson, *Essays: First Series*, 'Heroism,' passage underlined by Robert Kennedy"

The change that the counterculture made in American life has become nearly impossible to calculate—thanks partly to the exaggerations of people who hate the sixties, and partly to the exaggerations of people who hate the people who hate the sixties. The subject could use the attention of some people who really don't care.
—Louis Menand, "Life in the Stone Age"

MIDWAY through his 1986 memoir *Passing Time*, Vietnam veteran and Swarthmore undergraduate W. D. (Bill) Ehrhart, his antiwar sentiments stimulated by the debacle at Kent State, wonders, in a 1970 speech to the local Rotary Club, "who will be the heroes of the Vietnam War? Men like me who fought there, or those who argue for an end to further killing and senseless destruction?"[1] (96). Fifteen years later, near the end of *Fugitive Days*, his memoir about his Vietnam-era activism, Weather Underground veteran Bill Ayers describes a visit to the Greenwich Village townhouse where his then girlfriend Diana Oughton and two other Underground activists were killed in the famous 1970 bomb-building accident that propelled the Weather survivors underground and prompted a reconsideration of their commitment to violence as a means to end the war. Conflating his pilgrimage to the townhouse with vigils at the Vietnam Veterans Memorial in Washington, D.C., Ayers notes that now, belatedly, even the three men who intervened to stop the massacre at My Lai have been honored for their heroism and morality, and muses, "how much longer for the three who died on Eleventh Street? How much longer for Diana? When will she be remembered?" (277).

The September 2001 publication of *Fugitive Days* provided Ayers with a resounding answer to his question—and to Ehrhart's as well. On the very morning that terrorist-piloted commercial airplanes shattered America's complacent certainty about its world dominance, the *New York Times* ran a long profile of Bill Ayers and his wife, the former Weather Underground leader Bernadine Dohrn. The article, titled "No Regrets for a Love of Explosives," opened with the memoirist's audacious assertion that "I don't regret setting bombs. . . . I feel we didn't do enough." Fanned by the grief and anger and incredulity smoldering in the ruins of the World Trade Center, a small firestorm erupted over Ayers's unfortunately (if interestingly) timed memento mori of his youthful years in the radical wing of the New Left. Now, suddenly and unexpectedly, it was impossible to respond to *Fugitive Days* without considering it in light of the post-9/11 world order. The leftist press welcomed Ayers's illumination of "a dark, often misunderstood, crucial point within U.S. political history" as a cautionary tale for a contemporary resistance movement struggling to respond to "the recent military escalation, antiwar mobilizations, and the media hailstorm that seems to have crossed the line from grief to panic" (Shepard, 55). Conservative journalists sputtered with fury at "unrepentant terrorist" Ayers's refusal to repudiate his youthful antiwar actions (Tabin). The Julius and Ethel Rosenberg scholar Ronald Radosh, writing for *The Weekly Standard*, loathed Ayers's "disgusting" defense of the Weather Underground's campaign of symbolic violence and argued that, despite Ayers's insistence to the contrary, his book aimed to "encourage another generation of terrorists against the United States." "Bill Ayers has learned nothing in the years since he was a terrorist," Radosh concludes. "This man still hates America and seeks its destruction." In the *Wall Street Journal*, John Tabin berated a midwest Barnes & Noble bookstore for sponsoring a book-signing for Ayers, who "personifies the moral bankruptcy of the far left." William Norman Grigg, senior editor of *The New American*, proclaimed that Ayers and Dohrn were "an important part of the world Communist movement's terrorist fifth column within the United States" and expressed his "outrage that [they] are comfortably ensconced in the academic world." He expounded on the Soviets' 1960s international network of terrorists, which he claimed now sees its veterans holding "key positions of respect in government and academia." More mainstream commentators, too, framed their observations on *Fugitive Days* with the politically charged events of September 11. The political scientist Alan Wolfe, writing in the October 11, 2001, *Chronicle of Higher Education*, was only slightly less vituperative than the far right pundits in his denunciation of Ayers's "story of an unrepentant New Leftist who casually justifies violence." "*Fugitive Days*," he asserts, "is self-serving rather than searching, an apologia for extremism rather than an apology for arrogance." In *The New York Times Book Review*, Brent Staples also dismissed *Fugitive Days* as "maddeningly evasive" and fraught with "obfuscations," concluding that "in the aftermath of the terrorist attacks that killed thousands . . . readers will find this playacting with violence very difficult to forgive" (11).[2]

Although it is unlikely that a more fortuitously timed *Fugitive Days* would have elicited sympathetic reviews, the watershed events of 9/11 so compromised reception of Ayers's memoir that the paperback version, published in 2003, included "a new Afterword by the author," in which Ayers addresses the "bloody events" that "cracked open" the country on 9/11 and the ensuing "noisy upheaval surrounding and then overwhelming" *Fugitive Days*. After 9/11, Ayers unapologetically declaims, "suddenly the wildest, most ambitious agendas of the far, far Right seemed achievable." And so ensued a campaign to suppress dissent, consolidate American power, and "erase forever the history of decades of struggle by millions of people for peace and participatory democracy and social justice" (301). Attacked from all sides for his refusal to renounce his thirty-five-year-old actions, Ayers reiterates his commitment to dramatic social change. "I have no regrets for opposing the war with every ounce of my strength," he obstinately insists in his post-9/11 codicil. "In light of the indiscriminate murder of millions of Vietnamese, I still think we showed remarkable restraint, and that we probably didn't do enough" (298).

Bill Ayers's *Fugitive Days* is a recent entry among a large, diverse assemblage of autobiographical narratives—"participant histories," in the words of the movement historian Terry H. Anderson—by activists who were, during the 1960s and early 1970s, affiliated with or influenced by what its members called, simply, "the movement." Ayers's and his fellow memoirists' interpretations of the events of those turbulent years offer important testimony of the movement's varied attempts to bring the war home and a factual, if inevitably subjective, counterpart to the portrayals fictionalized in creative narratives about the New Left. The events of 9/11, the subsequent war in Iraq—and the responses to them—have only renewed the protracted national debate about the efficacy and morality of the Vietnam War–era protest movement. The politically charged, powerful reactions to Ayers's book are a synecdoche for the strong emotions and, often, near revulsion that the anti–Vietnam War home front movement evokes to this day. In contemporary America, if Diana Oughton *is* remembered at all, it is not, as Ayers hopes, as either "heroic" or "moral" (277).

Disagreements and misperceptions at once plague contemporary efforts to understand and learn from the American experience of the Vietnam War *and* engender our continued preoccupation with that seminal event of late-twentieth-century American history. We won in the long run—the cold war over, Soviet expansion thwarted. We lost miserably—the post-Vietnam syndrome responsible for America's compromised self-image and a timorous foreign policy until 9/11 and a second, bellicose President Bush delighted to flaunt American military might. We would have won but for a demoralized American public and irresolute elected officials who could not support the military effort necessary for a demonstrable victory. Explications and interpretations of the peace movement echo the fascination with and differences of opinion about the Vietnam War.

To reiterate, most historians and cultural critics of the movement, while emphasizing its internal dissensions and its many failures, ultimately affirm its essential role in ending the Vietnam War and—as important—fundamentally changing American society. Terry H. Anderson in *The Movement and the Sixties: Protest in America from Greensboro to Wounded Knee* (1995), James Miller in *Democracy Is in the Streets: From Port Huron to the Siege of Chicago* (1987), Tom Wells in *The War Within: America's Battle over Vietnam* (1994), Nancy Zaroulis and Gerald Sullivan in *Who Spoke Up? American Protest against the War in Vietnam 1963–1975* (1984), Charles DeBenedetti in *An American Ordeal: The Antiwar Movement of the Vietnam Era* (1990), and former SDS member Todd Gitlin in his 1987 historical autobiography *The Sixties: Years of Hope, Days of Rage* all concur with Melvin Small, who asserts in his 2002 *Antiwarriors: The Vietnam War and the Battle for America's Hearts and Minds* that the social protest movement that coalesced around opposition to American involvement in Vietnam was "the largest and most influential of all antiwar movements in the nation's history" (1).

Adam Garfinkle, in his contrarian 1995 book *Telltale Hearts: The Origins and Impact of the Vietnam Antiwar Movement*, concedes that the movement's influence on American society and culture was—though largely deleterious—profound. He insists, however, that the peace movement did not end—and, in fact, may have prolonged—the American war in Vietnam. "Antiwar demonstrations mounted and populated by radicals stifled at least as much if not more nonradical dissent against the war than they stimulated," Garfinkle maintains. "Most Americans, while concerned about a war seemingly without end or prospect of clearcut victory, were more prepared to suffer in silence than to associate themselves with lurid leftists and yelping Yippies" (266). The popular historian Stephen E. Ambrose, in his foreword to Garfinkle's book, sets out the familiar conservative-curmudgeon argument that the movement, in an "excess of free will and childish misjudgment seldom matched and never exceeded," alienated middle-class sympathizers and damagingly "extend[ed] the boundaries of the counterculture" (vii–viii). Compare the 1998 jeremiad by the self-titled "conservative champion" Michael Medved about baby boomers' misguided nostalgia for their youthful activism, which arose, he argues, not from "the robust health of the body politic," but from a "profound national sickness" (13A). More than a few of the retrospectives on the sixties that appeared in the popular press at the end of the 1990s suggested that we are fortunate—and wise—to have outgrown the political and cultural upheaval of the era. Walter Goodman, for instance, reviewing *The Whole World Was Watching*, an ABC documentary on the thirtieth anniversary of 1968, opines that the show offers us "the happy news ... that some of the antiwar radicals of the time, blessedly forgotten now, are busying themselves with worthy causes" (B5).

As the biographical notes in antiwar activists' memoirs and the "where are they now" conclusions of documentary films such as *The War at Home* (1979), *Berkeley in the Sixties* (1990), *Rebels with a Cause* (2000), and *The Weather Underground* (2003) indicate, Goodman's snide dismissal is accurate. Many of the young activists of the 1960s and early '70s (like fictional protagonists such as Piercy's Vida and Spiotta's Bobby De Soto) continue their fight for social justice in their middle age by working as teachers, social workers, and community organizers. Their personal accounts of their political awakening and youthful activism that propelled them to public, dramatic, even violent protest against their society are an important component of the still controversial Vietnam War and the similarly contested domestic war against it. During the Vietnam War, antiwar activists inhab-

210

ited the other side of the war more forcefully than any other constituency in that transforming experience. As Tom Hayden proclaims, "I first saw the war as America invading and dividing Vietnam. [Soon] it was Vietnam, like a malignant tumor, invading and dividing us" (195). Yet veterans of the movement recognize, in the years since the end of the war, that their presentation of their stories is complicated not only by politically charged disagreements about the probity and effectiveness of the movement, but by the fact that perceptions about the movement are themselves colored by the often simplistic myths and stereotypes about the movement and the 1960s.

"Memory Is a Motherfucker"

For some Americans, today as then, the sixties were dirty, foul-mouthed teenagers, violence in the streets, the cavalier dissevering of the American dream. Depending on your politics and, perhaps, your age at the time, the decade was the liberation or the dissolution of America. We may disagree about the era and its aftermath, but—as Louis Menand notes—most of us have an opinion on the subject. The historian David Farber, in a 1994 *Chronicle of Higher Education* article titled "The 60's: Myth and Reality," argues that the baby boomers who came of age in the 1960s are responsible for the misapprehension that "the decade [was] unique, an era out of time" (B1). Rick Perlstein concurs, wondering "was there ever a society more self-conscious about its own historical identity, its role as an *agent* of history, than America in the Sixties?" (37). Bill Ayers begins his 9/11-inspired afterword to his memoir with an acknowledgment of the difficulty of "writing about encompassing events that weigh so heavily upon us today as the received truths of history—the mythology of the 1960s and the lore of Viet Nam cast such deep, impenetrable shadows that they tend to wipe out the dense and nuanced landscape of actual life as it was lived" (294–295). The old joke is that if you can remember the sixties, you weren't there; the reality may be that if you were there, you can't remember the sixties accurately.

So the antiwarriors (the reflective, candid ones, at least) who offer their reminiscences about their roles in the movement write from the awareness that their stories are suffused with strong, dissonant opinions about the war and its protestors; that this political polarization is itself complicated by nostalgia and reductive cultural myths; and that these factors are confounded even more by the memoirist's nemesis: the mutability of memory. Ayers continues his defense of his wartime actions and his obdurate commitment to continue the fight today with his reiteration of the theme that recurs throughout *Fugitive Days*: the inconstancy of memory (exacerbated, as a result of his years underground, the reader soon perceives, by his own facility with deception). The book is prefaced with the disclaimer that "this story is only one version of events—it is a memory book rather than a transcript, an accounting of sorts without any pretense toward an authorized history." Throughout the book, he muses—in poetic, italicized passages set off from the narrative—about the verisimilitude of his version of events. "To revisit the past is to become, whether intended or not, a crusading editor—selecting, correcting, disappearing, rearranging, cutting, and pasting. There is an insistent voice that urges subversion or, at the very least, caution: hide the bodies, it says, erase the tracks, clean off the fingerprints, yours and others" (192). *Whether intended or not.* Ayers admits that he has changed the names to protect the innocent (or is it the guilty?); he worries, too, though, that "we remember in our favor": "the past is a foreign country and memory is always in translation—deciphering, paraphrasing, consulting the thesaurus. Memory rewrites rather than transcribes" (29, 46). Quite simply, as Ayers acknowledges, "memory is a motherfucker" (7).

Joan Baez, the sixties folksinger and self-proclaimed "counter-culture heroine," concludes the preface to her unreflective 1987 memoir *And a Voice to Sing With* with a statement about both the uncertainties of memory and the delusiveness of nostalgia: "I've told all as I have remembered it, knowing full well that, like everybody else, I am blessed with a selective memory and, perhaps more so than some, a vivid imagination. I have recorded these facts . . . because I . . . do not wish to be relegated to obscurity, antiquity, or somebody's dewy-eyed nostalgia about days gone by" (72, 13). Similarly, the National Public Radio reporter Margot Adler introduces her memoir, *Heretic's Heart: A Journey through Spirit and Revolution* (1997), with the confession that as she revisited her youthful past, "a few of my most vivid recollections turned out to be questionable" and that her aim is to recount accurately "an era that has suffered from such poisonous revisionism" (xii). In his memoir *Dreams Die Hard* David Harris notes that his effort to determine how "it all end[ed] up like this" is difficult because "my recollections are refracted at one end by who I was becoming at the time and at the other by who I have become since" (5). Most of the movement memoirists, then, caution their readers—and themselves—about this insidious trinity—controversy, nostalgia, selective memory—as they offer their backward glance at those "terrible, exquisite years" (Ayers, 284).

Red Diaper Babies, Baby Boomers, and Cultural Revolutionaries

Perhaps it is the consciousness—even in its own time—of the sixties as a unique era and phenomenon that accounts for the attractions of the subject for contemporary novelists and for the plethora of personal narratives by the era's actors in their later years. The pattern of publication of autobiographical narratives by participant-observers of the movement mirrors that of books, films, commentary, and other texts about the lost war. That is to say, a long period of silence, healing, and forgetting after America's withdrawal from Vietnam (with several exceptions: Ron Kovic's 1976 *Born on the Fourth of July*, for example), then a chorus of voices beginning in the early 1980s and continuing through Ayers's and Jane Fonda's recent contributions. The chronicles are diverse: some (Tom Hayden's *Reunion*, Abbie Hoffman's *Autobiography*) by high-profile celebrities of the movement and entertainers (Jane Fonda's *My Life So Far*; Joan Baez's *And a Voice to Sing With*); others (Jane Alpert's *Growing Up Underground*, Roger Rosenblatt's *Coming Apart*) from commentators whose experiences of the era's turmoil were less public; combat veterans (W. D. Ehrhart, Ron Kovic) and conscientious objectors (John Balaban); lifelong peace activists (David Dellinger) and jejune college students (Margot Adler).

Many of these texts are traditional autobiographies that offer a comprehensive history of their subject's life and times. David Horowitz's 1997 *Radical Son*, for instance, begins with his Jewish grandparents' flight from Russian pogroms to the "promised land" of early-twentieth-century America (9). A red diaper baby, like Turow's fictional Sonny Klonsky, Horowitz recounts his parents' quiet Communist Party activities, his own intellectual development at Columbia and Berkeley in the 1950s, his struggles to support a young, growing family by writing in Europe, his late-sixties return to Berkeley and editorship of the radical publication *Ramparts*, his embrace of—and life-changing betrayal by—the Black Panther Party in the early 1970s, and his increasing shift to the right throughout the 1980s and '90s. Now founding president of the conservative David Horowitz Freedom Center, Horowitz—self-anointed as "the most hated ex-radical of my generation"—punctuates his self-aggrandizing ("I am now as prominent on the conservative side of the ideological divide as I once was in the ranks of the Left") history of his odyssey through the 1960s with revisionist commentary that emphasizes his "second thoughts" about his intellectual involvement in the movement and his current disdain for the "company of killers" whom he had once welcomed as heirs of the Old Left (2, 3, 88).[3] Horowitz has written other critiques of the radical movement (*Destructive Generation: Second Thoughts about the 60's* [1989]; *Left Illusions* [2003]). *Radical Son* is his own story, an intelligent (if unusually self-serving), dense recounting of one man's life journey from idealism to disillusionment.

David Dellinger's *From Yale to Jail: The Life Story of a Moral Dissenter* (1993) is, like Horowitz's personal narrative, a traditional, straightforward autobiography. A lifelong pacifist-activist, Dellinger, who was a full generation older than the baby boomers who more famously populated the movement—and who was, therefore, like Daniel Berrigan, a reminder that the dedicated leaders of the antiwar movement were not all college-aged youth—describes his childhood during and just after World War I, his involvement with the Socialist Party after college at Yale, his imprisonments for resistance to the draft and refusal to pay taxes during World War II, and his communal family life and intellectual protest work in the 1950s. Like Horowitz, Dellinger, with his roots in the Old Left, regrets the student movement's apparent unwillingness to acknowledge the influence of earlier activists, but, cynical about the possibility for reform within the political system, he nonetheless embraces the new movement, specifically, the Students for a Democratic Society. Dellinger's viewpoint on the Vietnam-era peace movement is that of "an older brother ... old enough to" understand earlier movements for "justice and peace" but "drawn to stand with the rebellious kids" (189). As one of the Chicago 7 indicted for inciting a riot at the 1968 Democratic Convention and as a leader of the Mobe (Mobilization Committee to End the War in Vietnam), which during the Vietnam era sponsored the largest mass protests in American history, Dellinger was directly involved in antiwar activism to an extent that Horowitz was not. In *The Armies of the Night*, for example, Norman Mailer asserts that it was Dellinger's "extraordinary abilities" as chairman of the Mobe that held together the varied "cadres of that citizens' army [that would] march on the Pentagon" in October 1967 (246). Todd Gitlin calls him "the coalition-builder's coalition-builder" (*The Sixties*, 363). As the Yippies romped and the student movement lurched tragically toward violence, middle-aged Dellinger, in his polyester suit and comb-over hairstyle, emerges as a calm, wise participant-observer of the upheaval around him. His personal history, which concludes with his ongoing protests (in 1992, for instance, a forty-two day Fast for Justice and Peace in the Americas), is the story of a man for whom the Vietnam War and the movement were a single, if compelling, cause in a lifetime of peaceful efforts to effect fundamental social change. As Mailer notes, by 1967 Dellinger "had been involved for years in small not uncourageous acts of civil disobedience" (259).

The upstart in this small collection of conventional autobiographies that seek to explain their authors' pre-movement influences and post-movement reflections is Tom Hayden, who describes his method in the introduction to his 1988 *Reunion: A Memoir*: "this narrative outpouring [is] partly personal, partly historical. I have tried to convey my reflections as an ancient storyteller would, not by philosophizing, but by recounting those times as they happened on personal levels, letting the reader participate through his or her own memory, searching with me for meaning" (xi–xiii). Hayden—hailed as "the single greatest figure of the 1960s student movement" in an encomium by Paul Berman reprinted on the front cover of the paperback edition of *Reunion* (an interesting marketing technique for a book by and about the leader of an avowedly leaderless movement)—in fact offers considerably more analytical commentary on the hopes, failures, and long-term consequences of the movement than his acknowledged intentions seem to promise.

Hayden revisits his midwestern, middle-class, 1950s Catholic childhood, which is for him too smugly satisfied with the American dream. No son of radicals, he uncovers the seeds of his activism in a "boring and prearranged existence" that offered few challenges and stifled creativity in its society's young (14). Hayden arrives at the University of Michigan in 1957 primed to answer his contemporaries' early calls for "a new era of student social action and responsibility," and as editor of the university newspaper, he reports on even as he participates in the "new politics" that surround him (39, 29) Like most of the college-aged sixties activists, Hayden is energized, in the early part of the decade, by the civil rights movement. From Mississippi, it is a well-marked, febrile path to leadership in the Students for a Democratic Society; authorship of its 1962 manifesto, the Port Huron Statement; and organizing of the poor residents of the Newark, New Jersey, slums in SDS's Economic Research and Action Project (ERAP). By 1968, feeling that he is "living on the knife edge of history," Hayden and the SDS have turned their attention to Vietnam, "the central issue, the metaphor and mirror of our times, the moral and murderous experience that would mark our identity for the future" (253, 205). Hayden is ubiquitous as a movement leader, meeting with the NLF in Hanoi in late 1965 and again in the fall of 1967, intervening in the student strike at Columbia University in April 1968, standing vigil at Robert F. Kennedy's coffin in June, arrested at the debacle in Chicago later that summer. He is preoccupied with defending himself at the Chicago 7 trial when the radical remnants of the SDS, under the leadership of the Weather Underground ("not the conscience of a generation, but its id, finally surfacing"), blast into Chicago for their Days of Rage in October 1969, escalating the stakes and alienating the idealist Tom Hayden, who now loses hope for a "social revolution in America" (360). By the end of the decade, "our lives spiraling toward some personal and political abyss," Hayden begins to construct the postmovement life that will take him from "outlaw" to "minor celebrity" (415, 487). *Reunion* concludes, rather anticlimactically, with its author's election to public life, marriage to a movie star (the notorious "Hanoi Jane" Fonda), and ambivalent assessment of his hopeful young adulthood.

A handful of movement veterans and fellow travelers proffer autobiographical narratives that blur the generic line between autobiography and memoir. Texts such as *The Autobiography of Abbie Hoffman* (1980),[4] Ayers's *Fugitive Days*, James Carroll's *An American Requiem*, and most of the narratives by women considered here—Joan Baez's *And a Voice to Sing With*, Jane Alpert's *Growing Up Underground*, Margot Adler's *Heretic's Heart*—begin with a brief presentation of family or personal background, but move quickly to their authors' involvement in the movement. Though, like the testimonies of Hayden, Dellinger, and Horowitz, many of these narratives conclude with a contemporary update on their authors' post–Vietnam era activities, they offer considerably less analysis than those longer texts of the intellectual origins, internecine conflicts, and eventual legacy of the movement.

Yippie leader, Chicago 7 defendant, and self-proclaimed "cultural revolutionary" Abbie Hoffman (born, like Hayden and Horowitz, in the late 1930s and therefore a crucial decade or so older than most of the student activists) presents a linear, apparently realistic account of his emergence as leader (along with Jerry Rubin) of the Yippies, whom Hoffman defines as "political hippie[s]" (207, 137). The movement leader/celebrity who best understood the cultural implications of political activism, Hoffman recounts his in-your-face guerrilla theater efforts to unnerve and confront a complacent nation: dropping money on the floor of the New York Stock Exchange, claiming to exorcise and levitate the Pentagon at the October 1967 march that Mailer chronicles in *The Armies of the Night*, nominating a pig (Pigasus) for president at the notorious 1968 Democratic Convention. Hoffman's predictably irreverent saga of his revolutionary highjinks, his years underground, and his local activism before his 1989 suicide is a readable, if some-what superficial, record by the movement's clown prince.

Bill Ayers begins his book with the March 1970 townhouse explosion that debilitated the radical Weather Underground and serves as a watershed event in several fictional accounts of the radical wing of the movement. Like Hayden's, the chronological narrative that follows this "Prelude" recounts his idyllic childhood in the "privileged and padded suburbs" of 1950s America and his rapid evolution from prep school student to radical revolutionary (23). After a half-hearted and unsuccessful attempt to enlist in the civil rights movement, Ayers makes a second pass at the University of Michigan, where this time he finds the "shimmering vision of a democracy that would be par-ticipatory": the movement for social justice that he has been searching for (62). Joining "the rebels and the resistors, the anti-mob, the agnostics and the skeptics," Ayers baptizes himself "a charter member of a just-made society," ready to march, to be jailed, to stand up and be counted for a new, exciting campaign to change America (66). Ayers's breathless chronicle underscores the exhilaration and idealism that its young hero finds—and its middle-aged author invests—in the movement to end the war. For Ayers, the movement is love, sex, action. By spring 1968, he writes, "my particular inner longing came alive, linked to a huge outer quest, my youthful and personal vibra-tions aligned in some magical way with magnificent shocks and eruptions. I was filled with energy, intensity, and engagement" (120). Energized and self-important, Ayers and his fellow antiwarriors plunge headlong and in-nocently into an escalating crusade. "It was a time of transgression, and I was of a generation guided by the precept, Break as many rules as you can. The system was death; defiance and insubordination was life itself. Go further, we said. Shock, offend, outrage, overstep, disturb. Know no limits. Lose con-trol. Events cascaded on, new limits replaced old ones, standards were reas-sessed" (131). Ayers's use of the passive voice—the infamous "mistakes were made" construction that avoids ascribing ownership or accepting blame— is important here, for his description of his "up-against-the-wall-motherfucker politics of running confrontation" emphasizes action, adventure, and pas-sion over introspection, political ideology, planned strategy—or account-ability (153). The middle-aged Ayers seems unable or unwilling to examine the implications of his youthful actions, much as the young Ayers and his fellow "kids in combat, with little to lose" hurtle toward a violent revolution with scarcely a second thought. Only the March 1970 explosion mandates a Weatherbureau (i.e., the Weather leadership) retreat and a reevaluation of the group's hell-bent techniques (141). Ayers's partner-to-be, Bernadine Dohrn (christened by J. Edgar Hoover "the most dangerous woman in America," Ayers proudly reports) prevails, and the Weather Underground resolves to limit its violence to symbolic (rather than human) targets (194). And while Ayers and Dohrn struggle in their subterranean life, living the "Weathermyth" until 1980, when they turned themselves in, subsequent Underground bombings—New York City police headquarters and the Presidio army base in 1970, the U.S. Capitol in 1971, among others—wreak destruction only against property.

Women on the Margins

Compared with Hayden's, Hoffman's, and Ayers's, the female memoirists' lives on the fringes of the movement were apparently considerably less fun. Jane Alpert, like her livelier brothers-in-arms, does her four years' time underground and even serves two years in prison for her participation in antiwar bombings. *Growing Up Underground*, her unreflective and dour effort "to set the record straight on my role in a turbulent period of American history," replicates the structure of many of her cohorts' reminiscences: a relatively brief portrayal of a conventional family, childhood, and education followed by immersion in a renegade, unorganized group on the margins of the orgiastic movement, in which Alpert was always an outsider (18).

Margot Adler was even more removed from the "official" movement. Though she is the New York–born child of radical parents, Adler's "atheist, semi-Marxist" childhood is mitigated by idyllic summers in the 1950s on Martha's Vineyard and attendance at the upscale Greenwich Village City and Country School (42). She is radicalized as a mid-sixties Berkeley undergraduate, spends the summer of 1965 registering black voters in Mississippi, rejects Communist Party membership, and, back in New York for graduate school, in 1969 goes to Cuba with the Venceremos Brigade, a group of American radicals who supported the Cuban revolution. *Heretic's Heart* ends with Adler's postmovement involvement with paganism and spirituality, her always tenuous embrace of the movement acknowledged in the title of her book.

The least introspective of the memoirs discussed here, Joan Baez's banal *And a Voice to Sing With*, like the other somehow sketchy but full-scale autobiographies, begins with her peripatetic childhood as the daughter of a Mexican-born college professor. Early success as a folksinger and early

1960s college concerts led easily to support for the era's social causes. Baez sings "We Shall Overcome" with several hundred thousand people at the civil rights movement's August 1962 March on Washington. She performs Bob Dylan's "The Times They Are A-Changin'" at a campaign rally for LBJ. And, as the pregnant wife of the Stanford student activist and jailed draft resister David Harris (author of *Dreams Die Hard*), she sings at Woodstock, the "Technicolor, mud-splattered reflection of . . . the sixties, that outrageous, longed for, romanticized, lusted after, tragic, insane, bearded and bejeweled epoch" (165). Baez demonstrates that her politics are not merely career-driven when she establishes—and funds—an Institute for the Study of Nonviolence. Her post-sixties activism includes a Christmas 1972 visit to Hanoi and American POWs and trips in the mid-1970s to Northern Ireland and the USSR. By 1979, Baez notes, she is as content to forget Vietnam and the lost war as most other Americans are, but when "two boat people" plaintively ask her "where . . . were all the Americans who cared so much about the Vietnamese people in the sixties?" and tell her about the Communist victors' human rights abuses, she reluctantly investigates the postwar political situation in Vietnam (274). Because the United States reneged on the Paris Peace Accord agreement to provide reparations to Vietnam, Baez writes, "Vietnam had accordingly broken her promises of no reprisals, reconciliation for collaborations, and, of course, self-determination and democratic freedom for everyone" (275). Though eighty people (Daniel Berrigan, writers, Hollywood people) signed her 1979 *New York Times* letter to the Socialist Republic of Vietnam calling for an end to human rights abuses, she finds little support from the left (she describes specifically Jane Fonda's thoughtful but definitive refusal to accept that the Communist government of Vietnam was as abusive as Baez alleges) and "obnoxious" gloating from the right over her controversial actions.

The last few chapters of Baez's memoir, which recount her life and career through 1987, offer a gratuitous paean to actor Marlon Brando and tedious accounts of her waning career and the 1985 Live Aid concert in Philadelphia. Her sketch of that ersatz Woodstock—"Good Morning, Children of the Eighties! This is your Woodstock"—featuring minor celebrities like Cher, Don Johnson, and Duran Duran, is a sadly fitting conclusion to a book that adds little to our understanding of the movement and its participants (357).

In Lan Cao's 1997 novel *Monkey Bridge*, the middle-aged residents of Little Saigon in Arlington, Virginia, have read of Joan Baez's postwar sympathy for Vietnamese exiles, and the virulently anti-Communist expatriates have "granted absolution" to the woman "whose searing, melancholic voice had provided the antiwar movement with raw poetic beauty" (153). They angrily contrast the folksinger's change of heart about "America's most troubled war" with the apparent obduracy of fellow celebrity-activist Jane Fonda. The familiar photo of Hanoi Jane "draping herself flirtatiously" on an antiair-craft gun "was not," narrator Mai Nguyen notes, "something that could, or would be allowed to, recede permanently into the margin of history" (154). Further, Vietnamese Mrs. Bay and her American veteran friend Bill resent Fonda's role in a movie about a veteran's return home (*Coming Home*), and Mai knows that her defense of Fonda's right to star in the film is futile, since "she seemed a perennial and inexhaustible point of focus in the Little Saigon community" (210).

The always controversial Hanoi Jane acknowledges the lingering re-sentments—and her own regrets—about her notorious photo op in Hanoi (which has decidedly not receded into history) in her 2005 autobiography *My Life So Far*. It includes several chapters that recount her memories and perceptions of her peregrinations within the protest movement: the slow awakening of her social conscience, precipitated by an invitation from Mar-lon Brando to a 1965 fund-raiser for SNCC; her protracted efforts to make a Hollywood movie about a love triangle between two veterans and a vet's unhappy wife in the aftermath of the Vietnam War; her 1970s marriage to the former SDS leader and "movement icon" Tom Hayden (281).

Fonda presents her Vietnam-era activism as a defining theme of her life-long quest for self-actualization (and adds another twist on the complex father-child relationships that define the war's aftermath narratives), as she struggles to overcome a negative self-image created by her famous father's disapproval; bulimia; and an unhealthy dependence on controlling men (in-cluding second husband Hayden, whose "emotional coldness" and brilliant charisma make Fonda feel "stupid and superficial" [402]). "The activism upon which I embarked in 1970," Fonda notes, "changed me forever . . . and these changes remain to this day at the core of my being" (227).[5] Fonda ac-knowledges her mistakes as a celebrity-activist—naiveté, a grim shrillness, that ill-advised perch atop a North Vietnamese antiaircraft weapon, her at-tack on POWs who said that they had been tortured—admitting that "I made it easy for the media and others to choose a dubious if not downright hostile lens through which to view me"—Barbarella with a defiant fist in the air (227). Finally, however, Fonda tempers her apology for the confrontational actions that made her such a lightning rod with insistence on the fundamental probity of her outspoken opposition to the war: "I knew that . . . the killing in Vietnam needed to be stopped, and that using my celebrity to help people who were being bullied, deprived of safety and opportunity, was what I needed to do" (254).

Poets, Priests, and Professors

Another sizable group of movement memoirs presents interesting, and often acknowledged, variations on the conventions of the genre that the women and the celebrity men appropriate. The well-known antiwar protestor and Jesuit priest Daniel Berrigan's 1987 autobiography, *To Dwell in Peace*, offers a spiritual modulation of the traditional activist life story: four brothers, magnificent but unhappy mother, horrible father, poverty all around; seminary; antiwar activism culminating in the 1970 trial of the Catonsville 9; life underground; post-Vietnam antinuclear and AIDS activism. What makes Berrigan's book so unusual—and frustrating—is its poetic, ethereal style and tone. His record of events and activities is sketchy and impressionistic, the narrative punctuated with arcane rhapsodies such as "[the author] was in a strange position indeed. It came to this, that he was on only the most formal, distant terms with his own soul. He paid respects in passing, lifted his hat, so to speak, to that mysterious entity. A penetrating glance, body and soul; then they passed in the night" (346). Berrigan includes no commentary about his chimerical technique. Though he intends an ineffable meditation on his life and times, his amorphous book adds little to our comprehension of his and his compatriots' actions against the war.

In contrast, "peacenik priest" James Carroll offers, in his 1996 *An American Requiem: God, My Father, and the War That Came between Us*, a compelling if self-important account of how his growing opposition to the Vietnam War derails both his lifelong commitment to the Catholic church and his loving pride in his air force general father (217). He was a privileged self-proclaimed "prince" of that golden era in which the first Catholic president (John F. Kennedy), the powerful American cardinal (Spellman), and the charismatic new pope (John XXIII) came together to exert an unprecedented influence in international affairs—an era that Carroll calls "military Catholicism." Carroll, the son of the founding director of the Defense Intelligence Agency, created in 1961 by John F. Kennedy and Robert McNamara "to consolidate and objectify all military intelligence activities," is anointed to the priesthood by these leaders of the Catholic church (70,

183). Carroll's story of his emotional angst over his growing lack of trust in his spiritual and political mentors and the resulting heartbreaking rift in his relationship with his father is as self-aggrandizing as Hayden's and Horowitz's ego-ridden personal accounts; but his insider analysis of the political and interpersonal complexities of the Pentagon and the unusually close relationship between church and state during the Vietnam era make this an important and poignant memoir. And as a commentary on the patriarchy, Carroll's book echoes the preoccupation of many of the era's narratives. Throughout his young adulthood, Carroll variously, and quite consciously, adopts father figures who range from the poet Allen Tate to Elvis Presley to Daniel Berrigan (by whom Carroll feels betrayed when he learns that the priest who has espoused celibacy as a radical act in a sexual age has secretly married), to, as his subtitle implies, his own father: working-class FBI hero, air force general, and Vietnam War supporter. When in 1969 his powerful father refuses to support allegations by Defense Secretary Melvin Laird and the Joint Chiefs about Soviet advances in an antiballistic missile program, the proud general's career comes to "an abrupt and ignominious end." His painfully estranged second son years later (on another quintessentially healing visit to the Vietnam Veterans Memorial) recognizes that the father whom he'd once dismissed as a "war criminal" for his years of support for the war was, in fact, honorably living up to his obligations as a military officer: "How could he ever have said about these dead men that their sacrifice had been offered for a stupid mistake? Once he had helped dispatch thousands of young men to their deaths, certainly he'd have seen any subsequent denouncing of the war as breaking faith with them—his other sons" (or, as Arthur Miller puts it, "all my sons") (218, 220, 221). His father, Carroll belatedly recognizes, is as much a fatality of the Vietnam War as the men whose names engrave that granite wall. And the war, the war that comes between father and son, Carroll notes, "undergird[s] every aspect of the religious and political transformation I had been through" (253). Carroll begins and ends the story of his painful journey through the Vietnam era with his father, and, sincerely comparing himself to Jesus, who "came to understand Himself by understanding His father," acknowledges that "beneath every rumbling fault line and every quake was the steady, subterranean shifting of the tectonic plates of my relationship with Dad, Daddy" (122).

David Harris's 1982 autobiographical contribution is sui generis in yet another manner. Part biography, part memoir, part journalism, *Dreams*

Die Hard: Three Men's Journey through the Sixties is Harris's account of his relationship with fellow Stanford student and civil rights militant Dennis Sweeney and their mentor—another father figure—civil rights activist Allard Lowenstein (best remembered as the architect of the 1967 Dump Johnson campaign). As Harris presents them, the trio's intersecting stories, which culminate in Sweeney's spiraling descent into madness and his 1980 murder of Lowenstein, "frame the sixties in lives, the way it was when it was not yet history" (viii). Sweeney's story ("one of the saddest stories I know") becomes for Harris a synecdoche for the losses, mistakes, and misprision of a diverse movement in "an extraordinary time" (337, 338).

The sociologist, sixties scholar, and former SDS member Todd Gitlin's 1987 *The Sixties: Years of Hope, Days of Rage*, probably the best known of the movement veterans' narratives, is yet another mutation of the genre. Explaining that his book is an attempt "to claim the actual Sixties from 'the Sixties,' from [a] big bang theory of history, as well as to find out what I think," Gitlin avers that he writes from "the edge of history and autobiography" in a narrative that is "part historical reconstruction, part analysis, part memoir, part criticism, part celebration, part meditation" (3–4).

Gitlin interweaves his own story—normal fifties Bronx childhood, involvement in the early SDS at Harvard, writing for underground movement publications, the inevitable migration to Berkeley, frustration and alienation at the Weather Underground's highjacking of the student movement—with description and analysis of the momentous events and "unavoidable dilemmas" of the times (5).

Gitlin's insider/outsider perspective on his subject yields an interesting, problematic account and assessment of the movement. The scholar explains the relationship between the Old Left and the New Left that Horowitz and the historians recount. The participant is more interested in the fateful, fatal dissonance between the "early New Left"—his generation, the early members of the SDS, the authors of the Port Huron Statement, the "morally . . . serious, intellectually and culturally . . . ambitious" activists who "aspired to become the voice, conscience, and goad of its generation"—and the later New Left— the "unleashed young" who ran off the rails of the early commitment to create a better society and crashed into drugs, hedonistic personal expression, and violent anarchy (26, 213). Gitlin bemoans the increasing militancy of the movement, which, he claims, became less popular and effective as opposition to the war grew, and offers defensive explanations for his and other early New Leftists' inability to reclaim the movement from the "few hundred" Weather

Underground members who, by 1969, "held the rest of the Left enthralled" (395). Furious at the ascendance of the arrogant Weatherpeople, who, he says, were "the foam on a sea of rage," Gitlin insists that more reasoned activists could not counter the furious momentum of the radicals. "In the revolutionary mood," Gitlin writes, "no one could imagine how to translate compelling refutations into a compelling political practice. No alternative theory or action crystallized from the murk of the collective despair.... We could not imagine any life without the movement, but the movement no longer held any life for us" (397, 396). Denied the release valve of the women's movement, movement men, Gitlin claims, retreated in the 1970s and 1980s to "spiritual and psychological crisis" before recovering to continue "New Left politics . . . in a chastened, confused, and antiapocalyptic key" (424, 432). Although the nay-saying press featured the movement sell-outs ("as if a whole generation had moved en masse from 'J'accuse' to Jacuzzi"), many movement veterans, Gitlin explains, redirected their exhausted activism into the "professionalized reform" of careers in the professions and social justice organizations (433). Though Gitlin affirms that "the ideas and impulses [of the sixties] remain," his acknowledgment of the long-term efficacy of the movement is considerably more grudging than that of Gosse and others who object to the delimitation of "the Sixties" (xiv). In *The Sixties* the long view of the scholar is obscured by that murk of despair that envelops the once young and committed, still furious activist, for whom the movement was synonymous with the SDS. Finally, however, more objective than many of the memoirs, more personal than most of the histories, *The Sixties* succeeds because of Gitlin's compelling marriage of first-person testimony and scholarly, critical explication.

The journalist Roger Rosenblatt was a twenty-eight-year-old instructor of English and resident dean at Harvard University in "the momentous and shattering spring" of 1969, when three hundred student SDS members and supporters seized the administration building with demands about the university's ROTC programs, its relationship with its urban neighbors, and, of course, its position on the Vietnam War (6). Though avowedly apolitical ("This was the raging 1960s, but I felt no rage about anything, except civil rights. Like most everyone at Harvard, I opposed the war, but that was it. I rarely read a newspaper or watched TV news" [28]), when Harvard invited local police to forcibly remove the students, Rosenblatt was caught, like other junior faculty members, "by age and position, in the middle" of the turmoil of the ensuing weeks (54). In *Coming Apart* (1997), Rosenblatt briefly recounts his youthful apathy about school, his belated engagement with college, his distinguished graduate career at Harvard, and his too easily earned golden boy status as a young faculty member at his alma mater. Respected by students, faculty, and administration, he is a natural appointment to the faculty committee set up to investigate the illicit incidents. Young, articulate, and at least in principle sympathetic to the antiwar advocates, Rosenblatt is perceived as a supporter of the students in the adjudications of the committee. Yet, as he recounts the positions and actions of self-protecting senior faculty, the apathy of the faculty members who are a right-minded "silent majority," and the self-satisfied smugness of the student radicals, Rosenblatt reveals his creeping disaffection with academic life and his privileged students, whose "impulse to tear down traditional structures . . . was not followed up by the creation of new and improved structures" (159, 168). The middle-aged Rosenblatt reinforces the popular perception of the movement against the war as a children's cause, as he blames Harvard's vocal, self-congratulatory youth for "embolden[ing] right-wing America," destroying respect for the military, hamstringing contemporary foreign policy, evoking political correctness, and undermining liberal values (169). By the end of the eventful spring semester and of Rosenblatt's account of his crisis of conscience, the naïve, young teacher has given up on Harvard, an academic career, and the youth culture of the 1960s. "Harvard's upheaval," Rosenblatt concludes, "was not simply a typical war of the late 1960s between the radical students and the University officials. It was a deeper and more far-reaching conflict between older and younger sensibilities, between those who believed in institutions and those who wanted to tear them down, between those who were driven by sympathy for individual causes and those who stood with traditional social structures. The eruption . . . was the howl of the baby boom about to come into its own. . . . [It] exposed an entire generational rift and touched upon antagonisms that have not been mended to this day. For the country as a whole, 'fuck authority' would become . . . 'Fuck everybody'" (213). Rosenblatt's memoir, as witnessing by a marginal but engaged participant-observer who recognizes the profound shifting of his allegiances not years later but at the time of his grudging involvement in the era's turbulent events, is a unique, narrowly focused contribution to the genre.

The Vietnam veteran–poet Bill Ehrhart's narrative *Passing Time: Memoir of a Vietnam Veteran against the War* (originally published as *Marking Time*) is also more tightly focused than most, because it is one volume in a trilogy of autobiographical texts, which opens with *Vietnam-Perkasie* (1983) and concludes with *Busted: A Vietnam Veteran in Nixon's America* (1995). *Passing Time* begins with the gradual development of Ehrhart's antiwar sentiments during his post-Vietnam undergraduate years at Swarthmore College in the early 1970s and ends about 1973 with his post-college job as "seagoing janitor" in the engine room of an oil tanker. In the acknowledgments to the paperback edition of *Marking Time*, Ehrhart announces that "this book is not a novel, though you are welcome to read it as such. Except for a few instances where liberties have been taken in order to speed the flow of the narrative or simplify complex events," he continues, "whatever inaccuracies the book contains are errors of recollection or perception, not willful distortion of facts." Ehrhart does not linger over reservations about the reliability of memory that Ayers, Baez, Adler, and Harris confess, but his suggestion that the memoir works as a novel echoes the sensitivity about verisimilitude articulated by those other authors.

Concentrated on a single episode in the eventful tumult of the movement against the war, like *Coming Apart*, and consciously blurring the line between fact and fiction, like *Passing Time/Marking Time* and *Dispatches*, Norman Mailer's 1968 *The Armies of the Night* is the earliest of the personal narratives of the movement, and in many ways the most distinctive. It is, as Adam Garfinkle notes, "the perfect symbol of the fusion of the literary Left and the antiwar movement" (111). Mailer's rollicking, provocative, and typically egoistic tour de force won the National Book Award and the Pulitzer Prize for nonfiction and was welcomed as an exemplar of the "new journalism" of the era. The book—which in its subtitle, *History as a Novel, the Novel as History*, overtly conflates fiction and nonfiction—exemplifies the response of Vietnam-era American authors to the social transformations of the sixties with a new form of writing that combined the conventions and techniques of fiction and journalism. "Agitated by the contemporary crisis of values and energized by technological and scientific innovations," wrote one commentator on the so-called New Journalism in 1976, "many recent works break through the conventional boundaries of the established genres. . . . A new distribution of narrative energy in post–World War II American literature has pushed the traditional novel into the background and brought to prominence new forms of narrative" (Zavarzadeh, vii). Scholars of the nonfiction novel and New Journalism assert that novelists, overwhelmed by the social turmoil of the 1960s, eschewed the traditional novel for experiments with fantasy (Pynchon), myth (Barth, Hawkes), black comedy (Barthelme, Vonnegut), nonfiction (Mailer, Capote), even silence

(Salinger). John Hollowell wrote in 1977 that "the most frequently cited difficulty for writers of fiction was that of defining just what 'social reality' was. Everyday events continually blurred the comfortable distinctions between reality and unreality, between fantasy and fact. In a society so fluid and so elusive, the creation of social realism seemed continually to be upstaged by current events" (5). Therefore, many American writers were attracted by the objectivity of journalism and brought to it the techniques of the realistic novel that gave it its "immediacy": scene-by-scene construction, full recounting of dialogue, third-person point of view, recording of everyday details, gestures, etc. (Wolfe, 31–32). Like the New Journalism of Tom Wolfe, Truman Capote, and Joan Didion, Mailer's decidedly "immediate" account of the 1967 March on the Pentagon reflected the "increasing tendency toward documentary forms, toward personal confession, toward the exploration of public issues" (Hollowell, 10).[6]

The Armies of the Night is Mailer's application of the techniques of the innovative hybrid to writing about the antiwar march that became notorious for the Yippies' attempt to levitate the Pentagon, that five-sided "land of the enemy," the "high church of the corporation" (151, 255); for young protestors' confrontation of equally young, nervous army soldiers with taunts to join them as they placed photogenic flowers in the barrels of their rifles; for propelling the federal government "for the first time since the Bonus March of 1932" to order "its armed forces to protect the nation's capital against Americans" (Anderson, 178). In *The Armies of the Night*, as both actor in and contemporary analyst of the march, Mailer jauntily places himself— "an eyewitness who is a participant but not a vested partisan"—literally and metaphorically at the front of the cavalcade, claiming that only such a "comic hero," a "notable," can interpret such an ambiguous event (67).

The book begins with Mailer's drunken, obscene speech at a Thursday evening pre-march rally in D.C., where the "Beast," the "wild man" exhorts against "the progressive contamination of all American life in the abscess of Vietnam" (91). On Friday, the hung-over "historian" reports on an initiative led by William Sloane Coffin, Jr., in which a thousand college students propose to return their draft cards to the Department of Justice. "By handing in draft cards," Mailer observes, "these young men were committing their future either to prison, emigration, frustration, or at best, years where everything must be unknown, and that spoke of a readiness to take moral leaps which the acrobat must know when he flies off into space—one has to have faith in one's ability to react with grace en route, one has ultimately, it may be supposed, to believe in some kind of grace" (90). On Saturday, Mailer and his fellow intellectuals Dwight Macdonald and Robert Lowell— "the Critic, the Poet, and the Novelist" (123)—speechify and jostle to retain their honored position at the head of the march from the Lincoln Memorial to the Pentagon. At his first opportunity, Mailer, suggesting that his fame as "embattled aging enfant terrible of the literary world" makes him most useful to the cause in a public role, gets himself arrested and consequently feels "important in a new way" (153, 157). His release after an unexpected night in jail concludes the "history as a novel" that is the bulk of *The Armies of the Night* and allows Mailer's segue to the concluding section, in which the novelist yields to the historian, eschewing first-person testimony for reliance on "all newspaper accounts, eyewitness reports, and historic inductions available." Mailer nonetheless maintains that the ostensibly objective sources he consults are "so incoherent, inaccurate, contradictory, malicious, even based on error that no accurate history is available," that, indeed, the historian's account is more "collective novel" than history—much as he insists that the first document, though written as a novel, is faithful to his memory and therefore a "personal history" (284).

Mailer's sprightly account of the weekend's dramatic events and the disquisition on literary genre that makes *The Armies of the Night* a masterpiece of New Journalism complement his ruminations on the distinctly American sensibility that yielded at once a corrupt, corporation-dominated nation fighting "the unhappiest war America had ever fought" and the young, idealistic crusaders—shock troops in a marijuana haze—assailing the Apocalypse, creating their own inchoate Revolution, staking their claim on an essential American tradition of dissent (205). They are, Mailer notes, affirming the stereotype that the movement activists are children, despite his and his fellow intellectuals' participation in the march: "the spoiled children of a dead de-animalized middle class who had chosen most freely . . . to make an attack and then hold a testament before the most authoritative embodiment of the principle that America was right. . . . So it became a rite of passage for these tender drug-vitiated, jargon-mired children [and] they were forever different in the morning than they had been before the night, which is the meaning of a rite of passage" (311–312).

Throughout, Mailer's tone and his purpose are dramatic and apocalyptic. With the passion and power of its immediacy ("belief was reserved for the revelatory mystery of the happening where you did not know what was going to happen next"), *The Armies of the Night* captures the participants' sense that the stakes could hardly be higher—or more timely. The march is, claims Mailer, "that first major battle of a war which may go on for twenty years," which may, even, "in fifty years . . . loom in our history large as the ghosts of the Union dead" (103, 105). Embroidering and intensifying his colorful account of the weekend and his philosophical assessment of its importance is Mailer's iconoclastic, provocative meditation on the origins and conflicts of the New Left and its relationship with the Old Left and the civil rights movement: "Where the Arab-Israeli war had divided liberals from Old Leftists, and the Negro riots had quenched some of the militancy of the peace group liberals, the New Left was in a state of stimulation, and the hippies, dedicated to every turn of the unexpected, were obviously—as always—ready for anything" (251). *The Armies of the Night*—"the best book about sixties protest," according to Abbie Hoffman—combining as it does Mailer's own brittle, brilliant insights, his technical facility as an accomplished writer, his forty-four-year-old's perspective on the "mad middle class children," and the in-the-minute urgency of his prose, is a unique, powerful personal history of a "quintessentially American event" (47, 241). It complicates form and genre earlier, more egregiously—and more brilliantly—than the rest of this variegated congregation of "participant histories" of the movement to end the Vietnam War.

Forty years after the complex and contentious movement, Mailer's "ambiguity" remains a sagacious characterization, since the triple threat of internal dissension, myth, and the vagaries of memory shadows these authors' perceptions of their lives and times. Yet despite—*and because of*—all of the impediments, these texts—individually and in the aggregate—are an intriguing chapter of the cultural commentary on the Vietnam War and the home front war against it and an important counterpoint to the fictional representations of the lives of the more flamboyant among their participants. "The history of the war without is inseparable from that of the war within," Todd Gitlin reminds us. "Together they *are* America" (Wells, xii).

Again, the formal variations in this group of narratives underscore the broad range of values and attitudes that their authors brought to the movement, and the often heterogeneous experiences that they encountered in their activism. Like the fictitious protagonists Beth in *Home Front*, O'Brien's William Cowling, and Roth's Merry Levov, Joan Baez, Norman Mailer and Margot Adler, for example, were fringe players in the grassroots organizing, strategy sessions, and large-scale public protests that preoccupied acknowledged movement leaders such as Tom Hayden and David Dellinger.

Hayden and Gitlin disdained both the confrontational comedy of Abbie Hoffman and the Yippies and the "loveless barbarians" of the Weather Underground (Hayden, 358). Hoffman understands that Hayden dismisses his political theatrics and is "thankful there was more than one foxhole on our side of the barricades" (199). The male leaders of the movement share only the elegiac or angry perception that the movement ended with their hegemony. They are unable to consider the successes of the peace movement as it evolved into campaigns for women's and minority rights and environmentalism. The movement ended for them when it was no longer about them. The leveling mythology of the sixties presents a monolithic movement of pampered, draft-evading college kids with long hair and dirty jeans. The memoirs of movement participants belie that simplistic reduction as they both reiterate common unifying themes and clarify the significant differences in beliefs and behavior of the pluralistic group.

Pivotal Moments

In his introduction to *The Sixties*, Todd Gitlin explains that his book is "organized around pivotal moments"—"episodes when the movement collided with surrounding forces, or when the movement's own tensions erupted" (4). Gitlin's identification of these profound, memorable incidents delineates one of the recurring themes in reminiscences about the era: significant moments or sudden dramatic insights, watershed events that catapult the authors into the passionate protests of the time (4). In a movement compelled to escalate the drama continually to feed the media beast, spectacular actions prevailed. Echoes of historically profound events, such as the epiphanic townhouse explosion for the Weather Underground, resound throughout these narratives.

For the red diaper babies (Adler, Horowitz, Dellinger), as the moniker implies, the tradition of radical politics and public activism was a family heirloom. A childhood marked by political discussions and parental activism weathered into direct engagement with the pressing issues (civil rights, the Vietnam War, the women's movement) of one's adulthood. In contrast, Gitlin, "a liberal youth, raised by liberal parents," is radicalized by his romantic relationship, at age seventeen, with a red diaper baby (66, 67). "To the more or less liberal youth of my generation, with no family tradition of activism to draw on," Gitlin explains, "red-diaper babies were frequently our first contacts with the forbidden world of wholesale political criticism. . . .

[M]ine was a common experience: The majority of the original New Leftists were not the children of Communist or socialist parents, but sometime
in adolescence were touched, influenced, fascinated, by children who were.
From them the rest of us absorbed, by osmosis, the idea and precedent and
romance of a Left" (67).

Others were persuaded from the center, inspired by the resounding words
of the dazzling young president who challenged them at his inauguration,
now famously, to "ask not what your country can do for you—ask what
you can do for your country." Ron Kovic, for example, begins his memoir
of combat, recuperation, and antiwar activism, *Born on the Fourth of July*,
with JFK's inspirational call to action. Kovic recounts his grief and pain
when, during his final year of high school, the president is assassinated;
he is low-hanging fruit when marine recruiters visit his school and appeal
to the graduating boys to "serve our country like the young president has
asked us to" (74). If the example and inspiration of JFK propel Ron Kovic
into the muscular arms of the military recruiters, the same call to serve
thrusts Abbie Hoffman into the civil rights movement. "Kennedy," Hoffman notes, "heated our passion for change, and when he was killed that
chilly day in November, we mourned. Kennedy often lied to our generation,
but nevertheless he made us believe we could change the course of history.
Inspiration can come from strange and unusual places. In the early sixties,
we thought we were responding to Kennedy's inaugural call to do what we
could for our country" (59). Solipsistic, dramatic James Carroll recounts
many epiphanies, as Cardinal Spellman, Robert F. Kennedy, and even the
pope personally acknowledge his shining vocation. Martin Luther King, Jr.'s
"I Have a Dream" speech is another personal call to action: "I who, since my
childhood . . . had been looking for a way to join my private impulse to a
public crusade, was being shown it. . . . King had stopped being a prophet of
black liberation and had become, in a flash, a figure of my own" (138).

For some of the more radical leftists, Kennedy was too moderate, too
mainstream, too much part of the liberal Democratic Party apparatus that
they rejected. As Dellinger explains, "the difference between our [liberal or
radical] approaches had more to do with whether or not one thought there
was an essentially well-intentioned, genuinely democratic government in
Washington. If one did, one tried to play along with it, even while lobby-
ing and demonstrating for reform on a particular issue of concern" (190).
But for many of the New Left, JFK and the Democrats were—or became—
emblematic of the system that had to be overthrown. As Horowitz notes,

"we were Marxist revolutionaries when we began the New Left, and would have scorned *anyone* who supported Kennedy" (104). For others, the luminous promise of Camelot was the hopeful gleam in the distance, promising a better future for America. Tom Hayden best captures the bright allure of the dream and the tragedy of its sudden dimming. With JFK's assassination, Hayden notes, "[j]ust as we reached for it . . . the age of innocence was ended. . . . The tragic consciousness of the sixties generation began here, and would continue and grow" (103, 114–15).

Again, for many in the New Left, the seeds of anti-Vietnam activism first sprouted in the cotton fields of the Mississippi Delta in the early years of the 1960s, before many Americans had even heard of that small Asian country eight thousand miles to the east. In 1961, in her mid-teens, Jane Alpert, insecure, unpopular—a real-life Merry Levov—fantasizes that she is a freedom rider; and in her imaginary activism, she is, like an American Trung sister, brave, gracious, and independent of her oppressive family.[7] In the summer of 1965, Margot Adler, inspired at Berkeley by the free speech movement and perceiving that "the world was on the cusp of transformation," goes to Mississippi to work in the voter registration campaign (108). Tom Hayden went south, Abbie Hoffman did too; David Horowitz testifies that for him and his fellow New Leftists at Berkeley in the early sixties, "civil rights for Negroes was the cause through which we felt most morally ennobled and politically secure" (108). Gitlin—like Jay Cantor in *Great Neck*—clarifies the extent to which the civil rights movement was incubator, stimulus, and training ground for the later protests against American military involvement in Vietnam: "without the civil rights movement, the beat and Old Left and bohemian enclaves would not have opened into a revived politics. Youth culture might have remained just that—the transitional subculture of the young, a rite of passage on the route to normal adulthood—had it not been for the revolt of black youth, disrupting the American celebration in ways no one had imagined possible. From expressing youthful *difference*, many of the alienated, though hardly all, leaped into a self-conscious sense of *opposition*" (83). Or, as David Harris notes, "the movement that began in Mississippi . . . soon spread all the way to Southeast Asia" (vii).

Flaming crosses in Alabama sparked the fire that ignited the movement, and the flames were fanned by individual experiences and events throughout the era. In *Remembering Heaven's Face*, his 1992 memoir about his service in Vietnam as a conscientious objector and return trips in 1971 and 1989, the poet John Balaban recounts the catalyzing events that transform him from

a vaguely antiwar college student to a Vietnam-bound "diplomat of conscience" in the late sixties (22). Balaban had been "politically aware" since
hearing Martin Luther King, Jr., "speak his famous dream" in D.C. in 1963,
but his commitment to "another, possible society" is secondary to college life
until a Penn State friend is "clubbed, arrested, stripped, and handcuffed naked to a pole" at a 1965 march in Washington that was, Balaban notes, "one of
the first marches to turn ugly" (30). Recounting his friend's reports of police
violence against peaceful protestors—a girl with hanks of hair ripped from
her scalp, a bleeding boy staring "down into an open palm where one of his
eyes lay"—Balaban notes that "none of us was the same after that" (30). Two
years later, in spring 1967, the young scholar, now a half-hearted SDS member
and graduate student at Harvard, happens across a crowd of students protesting Defense Secretary Robert McNamara's Kennedy Institute address.[8] As the
"pleasant and amiable" group of students swarms around McNamara's car after his talk, the "formidable" defense secretary leaps to its roof to address the
crowd, which he berates for its rudeness, and bystander Balaban rankles at
the arrogant reproof: "That moment of public insolence—I mean McNamara's—made me suddenly ashamed of my books, my university, and the safety
of my student deferment. . . . It occurred to me that the only place to learn
anything, to do anything about Vietnam, was in Vietnam" (32–33). And so he
initiates the process that will send him to Vietnam as a conscientious objector,
to "bear witness, not arms," first as an English teacher with the International
Voluntary Services and later, after he is wounded during the Tet Offensive,
with the Committee of Responsibility to Save War-Burned and War-Injured
Children (17). Working in Can Tho, south of Saigon, in January 1968, Balaban
is pressed into medical service when he takes refuge in the regional hospital
during the Tet Offensive. Confronting the peril of Tet, Balaban pragmatically
eschews his commitment "not to take up arms." The violence and Vietnamese
civilian war injuries that he witnesses during the NLF's incursion into the
south are another turning point for Balaban: "I was ashamed to be alive, to
be human, let alone to be an American, to be one of those who had brought
the planes to this sad little country ten thousand miles away. . . . for me, after Tet, no philosophy or ideology—least of all, crusading American democracy—could justify or even remotely explain the slaughter of those civilians.
From that day on, I had no facts or beliefs except for what had been done
to those people" (104–105). When Balaban returns to the United States after
fulfilling his two years of CO duty, he, like so many returning combat veterans, feels out of place in a rapidly transforming nation. Missing Vietnam and

"experiencing revulsion" for America, Balaban returns to Vietnam with his new wife in 1971 on a National Endowment for the Humanities fellowship. In his account of this and the late-1980s return trip that concludes his memoir, Balaban expresses his affection and respect for the Vietnamese and, again like combat veterans, claims the war for those who served in Vietnam: "A total of 8,744,000 Americans—men and women, civilians and military—went to Vietnam. . . . No wonder this war won't go away. It lives in varying degrees of intensity in all those heads" (282). Evoking Michael Herr (who makes a brief appearance in *Remembering Heaven's Face*) and his pronouncement that Vietnam is what we had instead of childhoods (and thereby reinforcing the commonplace that participants in the war and the movement against it were young), Balaban asserts that "I grew up in Vietnam" (187).

In spring 1970, the severely wounded combat veteran Ron Kovic is home from Vietnam and the hospital, recuperating from his injuries, when he learns that the Ohio National Guard has killed student protestors at Kent State University. Admitting that while in-country he vowed retaliation against "the hippies and the draftcard burners" who were protesting the war back home, Kovic recognizes that he now must join "the traitors" (134). Police violence against protestors at the ensuing protest march in D.C. completes Kovic's transformation from warrior to antiwarrior: "I was no longer an observer. . . . I was never going to be the same. The demonstration had stirred something in my mind that would be there from now on" (139–140). Kovic joins Vietnam Veterans Against the War and begins to speak publicly, eventually becoming one of the more visible antiwar combat veterans in the movement (and, of course, the subject of Oliver Stone's 1989 Academy Award–winning film based on *Born on the Fourth of July*).

The Kent State disaster incites fellow veteran Bill Ehrhart's activism as well. "It isn't enough to send us halfway around the world to die, I thought. It isn't enough to turn us loose on Asians. Now you are turning the soldiers loose on your own children. Now you are killing your own children in the streets of America" (88). Overwhelmed by John Filo's now famous photograph of Mary Ann Vecchio crying with incredulous horror over slain student Jeffrey Miller (which Cantor calls "the pietà of Ohio"), Ehrhart breaks down: "And then I knew. It was time. . . . Time to face up to the hard, cold, utterly bitter truth. . . . The war was a horrible mistake, and my beloved country was dying because of it. . . . I did not want my country to die. I had to do something. It was time to stop the war. And I would have to do it"

(88). Ehrhart's dramatic epiphany sends him down Kovic's path: membership in Vietnam Veterans Against the War and fervid antiwar speeches.

In 1965, a vaguely alienated twenty-year-old Bill Ayers has been searching for something important, something relevant, to turn his energies to. Returning home after his brush with the civil rights movement, a disaffected but undirected Ayers contemplates joining the army to "go see about this war" but instead enrolls at the University of Michigan (49). Within a few pages, he has recognized that the "pacific and radical assumptions . . . familiar from the civil rights movement—nonviolent resistance, direct action and moral witness, breaking unjust laws" must be "applied in a challenging new context"—the movement to end the war (51). At a day-long teach-in, "totally mellow" from marijuana, Ayers hears SNCC legend Bob Moses articulate the connections between racism against southern blacks and war against Vietnamese peasants, and he is "transported."[9] Recognizing "with a jolt that I was at that moment standing in the middle of the elusive movement I'd been seeking," Ayers joins SDS "on the spot" (59, 61). A single blaze of insight transforms Ayers from disaffected youth to card-carrying militant. The Democratic Convention in Chicago cranks the wheel again ("from protest to resistance"), and the militant becomes a revolutionary. It is August 1968, and the "rebel troops," energized and frustrated by the painful events of the spring—the Tet Offensive, LBJ's withdrawal from the presidential race, the assassinations of Martin Luther King and Bobby Kennedy, the likely Democratic endorsement of Hubert Humphrey, and Mayor Daley's intransigence in dealing with pre-convention protest planners—are primed to wreak havoc in the streets of Chicago. Daley and his troops are similarly determined to prevent disorder, and, as Ayers asserts, "two Americas faced each other across a smoldering field" (128). The melee that ensues in Lincoln Park on the first night exhilarates Ayers: "In wreckage and celebration I felt, again, reborn" (130). But the stakes have escalated, and in the violence of the next night, (the infamous night on which "the whole world was watching," the night that Bill Ehrhart calls "Combat America"), something cracks, for Bill Ayers and for the movement. "Perhaps this is when the rage got started in the movement, this very night," Ayers conjectures. "I'm not sure, but before this, every meeting, every rally, every demonstration was filled with singing, and afterward the singing stopped. When we opened our mouths now, we could only scream. . . . The apocalypse approached" (Ehrhart, 29; Ayers, 131). Rejecting any critique of an increasingly confrontational movement—"You're hurting your own cause; I agree with your goals, but not your tactics. . . . It's all a problem of communication, really. On and on and on, I'd heard it all before"—Ayers confusedly presents the '68 convention as the point at which the movement turned violent *and* the announcement to the world that the U.S. government has lost the support of its own people *and* a personal moment of "sheer joy and wild relief to be there cherishing every lovely blow, bleeding a bit but neither broken nor murdered" (130–131, 135). Fourteen months later, with their return to Chicago for the Days of Rage, Ayers and his fellow Weather Underground members began to push America ever closer to that apocalypse: Yeats's "rough beast, its hour come round at last," not slouching, but screeching "toward Bethlehem to be born."

The narrative emphasis on pivotal moments that so many of these testimonies share captures the heady and headlong drama of the era and focuses the young protagonists' blinding epiphanies, but it arises from—and reinforces—that alluring but inaccurate appropriation of the myth of the sixties as a brief, glorious, youthful crusade derailed by cynicism and violence. Gitlin, for instance, asserts dramatically and definitively that the violence at the December 1969 Rolling Stones' Altamont concert (which "already felt like death") "burst the bubble of youth culture's illusions about itself" (406). Further, that "what Altamont was for the counterculture, the townhouse [explosion of March 1970] was for the student movement: the splattering rage of the 'death culture' lodged in the very heart of the 'life force'" (408). And that with the August 1970 bombing that killed a University of Wisconsin graduate student "the movement knew sin" (407). Yet the fact that the Kent State killings call Kovic and Ehrhart to home front action belies the claim by commentators such as historian James Miller that Kent State was "the death knell for the Movement" (310). Recent scholarship that affirms the post-sixties progress in environmental awareness and in rights for women, blacks, gays and lesbians, and ethnic minorities that evolved from the energy and organization of the movement similarly complicates the tidy, appealing mythology of the 1960s as an exhilarating, doomed decade, a transitory moment in Technicolor time.

Surrounded by Friends

These witnesses, inspired so often to activism by a powerful epiphany, remained in the movement for less distinct—and, ironically, less political—

reasons. Often frustrated by the failure of marches and rallies to end the war, sometimes caught up in the internal battles of an officially leaderless, often anarchic movement, occasionally indicted for crimes and driven underground, they remained dedicated and loyal to the struggle for a new society. Beyond the commitment to participatory democracy, an end to racism in Alabama and Vietnam, a desire for a more just and benevolent society, they, like their fictional counterparts, found in SDS and SNCC and other organized groups an affirmation and acceptance—a community—otherwise missing from their disaffected lives. In his preface to the 1993 edition of *The Sixties*, Todd Gitlin counters conservative critics of the individualistic impulses of "Sixties rebellion": "*the other side* of the counterculture," he insists, "was communitarian and . . . spiritual, a longing for group experience that would transcend the limits of the individual ego" (xix; emphasis mine). Bill Ayers recounts the attractiveness of the movement to newcomers in late 1967, as national demonstrations against the war became larger and more visible. "People floated into the movement now for a thousand reasons," he notes, "resistance to the war and the draft, certainly, to the gathering torment, and in opposition as well to segregation and racism, the lengthening American nightmare. People joined for love, too, because liberation was in the air and the idea of freedom was in full flood. . . . Everything was on the agenda now: justice and peace, education and culture and spirituality, work, sexuality, gender, art. The old god failed and the old truths left the world, and we asked: How shall I live?" (111–112).

The movement leaders among these authors do not much consider their motivations for organized mass activism—beyond the campaign to change America (and, though of course they do not admit this, acquisition of the perquisites of power and celebrity). Horowitz, Hayden, Hoffman, Mailer, Dellinger, Berrigan—none writes about the emotional or interpersonal dimensions of his movement activism. The war veterans (and Gitlin, who describes the early SDS as a "surrogate family"), interestingly, do—perhaps because their post-military, later-in-life, reluctant acceptance of their conversion to the cause is more emotional than intellectual (107).

When Ron Kovic, propelled to action by Kent State, rolls his wheelchair to Washington for the next massive march with the "traitors," he is struck by "the warmth" of the "weird carnival," the "feeling that we were all together in a very important place" (137).[10] And after the police attack the crowd, "flailing their clubs, smashing skulls," Kovic understands that he is changed forever. "There was a togetherness, just as there had been in Vietnam, but it was a togetherness of a different kind of people and for a much different reason. In the war we were killing and maiming people. In Washington on that Saturday afternoon in May we were trying to heal them and set them free" (139, 140). Two years later, when he joins Vietnam Veterans Against the War after the Dewey Canyon III Operation in D.C., Kovic again feels that his life has changed: "the loneliness seemed to vanish. I was surrounded by friends" (147). When Bill Ehrhart's Kent State epiphany propels him to a campus rally—wondering whether he is betraying his war buddies by consorting with "peaceniks"—he is impressed by the "tremendous unity, a sense of common purpose, a ferocious energy searching for constructive alternatives and solutions" (89, 90). Kovic and Ehrhart embrace the sense of community they discover in the movement, but even for them the camaraderie is more a happy accident than a motivation for signing on. For the women in the movement, however, who will learn by the mid-1970s in their own movement for equality that the personal is political, part of the attraction of the antiwar movement is that the political is personal.

Margot Adler was a freshman at the University of California at Berkeley in late September 1964 when the free speech movement (FSM) ignited. At first just watching student protests against the university's restrictive policies against student organizations, Adler is "excited by the growing sense of community among the protestors. . . . There was a feeling of instant community and internal power" (83). Soon active in the FSM, Adler has been arrested and jailed by December, and she is jubilant when Berkeley faculty vote to support students' demands for freedom of political speech: "the FSM gave me an experience of a new kind of freedom, not to speak, to act, or to buy, but to claim the power to come together with others in the community to transform and to change. . . . The Free Speech Movement gave me and many others a sense of personal power and control over our lives" (100–101). Terry Anderson quotes SNCC leader Mary King (who married Dennis Sweeney, of Harris's *Dreams Die Hard*), who wrote about the "intense feeling of interdependence" and "'spirit of comradeship' that became part of the sixties generation" (85), and Casey Hayden (Tom's wife, briefly), who recalls that "the movement 'was everything: home and family . . . love and a reason to live. . . . It was a holy time'" (86). Sara Evans echoes the spiritual metaphor: "Almost a mystical term, 'the movement' implied an experience, a sense of community and common purpose" (102).

For most of these women, this sense of community is a positive value, a journey toward a fuller, more enriched life. For Jane Alpert, however, the warm embrace of the movement is an escape from an unhappy childhood and adolescence and a desperate need for the affirmation of one man. Alpert has graduated from Swarthmore (a few years before Ehrhart's stint there) and is working as an editor at Cambridge University Press and taking graduate classes at Columbia when she meets Sam Melville, who works for a radical underground newspaper. She had been politically active locally in college and had gone to New York for the April 1967 Mobe rally in Central Park. But Alpert is merely an observer in the confrontation at Columbia in the spring of 1968, and she is alienated from the sex, drugs, and rock and roll movement: "In my straight job, straight clothes, straight apartment, I felt far away from them" (102). Only under the political and sexual tutelage of Sam Melville is Alpert radicalized. Reviewing her adolescent rebellion against her parents and her early incipient activism, Alpert avers in *Growing Up Underground* that "as much as my insecurity made me ripe for dependency on a man like Sam, my background and the state of the nation made me (and thousands of others my age) receptive to the ideas of the New Left. . . . The combination of sexual love and radical ideology . . . consumed me" (122, 124).

By summer 1969, Alpert, Melville, and their two closest radical friends have decided that they must escalate their activism and "smash a hole in the wall of imperialism" with daring and dynamite (175). Though she has reservations about the group's turn to violence, Alpert, ever more desperate to keep the wandering Sam's interest, convinces herself that her second thoughts are cowardice. She cannot bear the prospect of losing her lover or her cadre: "I came to think of the four of us as a family," Alpert writes. "At times we seemed a single consciousness. . . . I had never felt less alone" (175, 176). Alpert and her cohorts continue their bombing of banks and corporate offices in New York through the fall of 1969. Caught, eventually, by the FBI and released on bail, Alpert flees underground, with other radicals, after the March 1970 townhouse explosion. The final third of her memoir recounts her life on the run and her increasing involvement with the embryonic women's movement. Alpert recounts a long, convoluted story about feminist Robin Morgan, Catonsville 9 defendant Mary Moylan, and "weatherwoman" Kathy Boudin that leads her to wonder (with unusual insight) whether women in the movement were "interested in bombing buildings only when the men we slept with were urging us on" (275). She reads Shulamith Firestone's 1970 polemic, *The Dialectic of Sex*, which argues that "politico women," desperate for "male approval," are unable to evolve to a truly radical politics, and admits that "nearly every risk I'd ever taken had been urged on me by a man" (298). Alpert's feminism contributes to her renunciation of the left (for which, in her 1981 memoir, she expresses regret), her decision after more than four years underground to turn herself in, and her subsequent two-year prison sentence. Her struggle with the apparently incompatible goals of the antiwar movement and the inchoate women's movement sounds another recurring theme in these texts, as in the movement novels—namely, the role of women in the movement.

Girls Say No

At the beginning of the introduction to *Heretic's Heart*, Margot Adler, expressing the familiar perception that the sixties have been ill-served in contemporary commentary on the era, underscores the difference between her memories of the period and those presented by autobiographical accounts "by men of a certain fame" (ix). "I look back on the sixties differently," Adler writes. "Although I was part of many of the defining political events of the period . . . by position and gender I was never considered part of the dominant story. Accounts of the sixties by women are rare and our vision is somewhat different" (ix–x).[11] Later Adler describes her early recognition that women in the free speech movement were relegated to traditionally female tasks and summarizes the assertion by FSM leader and Communist Party member Bettina Aptheker, at a 1984 FSM reunion, that because most of the commentary on the sixties had been written by men, "our history of that era is partial." It is because of male appropriation of the history of the New Left, Aptheker continues, that "histories have emphasized power and control, whereas the women's stories might have emphasized the dailyness of struggle, connection, and the long slow process of meaningful change" (103). Though these insights glance at the complicated personal and political intersections between the antiwar movement and the incipient women's movement, Adler's own memoir—like Alpert's—fails to explore the vexing relationship and is therefore not the female perspective on the movement that she calls for. Neither does Joan Baez present any particular insight into women's experiences in the movement.[12] Yet as a group the memoirs of the "antiwar veterans" yield important, if inchoate, insights into women's participation in the movement and the movement's crucial significance to the mid-1970s women's movement that would evolve from it (Hoffman, 125).

Though women's antiwar groups such as Women Strike for Peace and Another Mother for Peace were active throughout the 1960s, in the early

years of the decade most young New Left activists were primarily committed to civil rights for African Americans and, later in the decade, to the
fight to end the war in Vietnam. Like nineteenth-century women who dedicated themselves to the abolitionist movement, New Left women, if they
were conscious of sexual politics at all, subsumed their own concerns to the
larger fight for a peaceful society promising equality for all. (Recall, from
Making Peace and *The Laws of Our Fathers*, for example, that young women
encouraged draft-resisting brothers by sporting buttons that promised that
"Girls Say Yes to Boys Who Say No.")[13] In retrospect, however, traces of
an incipient movement for women's liberation are apparent throughout the
era—and throughout these testimonies.

Late in 1964 and again in 1965 Mary King and Casey Hayden circulated
position papers criticizing women's second-class status in SNCC and the
SDS, and a women's-only workshop was convened at the December 1965
SDS conference. SDS, according to member Todd Gitlin, was "a young boys'
network," and women recognized increasingly that "men sought them out,
recruited them, took them seriously, honored their intelligence—then subtly demoted them to girlfriends, wives, note-takers, coffeemakers" (367).
Moderate women founded the National Organization for Women in 1966
and marched in the first all-female antiwar demonstration in Washington,
D.C., in January 1968. More radical women (which Gitlin calls "an early
phalanx of the women's liberation movement") traveled to Atlantic City
from the Chicago Democratic Convention in summer 1968 to protest the
Miss America Pageant as the symbol of women's enslavement by "ludicrous
beauty standards" (Gitlin, 342; qtd. in Anderson, 228–229). By early 1969,
as Anderson documents, "female activists discussed whether they should
remain in the male-dominated new left and antiwar movement or split and
form their own movement" (314–315).

The year 1970 brought women's consciousness-raising groups, the collective manifesto *Sisterhood Is Powerful*, and the NOW-sponsored Women's
Strike for Equality, a national women's march down New York City's Fifth
Avenue to celebrate the fiftieth anniversary of the Nineteenth Amendment and to call for women's rights. The campaign to pass an Equal Rights
Amendment, Title IX, the Equal Employment Opportunity Act, and the *Roe
v. Wade* Supreme Court decision guaranteeing reproductive rights followed
in the early 1970s. Gitlin, whose long, detailed account of the rise and fall of
the New Left in *The Sixties* continually emphasizes his disappointment with
the youth movement's turn toward violence and cultural anarchy, attributes

the gradual defection of New Left women to their own liberation movement not merely to the increasing radicalization of the times, but to the slow disintegration of the SDS and the student movement. "Sisterhood was powerful," he notes, "partly because movement brotherhood was not. . . . By 1969, the male-run movement was in convulsions, of which the women's movement was as much a product as a cause. . . . From the embers of the old movement, a new one rose scorching—sisterly, factional, wild, egomaniacal, furious . . . the voice of millions of women, living survivors of the death and transfiguration of the New Left" (Gitlin, 373–376).

Most histories of the movement and many of the novels and memoirs concede that women were relegated to the margins by young, macho male leaders. "There was sexism and discrimination within the movement," admits Bernadine Dohrn, one of the few acknowledged women leaders in movement organizations; "women . . . were leaders in the sense of being local and campus and community organizers and speakers, but it was always the men who were officers and who held official positions and gave the big debate speeches" (233). In *The Wars We Took to Vietnam*, the literary scholar Milton J. Bates suggests that "young men and women who shared the same goals, worked side by side, and even dressed alike were still separated by an abyss of misunderstanding" (136). Alpert and Adler and Dohrn know that the movement underestimated and eventually alienated its sisters; the historians know it too. The movement men? Sometimes. Sort of.[14]

In *Fugitive Days*, Dohrn's husband includes in his cursory review of the events of the riotous year of 1968 two inaccurate sentences about the Miss America bra-burning protest.[15] He quotes a long passage from the resolution of the women's workshop of the '67 SDS convention, but responds to the women's call for full participation in movement work with a dismissive "chicks in charge . . . you've got to love it." Further, he undercuts his predictable my-best-friends-are-women argument with the confession that, for him, relationships with women were always finally about sex. The excitable young Billy Ayers's gratitude that he is "alive in such a world, so many different women, so much variety" is not much tempered by the older, ostensibly wiser and more mature Bill Ayers (104–105, 68).

Post-Vietnam college and antiwar activism are largely about easy sex for Bill Ehrhart as well, whose memoirs reveal the male left's dismissal of women. Ehrhart riffs on familiar combat narrative themes: the in-country Dear John letter from his high school sweetheart; the old war buddy Gerry, whose wife, when Ehrhart visits, is "polite but distant." "She's, well, just a little jealous of you," Gerry assures Ehrhart; "she knows how close we were. . . . Vietnam's a whole part of my life that she wasn't a part of and can't ever be a part of. I think she sort of resents that, that's all, that you understand it and she doesn't"[16] (193). In *Passing Time*, Ehrhart expresses no interest in and certainly no insight about women in the movement. Horowitz is similarly indifferent and inordinately clueless. When he returns to Berkeley from Europe in early 1968, he is attracted by the new, flamboyant counterculture, its tie-dyed clothes and peace symbols, and the "air of a medieval pastoral" promising him that "a new world is possible." But for Horowitz, bra-less women signify only "a protest whose immediate effect was to raise the libidinal pulses of everyday life" (157). In his *Autobiography*, Abbie Hoffman glibly acknowledges that in "the hippie movement . . . sexist attitudes . . . prevailed. Women beaded, cooked, and screwed their way through the era while their 'old men' made the decisions" (99). More important, Hoffman agrees with Gitlin, who notes that "women had been the cement of the male-run movement; their desertion into their own circles completed the dissolution of the old boys' clan" (375). For Hoffman, too, the growth of the women's movement was the death knell for the antiwar movement: "once the idea of women's liberation was on the table for discussion, there was no way the seating order could remain the same or be quickly rearranged. Something had to give" (268). Near the end of the book, labeling himself a "macho feminist," Hoffman welcomes the changes in sex roles that the revolution demands but admits, "I do tend to see women as sex objects first" (281).

Tom Hayden's two comments, in his five-hundred-page memoir, about sexual politics in the movement are his superfluous acknowledgment that the language in the Port Huron Statement is sexist and his admission that "the movement was a chauvinist's paradise, the positions of power were dominated primarily by men, and the opportunities for unequal sexual liaisons were legion" (107–108). Apparently Hayden seized that amatory opportunity. In 1970, with the Chicago 7 guilty verdict on appeal, Hayden, frustrated by a deteriorating movement, retreated with his girlfriend to a small Berkeley commune, the Red Family. Hayden admits that for him the then popular group self-criticism meetings, inflicted largely an egoistic men, were "torture sessions" (421). Acknowledging his fame, his visibility in the movement, and his political interests, Hayden describes his eviction from the commune for being "an oppressive male chauvinist," and an obviously resentful Hayden, sans girlfriend, leaves Berkeley and its "radical claustrophobia. . . . The notorious New Left leader and national security threat alone in a world of hurt" (425).

In early 1970, the radical feminist Robin Morgan and Jane Alpert, the secretary of the New York underground newspaper *Rat Subterranean News*, took over the paper for a special issue on women (and later commandeered *Rat* altogether). In her polemic for it titled "Goodbye to All That," Morgan, expanding on Marge Piercy's invective of a year earlier, "The Grand Coolie Damn," attacks the sexism of the New Left and calls for women to unite for the "only real alternative: to seize our own power into our own hands, all women, separate and together, and make the Revolution the way it must be made—no priorities this time, no suffering group told to wait until after" (506). "Goodbye, goodbye forever, counterfeit Left," Morgan's manifesto concludes. ". . . We are rising with a fury older and potentially greater than any force in history, and this time we will be free or no one will survive. Power to all the people or to none" (507).

Though Morgan's call for a feminist revolution did not inspire all activist women to declare war on their movement brothers, it does reveal (and these memoirs underscore) many radical women's resentment and frustration with the male-dominated New Left. As the antiwar movement waned, young women radicalized by it united to change their lives and American society dramatically and forever. As the Berkeley activist Ruth Rosen notes in the 1990 documentary film *Berkeley in the '60s*, "one of the ways that the women's movement is the logical—and maybe even the inevitable—conclusion of the Sixties is that throughout the Sixties we were trying to imagine how to live differently, how to change the world. And the women's movement took much from the civil rights movement, from the New Left, from the antiwar movement, but we brought it home. We brought it into the kitchen. We brought it into the bedroom. We brought it into the most personal and intimate aspects of people's lives. It was hard to deny there. It was hard to ignore those issues." As Terry Anderson states unequivocally, "women's liberation was the most successful social movement of the sixties—and of American history" (421).

Morgan's call for "all male leadership out of the Left . . . whether through men stepping down or through women seizing the helm" was only one of the nails in the coffin of the male and SDS-dominated movement (506). Gradual U.S. withdrawal from the war in Vietnam, moderate leftists' repudiation of the increasing violence of the movement, and (some would say) the end of the draft contributed to its disintegration or metamorphosis (depending on your point of view) into more varied campaigns. However, as these memoirs make clear, the seeds of the chaotic ending of the formal movement were there from the very beginning. Indeed, acknowledgment of and struggles with the conflicting agendas, disparate strategies, and incompatible personalities of the movement are notable themes in the participants' testimonies.

Napalmed by Vietnam

The controversies, factions, and manifestations of anarchy are complex and varied; the intensifying feminism of the early 1970s was merely one of many intricate movement struggles. Radical black civil rights leaders ejected white activists from their movement in 1965 and 1966, even as they faced internal conflicts between the nonviolent principles of Martin Luther King and the more militant position of the Black Panther Party and Malcolm X that Cantor chronicles in *Great Neck*. The youthful New Left rejected the Old Left as too liberal, too committed to working within the system, while the Old Left damned the New Left as insufficiently anti-Communist. Within the New Left, significant (often generational) rifts developed between moderate leftists like the early SDS and groups—most famously exemplified by the Weather Underground—determined to escalate the movement, in the popular slogan of the time, "from protest to resistance." Serious radicals dismissed the counterculture's playful rebellion as frivolity that undermined the seriousness of the struggle and alienated potentially sympathetic American citizens. Margot Adler writes that "already in 1965 there were tensions emerging between the cultural and political wings of the radical movement. Today we tend to lump many aspects of the sixties together . . . but a continuing battle between the 'hippies,' on the one side, and the 'politicos,' on the other, defined much of the era" (110–111). From its beginnings, the movement, founded on the principles of participatory democracy, was, by definition, nonhierarchical and leaderless; and most historians agree that it was at once energized and compromised by its philosophical rejection of bureaucratic structures. As Melvin Small notes, "the amorphous, decentralized, and often anarchic nature of the movement was both its strength and its weakness. . . . [B]ecause the coalitions included people and organizations with dramatically different long-range strategies and short-range tactical preferences, a good deal of the movement's strength was dissipated in internecine political warfare" (4).

Many of the participant histories comment on the movement's internal problems, each of their interpretations determined, of course, by their authors' personal experiences. Jane Alpert's activism begins relatively late, in

1968; by then, she recognizes, "we radicals had nothing that could be called an army, no national unity or organization. Exhausted from demonstrations, trials, police brutality, and jailings, many leftists had already abandoned the cause for yoga, meditation, communes in Vermont and California, religious groups, or simply a hobo existence from city to city and job to job" (242). Tom Hayden, from his perspective as the author of the Port Huron Statement and as the celebrity his high-profile activities made him, claims to have understood the need for—and problems with—the "'anti-leader' organization" from the beginning (44). "There was a chronic competition and rivalry over status and power that few leaders survived, as if beneath the egalitarian rhetoric there was a resentment of anyone with significant authority," a defensive Hayden writes, ". . . even if that authority was based on achievement or could be useful in communicating with the media. Equally troubling was the near impossibility of giving such spontaneous movements a competent administrative framework, which resulted in a lack of stability and permanence" (44–45). David Dellinger blames Hayden (and Gitlin) for one of the schisms within the SDS, between the members who were committed single-mindedly to working to end the war in Vietnam and Hayden and others who turned to grassroots community organizing (through SDS's Economic Research and Action Project [ERAP]) "for economic and political changes that would . . . 'end the seventh war from now'" (201). These and other internecine conflicts within the SDS, claims Dellinger, manifested a "gradually developing competitive sectarianism that spread like a virus until it finally caused the entire organization to break up into rival vanguard groups at its June 1969 national convention [the Weather Underground coup d'état]" (201).

Abbie Hoffman acknowledges Hayden as a central figure as well, describing their disagreements as fellow Chicago 7 defendants. "In its way," Hoffman concedes, after criticizing Hayden for his arrogance (and betraying more than a little arrogance of his own), "the split served to keep the whole show afloat. Like perfectly balanced see-saw mates, the difference afforded us the ability to reach different kinds of people, and we became a kind of political version of the Beatles, each framing the events from his own perspective" (201). By 1970, Hayden notes sadly, "much of the movement had disintegrated from the 'beloved community' of the early SNCC to a Dostoyevskian nightmare. Blacks and whites had little in common. Women warred against the dominance of men. Declining structures like the Mobilization were filled with inbred quarrels over slogans and logistics; the newer radical structures were either small, communal groups or

246

invisible underground networks" (419). Hayden gets the final word on this issue because he understands (as the historians do in a way that some of the memoirists and most of the contrarians do not) that the Vietnam War was not the impetus for the early activists' vision for a new American society but the agent of what they consider to be the miscarriage of that vision. "The movement that had begun on the back roads of Mississippi saw its dreams napalmed by Vietnam," Hayden eulogizes (324). Fourteen years later, in a 2002 retrospective titled "The Port Huron Statement at 40," Hayden reiterates that "the visionary promise of Port Huron died on a battlefield that triggered a radical polarization instead of reform at home."

Sons of the Sons of Liberty

Each of the voices here grapples with the values and methods, the victories and sins, the disintegration and contemporary reputation of the movement. Some, such as Daniel Berrigan, Margot Adler, Joan Baez, Dave Dellinger, and Tom Hayden, affirm the fundamental efficacy of the movement while expressing ambivalence about the violence of the Weather Underground and other militant organizations or the irreverent lunacy of the Yippies. Others, most notably David Horowitz and Adam Garfinkle and to a lesser extent Roger Rosenblatt, are "second-thoughters" whose commentaries are an indictment of the movement and its era. Many—Terry Anderson, David Harris, Jane Alpert, James Miller, and, of course, Bill Ayers—enthusiastically embrace and in later life affirm the movement and its achievements. But whether unequivocally proud of their antiwar activism, ambivalent about their participation in the controversial movement, or decidedly regretful about it, each recognizes and acknowledges that the movement is part of a long, distinguished tradition of dissent and civil disobedience in American public life.

In 1960, Abbie Hoffman, a budding activist representing the American Civil Liberties Union, speaks to a group of Massachusetts American Legion members and local farmers in a protest of the showing of a House Un-American Activities Committee documentary film, *Operation Abolition*, which asserted that HUAC critics were communist fellow travelers. After the film and Hoffman's critique of it, the Legionnaires attack the inchoate revolutionary, who has recently discovered that he has "an ability to make outrage contagious," questioning his belief in God and his attitudes toward racial equality (48). But when one of the farmers supports Hoffman's review of the "factual errors" in the film, a proud dissident is born: "I fell in love with America that night," Hoffman proclaims. "Cornfields. Town meetings. Niagara Falls. . . . America was built by people who wanted to change things. It was founded on strong principles. I saw myself as a Son of Liberty riding through the night, sounding the alarm" (49). Heckled by pro-war construction workers, harassed by the FBI, dismissed as un-American by U.S. presidents, the New Left partisans defiantly and proudly claim their place in the long valiant line of American revolutionaries.

Toward the end of *Passing Time*, Bill Ehrhart attempts to convince his combat buddy that the war is a mistake, that they were wrong to participate in it. "We were on the wrong side, Gerry," Ehrhart sputters angrily. "We were the Redcoats" (200). When Gerry asks Bill how he plans to stop "the lunatics in Washington," Ehrhart admits that he doesn't know, but he summons the legacy of the first American patriots: "Think about guys like Thomas Paine and Patrick Henry. They'd be rolling over in their graves if they could see what we've done to Vietnam in the name of life, liberty, and the pursuit of happiness. What we've done to our own country" (200–201). Throughout *Fugitive Days*, Bill Ayers invokes the principles and patriots of the Revolution as the model for a new American insurrection. The young high school student reads Rousseau and Marx—and Thoreau, who "had argued in opposition to slavery and colonial wars, urging his fellow citizens to break unjust laws" (34). The lawless architects of the Days of Rage justify their violent actions by proclaiming that "we were freedom fighters, and we came to it in the spirit of John Brown and Nat Turner, in the name of liberty. We knew that others would brand us criminals . . . but they were wrong" (190). At the end of his story, the middle-aged Ayers, assessing American society at the dawn of the twenty-first century and admitting that "the important questions . . . remain unsettled," ruefully reminds us that "the democratic project is always a contested space in America, forever confronting opposition, resistance, and crisis" (285).

Norman Mailer, whose ingenious account of the march on the Pentagon is laced with grandiloquent philosophical pronouncements about the promise—and the failures—of America, invokes the American tradition of dissent throughout *The Armies of the Night*. The New Left, Mailer proposes, arose from the injustices of America and directed its "attention toward an American revolution; of what it might consist was another matter—one's idea of a better existence would be found or not found in the context of the revolution" (122). For Mailer, the October 1967 march is itself reminiscent of that other great domestic conflagration, and so he imagines that "in fifty years the day may loom in our history large as the ghosts of the Union dead" and wonders whether the secretary of defense sees the young night-time crowd camped on the Mall and notes that their campfires "cannot be unreminiscent of other campfires in Washington and Virginia little more than a century ago" (105, 293).[17] At the end of *The Armies of the Night*, as the morning dawns, Mailer rhapsodizes about the march as a rite of passage for a new American generation, a restive commencement ceremony that evokes "all the great American rites of passage when men and women man-acled themselves to a lost and painful principle and survived a day, a night, a week, a month, a year, a celebration of Thanksgiving—the country had been founded on a rite of passage. . . . each generation of Americans had forged their own rite, in the forest of the Alleghenies and the Adirondacks, at Valley Forge . . . at Gettysburg, the Alamo . . . Normandy" (311).

In the evaluative epilogue of *Reunion*, Tom Hayden evokes the spirit of American dissidence as well. He asserts that "the goal of the sixties was, in a sense, the completion of the vision of the early revolutionaries and aboli-tionists, for Tom Paine and Frederick Douglass wanted even more than the Bill of Rights or Emancipation Proclamation. True democrats, they wanted the fulfillment of the American promise through a different quality of rela-tions between people, between government and governed, a participatory democracy within a genuinely human community" (504).

The historians, with their apprehension of tradition and history, under-standably accede to—but complicate—the participants' evocation of a noble American past. Terry Anderson introduces and concludes his comprehen-sive history of the movement with the unqualified acknowledgment that "the activists succeeded in bringing about a sea change, a different America. Like their predecessors during the Jacksonian period, progressive era, and 1930s, sixties activists were provoked by the inconsistencies between the Founding Fathers' noble ideals and the disappointing reality for many citizens. . . . The debate . . . asks the central question of this democracy: What is the meaning of 'America'? Like reformers before, provoking a reevaluation of that ques-tion was the most significant legacy of the movement and the sixties" (423).

Adam Garfinkle offers the most sustained analysis of the roots of the movement in what he calls the "adversary culture" of the United States. The multifarious movement, Garfinkle argues, arose from the traditional intel-lectual frameworks of religious pacifism, liberal peace activism, and radical leftism, each of which emerged in the civil rights movement and the "birth of the nuclear age" to inspire the disaffected youth of the Vietnam generation

(42). For Garfinkle, the movement was the result, not of the Vietnam War and impassioned rejection of it, but of a confluence of cultural factors that formed "a unique generational personality" (46). "The Vietnam generation," Garfinkle asserts, "seems to have been predisposed to protest, to see official malfeasance, and to generate and then be lured by the enticements of the counterculture. . . . Had not civil rights and then Vietnam lit the fire, no doubt something else would have" (49).

Todd Gitlin is skeptical as well, though about the country rather than the protestors. He moves over time from a recognition that the early SDS was "steeped in a most traditional American individualism, especially the utopian edge of it expressed in the mid-nineteenth century middle-class transcendentalism of Emerson and Whitman," to the later fear that "the [movement intellectuals'] quest for American roots [was] forced and sentimental." By 1968 or so, he observes, "it seemed that the decent traditions were as good as dead in the American breast. America stood damned by original sins, compounded by an impressive history of imperial expeditions" (107, 257). Compare David Horowitz's unsurprising inversion of the militants' claim of traditional patriotism. Horowitz unearths his recantation of his acceptance of the New Left from the very hallowed ground that his former comrades arrogate. Social injustice, Horowitz explains, arises from human—not institutional—flaws, and controlling humanity requires "institutions of constraint": "It was this perspective—conservative in its essence—that had inspired the creators of the American republic. In the *Federalist Papers*, Madison had defended the American idea of liberty by means of checks and balances as a design to thwart the leveling agendas of the Left. . . . The conservatism I had arrived at," Horowitz continues, "could be expressed in a single patriotic idea: The revolutionary failures of the Twentieth Century had demonstrated the wisdom of the American founding, and validated its tenets: private property, individual rights, and a limited state" (397). And the historian Andrew Wiest emphasizes the negative connotations of the Movement's ancestry when, in *The Vietnam War, 1956–1975*, he twice notes that "the volatile mixture of Vietnam, the counter culture, and the Civil Rights Movement led to a near breakdown in the American body politic. In 1968, amid a spate of riots and assassinations, many observers thought that the United States was on the brink of a second American Revolution" (7).

Much as they acknowledge not only the energy and passion but the internal rancor and consequent collapse of the movement, both the memoirists and the historians recognize that the movement was heir at once to a significant tradition of resistance in American life and to the repudiation of that tradition. Nonetheless, most participants and commentators accept that, whether it was America's most audacious experiment in democracy or the nadir of American democracy, the movement against the war—what Michael Herr in *Dispatches* calls "the other extreme of the same theater"— was "a fight for the soul of America" (6; Gitlin, Foreword, xvii). The memoirs by the peace activists of the 1960s both reflect and foster the myths, misapprehensions, and disagreements about the legacy of the movement that created them: that it was birthed and nurtured by idealistic young adults on college campuses; that it died definitively and violently not long after the end of the decade that spawned it. Right-wing David Horowitz's fury, unabashed Bill Ayers's steadfastness, Tom Hayden's sorrow, Todd Gitlin's disappointment—the personal testimonies of the participants offer an array of responses to America's most sustained experiment in mass protest.

As the September 2001 responses to Bill Ayers's *Fugitive Days* portended, today the escalating unpopularity of another apparently misguided military quagmire, the war in Iraq, highlights the ongoing argument about the legacy of the Vietnam antiwar movement. There is little disagreement that the massive antiwar demonstrations of the waning years of the Vietnam War dissuaded one beleaguered U.S. president from seeking a second term and compelled a subsequent, paranoid commander-in-chief to launch the domestic espionage program that would topple his presidency and append the postscript "-gate" to every public national scandal since. And American popular culture was permanently transformed by the counterculture's challenge to mid-twentieth-century notions of propriety, parental authority, and personal responsibility.

So, whether the bequests of the antiwar movement are a more inclusive, enlightened society or a vulgar, violent, narcissistic culture is an argument that persists. As the historian and sixties SDS member Maurice Isserman notes in a March 2007 essay about the reinvigoration of the SDS on contemporary college campuses, "for the right, the [sixties] is often used as shorthand source for all that went wrong in the United States toward the end of the 20th century. For the left, it continues to seem an era of heroic political possibilities, partially realized, mostly lost. The right would like to obliterate the 60s; the left (or some on the left, anyway) would like to relive them" (B10). If the substance of the ongoing legacy of the 1960s remains controversial and debatable, few would argue that contemporary America was transformed by the social movements that the 1960s introduced.

Chapter Six

People Singing a Sad Song: Vietnamese Exiles in American Literature

The foreign-born, the exotically raised Third World immigrant . . . can be as American as any steerage passenger from Ireland, Italy, or the Russian Pale. . . . I can be a brash and raucous homesteader, Huck Finn and Woman Warrior, on the unclaimed plains of American literature.
—Bharati Mukherjee

I am going away . . . to an unknown country where I shall have no past and no name, and where I shall be born again with a new face and an untried heart.
—Collette

War has no beginning and no end. It crosses oceans like a splintered boat filled with people singing a sad song.
—lê thi diem thúy, *The Gangster We Are All Looking For*

I thought that for the rest of our lifetimes, wherever we go, we will find Vietnamese.
—Ward Just, *The American Blues*

IN the spring of 2007, Together Higher, a contemporary dance company from Hanoi, presented its show *Stories of Us* in Seattle, Portland, Chicago, and Manhattan. American audiences for *Stories of Us*, which featured deaf and hearing-impaired performers, were primarily members of the deaf community, for "Vietnamese-Americans largely stayed home," Claudia La Rocco reported in the *New York Times*. The Vietnamese American communities' lack of support for Together Higher, La Rocco notes, underscores the "protests and boycotts" that, in America, commonly greet artists from North Vietnam, whose work American Vietnamese—most of whom emigrated from South Vietnam—reject as "promot[ing] communism or serv[ing] as propaganda for the Vietnamese government." For many Vietnamese in America, a generation and more after emigration from their homeland, responses to the American war, its victors, and the Communist government of contemporary Vietnam remain personal, diverse, and occasionally violent.

Since the 1980s, in large Vietnamese American communities ("Little Saigons") in American cities, Vietnamese American journalists and activists have been attacked, even murdered, apparently by anti-Communist partisans, for advocating accommodation with the current government of Vietnam. Vietnam veteran–author Robert Olen Butler offers a fictional version of such internecine enmity in the title story of *A Good Scent from a Strange Mountain*, his Pulitzer Prize–winning 1992 short story collection about Vietnamese refugees in New Orleans and Lake Charles, Louisiana. In it, Đạo, the aged Vietnamese narrator—now, ten years after the end of the war, a resident of New Orleans—overhears his son-in-law and grandson, former officers in the army of the Republic of Vietnam, discuss their apparent complicity in the murder of a local Vietnamese American journalist who has proposed that his community accept the Communist government of Vietnam. Mr. Lê's "fatal error . . . should not be that in America," notes the apolitical Đạo, who acknowledges, sadly, that no one is interested in "an old man's opinion on this whole matter" (238).

There are more than 1.2 million people of Vietnamese ancestry currently residing in the United States. Burgeoning numbers among this disproportionately young population and America's important history with Vietnam and the Vietnamese make the Vietnamese community a significant minority group in contemporary America. Yet a recent *Chronicle of Higher Education* article about the coming of age of Asian American history fails even to mention the Vietnamese as a viable Asian ethnic group in the United States. Indeed, the history of what Kate Gadbow, in *Pushed to Shore*, her 2003 novel about Vietnamese and Hmong refugees in Missoula, Montana, calls the "Asian invasion" is brief and recent (49). Nearly all of the million-plus Vietnamese (and nearly six hundred thousand Hmong, Laotians, and Cambodians) in the United States—which Le Ly Hayslip calls "apprentice Americans"—arrived or were born here since the end of—and as a result of—Vietnam's American War (*Child*, 7).

The Vietnamese who fled their shattered country for the United States in the spring of 1975, and subsequent waves in the late 1970s and late 1980s, left hastily, with few possessions and uncertain hopes. Yet the weight of the emotional and psychological baggage that they unpacked in the United

States belies the exiles' numbers, then and now. Though social scientists have in recent years offered considerable anthropological and sociological commentary on the late-twentieth-century diaspora of the Vietnamese and other Southeast Asians and on their subsequent adjustment to the United States, American culture is only now exploring the lives of its new citizens from a small, ancient country halfway around the world. Of all the narratives of the legacy of America's Vietnam War, perhaps none promises to teach and challenge us—to bring the war home, to chronicle its other side—in the coming years as much as the collective story of the refugees and their descendants who fled their war-torn country to create new lives in the land of their vanquished invaders.

In a brief 1997 article, "Vietnamese in America: Literary Representations," Philip K. Jason reviewed the traditional critical paradigms of literary texts of the Vietnam War, beginning with John Clark Pratt's 1987 classification of all such books as combat literature and continuing with William J. Searle's recognition of an important second category of aftermath texts; or, to use different terminology, Vince Gotera's "The 'Nam'" and "The World." Only recently, Jason asserted, had writers and scholars begun to acknowledge another strain of Vietnam texts, those that represent the Vietnamese in America. In *The Viet Nam War/The American War*, her 1995 study of "images and representations in Euro-American and Vietnamese exile narratives," Renny Christopher insists that simplistic rubrics like "The 'Nam'" and "The World" reflect and perpetuate narrow and racist stereotypes that have written the Vietnamese out of the American story of its Vietnam War and Vietnam's American War. Long-standing racist attitudes about Asians, the privileging of firsthand accounts of the war by American soldiers (the you-had-to-be-there syndrome), and the commonly accepted perception that the Vietnam War was unique among American conflicts have, Christopher argues, arisen from and contributed to an Americanization of the Vietnam War that stereotypes or ignores the voices and stories of the Vietnamese.

Indeed, as Christopher demonstrates, few of the major, canonical texts arising from the Vietnam War offer anything other than brief, often racist presentations of minor and simplistic Vietnamese characters. In her analysis of well-known American war narratives such as Michael Herr's *Dispatches*, Larry Heinemann's *Close Quarters*, and Oliver Stone's *Platoon* she discusses their ethnocentric adherence to common stereotypes about the Vietnamese as small, sneaky "gooks" who are alien, mysterious, and distinctly "other." There are, indeed, countless novels and films about the war that offer now familiar scenes with the cunning, deceitful Vietnamese: the cherubic child who approaches a platoon of American GIs with a smile and a concealed hand grenade; the wizened old peasant woman with the betel-blackened smile who is a spy for the Vietcong; the Saigon bar girl; the Saigon cowboy. . . . The recurrence of such predictable and simplistic representations of the Vietnamese during the war only underscores the novels, memoirs, and films by Americans that offer more complex Vietnamese characters and significant relationships between Vietnamese and Americans. An even smaller but intriguing—and growing—body of work is the collection of texts that present the lives of the Vietnamese who have settled in the United States, those new Americans whom journalist Andrew Lam labels "prophets of migration" (15). Fictional representations of the Vietnamese in America—exiles and native-born Asian Americans—by American veterans, by Americans who have come to know and embrace the Vietnamese on American soil, and, most recently, by these new hyphenated Americans themselves bring the war home in instructive and fascinating new ways. As Philip Jason writes, "if Vietnam as a set of cultural conditions has always had its home in the United States, now, in a more literal and permanent way, Vietnam is here for good" (44).

Happily assimilated Gabrielle Tran narrates "The American Couple," the longest and richest story in Butler's *A Good Scent from a Strange Mountain*. Gabrielle loves "the wonderful lightness" of America; she likes game shows and soap operas and the fact that in America "there is always improvisation, something new, and when things get strained, you don't fall back on tradition but you make up something new" (157, 158). But Gabrielle's husband Vinh, a twice-successful businessman and a veteran of the American War, is more ambivalent about his new country. "We are American citizens and so are our children and so will be our children's children," he announces stiffly to the American veteran who befriends the couple at a Mexican resort. But Gabrielle knows that though her husband "appreciates America very much for being the sort of place where a man like him can succeed," he resists "the light and lively and less filling and soft as a cloud and reach out and touch someone culture that America had to offer. All the things that I had a sweet tooth for, my husband couldn't stand, not this man who'd been through a war and survived, the man who'd made his way in a strange land" (176, 213–214). Collectively, the Trans—fortunate to have escaped Vietnam, successful in America, and alternately seduced by and suspicious of America's "feel-good culture"—represent the variety of experiences and responses to

American society presented in prose texts by and about the Vietnamese in contemporary America (230).

Vinh and Gabrielle Tran undoubtedly would have been among the first South Vietnamese to flee their collapsing country for the United States in the spring of 1975. This first wave of refugees, some 125,000 to 250,000 in number, were generally well educated, English-speaking, urban, often Catholic professionals, many of whom had worked with the Americans during the war. As friends of America, as Christians, as early arrivals, they met a comparatively friendly reception in the United States; and after a precipitous but organized exodus on American planes and ships, most of the first wave of Vietnamese refugees settled in the United States with relative ease. The so-called boat people, the exiles in the second wave of Vietnamese emigration, began arriving in the United States in the late 1970s as, after the Communist victory in 1975, internal problems in Vietnam—famine, banishment to re-education camps and New Economic Zones, war with Cambodia—sent another 200,000 to 400,000 Vietnamese on a complicated and perilous journey: first in small, leaky boats to refugee centers in Thailand, Malaysia, Indonesia, or Hong Kong; then to resettlement centers in California, Arkansas, Florida, or Pennsylvania; finally to U.S. government-sponsored dispersal throughout the United States.[1] In this second wave, the boat people who survived capsized boats and Thai pirates (some estimates suggest that as many as half of the boat people died en route) reached the United States, sometimes with relatives already living here, but often as uneducated, rural Vietnamese with no facility with English and with "few financial resources, deep emotional scars, and in many more ways less prepared than the first wave to make a smooth transition" (Smith and Tarallo, 27). In 1979, responding to growing numbers of Vietnamese fleeing in unsafe conditions and arriving as economic rather than political refugees, the United Nations High Commission for Refugees and the Socialist Republic of Vietnam established the Orderly Departure Program. Under the ODP, the United States agreed to admit Vietnamese with close family members already living in the United States (the family reunification program); former employees of the U.S. government or American businesses in Vietnam and former members of the military of the Republic of Vietnam; and Amerasians, persons born in Vietnam during the American War and fathered by a U.S. citizen. As these legal categories and the timing and circumstances of their arrival indicate, refugees from Vietnam settled in the United States for quite dissimilar reasons, with varying backgrounds, experiences, and

256

prospects. Their stories are a powerful, vital chapter in the cultural history of the aftermath of the war in America and a salient component of the collective American narrative of the Vietnam War. As essayist Andrew Lam, who was eleven years old when he fled Vietnam for the United States, notes, "my story, too . . . is an American experience" (46).

An Encounter with the Orient

Among the first witnesses to the lives of Vietnamese in America were American participants in the conflagration that drove the Vietnamese so abruptly out of their native land. In his first novel, *The Alleys of Eden* (1981), Robert Olen Butler offers a rare early portrait of a complex Vietnamese character, central to the novel, as she decides to flee her home in Saigon just ahead of the advancing Communist forces and then struggles to begin a life in the United States.

Four years after his desertion from the American army, in the early hours of the late April day in 1975 on which the war will finally end, Cliff Wilkes lies in his small Saigon room in his "own and alien home," mentally revisiting his past life: his relationships with his ex-wife, his father, and Lanh, the Vietnamese former bar girl with whom he lives; his work as a student activist; and his experience in the army (7). The first half of *The Alleys of Eden* presents Cliff's protracted nocturnal reflections, ending with his and Lanh's frantic flight through the streets of Saigon to the American embassy and their escape on one of the last helicopters out of the city. Book Two, the second half of the novel, begins with their parlous journey to the United States, continues with their temporary separation and subsequent settlement in a quiet suburb of Chicago, and ends with Cliff's departure—without Lanh—for Canada, when he recognizes that, neither Vietnamese nor American, he is a man alone and "full of detritus. Pot shards, bone fragments, a vanished civilization" (255).

For Cliff, the point-of-view character in the novel, Lanh exists only for and through him. He obviously believes that he has rescued and affirmed her, and once they come together in Vietnam, "she stopped being anything but his mate almost at once" (12). Throughout his long Saigon reverie, while Lanh sleeps beside him (her body "a mere fragment of himself laid out there to keep him from going mad"), Cliff considers whether, if he returns to America, he should take his lover with him or leave her behind to almost certain punishment by the Communists for her relationship with their enemy (70). Later, awake, Lanh, though afraid of life in America, decides to

257

accompany Cliff on his reluctant return to the United States because she cannot bear to let him go without her. And for Cliff, up until the moment at the end of the novel when he abandons her, Lanh remains part of him: "She was an extension of himself. After the years of love and fear in an alley room she had been grafted to him" (123).

In fact, Lanh is considerably more multifaceted than Cliff allows. By his own acknowledgment quick-witted, like many of the bar girls, "but with an edge to her mind, to her feelings that the others couldn't even begin to understand," Lanh has been educated by her now dead mother (11–12). She understands the risks of fleeing with Cliff; she knows that their safe, secret world together must end when they leave Saigon, and she presciently recognizes that once Cliff returns to his old life, she might lose him. As he deliberates about his few options as Saigon begins to fall, Cliff imagines Lanh's reaction if he proposes fleeing Vietnam without her:

> Go, she would say. What is this place and its people to you? The best of you, the most compassionate of heart, the most tolerant and appreciative of mind, have come here and used Vietnam as a stage to play the high drama of your own conscience. A place to suffer grandly, to define your own evil, and then to leave. To leave utterly. And whether you treated us good or treated us bad, it makes no difference. You used us. You came and gave us scraps of your awareness, one year each of your heart. You came and made us feel, feel deeply, stirred us, set us seeking new things, and then you go. Vietnam is a foreign place to you. You feel here, suffer, for a time, but you return to a home far away. But there is no home away from here for me. You come and you make me suffer, I suffer with you, you give me joy, we share joy, and all those things alter this place for me. The sun shows differently on the clouds now, the trees are different. You go back to other places, old feelings. It was a terrible thing you suffered here. But it was only a dream, after all. It was another time, another place, the far side of the world, and it is all over. Go back. It is all you can do. But I hated you and loved you and I cannot be the same and there is nowhere for me to go. (91–92)

Cliff's typically narcissistic response to Lanh's imagined statement is to appropriate her perception of dislocation. "What happened to you happened to me as well," he insists. "I still have nowhere" (92). What Cliff cannot understand—though Lanh does, and the second half of the novel demonstrates—is that he, despite his almost willful refusal to accept his Americanness, does indeed have someplace to go, does indeed reconnect with his country and his life when he returns to the States, and that the price of this reassimilation is his separation from Lanh.

There is nothing in *The Alleys of Eden* to make the reader or Lanh doubt Cliff's genuine love for her. But Cliff's attraction to Lanh is more about his affinity for Vietnam than for any individual woman. Though Lanh is insecure about her small breasts ("you'd trade me in for the first pair of size 36 American breasts you could get your hands on," she accuses him), her dark skin, her otherness, Cliff loves Lanh precisely because she is, for him, the personification of the Orient (51). Arguably, his affection for Lanh and his attraction to Vietnam arise from his need to remain superior and in control. In his important, controversial 1979 book *Orientalism*, Edward Said exposes traditional Western stereotypes about the East, which, he insists, is typically portrayed by Westerners as a "weak partner for the West." Furthermore, Said asserts, the East is "linked . . . to elements in Western society (delinquents, the insane, women, the poor) having in common an identity best described as lamentably alien" (208, 207). In *The Alleys of Eden*, Lanh—Vietnamese, female, and a former prostitute—embodies the alien for which Cliff exhibits so little empathy. As their relationship deteriorates under the strain of life in the States, Lanh begs Cliff not to pressure her to adapt to America. "You can be glib about all this—you grew up in this country," she says, acknowledging (as Cliff cannot) his congruity with American life. "Don't you understand there's too much for me to take in, to worry about the language right now?" (215). Then Lanh, demonstrating the associations between sex and the Orient that Said elucidates, does what she has "not done . . . in this way since they'd come to America":

> Instead of English words, she filled her mouth with him. She articulated him, spoke him, her tongue shaping at him, speaking him. She had felt keenly Vietnamese at this moment, he knew, and she had crouched to suck him. To suck out what he'd been secreting in his body, to suck out the seeds of his Americanism, wasted seeds, the crust of an old fuck on a bedspread. He felt the shadows of so many moments like this—all in the fish air and lute tongue of Saigon. . . . Lanh was pulling it from him—sucking out of him everything that he wanted to shun anyway. . . . she protected him, he was safe inside her. (216–217)

Late in the novel, after he has left Lanh, feeling himself slipping further and further away from his connections with Vietnam, where he has been able to hide, Cliff returns for one last act of intercourse with her. Seeking "an encounter with the Orient, a scale against his virility," Cliff holds Lanh and swells "with the countryside, with the sprawl of the city, Saigon. . . . In her body he was Vietnamese" (254, 252). Cliff is, of course, not Vietnamese, but neither can he accept being American. He is a man without a country, a man without human relationships of any kind, and after his interminable, excruciating anxieties about whether to bring Lanh to the United States, he abandons her at the end of the novel—to an unfamiliar country and an adopted Vietnamese family—with cavalier nonchalance. When Vietnam and Lanh no longer offer an escape from the reality of life in America, Cliff abjures Lanh by re-Vietnamizing her. In America, Lanh can no longer suck out Cliff's Americanness, can no longer function as the vessel for his forgetting. So he repatriates her, makes her the whore that she once was, and relegates her to the cold company of others in his life who have let him down. And so he can go.

Ironically, having recognized that she had to leave Vietnam, and inevitably adjusting to life in the United States, Lanh too seems to become, and accept becoming, more Vietnamese in America than she was in Saigon. Lanh is frightened in a country "filled with . . . enormous people," and her limited ability to speak English (facilitated by Cliff's fluency in Vietnamese) leaves her feeling "like a child or a fool" (81, 167). When she learns that there is another refugee family from Vietnam in their Illinois community, she seeks them out immediately. And when Cliff admonishes her for her uncharacteristic interest in other Vietnamese exiles ("in Saigon . . . you and I were enough"), Lanh expresses her own surprise at her attraction to the familiar: "'I don't understand it myself,' she said. 'I did not feel Vietnamese in Vietnam. I felt part of you and that was all. . . . But now, even this moment, speaking of the Vietnamese family makes my heart flutter. I don't understand'" (207). "In Saigon," Renny Christopher asserts, "Lanh has been separated from her Vietnamese identity by her work as a bar girl, which is shameful in her culture. In America, she can leave her bar girl past behind her and rejoin her Vietnamese culture" (272). Yet Lanh's embrace of her true identity is a meager consolation for her. As The Alleys of Eden ends, as Cliff sadly leaves for Canada, Lanh will go to live with that Vietnamese family, the Binhs, "the unfortunates from that troubled land" (171). As Christopher notes, "the book ends in desolation; neither character finds a home, a culture" (273).

Unlike Cliff Wilkes—the man without a home—Emmett Wheeler, the protagonist of veteran Wayne Karlin's Lost Armies (1988), returns from war and postwar wandering to the marshes of southern Maryland that have been his family's home for generations. Seeing his home county from the perspective of its Vietnamese refugees, his students, Wheeler "realize[s] how strange the country was to him," but Xuan, his refugee girlfriend, recognizes that he loves the place, "not only as it is, but because its time is in you," and confesses that "I never thought of Americans as having that kind of connection to land, a place" (22, 79).

When Wheeler, a failed journalist, now part-time English-as-a-Second Language teacher, meets Xuan, he has been asked by the local newspaper editor and the county sheriff—both old friends—to help determine the origin of dead, mutilated deer that are being dumped in the local Vietnamese trailer park. The ghost-haunted Vietnamese believe that a spirit is killing the deer and will soon murder their children; but for Wheeler and the other locals, all signs point to Dennis Slagel, outlier, troublemaker, and Wheeler's fellow veteran and childhood friend. The complicated suspense story that ensues involves Wheeler's attempt to discover the fate of Dennis's Kit Carson scout, whom Dennis has christened "Willy the Gook" in honor of his friend, a local black man named Willy Looms, who died in Vietnam. A backdrop to the mystery of the dead deer is the campaign by a Madame Nhu–like Vietnamese restaurateur, Lily Minh, to relocate to the Tidewater area of southern Maryland the disaffected rural refugees who cannot adjust to urban life in the established Vietnamese community in Arlington, Virginia.[2] Collaborating with racist congressman Elliot Mundy (who, though Wheeler's and Dennis's contemporary, did not fight in Vietnam and now tells Wheeler he regrets his failure to serve), Lily Minh plans to set up the local Vietnamese in the area's commercial crabbing and oystering industry (43).

Xuan is Lanh with a voice; fluent in English, like Lan Cao's Mai ("Our father understood the world: he prepared us for a future as refugees by making sure we grew up able to speak the language I write in now," Xuan explains in her English exercise book, entries from which punctuate the short novel [136]), she claims to have been, like Lanh, a "whore for the Americans": "I let them empty their nightmares of the murder of my people into me. Then I made them look into my eyes until they saw me. I knew that one day they would raise a weapon and see me again in the face of their enemy and they would hesitate and die. When they left I knew I had birthed their corpses" (12–13). Only late in the novel does Wheeler learn, from Xuan's acidulous brother Tho (who turns out to be Willy the Gook and the source of the dead deer), that Xuan was not a whore and that she pretends to be only to punish herself for leaving Vietnam. Tho explains to Wheeler that he secretly fought for the Vietcong during the war—and why: "You Americans have the freedom to invent your own lives—it gives you the illusion you can invent other people's lives also. Invent and then grow tired of your inventions. You came to us to kill us and to love us, all to prove some idea you had about yourselves. But we were nothing to you. Only your dreams, your shadows, your whores" (129). Tho's angry assessment of America's seduction and betrayal of Vietnam and its people echoes Lanh's ostensible accusation—"You used us"—in *The Alleys of Eden*. At the end of *Lost Armies*, with Dennis and Tho both dead, Xuan imagines that she and Wheeler "forgive each other. And find together an imperfect peace"; but her embrace of Tho demonstrates her acceptance of her brother's caustic attitude about the lost war. "There's echoes of him in my heart and bones and blood," Xuan tells Wheeler. "If you want me, you get him too" (150, 135).

It is perhaps too commonly accepted by students of the Vietnam War that the Vietnamese—unlike Americans—have put their American War behind them, despite millions of Vietnamese, combatants and civilians, killed, two million displaced, and countless survivors left wounded or poisoned by American dioxin.[3] But the Vietnamese have been fighting for their independence for two thousand years, and, as Thomas Bass notes, "the American War . . . is already three wars ago for the Vietnamese" (116). It would be simplistic and inaccurate to suggest that the American War was insignificant for Vietnam, but in relative terms it was a brief calamity in a long, strife-filled history. It was also, for the National Liberation Front and its supporters, a victory that at long last unified the divided country. As Vietnamese American Andrew X. Pham writes in *Catfish and Mandala*, his 1999 travel memoir about his return to the country of his birth, "Vietnamese have a saying: *'A thousand years of Chinese rule, a hundred years of French subjugation, and ten years of American domination, but we survived, unified*'" (282).

The Vietnamese who fled to the United States in the years after 1975 were, of course, not the victors of the American War; vanquished and exiled, some Vietnamese expatriates might well be expected to want to abjure the conflict that changed their lives dramatically and forever. For other émigrés, sudden exile from their country could be an experience so profound that they can never overcome it. Lanh's and Tho's resentment about the war is replicated today in the real U.S. Vietnamese community by that intra-ethnic dissension among stateside Vietnamese about whether to wait for (or foment) the demise of Communist leadership in Vietnam; by the prolonged, painful, and finally unsuccessful efforts to relocate by some 110,000 boat people deemed to be economic immigrants rather than political refugees and therefore denied admission to America or another Western country;[4] and by the increasing numbers of Viet Kieu (refugees and next-generation Vietnamese who return to Vietnam). The literature by and about Vietnamese Americans presents postwar memories, ghosts, and a legacy as complicated and painful as those that haunt America more than thirty years after the fall of Saigon.

When Xuan writes in her English journal that she birthed the corpses of American soldiers, she (offering a variation on the theme embodied in the POW memoirs) articulates a theme of regeneration through violence that demonstrates both the refugees' need to start afresh in America and the remorseful pain that that process brings, as well as her feelings about the war that drove her from her country.[5] Wheeler asks Xuan her full name, and she tells him the name that is on her green card, explaining that the Vietnamese are given new names when they die and acknowledging that, for her (as, indeed, for many of these characters), exile from Vietnam is a kind of death. "Once upon a time, in another life," Xuan explains, "I was a student—I studied history and then history ate me. I died and was born in a boat in the Gulf of Siam"[6] (115). Or, as Andrew Lam asserts, "the past is irretrievable yet I can never be free from it" (13).

Behind Enemy Lines

Xuan's dramatic assertion that she was eaten by history is a metaphor about their involvement with the war that is echoed throughout the fictional stories of the exodus from Vietnam, for these are characters for whom expatriation means diminution. In *Monkey Bridge*, Vietnamese American Lan Cao's novel about a young girl's adolescence in the United States after she flees Vietnam with her mother in 1975, narrator Mai Nguyen contemplates her mother's preoccupation with the danger in the world around her and her now dead father's reaction to ominous political developments. "It was 'one wrong move' which had irrevocably changed our lives. 'One wrong move,' according to him, and 'the entire course of a country changed'. . . . To be guilty of 'one wrong move' was to be caught in the web of history, the way my family and other Southerners found themselves, in the Southern half of the country, reinforced by the United States in a war against the Northern half, led by Ho Chi Minh and supported by the Soviets and the Chinese" (25, 27). Caught in the web of history. In "Love," Robert Olen Butler presents the story of a Louisiana phone company employee, once a Vietnamese spy for the Americans in Biên Hòa, and his efforts to recapture his beautiful wife's affections from the Vietnamese former airborne ranger, now restaurateur who has claimed them. Though in Vietnam the unnamed narrator used his position with the Americans to order attacks on his wife's suitors, in America—until this new competitor—his wife has not threatened to cuckold him. "So finally history caught up with my country," the narrator states, and "it seems as if somehow the men of Vietnam have lost their nerve in America . . . these men are beaten down" (77). Expatriated to the United States, the narrator, a man who could once summon American artillery strikes to vanquish his wife's admirers, now finds himself "in a foreign country, behind enemy lines, as it were, without any resources but my own" (83, 80). His elaborate plan to humble his opponent with a voodoo curse is a comical, calamitous fiasco; and though the injured narrator succeeds in regaining his wife's attention, he is clearly no longer "the man who could bring fire from heaven" (92).

Mr. Thinh, the protagonist of Vietnamese American author Thanhha Lai's "The Walls, the House, the Sky" (1994), disapproves of his American-ized teenaged daughter's bold American boyfriend (a "blond devil"), her yogurt and granola, her haughty defiance toward her uncommunicative father (258). His lovely daughter reminds him of his young lover from "back in those Saigon days when he was important" (258). Now, in America with his frowzy wife and his unloving daughter, Mr. Thinh, who both admires and slightly disapproves of a successful Vietnamese friend who has "found a place in this society, never has moments of doubt if he, a Vietnamese, should be doing this or that," cannot reach out to either (264). When, at the story's conclusion, Mr. Thinh sees his daughter dressed for a formal dance, he knows that he should tell her that she is beautiful (like the long-lost lover), but, as ever, he cannot speak. As Tina and the blond devil depart for the dance, Mr. Thinh can utter only a silent scream.

Thiêu, now called Ted, the narrator of Butler's "Crickets," is self-conscious in America, where he is "the size of a woman" (60). He futilely tries to share his childhood with his Americanized son by introducing him to fighting crickets, explaining that in Vietnam there are two types of crickets—large, strong ones that are slow and easily confused and small fire crickets, weaker (like Ted) but smart and quick (like Ted). As he searches his Louisiana yard for crickets, Ted discovers that there are no fire crickets in his new home. In Vietnam, Ted wryly notes, "a fire cricket was a very precious and admirable thing," but "this is another country" (64).

Veterans Tran Vinh and Frank Davies, in Butler's "The American Couple," are successful businessmen in their postwar American lives, but they too are like little boys playing at war when they square off for an ersatz battle among the ruins of an abandoned movie set in Puerto Vallarta, Mexico. Engaging in what Vinh's wife, narrator Gabrielle, recognizes as "some kind of little war game," the men stalk and wrestle each other because "they had shared something once, something important—rage, fear, the urge to violence, just causes, life and death. They'd both felt those things in service of the same war. And neither of them wanted to let go of all that" (222, 230). Gabrielle worries that her husband seems to have more to say to a fellow vet, a stranger, an American, than he does to his Americanized wife; but she is reassured when she recognizes that "Vinh, too, has been distracted by the American culture. He is a seller of Swedish meatballs and cocktail franks, after all. He wears his dark gray suit and he studies his spreadsheets and he flies here and there carrying a leather briefcase with all the other Americans and he makes much money from food that people eat with toothpicks. But in Vietnam, in the war, there was passion. And there is a passion still inside him" (233). Like Xuan birthing the soldiers' corpses, Vinh "purg[es] . . . the war," but also like the narrator of "Love," he is a man diminished by exile (232).

Shared Suffering

In these texts, American veterans, like Frank Davies of "The American Couple," years after their own passionate experience of war are no less entangled in the web of history than their Vietnamese veteran brothers. The war has been over for twenty years, but Frank still wears his dog-tags and a T-shirt with "a map of Vietnam and the words I'VE BEEN AND I'M PROUD," and Gabrielle classifies him as "one of those [vets] who was either unable or reluctant to forget where he has been" (172, 164). As her husband and Frank compare war stories, Gabrielle befriends Frank's long-suffering wife Eileen. The men are walking far in the distance when Frank gestures a detonation. "'I know that story,' Eileen said with a sigh. 'An ammunition dump has just exploded in Qui Nhon'" (189). Like so many fictional Vietnam veterans, Frank is a middle-aged man who remains obsessed with his youthful wartime experience.

Although Gabrielle thinks that American veterans perceive the Vietnamese as "fascinating and long-suffering and unreal" or "sly and dangerous and unreal" (174), these narratives emphasize the bond that is the legacy of the war for Americans who fought in Vietnam and the people they fought with, for, and against. As James W. Tollefson notes, "Americans and Indochinese have in common . . . shared suffering in the war and its aftermath, and no two groups symbolize that shared suffering more than the Indochinese refugees and America's Vietnam veterans" (qtd. in Christopher, 265). The bond is often a recognition of their mutually tenuous place in contemporary American life.

When Amerasian teenager Tony Hatcher (known in the novel also as The Deuce) flees New Jersey for the dangerous streets of New York City in Robert Olen Butler's 1989 novel *The Deuce*, he rejects his comfortable middle-class life with his successful veteran father and embraces as his surrogate father a homeless vet who is haunted by the war. In Vietnamese veteran Hoang Khoi Phong's 1991 story "Twilight," American War veteran Nguyen feels out of place living in a mobile home park in his "adopted land," where the other residents are elderly Americans (266). Though welcomed by the extroverted veteran Bill, Nguyen is drawn to a sadder man damaged by war. Though he cannot speak, Sarkissian, a wheelchair-bound World War II–era Armenian refugee, silently welcomes Nguyen, but only later, when he learns from Bill that the old man lost a son in the Vietnam War, does Nguyen understand why Mrs. Sarkissian looks at him with eyes of "indescribable darkness" (267). From the moment that he discovers that the Armenian is a fellow refugee, he feels close to the frail old man—"he had left his country against his will, and then his son had died on the soil of my land"—but the man's silence and his wife's coldness obviate any relationship between the fellow exiles (272). And yet, after Sarkissian dies, a saddened Nguyen lights incense at his grave "to commemorate a compatriot" (273). When Nguyen moves on from the trailer park, he sells his mobile home to a young Korean immigrant, who appears affluent and optimistic because "backing him was a country embarked on a successful road to development" (271). Nguyen concludes his first-person tale with his confession that he is the sad, etiolated brother of Robert Olen Butler's displaced and emasculated men: "The difference between" him and his Korean successor, Nguyen notes, is "that he always walked with his head high, while for the last ten years it seemed that I had always looked down" (274).

As Lan Cao and Wayne Karlin understand, the attitudes of Americans toward the Vietnamese are intertwined with Americans' feelings about the war that made so many Vietnamese a part of American life. "We were," Lan Cao's Mai Nguyen recognizes, "a ragtag accumulation of unwanted, an awkward reminder of a war the whole country was trying to forget" (15). At the Vietnam Veterans Memorial on the Mall in Washington, D.C., Wayne Karlin's Kiet—the streetwise Amerasian teenager in his 1998 novel *Prisoners*—gravitates to a bamboo cage with a sign that announces: "AMERICANS ARE STILL HELD CAPTIVE BY ASIA: POW'S NEVER HAVE A NICE DAY." The cage is the makeshift home of an American veteran, an amputee who challenges Kiet: "You don't remember nothing, do you? . . . Got on the boat, got off the boat. Got welcomed with open arms. Meanwhile, me, I never got back. I'm missing. . . . People'd treat me just like I was a gook. . . . Me, you, same-same, right?"[7] (97–98).

Even veterans who embrace rather than resent the Vietnamese recognize that they are aliens together. The Mekong Grocery in Lan Cao's Arlington, Virginia, Little Saigon is a sanctuary for local Vietnam veterans. Mrs. Bay, Mai's mother's friend who works at the grocery, senses "a continuing connection with the American soldiers who visited the store, for the simple reason that a common base, she believed, existed to connect us exiles, on one point, to these lost men, on another point on the American triangle." In the Mekong Grocery, the veteran "would bring his little piece of a big history with him, and even though it was not the same as ours, we were in fact parts of a shared experience" (209).

For American veterans in the years after the war, the burgeoning presence of Vietnamese refugees in U.S. communities can—for good or for ill—bring the war home forcefully. As Alex Hallam, a Vietnam veteran and the county sheriff in Karlin's *Prisoners*, says about the local Vietnamese, "It was so unreal then. . . . Only now it's gotten real. Like it's been given a shape" (134). With the arrival of the hard-working Vietnamese in Port Alamo, Texas, the setting of Louis Malle's 1985 film *Alamo Bay*, the competition to make a living by shrimping and crabbing is increased dramatically. The bank has just repossessed Shang Pierce's boat when the Vietnam veteran and shrimper angrily orders the local Vietnamese priest to keep his people "out of my family's fishing grounds." Shang's claim of ancestral space is more a desperate response to immediate economic pressures than a proud Texan's commitment to family and tradition. And, significantly, Shang's working-class life is threatened, not by other Texans or even by Mexicans, whom the native shrimpers have obviously accommodated; it is the fear of the other that Shang articulates: the odd, new foreigners who work hard, "work cheaper than Americans," and don't follow the rules. As the town grocer/city councilman complains, "the federal government abandoned these people here in our town without educating them on how we do things." Joining forces with the Ku Klux Klan, whose local organizer asserts that the coming of the Vietnamese to Port Alamo is a Catholic and Communist plot, Shang and his threatened fellow native shrimpers do run the Vietnamese out of Galveston Bay (though only temporarily; at the end of the movie we are told that "today, more than 15,000 Vietnamese live and work on the Gulf Coast of Texas").

Charlie McDade's 1986 novel *The Gulf* presents a similar story of native Texas fishermen's resentment of new—and foreign—competition in their shrimp grounds. Like Malle's Shang, Pat Riley, the villain of *The Gulf*, is a Vietnam vet, and like *Alamo Bay*, *The Gulf* culminates in a violent attack on the Vietnamese, and on Peter Hodges, the war resister who teaches the refugees English. David Hodges, Peter's brother and a Vietnam veteran who is struggling with his actions during the war, refuses to get involved in the community's showdown with the Vietnamese, despite his recognition that "now the war had come home, and promised to be just as bloody" (249).

Boat People, Mary Gardner's 1995 novel about Vietnamese living in Galveston, presents the lives of Lang Nguyen, a Vietnamese medical resident, and the Vietnamese fishermen's families who live in a local housing project. Lang feels superior to these working-class Vietnamese, with their crude, rural accents, but he knows that to Americans "all the yellow people . . . look alike" (40). And indeed, the local policeman who stops Lang for speeding is an equal opportunity racist, happy to write a ticket for a "gook doctor" whom he resents: "you come to our country and we put you through school, feed you, give you a good life you'd never have in that Vit-nahm. . . . Buy your cars . . . send our good money back to all your gook family in that Vit-nahm" (90).

"All those damn names," complains veteran Alex Hallam in *Lost Armies*. "Phuong and Huong and Nguyen and Pham Dam and Phuc Duc and Duct Tape and Fuck a Duck. . . . I get with those people and suddenly I'm sounding like a redneck jarhead again" (16–17). In recognizing his own racism, Alex illustrates a self-consciousness about race and implies an identification between African Americans and the Vietnamese that is developed throughout these texts. In Butler's "Love," the narrator resorts to voodoo to discourage his alluring wife's suitors: "You can't live around New Orleans without hearing about voodoo," he reports, and sets off for the French Quarter to consult an expert. Eschewing the "phony" voodoo shops on Bourbon Street, the narrator makes his way to the black neighborhood, where he acquires some black magic from an elderly African American "low-down papa" named Dr. Joseph. "I have learned the lessons of history and I felt a kinship with these people," the narrator observes about the black people in the Quarter (81).

In *Boat People*, too, the lessons of history teach the kinship between Vietnamese refugees and African Americans, who live together in the public housing project. Since her mother died there, Azelita Simpson, a black school aide, volunteers at the hospital where Lang Nguyen practices. "She was very close to her mother," nurse Shirley explains to Lang, who observes that "the black people were like the Vietnamese in this regard" (30). Wilson, Azelita's new African American boyfriend and a Vietnam vet, at first dislikes the Vietnamese who are Azelita's neighbors and whose children she works with at the school, but the motherly black woman is drawn to the small, silent children: "I like those little Viet kids," she says. "They got their own kind of slavery to grow out of" (166). Gardner develops this theme of shared slavery. When one of the Vietnamese children identifies Azelita's house as "the nigger house," Trang, an Amerasian teenager who is searching for her American father, admonishes him: "Why you talking? . . . Americans just call you little gook shit. Black people came here by boat too. Just like us. . . . They talk funny because they have to keep their mouths shut for so long. Otherwise they get killed by the people who own them" (254). At the novel's sentimental end, Wilson assures Trang that he is not her father, but that the identity of her father doesn't matter: "What matters is who *you* are. . . . We boat people, we all special. . . . We worked so hard and hurt so much, we gonna get every single thing we got coming to us" (272). It is significant that it is Vietnam vets, those fathers and could-be fathers (Malle's Shang Pierce, Gardner's Wilson) of the mixed-race *bui doi*, who demonstrate most blatantly the resentment and fear of the refugees that reverberate throughout these texts. How could these ineffectual warriors fail to recognize—and resent—that they, like the Vietnamese exiles, "were custodians of a loss everyone knew about but refused to acknowledge. . . . [that] Vietnam had been their life, and now it must become nothing" (Lan Cao, 64).

Prophets of Migration, Custodians of Loss

And for the Vietnamese exiled to America—even those too young to remember the land their parents fled—the experience of war shimmers under the surface of their lives like minnows, shadowy, even invisible in the rough water, but always there. Thuy, the primary narrator of Dao Strom's 2003 novel *Grass Roof, Tin Roof,* leaves Vietnam as a young child. "It is true I was born on the fringes of several wars. It is true no bullets grazed me, no mortar blast stunned me, no tear gas blinded me, and no mother was actually taken from me; nevertheless," she writes, "I hold images" (161). "The first form of war," Thuy observes, is "all the visible losses"—soldiers and guns and damage. But the second form is less often acknowledged, she asserts, and that is "the soul's experience of war" (162). lê thi diem thúy's unnamed narrator in *The Gangster We Are All Looking For* (2003) also escapes Vietnam as a child. Born while her father is away fighting and too young to remember the war, she, like Thuy, nonetheless understands its immanence in her life: "Ma says war is a bird with a broken wing flying over the country-side, trailing blood and burying crops in sorrow. If something grows in spite of this, it is both a curse and a miracle. When I was born, she cried to know that it was war I was breathing in, and she could never shake it out of me. . . . War has no beginning and no end. It crosses oceans like a splintered boat filled with people singing a sad song" (87). Years after the end of the Vietnam War, American veterans may still wear their dogtags, but the Vietnamese bear the war quietly inside—in their souls. As Andrew Lam reminds us, "to grow up Vietnamese in America, after all, is to grow up with the legacy of the loser's side" (57). Yet, though the war lingers for them, much like home, family, and ancestors, their stories are as much about looking forward and struggling to start over as they are embedded in the past. *Lost Armies*'s Xuan's new name is a death name, but it is a (re)birth name as well.

These books present the lives of Vietnamese exiles through an exploration of tensions between Vietnam and America; between ancient, ancestral mores and new American values; and—in a variation on the generation gap theme that appears in so many of the antiwar movement narratives—between the older, exile generation and the younger, American-born Vietnamese. As *Grass Roof, Tin Roof*'s Thuy (or, in America, April) notes, "whether the end of a people comes as a grand elegy or as a consequence of all they have abused, lost, and ruined, the end does come. . . . Home—whatever that is—will be extinguished or rearranged. And what remains afterward, the survivors, eventually they are scattered too, like seeds, or sent out like scouts but bearing messages they've forgotten by the time they land and begin to roam amid other populations of people. They set up smaller, sadder camps of the old life, always with the same sense of something shattered and undistilled behind them" (163–164). Survivors bearing uncertain messages, the refugees arrive from a fractured world to find each other, forming new families, new communities, much as POWs, peace activists, and others displaced by the war do; regroup, and make a new life in a foreign land, acculturating to America as they change it.

Renny Christopher notes the bifurcated sensibility that the stories of the displaced Vietnamese manifest; while Americans' novels about the Vietnam War are invariably about America, she asserts, "Vietnamese exile writers' representations are focused on cultural negotiations, on the process of becoming bicultural. This process is not the same as assimilating, which is to leave behind one's culture of origin. Biculturality is one of the important ways in which Vietnamese American literature differs from much of the tradition of Asian American literature. Vietnamese exile authors, while becoming 'American,' insist on remaining Vietnamese at the same time" (30). Shirley Geok-Lin Lim generalizes that recent Asian American literature "foreground[s] . . . 'the instability of identity' in Asian American culture today, representing the oscillating and crisscrossing of national, racial, and subjective boundaries that characterize the experience of biculturalism and multiculturalism" (156). Paul Rutledge agrees that "Vietnamese-Americans do not tend to discard former customs, nor do they ignore or refuse to engage the new cultural standards. . . . the Vietnamese have effectively maintained the viability of both indigenous and host cultural units." Or, to put it another way, "Vietnamese-Americans have chosen a course which cannot be definitively described as either acculturation or assimilation" (145, 146).

And, as these storytellers demonstrate, achieving biculturality—learning to live in America without forgetting one's Vietnamese heritage—is a delicate balance. These texts are filled with bemusing episodes that illustrate the most basic, immediate challenges of habituating to an unfamiliar culture. Ten-year-old Linh Nguyen and her younger brothers, in *Boat People*, are regular patrons at the community public library, but when their father, Phuong, inexplicably decides to join his children, Linh anticipates trouble. And indeed, the library's revolving door confuses and paralyzes him. The young narrator of *The Gangster We Are All Looking For* and her father arrive in the United States several years before their mother and wife joins them; sad, lonely, and sleepless, father and daughter pass the time by exploring their unfamiliar California neighborhood, and their midnight rambles make the *Neighborhood News*: "According to the store manager, their behavior was 'strange' but not in any way threatening. . . . 'Everything seemed to interest them. I mean, everything, from the TV dinners to the 10-pound bags of dog food'" (110).

Memoirist Le Ly Hayslip and Mai Nguyen's mother Thanh are more over-whelmed than entranced by a large, well-stocked American supermarket, with its colorful explosion of products and brands. Paul Rutledge recounts the confusion of another refugee unnerved by her initial supermarket expe-rience: "Assuming that the picture on the package literally showed what the contents would be, the mother was horrified at jars of Gerber's baby food with a picture of a small child on the front. Misunderstanding the message, she worried that Americans practiced cannibalism" (59). In many of these books, the first dramatic instance of cultural negotiation is a frightening but alluring brush with America's commercial, capitalist culture—the old myth of America as the land of plenty behind the golden door.

Most of the texts about Vietnamese exiles include a similar scene illus-trating their perception of the "foreignness" of contemporary American life. More important, each offers complex—and interesting—explorations of in-dividual efforts to chart the difficult course of a life in the new world that accepts the values of the old. A danger for some of these fictional émigrés is that once accustomed to the United States, they embrace their new coun-try so successfully that their hold on the past is undermined, their loyalty to obsolete communities attenuated; and the recognition of losing touch with their heritage invariably evokes regret and guilt rather than a sense of freedom.[8] Lang Nguyen receives a letter from home announcing that his mother is dead, and the grief-stricken doctor hurriedly constructs an altar so that he can honor his mother. "I never built the altar. . . . I put my feet on the face of my homeland. I forgot my own people," he berates himself. When his American roommate tells him that "you're American now," Lang insists "I am *not* American" (202).

Butler's unnamed narrator in "The Trip Back"—another attenuated, in-effectual middle-aged Vietnamese man—drives from his home in Lake Charles, Louisiana, to Houston to retrieve his wife's elderly grandfather from the airport. As he tries to engage the old man in conversation on the long ride home, the narrator, a successful businessman in the States, observes si-lently, "I found that I myself was no longer comfortable with the old ways. Like the extended family. Like other things, too. The Vietnamese indirect-ness, for instance. The superstition. I was a good American now, and . . . it was not an unpleasant thought that I had finally left Vietnam behind" (36). The elderly man, the narrator discovers, does not recall that he has a grand-daughter—but he remembers his favorite 1934 Hotchkiss car; he remembers the South China Sea; he remembers Vietnam. And eventually the narrator sadly recognizes that he himself has "lost a whole country and . . . didn't give it a thought" (42). As the old grandfather "sort[s] out his life as it was about to end," the narrator fears that "deep down I am built on a much smaller scale than the surface of my mind aspires to. . . . Deep down, secretly, I may be prepared to betray all that I think I love the most" (42–43).

Both Lang and the narrator of "The Trip Back" experience an epiphany that awakens them to the impossibility—and inadvisability—of becoming too Americanized. Other protagonists articulate their ambivalence about the peculiar state of biculturality that their exile demands. The unnamed narrator in Butler's "In the Clearing" writes to the son whom he unwittingly left in Vietnam, offering a story he shares with his lieutenant during his youthful war experience, the well-known folk tale about the dragon and the fairy princess who founded Vietnam, along with the sad confession that the lieutenant, who facilitated his unexpected escape from Vietnam "thought he was helping me save my life, and maybe that was true, but maybe it wasn't true at all" (109). Another businessman tells us, in Butler's "Relic," about his decision to flee his country—without the wife and children who "belonged in Vietnam"—and start afresh and alone in a new country. The Catholic collector who believes in the power of relics and who buys one of John Lennon's shoes struggles to surmount his past. He has the money to "become the American that I must be," but finds that "it isn't so simple. Something is missing" (141, 140). As the story ends, he can only hope that John Lennon's shoe will take him to "the place where I belong" (142). The elderly Vietnamese narrator of Butler's "A Ghost Story" knows that many listeners will doubt his "true story" of Miss Linh, the beautiful ghost who saved the life of an ARVN major near An Khê in 1971. But he knows that the story is true, because in April 1975 the ghost saved him too, and as he drove away to safety in the United States, he "looked out the window and saw Miss Ling's tongue slip from her mouth and lick her lips, as if she had just eaten me up. And," the story ends, "indeed she has" (123).

After her mother's suicide, at the end of *Monkey Bridge*, Mai Nguyen reflects on the bereft older woman's inability to adapt to her new life in the States: "In one way or another, my mother and her friends were not much unlike the physically wounded. They had continued to hang on to their Vietnam lives, caressing the shape of a country that was no longer there, in a way not much different from amputees who continued to feel the silhouette of their absent limbs. Years later, they continued to deny the fact that some tender and unexpendable part of them had been exiled into a space that could not be reached, and so they would continue to live their lives, like my mother, in a long wail of denial" (255–256). For some of these characters, exile from home and community, and a compromised life in America—the "odd new life" that Dao Strom's Su Heng has "come to inhabit" in a new land—are a kind of annihilation (*Gentle Order*, 169). Often their dislocation manifests itself in physical or mental illness, and their attitude toward ill health highlights the cultural differences between their old world and the new.

Wandering Souls

Pao Lor is a young Hmong from Laos studying English in Janet Hunter's high school class in Kate Gadbow's *Pushed to Shore*. After Pao is arrested for hunting out of season, he falls ill.[9] Janet knows that the Hmong believe that a person's soul can leave his body "if the person is afraid, or alone, or depressed by separation from loved ones or home" (134). When the community's shaman is unable to help Pao, American doctors diagnose depression, but their drugs fail too, and Pao commits suicide. An angry Janet rails against the

> huge lie [that] has been told to these people. They trusted us and we betrayed them. In our bloated American pride, our self-satisfaction, we've brought them here, and now we have to convince them everything about us is wonderful—the best in the world. We talked Pao into giving up his own healers with their superstitious—and messy—rituals. We put him on our dandy little pills, because they're ours and they're scientifically proven. And then one day they stopped working, or maybe he took too many, or forgot to take them at all, and his world went black. Oops! Too bad. Such a pity. But look how much better off the rest of them are. (280–281)

Boat People's Hai Truong, Linh's mother, believes that her true husband is not the fisherman father of her children, but a lonely spirit who has come to live in her and make her sad. Like the depressed narrator of Charlotte Perkins Gilman's feminist classic *The Yellow Wallpaper*, Hai circumnavigates her kitchen, rubbing a mark on the wall, grounding herself to the house, in which she feels safe. But now Hai is hospitalized—not for the first time—and Linh prays for her mother to return home, though she knows that American medicine will not cure the woman: "It was all right to get hit by a car, or catch your arm in a fishing winch . . . But if you had a ghost in you, that was not all right. In America, they put you in the hospital and made you stay in a room with no other Vietnamese to talk to. They made you sign papers. They gave you lumps to eat that tasted like dishcloths" (20). As Rutledge explains, traditional Southeast Asian health care acknowledges supernatural as well as physical sources of sickness. "Ill health," he notes, "may be the result of demons, deities of various descriptions, or wandering souls who have returned to earth in anger" (99). Called in to interpret, Dr. Lang tries to explain to his American colleagues that Hai is not crazy. But he knows that this is one reality that will not translate: "It is very hard to explain," Lang insists. "A spirit has come to live in her. . . . It would not work for an American. . . . It is true only for a Vietnamese" (178).

Indeed, there is much that doesn't translate about Vietnam, an eastern culture and a predominantly Buddhist country. "While Americans are, according to myth, forward-looking and optimistic," writes Frances Fitzgerald in *Fire in the Lake*, her early important study of Vietnamese and Americans in Vietnam, "the traditional Vietnamese were directed towards the past, both by the small tradition of the family and the great tradition of the state" (15). The loyalties of the Vietnamese are therefore to family, village, and state; and Vietnamese removed from their ancestral lands are "without a social identity" (13). *Boat People*'s Lang confirms that "Vietnamese have many responsibilities. To their ancestors. To their families. To their land. We cannot set them aside" (230). The narrator of "The Trip Back" welcomes his wife's grandfather because in Vietnam "we honor our families" (31). Bac Nguyen, the recently emigrated elderly man who is befriended (and later robbed and beaten) by the orphan Vinh in Aimee Phan's "Visitors," challenges the younger man's resentment of Americans—who, Vinh says, "destroyed our country, then . . . left"—with the admonition that family always matters more than politics. "We spend so much energy and time on the larger issues, religion, country, political parties," Bac Nguyen proselytizes, "that we ignore the smaller ones, like family and our homes, which are ultimately more important" (98). Gail Dolgin and Vicente Franco's 2002 documentary film *Daughter from Danang* begins with Tennessee-raised Heidi (once Hiep) Bub's return to Vietnam to visit the mother who gave her up for American adoption in the mid-1970s. Heidi happily anticipates her reunion with her birth family, but she worries that "I've been 101% Americanized, and I have no earthly idea of their expectations." Yet even that awareness does not prepare Heidi for the cultural dissonance that sends her rushing away from Danang in tears at the end of her week-long visit. During their formal farewell, Heidi's siblings ask her quite directly to take their dependent mother home with her, or at least to commit to a monthly stipend for her support. There is more going on in Heidi's family's expectations than their understandable perception that she is a rich American; for them, as Vietnamese, loyalty to family and respect for the aged are the consummate values. It would simply not occur to them that Heidi would object to caring for her mother—even a mother whom she cannot remember. As Rutledge states, "In Vietnam, the family took precedence over the individual. . . . All family members, regardless of where they reside, are expected to assist each other in times of crisis" (83, 123). And for the Vietnamese, as Fitzgerald notes, family means not just close relatives, but community as well. *The Alleys of Eden*'s Lanh is embraced by the Binh family; though strangers in Vietnam, they are—by virtue of their exile status—family in America. The "uncles" who arrive in America with lê thi diem thúy's young narrator and her father search their San Diego neighborhood "looking for signs of other Vietnamese people" (15). For these characters, their communities of fellow displaced Vietnamese provide emotional (and sometimes financial) support; and help, however feebly, to assuage the grief and guilt caused by separation from ancestors and ancestral lands.

Before her exodus for the United States, Mai's grandfather, Thanh's father, whose failure to make the trip from Vietnam haunts Thanh throughout *Monkey Bridge*, teaches a young Mai about "the Confucian custom of ancestor worship": "The soul becomes sad if it is left unattended by its descendants. . . . The farther we wander from the earth and water of our burial ground, the weaker our ties to our ancestors become, and the separation is not good for the soul! It drains the heart of blood and leaves a profound hollowness in the center of our veins" (59–60). Mai wonders, throughout the four years since she and her mother settled uncertainly in the States, why her grandfather had failed to meet Thanh, as arranged, for the trip. Not until late in the novel does Mai learn the tragic truth of her mother's life and the secret that her grandfather was (like Karlin's Tho) a Vietcong sympathizer. Until then, Mai accepts the quite plausible scenario that her grandfather simply could not bear to leave his home: "The constancy of the ancestral land and the village burial ground . . . these were things that mattered to him. My grandfather would not be easily convinced of the need to cross the ocean's depths for the purpose of starting a more convenient and modern life" (159). And Mai's mother knows, when her own mother dies after being relocated to a strategic hamlet, that "I would have to find a way back there, back to the graves of my ancestors, back to the sacred land. . . . She would have to die where she was born, and I would have to construct this circle for her, a beginning and an end that converged toward and occupied one single, concentrated space"[10] (248). That she, caught in the horrors of the conflagration, fails to bury her mother is one of Thanh's most profound and lingering war wounds. A Vietnamese refugee in a Malaysian relocation camp tells Lady Borton, in *Sensing the Enemy*, that "more than anything . . . I want to return to my *quê hương*—my home, the location of my ancestors' graves. . . . I'm just like every other Vietnamese, as rooted to my *quê hương* as a banyan tree." (46).

Prisoners's Russell Hallam, an African American Vietnam veteran and the descendant of an extended family that has lived for generations in the Tidewater area of southern Maryland, understands the profound importance of ancestry for the Vietnamese: "Time touched him back. It wasn't a matter of searching it out. It was simply there, the weight of an internal presence. It was something the Vietnamese would probably understand: their ancestry and history were felt as points of reference, of lookout, in a person's soul" (64). Hip, cynical Tony Hatcher/Võ Đình Thanh—Butler's "The Deuce"—glibly rejects his bar girl mother's superstitiousness and Buddhist beliefs as "Vietnamese voodoo": "You do what you can for yourself, but you don't have to believe in wandering souls and celestial drinks and incense for your dead kin to realize that somebody is running this fucking show" (10, 81). But at the end of the novel, a more mature Thanh resolves to pray for his mother "just in case she's dead and just in case the Buddhists are right about all that. She believed in it, even if I don't, so it's the least I can do for her" (302).

Life in Reverse

The significance of family and ancestors and Tony/Thanh's disdain for his mother's values underscore these narratives' recurring exploration of the stresses of "cultural negotiations" as they are demonstrated through a generation gap between the older generation and the younger and the era's problematic but important relationship between father and child. In *The Unwanted*, Kien Nguyen's memoir about growing up as a reviled "half breed" in Nhatrang and Saigon, Kien's mother prepares to flee with the eight-year-old and his younger brother in April 1975, as the end approaches. But Kien's grandparents refuse to leave. "I can't go to America," the grandfather insists. "I don't want to go to any foreign land where I don't speak the language or know the customs. I'd rather die here by the Vietcong's hands, among my ancestors, than live like a ghost among strangers" (21–22).

Social scientists confirm that emigration by elderly Vietnamese in the years after 1975 was relatively rare. U.S. census figures indicate that while people over the age of sixty-five made up 13 percent of the total American population in 1990, the same age group constituted only 3 percent of the American Vietnamese population (Zhou and Bankston, 50). When hospitalized Hai Troung cries out for her mother, Lang explains to her American nurse: "'Not many mothers come on the boats.' A whole kingdom of elders had been left behind. Lang didn't know a single Vietnamese woman over forty in Galveston. . . . 'It is not the way life should be'".(30). And as Min Zhou and Carl Bankston explain, in their sociological study of Vietnamese children in the United States—and Rutledge and common sense confirm—the younger the immigrant, the easier and more absolute the adaptation to a new culture. Throughout these books, as Linh's familiarity with the local library indicates, children function as translators, shoppers, diminutive Virgils guiding their flummoxed parents through a bewildering new world. When her father is able to start a small gardening business, lê thi diem thúy's narrator becomes his "secretary," because "I speak the best English" (90). The Vietnamese child of refugees, notes Andrew Lam, "learns that . . . he is a better navigator in the New World where his parents, clinging desperately to the past, to traditional values to guide them, fumble and lurch and retreat into smallness—private world, . . . private sorrows. The immigrant child, wanting the larger world, shunning the old ways, inexorably breaks his parents' hearts" (35). Mai Nguyen recognizes, in *Monkey Bridge*, that mother and daughter have switched roles: "we were going through life in reverse, and I was the one who would help my mother through the hard scrutiny of ordinary suburban life. I would have to forego the luxury of adolescent experiments and temper tantrums, so that I could scoop my mother out of harm's way and give her sanctuary. Now, when we stepped into the exterior world, I was the one who told my mother what was acceptable or unacceptable behavior" (35).

Mai casts "an anthropologist's eye" on her mother Thanh and Thanh's contemporaries in Falls Church, Virginia's Little Saigon, and, ironically, sees *them* as the children:

Detached, I could see this community as a riot of adolescents, obstreperous, awkward, out of sync with the subscribed norms of American life, and beyond

the reach of my authority. I could feel for them, their sad shuffles and anach-
ronistic modes of behavior, the peculiar and timid way they held their bodies
and occupied the physical space, the unfailing well-manneredness with which
they conducted themselves in public—their foreigners' ragged edges. Here,
in one corner, was a grouping of elderly women and men too unattached to
the ways of the United States even to be aware of their differences. They had
never managed, nor had the desire to manage, the eye-blinking, arm-folding
maneuvers needed for a makeover. Here, in a walk-up apartment in a suburban neighborhood thirty minutes from Washington, D.C., they continued to
present themselves as reproductions from the tropics. (146)

The older Vietnamese in *Monkey Bridge* cling together, in their "smaller,
sadder camps of the old life" that Dao Strom defines. And if the younger
Vietnamese Americans are sometimes impatient with their parents' intractable death grip on their fading lost lives, the older generation—like the
grandfather in "The Trip Back"—recognizes the high price of assimilation.

Đạo, the narrator of the title story in Butler's *A Good Scent from a Strange
Mountain*, is almost a hundred years old—so old that he knew Hô Chí Minh
in 1917 when the great patriot was Nguyên Aí Quôc, a pastry chef at the Carlton Hotel in London. Now in New Orleans, nearing the end of his life, the
narrator honors the Vietnamese death custom of formally bidding farewell
to family and friends, and he is disheartened about the prospects for harmony in his expanded family: "A Vietnamese family is extended as far as the
bloodline strings us together, like so many paper lanterns around a village
square. And we all give off light together. That's the way it has always been
in our culture. But these people who come to visit me have been in America
for a long time and there are very strange things going on that I can see in
their faces" (237). As the older Vietnamese understand, pursuing biculturality is like negotiating a monkey bridge, that primitive, precarious handmade
overpass that spans the waterways of rural Vietnam; the monkey bridge, as
Lan Cao notes, is a "thin, unsteady shimmer of bamboo" that "only the least
fainthearted, the most agile would think about using" (179, 109).

Of all the texts considered here, Lan Cao's *Monkey Bridge* (1997), the
first novel written by a Vietnamese American, presents most cogently the
strains, stresses, and consolations of biculturality for the Vietnamese in
America as it explores themes echoed by nearly all of the other stories of
Vietnamese in exile. In the tradition of earlier bicultural autobiographical
narratives and mother-daughter stories like Amy Tan's *The Joy Luck Club*

and Maxine Hong Kingston's *The Woman Warrior* (and therefore a variation on the more common father-child tales related in many of these narratives), *Monkey Bridge* is the first-person account of nineteen-year-old Mai Nguyen's relationship with her lugubrious mother and her efforts to learn and comprehend the mysterious "truth of sin, illegitimacy, and murder" that haunts the older woman (228–229). The novel is set in Little Saigon in Arlington, Virginia, in 1979, four years after Mai and her mother have fled the North Vietnamese takeover of Saigon. Younger, more successfully assimilated into American culture than her mother (who is, like Hai Truong in Mary Gardner's *Boat People*, a haunted middle-aged Vietnamese woman), Mai, is in fact, caught between two worlds: the transplanted ancestral community of her mother and the other refugees, with their "foreigners' ragged edges," and the promise of another escape, to college, to an unencumbered, acculturated adulthood in America, "a country in love with itself, beckoning us to feel the same" (146, 31).

Mai, who has left Vietnam several months before her mother in the care of "Uncle Michael," the American army colonel whom she and her family befriend while he is serving in Vietnam, adapts to life in America with relative ease because of her facility with the language, a counterpoint to Butler's Lanh and so many of the adult immigrants in these texts, who struggle because of their inability to communicate in English. During those months that Mai waits with her adoptive American family for her mother to arrive from a disintegrating Vietnam, she studies English with "Aunt Mary." By the time Mai leaves Connecticut to live with her mother in Arlington—where they settle because it is near their new country's capital and therefore, Mai's fearful mother Thanh believes, the safest place in America—Mai recognizes that her familiarity with English brings "an astonishing new power. For my mother and her Vietnamese neighbors, I became the keeper of the word" (37). Again, in America, teenaged Mai functions as the mother, and her napalm-scarred, ill mother—who is "undone in our new life"—becomes the child (34).

Keepers of the Word

Not surprisingly, fluency in or ignorance of spoken English is a central theme throughout the stories of the Vietnamese in America. Paul Rutledge emphasizes the difficulty that native speakers of Vietnamese, which is a tonal language, have learning English (despite English classes offered by volunteer agencies and at refugee camps), as well as the quite practical necessity for doing so. He quotes 1987 Office of Refugee Resettlement reports, which document that while 51 percent of refugees who had some fluency in English found employment in the United States, only 6 to 9 percent of non-English speakers did (115, 80). Kate Godbow's Janet Hunter, Emmett Wheeler of *Lost Armies*, the unnamed narrator of Linh Dinh's story "The Hippie Chick," Peter Hodges, the former draft evader in Charlie McDade's *The Gulf*, and scholar Renny Christopher are all introduced to their local Vietnamese communities by teaching English-as-a-second-language classes to eager students. Janet Hunter acknowledges that her teenaged students' essays are "in contorted, refugee-camp English. Short" (4). They are also "heartbreaking"—the reason she is furious when a creative writing teacher who does not teach the Vietnamese students dismisses a story by Hunter's prize student, Vinh, about his escape from Vietnam as "accidental poetry" (4, 6). Emmett Wheeler feels "ridiculous" correcting the grammar and syntax of Mr. Dinh's account of his wife's murder by Thai fishermen. His students' essays, he recognizes, are "pits of pain" (2). Azelita, the school aide who befriends Linh and the other children of *Boat People*, understands that "when you don't own your own words, you don't own your own soul either. I see those Vietnamese kids at school, working their little tails off to learn how to do ABC in English, and wonder if they know who they are from one day to the next" (164–165).

Cliff Wilkes is embarrassed and angry at Lanh's "inarticulateness" in English. Away from Vietnam, Lanh "had no language . . . and . . . no country now and everything was alien to her and turned her into a stranger" (239). Lanh's difficulty communicating in English is both cause and symbol of the deterioration of her relationship with Cliff. Mai Lan's American husband, in Linh Dinh's "The Hippie Chick," is visiting Vietnam with his younger wife. In the United States, they speak "a permutation of English" to each other, and now, in her home country, he is unnerved by her fluency in her native language: "In her own language she could babble on to almost anyone. It was disturbing to detect a whole new range of expressions on her face. The nuances and complexities. I found myself keeping an uneasy tab on this development, to store away her hidden repertoire for my future reference in the United States" (161). Yet, reinforcing the challenges of biculturality, these texts acknowledge that for these characters, facility with English, though necessary for successful adaptation to America, comes, ironically, at a price. As a young child in Vietnam, Tony, in Butler's *The Deuce*, learned his profane, street-slick English palaver from his mother's American lovers, and he resents his mother Nghi's broken pigeon-English, blaming her childlike English for his American father's decision to take Tony, but not Nghi, back to America: "Chop chop. Can you believe that shit? If she'd tried as hard as me to learn English, maybe things would've turned out differently that day. Who can love a woman who talks like that?" (14). But when his mother writes to him, several years after his resettlement in the States, Tony cannot read her Vietnamese words, admitting that "as the years went on, I sort of lost my command of the spoken Vietnamese language because I never used it" (42). Their Danish stepfather insists that his Vietnamese children speak proper English when they arrive in America, in Dao Strom's *Grass Roof, Tin Roof*, and encourages them to adopt American names. As Thuy (renamed April) tells us, "he believed that it was more important for the children to speak the language of the country they were growing up in than for them to cling to a culture they had left" (56). Hus angrily corrects his wife Tran's English and is impatient when she speaks Vietnamese, with its "garrulous and aggressive and shrill" tones (60). At the end of the novel, when Thuy returns to Vietnam, which she left as a young child, she regrets her inability to understand her Vietnamese relatives. "I'm twenty-three years old, twenty-one years past the last time some of these people leaned down and spoke to me in a language I can't remember I ever knew" (206).

For Lan Cao's Mai, fluency in English means more than her role as newly empowered "keeper of the word." Her mother worries about Mai's easy accommodation to a new life, confiding to her diary that "everything that smells of life before, my daughter thinks she can scour clean. She has disengaged and unremembered so swiftly something as big as a life, disassembling it from her mind as if it had never been" (53). Though the story and Mai's awareness of the strains and sacrifices of her bicultural life belie her mother's concerns, Mai recognizes too that once she becomes fluent in English, "the American dream" exerts "a sly but seductive pull" (53, 37). At the end of *Monkey Bridge*, Mai embarks upon her journey toward that American dream. Mount Holyoke College's recruitment brochure promises "the openness of an unexplored future and the safety of its sanctuary" (260). Thanh's suicide note is the tragic story of her life of lies: her illegitimate birth, her putative father's murder of her biological father, her mother's unburied, wandering soul. Although the novel ends with Mai's recognition that the part of her that had always wanted to break free of her mother has "made a sudden turn in reverse to rush backward into the folds of my mother's womb," that "a part of her would always pass itself through me," Mai's unexplored future is full of promise: college, apparent financial security, adoption by Uncle Michael (259).

Dust of Life

How different is Mai's life from those of mixed-blood characters such as Karlin's Kiet, Gardner's Trang, and The Deuce. For the young Vietnamese with the key to the golden door—American blood—settlement in the States and biculturality are at once a genetic demand and an extraordinary challenge. The twenty-five to sixty-five thousand "Amerasians"—officially defined as any person born in Vietnam between 1962 and 1976 and fathered by an American citizen—who emigrated to the United States in the 1980s and 1990s under the Amerasian Immigration Act, the Orderly Departure Program, and finally, after 1988, the Amerasian Homecoming Act are, physically and psychologically, neither American nor Vietnamese. Reviled in Vietnam as *bui doi*—the dust of life—most emigrated to find in America a Vietnamese refugee community that rejected them as not truly Vietnamese and an American society at best ambivalent about this very visible legacy of a painful experience that most Americans wanted only to forget.

The journalist Philip Gourevitch described Amerasians' status in Vietnam in a 1995 *Granta* article, "The Boat People": "The Amerasians were a pariah caste in post-war Vietnam—fatherless, often the children of prostitutes, reviled in a nationalist society ill-disposed to half-breeds, and doubly reviled as the monster spawn of the imperialist foe. Many had been abandoned by their mothers; they were often barred from schools, or tormented by their fellow students, and they were denied higher education and most employment opportunities. . . . To be an Amerasian, or related to an Amerasian, was often a ticket to time in a New Economic Zone or a jail" (51). At the beginning of *Daughter from Danang*, Heidi Bub's mother explains that she handed her young child over to Americans rescuing orphans in April 1975 because "if you had worked for the Americans and had racially mixed children, they said those kids would be gathered up. They would be soaked in gasoline and burnt." The fate of Amerasian children in a Communist Vietnam was hardly this horrific, but Kien Nguyen surely does not exaggerate in *The Unwanted* when in 1984 he receives a letter informing him of his eligibility for emigration to the United States under the Orderly Departure Program and declares that "there had not been a moment of happiness since the day I was taught the word *half-breed*" (281). Kien Nguyen eventually departs Vietnam, and after a time in a refugee camp in the Philippines, settles in America, where he completes dental school and, sixteen years later, publishes his memoir, which he has written to heal himself and to acknowledge the many stories of "terror and repression, abuse and neglect, strength, and ultimately—for the lucky ones—survival" (342). Nguyen apparently thrives in the States—land of the fabled Asian "model minority"—but not all Amerasians, however bleak their prospects in Vietnam, qualify as among "the lucky ones" once they arrive in the land of their fathers.

Fifteen-year-old Trang, in *Boat People*, is a more typical Amerasian in the States—young, alone, uneducated, and aimless. Trang has come to America with her aunt, who abuses her, and her ineffectual search for her American father promises to end in disappointment. Her younger friend Linh understands that Trang is disenfranchised—maybe even "evil," as people claim about the *bui doi*—and concludes that therefore "perhaps it was all right to hurt her" (243, 22). Trang's story is common among young Amerasians in the United States in the 1980s and '90s. The 1988 Amerasian Homecoming Act lifted quotas on Amerasian immigration and loosened documentary requirements by which such children proved their half-American ethnicity, and "overnight," Bass asserts, "Amerasians of Vietnam went from being . . . 'the dust of life,' to 'gold children' endowed with the power to fly themselves and their family members around the world" (3). Children orphaned or abandoned to beg in the streets of Saigon suddenly found themselves with tenacious real or faux relatives who wanted to emigrate to the United States. As Gourevitch writes, "people who had some biological or semi-familial relationship to an Amerasian often agreed, for a price, to take on a few new family members. Others would find an unattached Amerasian and attach themselves and their real or newly assembled 'families' to him as kin" (52). In the United States, Trang is a second-class citizen in the home of her aunt and uncle, with whom she has fled from Vietnam, leaving her mother behind. In *Prisoners*, social worker Louise Hallam is describing Trang as much as Kiet, her fictional sister, when she explains to her husband Alex, "In Vietnam, kids like her were despised until people found out that American features could get entry visas. . . . Then they were called golden children. Only a lot of them were abandoned once they got here" (123). Very few Amerasians were reunited with their American fathers when they arrived in the United States, and many, like Trang, know nothing about the fathers whose country they now call home. Trang tries to claim Azelita's veteran-boyfriend Wilson as her father: "You were in my country. You were soldier. You are an American!" she insists, but Wilson's response is Gardner's lesson in *Boat People*: "It don't matter who's your daddy, sugar. What matters is who *you* are" (272). Wilson had better be right, for Trang will never find her father. The Amerasians' futile search for their American fathers offers another compelling twist to the father-child theme that resonates throughout the narratives of the aftermath of the Vietnam War.

Fourteen-year-old Kien Nguyen is in Nhatrang when he writes to his American father, begging him to take him to America. Three months later his unopened letter returns marked "Return to sender, address unknown" (274). Kien Nguyen is indeed "The Unwanted." Twenty-something Binh (Damien Nguyen) finds his father—a literally and metaphorically blind ranch hand named Steve Cole (played by Nick Nolte)—at the end of Hans Petter Moland's 2004 film *The Beautiful Country*, but his flight from Vietnam to the beautiful country of America is precipitated less by a desire to meet his father, or even to leave Vietnam and his mother, than by an accident instigated by his pariah status in Vietnam. Because he has the "face of [the] enemy," the unusually tall Binh grows up reviled as ugly and not truly Vietnamese. The movie recounts Binh's life and forced emigration from Vietnam; the terrors and privations of the refugee boat and his escape from a Malaysian refugee camp; his indentured menial work in New York City to pay the cost of his escape; his belated discovery that, as the son of an American GI, he could have left Vietnam legally; and his successful quest to find his father. Binh knows that, as the English captain of the hazardous rag ship tells him, he will "always be out of place wherever [he] go[es]." *The Beautiful Country* presents in Binh a young man who, despite his paternity, is Vietnamese; he sends his meager wages back to his mother in Vietnam, because "she have nothing." He accepts responsibility for his young brother's death on the disease-infested refugee ship. Soft-spoken and unassuming, Binh is nothing like the street-savvy, in-your-face *bui doi* who have been in America for a while.

Karlin's Kiet, for example, is only sixteen, but her troubled life in the States has already been eventful and nomadic. Abused by the latest of a series of foster fathers, sent to a detention center, then to a group home for troubled adolescent girls, Kiet runs away when watching the movie *Platoon* evokes vague memories of seeing her mother murdered by GIs in Vietnam. Turned away by a local Vietnamese family to whom she appeals for help—"We're all dust in this country, little sister. But I can't afford the trouble"—Kiet makes her way from southern Maryland to Washington, D.C. (52). Kiet is angry, confrontational—an "off-brand grrrl ghost. . . . VCWA: Viet Cong With an Attitude" (93, 11). She applauds the "VC homies" on the streets of "the enemy capital" who sell "t-shirts saying *tough shit yeah we're here now*" and "hot dogs and egg rolls and copper Washington Monuments and Sno-Globes (turn them over and shake them and napalm falls on a thatched roof village)" (92, 91). At the Vietnam Veterans Memorial, Kiet looks for her African American father in the "phone book of the dead," though she admits that she doesn't know her father's real name (93). Intrigued by the Wall, she wonders "since when Americans build altars for wandering souls, come here, talk to em, leave offerings?," but she knows that "you gotta build them an altar, so they won't wander around, fuck with the living" (99). In the darkness, Kiet "pushes [her] whole body against the wall. Daddy daddy daddy daddy daddy 58,108 times" (99). Echoing the rebirth of *Lost Armies*'s Xuan, Kiet enacts her own regeneration through violence, pulling away from the Wall, "feeling myself being named and born out of the black living wedge of the dead" (100). Reborn, Kiet returns to Point Lookout in rural Maryland, where she kills the foster father who has abused her and finds a true—if not biological—father in Baxter, the reclusive blind African American veteran whom sheriff Alex looks after and who, Alex remembers, tried to adopt an orphan in Vietnam before he was wounded.

Trang wanders through her life without a father, and a luckier Kiet settles for a disabled substitute paternal parent, but The Deuce runs away from his American father when Kenneth, a respectable if dull lawyer, returns to Saigon in 1974 to claim his half-Vietnamese son.[11] *The Deuce* is the first-person narrative of another Amerasian teenager who runs and runs and runs some more before coming to terms with his mixed blood and his ineffectual father, and negotiating through his confusing and multiple identities to discover who he really is. Võ Đình Thanh is six years old when his Vietnamese mother lets his American father take him to live in Point Pleasant, New Jersey, with a bedroom full of "furniture, toys, a record player, a tape machine, a TV . . . things," Thanh (now called Tony) tells us, "I'd always figured someday I'd be able to steal for myself" (31). But the price of the TV and the expensive sneakers is a silent, distant stepmother who takes off a couple of years after Tony arrives and a father who tries—but fails—to establish a meaningful relationship with his son. "I feel very stupid sometimes," Kenneth explains to Tony just before the teenager runs away from his suburban life, "because I took for granted that you could be plucked out of your home and family, such as it was, and taken to the other side of the world by a stranger who says he's your father, and you'd naturally understand why he did that" (64). Tony *can* understand that; what he cannot understand or forgive is why his father left his mother Nghi—a bar girl with a drug problem, who, according to Kenneth, sold her son to his American father—behind in Vietnam.

After ten years of suburban life, when Kenneth announces his plans to remarry, sixteen-year-old Tony sets out to find the Vietnamese community in Montreal, figuring that "since I wasn't American, there was no sense in staying in America" (71). But en route Tony, who tells a stranger that his name is Thanh (thereby rejecting his American heritage and embracing his Vietnamese identity), is robbed and stranded in New York City. After a dangerous time alone, living on the streets, Tony/Thanh meets Joey Cipriani, an unemployed Vietnam vet who panhandles in the Port Authority Bus Terminal and who eventually takes Thanh to his "home" in an abandoned building on the Lower East Side. When a Port Authority police officer and Treen, a homosexual pimp, both display an interest in Thanh, Joey claims that the teenager—whom he christens "The Deuce" after nearby seedy, pre-Disneyized Forty-second Street and because "you're two things. You're Vietnamese and you're American. A deuce"—is his son (122). And when Treen murders Joey for protecting Thanh, just as Kenneth finds Tranh, the boy knows that the police will do nothing to prosecute Treen for a crime against a homeless Vietnam veteran, and that he will therefore have to avenge his surrogate father's death.

In *The Deuce*, Butler emphasizes Tony/Thanh/The Deuce's struggle to learn and decide who and what he is. In a bicultural twist on Herman Melville's "Call Me Ishmael," Tony begins his story with the announcement of his complex identity: "I wish it was simple just to say who I am, just to say my name is so-and-so and that makes you think of a certain kind of person and that would be me.... But me, I've got three names. And so I've got to go through all this bullshit just to start talking" (7). Tony recognizes the visible manifestation of his complicated identity. "You look at me and there's something a little odd," Tony explains. With one glance, he tells us, he looks like "any of the all-American types in school"; with another, "the look of the gook" comes through: "these are the eyes of an American, then they're the eyes of a Vietnamese" (23, 237). The other Amerasian characters here echo Thanh's sensitivity about the physical characteristics that mark them as "half-breeds," outcast in two societies. *Boat People*'s Trang pours yellow paint on the brown—not, to her chagrin, black—hair that announces her otherness in the Galveston Vietnamese community, while in Vietnam, Kien Nguyen's mother dyes his curly blond hair black in an attempt to safeguard him from prejudice against his mixed blood. Like The Deuce, Trán (in America, Fran), the first-person narrator of Robert Olen Butler's "Letters from My Father," recognizes the symbolic significance of her ambiguous face:

> I was a child of dust. . . . that's what we were called, those of us who had faces like those drawings you see in some bookstalls on Nguyen Hue Street. You look once and you see a beautiful woman sitting at her mirror, but then you look again and you see the skull of a dead person, no skin on the face, just the wide eyes of the skull and the bared teeth. We were like that, the children of dust in Saigon. At one look we were Vietnamese and at another look we were American and after that you couldn't get your eyes to stay still when they turned to us, they kept seeing first one thing and then another. (66)

The Deuce reluctantly admits that his aborted plan to join the Vietnamese community in Montreal was probably doomed. "Could I have convinced the Vietnamese that I was one of them? They had eyes to see. Fucking blend in. I doubt it. It would've been fuck yous, child of the dust, and the bus you rode in on" (72). Later he wonders whether, if he had made it to Canada, he'd "be Vietnamese right now. Could I have done it? Could I have been Vietnamese?" (222). Thanh tries to embrace his Vietnamese heritage. When Joey asks him whether he's half Vietnamese, he responds "I'm Vietnamese" (118). But in this novel that is in many ways a traditional bildungsroman, as Thanh struggles to survive on the streets of New York City, he continues to grapple with his identity. Though when he proclaims to Joey that he's "not part American," he concedes that his insistent assertion is a lie (120). The owner of a small Korean grocery store near Forty-second Street gives Thanh some food and attempts to befriend him. He recognizes Thanh as Vietnamese, and the boy is somewhat melodramatically surprised that he is not pleased by a fellow Asian's acknowledgment of his ethnicity: "There's no fucking flash of light or ringing bells or any goddam thing that would say, Kid this is you, you've found yourself at last, rest easy now, you really are Vietnamese. . . . Am I Vietnamese? Am I Võ Đình Thanh after all? What the fuck good would that do me?" (209). Late in the novel, when he learns of Joey's death, a slowly maturing Thanh moves closer to an understanding and acceptance of his bifurcated identity. Admitting that the American Tony wants to cry and the Vietnamese Thanh wants to "head for the alleys,"

The Deuce recognizes that he's "like two different people," one fleeing but the other weeping for his murdered friend (256). As the novel ends, Tony/Thanh/The Deuce accepts that he is a lost Vietnamese woman's son *and* Kenneth Hatcher's son *and* "I'm a lot of things but I'm one thing, and I have no doubt about that. I'm the Deuce" (303).

As The Deuce's ruminations about his name suggest, for these Amerasian and Asian characters—as for the underground fugitives in the movement who adopted multiple identities in their subterranean lives—naming is an important metaphor for and marker of identity. In *Lost Armies*, Xuan tells Wheeler about the Vietnamese practice of death names, a theme reinforced by Wheeler's—and later, in *Prisoners*, Kiet's—visit to the Vietnam Veterans Memorial and its "death names" (*Lost Armies*, 52). *Prisoners*'s peripatetic Kiet has had several names in her American life—Keisha, and, most recently, K-K—but in the girls' home that she escapes early in the novel, Larry, a counselor and veteran (the same Larry who so thoughtlessly rents *Platoon* for the girls to watch), finds her real name, Kiet, in her papers. "I had to explain to him that name was all drowned . . . and said go with K-K," Kiet asserts, "but he tells me no, you need to be proud of your heritage. Meaning the gook part I didn't know fuck-all about" (13). Fran, the narrator of Butler's "Letters from My Father," adopts the name Trán when she lives with her mother in Saigon. Fran, short for Francine, is "something like a Vietnamese name," but, Fran tells us, "it isn't, really" (66). The story underscores the ambiguous identity that Fran/Trán's names imply. Like The Deuce, Fran is in search of her father. It's true that she lives in her American father's house in Louisiana, but when she discovers the hundreds of letters from her father to the authorities, written over nine years in an effort to get his daughter and her mother out of Vietnam, she knows that the man who wrote those indignant, passionate letters is not the distant, uncommunicative father with whom she lives now. At the end of the story, hidden in a storeroom, Fran waits for her father, so she can "ask him to talk to me like in these letters, like when he was so angry with some stranger that he knew what to say" (72).

The eight interrelated stories in Aimee Phan's 2004 collection *We Should Never Meet* present the stories of Vietnamese American orphans who left Saigon during the last days of the war on the Operation Babylift program that evacuated 2,600 babies and children to the United States. Huan is adopted, and Mai is raised by comfortable and attentive foster parents, but high school dropout Kim and her gang leader boyfriend Vinh are shuffled through the foster care system until they are eighteen and thrust into a difficult life of burglary, abortions, and bad times. Phan outlines the controversy about whether Vietnam's children should have been brought to the States, where, some Vietnamese partisans insist, they would become for Americans "fashionable . . . souvenirs of the war," embraced merely to assuage America's guilt about destroying the orphans' home (132). Phan's characters—like Sage, the half-Vietnamese protagonist of the final novella in Dao Strom's *The Gentle Order of Girls and Boys* (2006), and unlike most of the *bui doi* in these texts—show little interest in their American fathers. Kim tires of Americans asking her whether she is searching for her American father, but she knows that "the other orphans" do struggle with their identity.

Thomas Bass declares that "no more than a couple of hundred Amerasians, out of the twenty-five thousand airlifted to the States, have found their fathers" (189–190). Searching for a home, an identity, the young Amerasian characters in these texts—whether literally alone like Trang and Kiet or emotionally isolated like The Deuce and Fran—are the particularly poignant and powerful residue of America's misadventure in Vietnam. With their American features and their curly hair, they are the physical manifestation of biculturality. Pariahs in Vietnam and a "political embarrassment" in the States, they are also, as Bass notes, "a bridge between cultures, a mirror held to our unsuspecting faces, and the first thing one might remark is that America's newest refugees are also its children" (4).

"My Skin Felt at Home"

As America learns to accept its hybrid children and their Asian half-siblings, time, the lifting of the trade embargo, and the restoration of diplomatic relations between Vietnam and the United States have allowed Vietnam's children—and their children—to return to their ancestral land. A 1994 *New York Times* article subtitled "Reversing an Exodus" asserts that "as many as 10,000 Vietnamese a month are returning for visits to a country hungry for their cash but often suspicious of their western ways" (A1). Vietnam-born, California-raised Andrew X. Pham recounts his visit to Vietnam in his travel memoir *Catfish and Mandala*. Some overseas Vietnamese, or Viet Kieu, have repatriated permanently—such as the young professionals profiled in the *Times* article and Tony Nong, who left Vietnam at age eight, was raised in California, and returned to Vietnam in 1992 to work with his mother Ann, in her successful tour company (and who is profiled in Sandy Northrop's 2002 documentary *Vietnam Passage: Journeys from War to Peace*). Lan Vu, twenty-seven years old in 1994, returned to Vietnam from Portland, Oregon, where she was raised, to work for a Swiss chemical company. "Learning to tread the narrow path between being an outsider and a native," she tells the *New York Times* that she feels increasingly at home in Vietnam: "Probably intellectually I'm American, but the emotional part of me is Vietnamese" (A7).

A number of the most recent of the texts considered here, those written by Vietnamese Americans who were born in Vietnam but grew up in the United States, present protagonists whose narratives conclude with a trip back—a peregrination to the land of their birth, a pilgrimage that parallels American veterans' therapeutic journey to the Vietnam Veterans Memorial in the nation's capital. The fictional protagonists offer a more considered, complex response to their journeys and enjoy a more auspicious reunion with distant relatives than the real-life Viet Kieu, whose return to Vietnam is often unsatisfying. *Daughter from Danang*'s Heidi, back in the States, two years after her tearful farewell to her Vietnamese family, has stopped answering their letters and admits at the end of the film, "I wish this trip never happened. It's not how I wanted it to be. . . . They're strangers to me." A more analytical and introspective Andrew Pham struggles, too, with his recognition that he is "too American. Too refined, too removed from my *que*, my birth village" to find in Vietnam the direction for his life that he is seeking (183). As he cycles throughout Vietnam, the frisson of surprised pleasure that the local Vietnamese betray when they discover that Pham (who looks more Japanese than Vietnamese) speaks their language is undermined by a more deeply felt and pervasive resentment of his safe, privileged American life. Calvin, a new Vietnamese friend, assures Pham that "*Vietnamese are Vietnamese if they believe they are,*" but concedes that "*some call you lost brothers. Look at you. Living in America has lightened your skin, made you forget your language. You have tasted Western women and you're probably not as attracted to Vietnamese women anymore. You eat nutritious Western food and you are bigger and stronger than us. You know better than to smoke and drink like Vietnamese. . . . Someday, your blood will mix so well with Western blood that there will be no difference between you and them. You are already lost to us*" (326, 330). Le Ly Hayslip, whose 1989 memoir *When Heaven and Earth Changed Places: A Vietnamese Woman's Journey from War to Peace* juxtaposes her account of her 1986 trip back to Vietnam, after sixteen years in the States, with her childhood memories of her country in wartime, recognizes her Vietnamese family's ambivalent embrace of their expatriate daughter: "Do I," she wonders, resentfully, "deserve envy for my painted fingernails and hygienist-cleaned teeth and four-bedroom home in California, or pity for the spiritual things—a life with my family in the land of my ancestors—I gave up to obtain them?" (193). And Andrew Lam recognizes at the conclusion of "Viet Kieu," his essay about his journey back to his childhood home, "If I am some archetype in Vietnam's new narrative of itself—a modern-day Odysseus of sorts, someone that those who stayed imagine that they can become if they were to flee overseas—I feel a stranger in my own homeland. . . . The jet plane does and does not take me home again. Or rather, I go home but the country of my childhood memories is long gone, replaced by a collective yearning of possibilities beyond the provincial" (130).

lê thi diem thúy's protagonist has already run away from her parents and her California home (like Pham's sister-suicide Chi) and at the end of *The Gangster We Are All Looking For* is rumored to live near New York City and to write stories. All of her life, she has felt the invisible presence of her brother, who, we learn late in the novel, has drowned in the South China Sea. Though she gradually comes to accept that he is dead, *Gangster*'s narrator goes back to Vietnam, still looking for her sibling: "I don't know how time moves or which of our sorrows or our desires it is able to wash away. I return after twenty years still expecting my brother to step out of the sea. Though I'm taken to the cemetery the first day back, no part of me believes he is actually beneath the light blue plaster headstone. . . . Walking along the streets and among the market stalls, I half expect to turn and find him, a young man moving along beside me, someone whose face I may no longer recognize but whose body my body will recall" (154). Huan, the half-black, half-Vietnamese protagonist of Aimee Phan's final story, "Motherland," returns reluctantly to the land of his birth, coerced by his American adoptive mother and his former girlfriend, a Korean who has left him because her family disapproves of his mixed heritage, into "a belated quest to discover his roots" (217). Huan and Mai, his childhood friend and fellow Babylifter, return to Vietnam tentatively, resentful about both the parents who abandoned them and the Americans who accepted them. Huan is aware that the Vietnamese hate him for his American blood and his ostensibly wealthy, privileged American life, but at the end of the story, Huan and Mai make their peace with Vietnam and their missing parents, acknowledging that parents could not do right "when everything here was wrong. . . . It was a war" (243).

Dao Strom's Thuy/April writes daily letters to her Danish stepfather recounting her reactions to her journey back to Vietnam, at the end of *Grass Roof, Tin Roof*, when she is twenty-three years old. Though Vietnam does not feel like home, and Thuy admits that she has "never quite grasped" that she was born there, her responses to Vietnam are profound. "My skin felt at home for the first time anywhere, unfettered, natural," Thuy confides to her father. "I recognized things I shared, like my relatives' gestures, the shapes of people's faces, their body types, their smiles and tired expressions" (204). An English-speaking cousin tells Thuy about her husband, whose family forced him to divorce his wife and emigrate with them to the United States, but who, after six months in San Francisco, jumped off the Bay Bridge. Thuy understands "how it must've been incomprehensible, to go from here to there, to be suddenly in a place where all you had previously known no longer counts and you know you cannot go back" (211).

Fundamentally incomprehensible though the wrenching loss, homesickness, and confusion of the emigrant's experience may be, the flourishing assemblage of creative texts about the Vietnamese in America offers rich insights into the Vietnamese diaspora and America's responses to its newest citizens. As the Vietnamese and Southeast Asian communities in the United States age and grow, these novels, films, and memoirs—surely to be complemented by other new narratives—offer poignant commentary on another side of the Vietnam War.

Conclusion

We Were All There

War Stories aren't really anything more than stories about people anyway.

—Michael Herr, *Dispatches*

N his early combat memoir *A Rumor of War* (1977), Philip Caputo recognized that the Vietnam War would be "the dominant event in the life of my generation" (xx). The powerful combat narratives that succeeded Caputo's affirm his prescience, for the war in Vietnam, more than any other historical event, defined late-twentieth-century America. Complementing the diverse interpretations of the experience of Americans serving in Vietnam, similarly sundry, poignant cultural texts that at once create and illuminate the other sides of the war—the acrimonious home front during the long years of America's presence in Vietnam and the postwar experiences of the myriad Americans whose lives were touched, destroyed, or profoundly changed by it—testify to the reverberating significance of the war at home, well beyond the jungles of Vietnam and long after the M-16s and boonie hats disappeared into musty khaki-colored trunks.

Bringing the War Home

The novels, memoirs, and films written about the Vietnam era in the past generation (and, evidence indicates, in the years to come) offer varied, cogent commentary on an era unsettled and inscribed by racial divisions and painful progress, by fundamental challenges to traditional expectations for women and other historically disenfranchised groups, by a war so prolonged and controversial that those struggles for individual rights coalesced around it. In these narratives, the violent drama of the combat experience is complemented by comparably disruptive events on the home front: assassinations, urban riots, massive demonstrations, chaos in the streets of Chicago, deaths on university campuses. At the beginning of the era, the young revolutionaries of the SDS pledged to create a new, truly participatory democracy, but by the waning years of the war, for many of these authors, as for Philip Roth, "the outlaws [were] . . . inside the gates." The repercussions of the profound, widespread social disruptiveness of the era's movements remain, for contemporary American culture, at once unsettled and riveting. As Tom Brokaw suggests, "The bottom line has yet to be drawn under those turbulent times. Conclusions have yet to be established" (xiv).

Narratives such as *The Waiting Room, The Darling,* and *Running on Empty* demonstrate variously and compellingly that the cultural tentacles of the war extended well beyond the military arena. Women writers emphasize a home front battlefield as their female protagonists stoically embrace a wartime vigil, then a long postwar journey with war-damaged husbands, brothers, and fathers that brings the war home literally and poignantly. Memoirs by Vietnam prisoners of war underscore the continuing controversy of the allegation that some of the combatants whose wartime fate remains ambiguous may have been left behind in Vietnam—a contention that to this day demonstrates America's enduring preoccupation with the Vietnam phenomenon. The POW wives' long years of waiting—of living on hold—parallel the experience not only of their prisoner husbands but of the wives, sisters, and daughters who stand guard, waiting, long after the Paris Peace accords, for their men truly to return from war. The theme of liminality recurs throughout these narratives—in Vietnamese refugees immured in relocation camps, in lonely radical activists lurking furtively underground, in veterans who cannot move beyond the horrific legacy of war.

The narratives about home front dissidents—idealistic college students, lifelong pacifists, antiwar veterans—display most clearly the angry passions that the war evoked and the misapprehensions about the era and its participants that have prevailed in the decades since. They examine as well the larger tapestry of the Vietnam era and the evocative ways in which equality for African Americans and women, a new awareness of the environment, and other movements of the 1960s and '70s distended the Vietnam experience. And the stories of the Vietnamese in America challenge Americans' provincial perception of the war, demonstrating that the Vietnam War was, for the majority of those who engaged it directly, daily, often disastrously, an American War. It is the creative narratives of the Vietnamese displaced by America's sojourn in Vietnam—and their children—that disclose most evocatively the inclusive apprehension of the war that all of these narratives offer.

And yet, despite the breadth and diversity of these narratives of the "other sides" of the war, prevailing themes emerge with intriguing consistency. The true and fictional stories of waiting wives, forsaken children, disaffected rescusants, unsettled refugees, and others touched by the calamitous war and its reverberations subvert the combatant's claim that "you had to be there," which has been a sacrosanct axiom of American war literature at least since Ernest Hemingway dismissed Willa Cather's 1922 Pulitzer Prize–winning World War I novel, *One of Ours*, with the acerbic suggestion that her novel's battle scenes were indebted to the movie *Birth of a Nation*. "Catherized," sniffs the war novelist. "Poor woman she has to get her war experience somewhere" (Wilson, 118). Again and again, these narratives suggest that well-intentioned, respectful citizens—and readers—can, in fact, comprehend the combat experience. You didn't have to be there after all, they demonstrate; *we were all there.*

Throughout these works, the response to displacement and upheaval is the search for community and camaraderie—in the Hanoi Hilton, in cadres of counterculture communicants, in the Little Saigons of American cities. Under the exigencies of combat, imprisonment, and diaspora, the war's constituents create alternative communities that lend support to their partisans and consequence to the charged circumstances. And those idealistic sixties searchers for a better way to live show, finally, that their rejection of the inequitable status quo brings not a repudiation of traditional familial structures so much as a quest for a new kind of family.

Another prevalent—and related—theme is the complicated, contested campaign to come to terms with the fathers. Acknowledging the patriarchal origins of war and the alluring perfidy of the legacy of the fathers' triumphant victory in World War II, the aftermath narratives—from John McCain's encomium to his military ancestors, to Mason's Sam Hughes's adolescent summer sortie to learn about the father who died in combat before her birth, to Karlin's Kiet's doomed search for her American soldier-daddy—enact a confused generation's quest for clarity and meaning through countless, variant iterations of the generation gap and the often heartbreaking, captious relationship between father and child. The comcomitant frustrated project of the fathers—Philip Roth's Swede Levov, Jay Cantor's Leo Jacobs, Christopher Sorrentino's Hank Galton—to understand the "family of lost boys and girls" reinforces the theme and highlights one of the seminal myths of the era, that is, the youth of its participants (Cantor, 174).

We've Been Here Before

Today, the United States wallows in twenty-first-century wars whose parallels with the more frustrating aspects of the imbroglio in Vietnam become ever more apparent. Comparisons between the Vietnam War and America's military enterprise in Iraq are, of course, ubiquitous. The Iraq War, like the Vietnam War, is, it is said, an unconventional guerrilla war waged in an environment geographically, politically, culturally—and dangerously—unfamiliar to the American military. It is an incursion compromised—like the Southeast Asia misadventure—by dubious motivations for U.S. involvement, a questionable military strategy, and no clear exit plan. "Quagmire" is again a familiar appellation for a frustrating foreign fiasco. Today, senior army officials, seeking clarity about the Iraq War, read revisionist critiques of the Vietnam War that question the Pentagon's post-Vietnam "big-war" strategy, which reinforced the late-twentieth-century maxim that America lost in Vietnam because it fought "with one hand tied behind its back." The "newer analyses of Vietnam," Greg Jaffe writes in the *Wall Street Journal*, "are . . . changing the way the Army fights. The argument that the military must exercise restraint is a central point of the Army's new counterinsurgency doctrine." Social critic Anna Quindlen, reinforcing the sentiment that "We've Been Here Before" (and staking another claim on the Wall as resonant metaphor), suggests, in her October 2005 *Newsweek* Last Word column, that "the Vietnam Memorial stands, in part, as a monument to blind incrementalism, to men who refused to stop, not because of wisdom but because of ego, because of the fear of looking weak. Not enough troops, not enough planning, no real understanding of the people or the power of the insurgency, dwindling public support. The war in Iraq is a disaster in the image and likeness of its predecessor." Quindlen wonders, "If we are such a great nation, why are we utterly incapable of learning from our mistakes?" (70).

And though there is no large-scale movement opposing the increasingly unpopular war in Iraq and the largely forgotten conflict in Afghanistan (arguably, if simplistically, because the absence of a draft renders more American citizens largely invulnerable to direct participation in today's wars), the still fervid resentment against Vietnam antiwar activists was recently evident in the army's decision to prevent Joan Baez—an outspoken opponent to the Iraq War—from performing in the April 2007 concert by singer and war critic John Mellencamp for injured soldiers at Walter Reed Army Medical Center. Though the army insists that Baez was barred because of a late invitation, she, Mellancamp, and the national media suspect that old resentments about her Vietnam-era activism explain the rejection. Although Americans have apparently learned, since the antipathies of the Vietnam era, not to blame the warrior for the war, they are more willing than ever to excoriate the antiwarrior. In short, the sad correlations between the current war and the war in Vietnam are increasingly apparent.

Undoubtedly, over time, American attitudes about the Vietnam War will continue to evolve. Creative narratives about the Iraq War have begun to appear, and as the length, destructiveness, and dissatisfaction with the current war grow, it will surely supplant the Vietnam War as cultural touchstone, at least for a younger generation. Today, U.S.-Vietnamese relations are in flux, as Vietnam's rapid modernization influences current American economic and foreign policy. The United States reestablished economic and diplomatic relations with Vietnam in the 1990s, thereby expediting what is now $8 billion in mutual trade between the two former enemies. Young, ambitious Vietnamese—would-be capitalists—greeted Microsoft founder Bill Gates like a rock star when he visited Vietnam, and the American microchip company Intel plans to build a $600 million plant in Ho Chi Minh City.

Closer interactions between the United States and a young, more affluent Vietnam may, in fact, effectuate a revisionist perspective on the place of Vietnam and the Vietnamese in American history and memory. Yet the unrelenting passage of time surely promises a more incontrovertible transformation. For example, in his stump speeches and his best-selling manifesto, *The Audacity of Hope*, presidential aspirant Barack Obama (who was born in 1961, at the tail end of the baby boom) calls for a political philosophy that—and a candidate who—transcends the divisive ideologies that have prevailed in American politics for the past half century. Claiming that the real and important social advances of the 1960s were compromised by an attendant loss of a "quality of trust" in American democracy, the Illinois senator suggests that a renewed liberal agenda (and an Obama presidency) would surmount the "psychodrama of the Baby Boom generation" that has defiled American politics and public life in recent years (37). Barack Obama is the first—but only the first—ambitious American politician to repudiate as fractured and outmoded the social and political legacy of the baby boomers and the 1960s. As a generation of Americans for whom the Vietnam War is ancient history takes center stage, the power of the war and its reverberations will inevitably abate. Yet the enormous canon of cultural narratives about the Vietnam War and complementary movements of the 1960s, which constitute a prodigious and growing re-examination of late-twentieth-century American life, will continue to disclose that the baby boomers' war still resonates.

Early in *Monkey Bridge*, Lan Cao's "ragtag" refugees, seduced into pursuing a "Vietnamese version of the American Dream," emend their personal histories, change their birth dates, and embrace America's promise of "a truly uncluttered beginning" (15, 40–41). As the novel slowly reveals the tragic history of Mai's family, the young narrator gradually understands that neither she nor her tortured mother can escape the karmic burdens of their shared past. But, at the end of the novel, in liberating Mai to pursue her own dreams and live her own life, Thanh, her haunted mother, affirms the seductive dream of a "brand new tomorrow" and empowers her daughter to "rewrite the endings" of her own predetermined life (204, 40). The narratives that tell the varied and powerful stories of the other sides of the Vietnam War similarly rewrite the endings of America's haunting liaison with Vietnam and the Vietnamese.

More important, this vibrant collection of cultural narratives amplifies the large, always growing canon of literature about the Vietnam War beyond the memoirs, fiction, and films—*Platoon*, *Fields of Fire*, *The Things They Carried*, and thousands more—that capture the traumatic, dramatic in-country combat experience. The legacy of the Vietnam War has "leaked into the matrix. . . . We are all at the party," proclaims Wayne Karlin's frustrated Louise (*Prisoners*, 104). Thomas Myers suggests that in history and memory, "there are only Vietnams" ("Dispatches," 411). And Ward Just, Michael Herr, and Bobbie Ann Mason remind us that everyone in America fought the Vietnam War—and fights it still.

Notes

Chapter One. MIA in America

1 See Timothy J. Lomperis, *"Reading the Wind": The Literature of the Vietnam War* (1987).

2 David Langness, in a recent *Paste* magazine article about American war fiction, takes the "you had to be there" aphorism even further. "By definition," he cautions, "only survivors write war stories.... When you read a war story, take it with a salt tablet. It was written by someone who lived, who didn't pay the full freight, who made it out somehow." Taken to its illogical extreme, the presumption that only combat veterans can truly understand the experience mandates that really only war *fatalities* are its true claimants.

3 Published originally as *Marking Time*.

4 Standard combat jargon: fucking new guy.

5 Ward Just proves the exception to the rule. At the conclusion of *The American Blues*, Just's journalist-narrator finally comes to terms with his inability to finish his book—or his preoccupation with the Vietnam War: "For many years I had accepted the thesis, half a century old now, that the large abstract words such as glory, honor, courage, and cowardice, were obscene. That which was chaste was factual . . . Now I knew I was mistaken and in this war all we had were the large abstract words . . . I had a skull overflowing with facts—untainted, innocent—and none of them described the war. . . . Only the large words were equal to the experience, in which the sacrifice was so out of balance and the results so confounding. Glory or disgrace, sacred or profane; pick the words you want. Only in this way would the deepest secrets, those closest to the heart, be disclosed" (203–204).

6 An important exception is the veterans who become antiwar activists. While most of the fictional veterans of the war cannot, or will not, talk about their Vietnam experience, activists like Ron Kovic and Bill Ehrhart (both real rather than fictional creations, interestingly) positively scream their opposition to the war and their own war experiences throughout their respective memoirs.

7 Real-life non-veterans who have publicly regretted their failure to serve include James Fallows ("What Did You Do in the Class War, Daddy?," 1975) and Christopher Buckley ("Viet Guilt," 1983).

8 Pete, one of the struggling Vietnam vets in Bobbie Ann Mason's *In Country* (1985), and the terminally ill Vietnam and career military vet Henry Teeter in John A. Miller's 1995 story "Guns" express similar enjoyment of, and nostalgia for, their tours of duty in Vietnam.

9 Kidder's dismissal parallels Jerry Lembcke's thesis in his controversial *The Spitting Image: Myth, Memory, and the Legacy of Vietnam* (2000).

10   Prominent among the Vietnam-era activities of Senator John Kerry that propelled angry Vietnam veterans to derail his 2004 Democratic presidential campaign through their "Swift Boat Veterans and POWs for Truth" attacks were Kerry's 1971 testimonies. Under the Swiftvets.com link, "Phony War Crimes," the anti-Kerry vets counter his testimonies at the Winter Soldier hearings and the April 1971 Senate Committee on Foreign Relations hearing with the insistence that "false testimony and exaggerations were primary characteristics of the war crimes disinformation campaign, and also of the VVAW itself."

11   Interestingly, these novels and memoirs—no doubt because of the irresistibly dramatic, narrative power of the atrocity—do not quibble about what qualifies as an immoral or illicit activity. As the journalist Jonathan Schell demonstrates in *The Military Half*, his 1968 "Account of Destruction in Quang Ngai and Quang Tin," official rules of engagement allowed considerable latitude in identifying and responding to actionable civilian activities. "A village could be bombed immediately and without the issuing of any warning to the villagers if Americans or other friendly troops or aircraft had received fire from within it," Schell notes. Also, "a village could . . . be destroyed if intelligence reports indicated that the villagers had been supporting the Vietcong by offering them food and labour" (13–14, 15).

12   The sole survivor is a seductive dramatic conceit. Like Paco, O'Nan's Larry Markham, Estevez's Jeremy, Bausch's Michael, and the movie Rambo, among others of these protagonists, carry the guilt, the shame, and the burden of memory of being the last man standing in their combat group.

13   Scott Ely's 1988 novel *Pit Bull* presents another young woman oddly fascinated with the scarred body of an older Vietnam vet. *Dirty Work* offers an unusual inversion of the theme in that Walter James befriends a scarred young girl.

14   When O'Brien's narrator, about halfway through the novel, clarifies what has been becoming increasingly evident—that John Wade was one of Calley's soldiers at My Lai—he explains that the Vietnamese names for the subhamlets in Son My Village, near Quang Ngai City, were different from the names that the Americans used. My Lai, he tells us, is actually named Thuan Yen. Throughout *In the Lake of the Woods*, O'Brien refers to Thuan Yen, not My Lai, which emphasizes the accuracy of his treatment of the events of the war (an accuracy reinforced by his frequent quotation of testimony from the actual Calley trial and other factual documents); and this, in turn, underscores the documentary aspect of the novel. It also, it seems to me, attenuates Wade's guilt. Somehow, although we learn that Thuan Yen is My Lai, the former name does not reverberate with the same significance that My Lai has for Americans: in 1969, when we first learned about My Lai; in 1994, when *In the Lake of the Woods* was published; or today.

15   Unlike several of the POW memoirs that are co-authored by husband and wife, none of the veterans' aftermath memoirs presents the author's spouse as a significant presence in the author's life, or in the narrative.

16 Albert French's 1997 memoir *Patches of Fire* and Tim O'Brien's 1975 novel *Northern Lights* present main characters whose lives are defined, respectively, by nonexistent and problematic relationships with their fathers.

17 In his 2007 memoir, *The Father of All Things*, Tom Bissell follows the troubling father-son relationship into the next generation. Bissell's book—an unusual generic hybrid of family memoir, travelogue, historical/political commentary on the Vietnam War, and oral history by the children of American and Vietnamese veterans—explores the awkward, unresolved relationship between his alcoholic father and the Vietnam veteran's second son, who, Bissell insists, loves but cannot understand his former marine father.

18 An interesting exception is Peter Dimock's odd, slim 1998 novel, *A Short Rhetoric for Leaving the Family*, a tour-de-force rhetorical exercise that is a former mental patient's disquisition to two young relatives about his father's position as special assistant to an unnamed U.S. president and his consequent responsibility for escalation of the war in Vietnam.

Chapter Two. *The Other Side of Grief*

1 Remember Ward Just's suggestion that men go to war because the women are watching.

2 Fifty-four civilian and eight military women died in Vietnam; most of the nurses who perished were among the approximately one hundred fifty people who died in the crash of the C-5A Galaxy outside Saigon on April 4, 1975, during Operation Babylift, the U.S. effort to evacuate Vietnamese orphans before the Communist takeover.

3 Lynda Van Devanter, who established the Women's Project of the Vietnam Veterans of America, died in 2002, ostensibly as a result of exposure in Vietnam to Agent Orange.

4 Today, with one in ten soldiers in the Iraq War female, one wonders how women's increasingly legitimate claims to direct war experience will mitigate the traditional male monopoly of the combat story.

5 Though Susanne Carter agrees that "most women have written in the tradition of realism," her 1991 and 1992 articles analyze more uncommon "innovative interpretations" such as Ursula LeGuin's futuristic *The Word for World Is Forest* and Elizabeth Ann Scarborough's fantasy *The Healer's War* ("Creating a Landscape," 290).

6 Compare Tom Bissell's memoir, *The Father of All Things*, about his journey to Vietnam with his veteran-father, Bissell's attempt to understand the youthful experience that defined his father's life. "Our fathers," Bissell writes, "were remote because the war itself was impossibly remote. . . . Despite its remoteness, the war's aftereffects were inescapably intimate. At every meal Vietnam sat down, invisibly, with our families" (101).

7   A bizarre and wonderful exception is Tim O'Brien's "Sweetheart of the Song Tra Bong," a story from *The Things They Carried* in which seventeen-year-old Mary Anne Bell's GI boyfriend flies her to his remote posting in the mountains near Chu Lai, and Mary Anne promptly goes native with a group of seriously gungy Green Berets.

8   As with the male-authored narratives, a pilgrimage to the Vietnam Veterans Memorial features prominently in many of these texts. On her 1984 visit (well before the addition of the women's memorial), Winnie Smith resents the exclusion of women veterans from the memorial and Veterans Day celebrations there, but she rejects the "jabbering" crowd of visitors who "have no connection to the war." She embraces the Wall in yet another variation of veterans' insistence that those who weren't there don't get it: "Let the outsiders be damned. We have this place, and we are finding one another. We will grow strong together again" (318, 319). This notion of the Wall as a site of healing recurs throughout these texts—in *Private Woods* and *Snake's Daughter* and *Lonely Girls with Burning Eyes* as well as in *In Country* and *Let Their Spirits Dance*.

Chapter Three. Years of Darkness

1   The president's confederates were apparently happy enough to exploit the POW myth against fellow Republicans as well. Connie Bruck's May 2005 *New Yorker* profile of John McCain recounts Bush supporters' infamous and successful campaign to sabotage McCain's presidential aspirations in the 2000 South Carolina primary. The media campaign mounted by Ralph Reed and Pat Robertson derailed McCain with allegations (among others) that he "had committed treason in Hanoi, or was crazed from his captivity" (Bruck, 62).

2   See H. Bruce Franklin's *M.I.A. or Mythmaking in America* for an account of the intermingling of statistics on POWs and MIAs during the Vietnam War.

3   Many books reinforce the popular belief that America left men behind: see Nigel Cawthorne's *The Bamboo Cage*; Rod Colvin's *First Heroes*; and Monika Jenson-Stevenson and William Stevenson's *Kiss the Boys Goodbye*. Susan Katz Keating's *Prisoners of Hope: Exploiting the POW/MIA Myth in America* and Malcolm McConnell's *Inside Hanoi's Secret Archives: Solving the MIA Mystery* offer a refutation of these claims. See too the POW/MIA websites and listservs on the Internet, many of which fuel the ongoing arguments about whether or not American POWs/MIAs still remain in Southeast Asia.

4   In the years since the original postwar accounting, some MIAs have been classified as unrecoverable, in a category labeled "no further pursuit." Vietnamese French author Phan Huy Duong's "The Billion Dollar Skeleton" is a satiric story about the efforts of the richest man in the world to recover the remains of his American MIA son.

5   Published originally in 1975 as *A Hero's Welcome: The Conscience of Sergeant James Daly versus the United States Army*.

6   Compare conscientious objector John Balaban's recognition, in his memoir *Re-membering Heaven's Face*, that "the real force" of young American International Voluntary Services volunteers in Vietnam was "in propaganda" (69).

7   In which, of course, the second North Vietnamese attack, which was Lyndon John-son's impellent for sending ground troops to Vietnam, therefore formally involving American combatants in a war with Vietnam, was later determined never to have occurred.

8   In both the novels and the memoirs discussed here, the suddenly solitary POW/MIA wife receives almost no emotional support or tangible assistance from her parents and siblings. Does the mobility dictated by the military culture enforce a separation from traditional familial support structures? Or do the authors under-estimate such relationships in order to dramatize the unnerving isolation that their protagonists feel? Also, Pat Hall reinforces Moreau's point about "the last genera-tion" when, in *Commitment to Honor*, she describes her difficulty readjusting to military life *after* her POW husband returns from Vietnam, in part because "some of the young wives were now employed and did not attend all the functions the older women expected them to attend" (138).

9   Compare the wives' incarcerated husbands. Most of the male memoirists, when they mention their sexuality at all, insist that the privations of imprisonment ren-dered sexual activity—or its absence—insignificant during their years as a POW. Descriptions of the clever communication methods occasionally allude to the transmission of an off-color joke; a few POWs recount their relief at the infrequent wet dream. With the unexpected (and fictional) exception of James Kirkwood's de-scription of homosexual sex and affection in *Some Kind of Hero*, the narratives con-sciously offer not even the hint of homosexual desire or activity—in the American POWs, that is; more than a few allege that their Vietnamese guards were interested in each other, or in the comparatively well-endowed American prisoners. In the macho, blatantly Christian exegesis that was the official story, the POWs, like their wives, are asexual.

10 The supercilious antiwar activist in *Limbo* is, ironically, like contemporary conser-vative pundit Ann Coulter, who, in her 2006 book *Godless: The Church of Liberal-ism*, accuses the widows of men killed in the 9/11 terrorist attacks of exploiting and enjoying their husbands' deaths.

11 The *New York Times* May 15, 2007, obituary for Kate Webb, who died at age sixty-four, was its second acknowledgment of the death of the intrepid life-long journalist.

12 It is because the Vietnamese will not touch her, Schwinn notes, that she—unlike her male colleague—is able to smuggle out her notes when she is released.

13 Nineteen-year-old marine PFC Bobby Garwood was captured in DaNang in Sep-tember 1965, near the end of his Vietnam tour. In 1979, fourteen years after his capture and six years after the release of the American POWs, Garwood asked an English-speaking Finnish economist visiting Hanoi to tell American authorities that he wanted to come home. Several of the Southern memoirists (Daly, Schwinn

and Diehl, some of the Survivors) recount their interactions with Garwood, whom they present as a Vietnamese collaborator. But the mysterious Garwood case, which fuels the claims of the conspiracy theorists who insist that America left POWs in Vietnam, remains controversial and unclear. Monika Jensen-Stevenson (in *Spite House: The Last Secret of the Vietnam War*) and others argue that Garwood was a scapegoat, sacrificed by a craven military determined to cover up its mistakes in Vietnam and its abandonment of American prisoners.

14   Grant's subjects, except for Ted Guy, were all between twenty and twenty-four years old. All were captured early in that watershed year, 1968.

Chapter Four. *The Fugitive's Hour*

1   See David Farber's article "The 60's: Myth and Reality," (*Chronicle of Higher Education*, December 7, 1994) and Rick Perlstein's "Who Owns the Sixties?: The Opening of a Scholarly Generation Gap" (*Lingua Franca*, May/June 1996) for overviews of trends in late 1990s scholarship on the 1960s. See also "The Other Sixties," by Mark Feeney in *The Boston Globe*, April 6, 2003, C2. And in his 2006 manifesto *The Good Fight: Why Liberals—and Only Liberals—Can Win the War on Terror and Make America Great Again*, Peter Beinart traces the decline of the Democratic Party in the second half of the twentieth century. His second chapter, "Losing America," particularly blames the increasingly radical civil rights movement and the SDS for jettisoning "liberalism's ideological foundations" (33).

2   That 2004 Swift vets' attack on John Kerry proves the point. While the irate veterans questioned Kerry's conduct in Vietnam, they were more enraged by his postwar involvement with Vietnam Veterans Against the War.

3   It is those "speed freaks and junkie moochers" who "come and piss in your streams and you're supposed to mop their brows and nurse their strung-out parasitic hearts until the whole place becomes a flophouse, you know, Bowery in the foothills" who turn the women's commune where Caroline Sherman takes shelter in Spiotta's *Eat the Document* into a cautious, closed community. And in their 2007 documentary film *Summer of Love*, filmmakers Gail Dolgin and Vicente Franco (who made *Daughter from Danang*) identify rubber-necking weekend hippies as one of the reasons that San Francisco's 1967 "celebration of free love, music, and an alternative lifestyle . . . descended into a maelstrom of drug abuse, broken dreams, and occasional violence."

4   The fallout shelter appears as a plot device, symbol, and motif in O'Brien's 1975 debut novel, *Northern Lights*.

5   More recently, Oates was the liaison of the gay and lesbian community to the John Kerry presidential campaign finance committee; she is the wife of Robert Shrum, well-known adviser to national Democratic candidates and author of the 2007 memoir *No Excuses: Concessions of a Serial Campaigner*.

6   An interesting—and not uncommon—variation on the familiar soldier's theme: you had to be there. Compare Weather Underground fugitive Beth Jacobs's appre-

hension, in Jay Cantor's *Great Neck*, that "Her Life So Far could only really make sense to comrades who had shared it" (556).

7   Scenes in *Drop City* and other movement narratives of industrious women bustling about sedentary men are replicated throughout contemporary Vietnam.

8   At his most directive, Juan organizes his quartet for combat drills and physical conditioning. His schedule:

> 8–8:30 washing, eating
> 8:30–11:30 field training
> 11:30–12 ego reconstruction

is an eerie radical inversion of Benjamin Franklin's and Jay Gatsby's more individualistic self-improvement regimens (134). In *Trance*, Sorrentino offers another variation on the theme with Teko's (Choi's Juan) "Revolutionary Diary," which recounts Teko's disappointment when he discovers Tania reading *Fear of Flying* and when his female charges (as only he considers them) exhibit a "disrespectful, undisciplined response" to the daily Criticism/Self-Criticism session. Teko carefully enumerates individual confederates' daily intake of "cigarets" and beer, objecting to Yolanda's, Joan's, and Tania's indulgence because it compromises "expense, physical readiness, usual discipline" (263).

9   *Eat the Document*'s Bobby Nash similarly—and tragically—battles his self-doubts about his ability to fight the war by any means necessary. When at the end of the novel he and Louise Barrot meet, after twenty-eight years underground, having pronounced their shared violent action "a huge mistake," Louise tells Bobby that she never expected anyone to die. Bobby confesses that he did indeed anticipate the fatal results of their final bombing; he confides, "I did it as a testament to my own certainty, as a test of my conviction. I needed to prove to myself I could go all the way" (274, 279).

Chapter Five. Something Strange and Extravagant

1   *Passing Time* was originally published as *Marking Time*.

2   9/11-influenced negative reaction to the publication of *Fugitive Days* was not merely literary. A November 16 *Chronicle of Higher Education* story that begins, "Since the attacks of September 11 . . . ," recounts that angry alumni of Northwestern University (where Bernadine Dohrn is director of the Children and Family Justice Center and a faculty member of the law school) and of the University of Illinois at Chicago (professional home of Professor of Education Bill Ayers) protested the employment of the former radicals and threatened to withhold donations to the institutions.

3   Horowitz's current, and quite visible, campaign is his effort, through his national conservative watchdog group, Students for Academic Freedom, to force American universities and colleges to adopt an Academic Bill of Rights that will protect "dissenting" (read conservative) viewpoints in the classroom.

4   Published originally as *Soon to Be a Major Motion Picture.*

5   Like many Vietnam-era activists, Fonda continues her work for social progress, today complementing movie acting with leadership of her Georgia Campaign for Adolescent Pregnancy Prevention (G-CAPP).

6   For more on the New Journalism (in another context), see my "Green Visors and Ivory Towers: Jean Stafford and the New Journalism," *Kenyon Review* 16, no. 4 (Fall 1994): 104–119.

7   In Vietnamese lore, the Trung Sisters, daughters of a Vietnam lord in the first century CE, heroically led their army of 80,000 against Chinese invaders. They are honored annually in Vietnam as national heroes.

8   Though Balaban clearly notes that McNamara "brought the war home to me one warm spring afternoon in 1967," Rosenblatt in *Coming Apart* and historians (including Small in *Antiwarriors* and Wells in *The War Within*) agree that the defense secretary's donnybrook with protesting students at Harvard occurred on November 11, 1966.

9   An interesting variation of this conceit recurs throughout the memoirs of the movement participants, who repeatedly envision themselves as Vietnamese. Bill Ehrhart's reaction to police versus protestor violence at the April 1971 New Mobilization march on Washington is the angry assertion that "it was just like the war—only this time I had no weapon, no flak jacket or helmet, no way to defend myself, no protection of any kind. Was this what it felt like to be a peasant in Vietnam, I wondered, wanting to throw up" (166). Bill Ayers describes the "implosion" of the 1968 Democratic Convention in Chicago: "we would be Viet Cong guerrillas attacking an American outpost, the audience of convention-goers would play the unhappy Americans, besieged" (134). As Bruce Franklin concludes, in his discourse on the postwar demonization of the Vietnamese and of the movement veterans, first the Vietnamese people were denounced (largely through the exploitation of the myth that POWs and MIAs were left behind in Vietnam), then "soon those tens of millions of Americans who had fought against the war themselves became, as a corollary, a truly hateful enemy as envisioned by the dominant American culture" (48).

10 Though Kovic doesn't say so, the march is surely the May 9, 1970, New Mobe, post–Kent State demonstration, the occasion of Nixon's infamous early morning visit with protestors at the Lincoln Memorial.

11 Compare Adler's recognition of a movement "dominant story" complemented by the women's story and the notion of official and unofficial versions of the POW experience by the strong, heroic pilots and the younger, weaker, dissident prisoners, respectively.

12 In *And a Voice to Sing With*, Baez, who posed with her two sisters for the iconic "Girls Say Yes to Boys Who Say No" antiwar poster, dismisses feminists' objections to the apothegm. "I thought it was clever," she notes. "I honest to God didn't know what they were talking about" (152–153). Susan J. Douglas, however, acknowledges Baez not only as the "pioneer" of folk music that invited less activist youth into the

civil rights movement but as "a new kind of female performer" who rejected "gender norms about proper female behavior and appearance" (146–147).

13 While one might argue that its acknowledgment of women's control of their own sexuality is empowering for women, more women, as Joan Baez notes, perceived the maxim as another example of women's marginal status in the movement. Katherine Kinney writes that "women's subordinate role in the antidraft movement was emblematized by the popular slogan, "Girls Say Yes to Guys Who Say No," and Milton J. Bates notes that the slogan is a revision of a World War I motto and illustrates that "women were not allowed to forget that they had less at stake in opposing the war, since they were exempt from the draft. They were to be, in effect, camp followers of the antiwarriors" (Kinney, 147; Bates, 137).

14 The Weathermen got it, enough, at least, to change their name to the less sexist (or, as Gitlin would have it, "feminized") Weather Underground (402).

15 Inaccurate because activist women did not burn their bras in Atlantic City. Ayers can perhaps be forgiven for his mistake, for this media-created misperception about the Miss America protest—which Susan J. Douglas describes as "a watershed in American history . . . virtually ignored in retrospectives on the 1960s"—is still widely held (139–140). The nearly four hundred energized women who protested on the Boardwalk that September day did everything *but* burn their bras, as they responded spiritedly to the official call to "reject the Pageant Farce and join us; a huge Freedom Trash Can (into which we will throw bras, girdles, curlers, false eyelashes, wigs, and representative issues of *Cosmopolitan, Ladies' Home Journal, Family Circle*, etc.—bring any such woman-garbage you have around the house)" (*Sisterhood Is Powerful*, 521).

16 The antiwarriors represented here offer their own you-had-to-be-there claim on their wartime activities. "It is very hard for people who came of age after the war ended to understand how the Vietnam War became part of our skin and bones," Margot Adler asserts. ". . . it became the fabric of our nightmares" (173–174). Bill Ayers, insisting again that he feels no regret for his movement actions, is "sorry only for those who are perpetually blind to the cruel side of the world, those who never feel stirred to fight for something infinite, for humanity itself" (284). The combat veteran-activists feel doubly privileged. Ron Kovic is in demand as an antiwar speaker; he claims in *Born on the Fourth of July*: "I think I honestly believed that if only I could speak out to enough people I could stop the war myself. I honestly believed people would listen to me because of who I was, a wounded American veteran" (149–150). And Bill Ehrhart, having insisted of his combat experience early in *Passing Time* that "nobody back in the World has any idea what it's like," later applies his privileged voice in that World: "if guys like you and me don't speak out now," Ehrhart implores his veteran-friend, "where's it gonna stop? . . . Maybe if guys like us can manage to turn this country around, maybe it might turn out to have been worth it after all" (52, 201).

17 In *Monkey Bridge* Mai Nguyen's newly immigrant mother insists that she and Mai settle near Washington, D.C., because it is "the safest place in the world." Mai notes

that "it hardly mattered that all around us the ghosts of a different war lingered, the Battle of Fredericksburg, the Battle of Bull Run, Confederate victories secured by Robert E. Lee's Army of Northern Virginia" (31).

Chapter Six. People Singing a Sad Song

1   Few of the texts by and about Vietnamese refugees devote much attention to the refugee camps and resettlement centers that were interim stops for many Vietnamese emigrants. Interesting exceptions are Paul Eggers's novel *Saviors* and short story collection *How the Water Feels*, Tran Vu's story "The Coral Reef" (from *Dragon Hunt*), Lady Borton's memoir *Sensing the Enemy*, and Timothy Linh Bui's film *Green Dragon*.

2   A Kit Carson scout is a former National Liberation Front (NLF) soldier who surrendered under a program called "Chieu Hoi," or "open arms," to help the Army of the Republic of Vietnam (ARVN) and the Americans. Robert Olen Butler presents another such narrative in "Open Arms," the first story in his collection *A Good Scent from a Strange Mountain*. Madame Ngo Dinh Nhu, the elegant, acerbic "Dragon Lady of Vietnam," served as first lady of South Vietnam for her widowed brother-in-law, Ngo Dinh Diem. Her husband was chief of the secret police.

3   A June 2006 *New York Times* article describes how *Last Night I Dreamed of Peace*, a recently discovered and published diary by Dang Thuy Tram, a female doctor who was killed in 1970, is a surprise best-seller in Vietnam, where it is "bringing the war alive for a new generation of readers." Noting that "two-thirds of Vietnam's 83 million people were born after the war ended in 1975," it quotes a Vietnamese professor at Harvard, who suggests that for this young population, "the Vietnam War is ancient history."

4   The last of the refugee camps for asylum seekers from Southeast Asia closed, in Hong Kong, in mid-1997. Many of the would-be refugees who were forcibly repatriated between 1989 and 1997 protested their forced return to Vietnam by hunger strikes, riots, and other violent protests.

5   "Regeneration through violence"—the term, and the concept—are Richard Slotkin's. Though Slotkin writes about the traditional American myth of the West, his theory suggests interesting parallels in these stories of Vietnamese exiles.

6   Compare veterans Jeremy in *The War at Home* and Red in *Missing in America*, who, we are told, "died" in Vietnam.

7   Compare Bill Ehrhart and Bill Ayers, who think of themselves as Vietnamese.

8   Robert Olen Butler offers a slyly subtle exception in his story, "Mr. Green." In it the nameless forty-one-year-old female narrator takes an understated but liberating revenge on her sexist, dismissive, long-dead grandfather by murdering his alter ego and legacy, an annoying parrot whose name gives the story its title.

9   Life tragically imitated art in late November 2004, when Chai Soua Vang, a Hmong immigrant and resident of "the Hmong capital of America," St. Paul, Minnesota,

killed six local deer hunters near a small Wisconsin town. Stephen Kinzer's late 2004 *New York Times* accounts of the incident emphasized the importance of hunting in Hmong culture, racial tensions within the community, and the possibility that the accused's role as a shaman in the Hmong community would factor into his lawyer's defense. Chai Soua Vang was convicted of murder and, in November 2005, sentenced to life in prison with no chance of parole. Subsequent hunting-related violent racial incidents have also occurred in Wisconsin's northern woods.

10 Designed by American military advisers and implemented in 1962, the strategic hamlet program was a plan to isolate rural villagers in newly constructed compounds—sometimes called "sunrise villages"—that would protect them from infiltration by the Vietcong and from the firepower of the Americans, while allowing the Americans to separate friend from foe. Though shoddy construction, concentration camp conditions, and easy penetration by the Vietcong doomed the strategic hamlet program, its failure was guaranteed for reasons more fundamental and more profound. Ignorant about Vietnamese culture, American military strategists did not comprehend the deep connections to family, the past, and place that are the essential values of the Vietnamese. The cultural miscommunication and ignorance that predestined this program to failure are a synecdoche for America's myriad miscalculations in the Vietnam War.

11 Almost always it is a search for the father for these characters. An exception is Patricia Henley's novel *In the River Sweet*, which presents a middle-aged American woman who is contacted by her Amerasian son, to whom she gave birth while volunteering in a French convent in Saigon in 1968 and whom she left behind with her blind Vietnamese lover and his imposing mother.

Works Cited

Note: In Vietnamese, the first name is the family surname, and the second name is the given name—i.e., the opposite of name order in English. American publishers list Vietnamese names, in bibliographic form, both ways. For clarity, here, for all Vietnamese names I use the standard American English practice of last name, first name, though doing so is not strictly accurate.

Aaron, Jason, and Cameron Stewart. *The Other Side*. New York: DC Comics, 2007.

Adler, Margot. *Heretic's Heart: A Journey through Spirit and Revolution*. Boston: Beacon Press, 1997.

Alamo Bay. Directed by Louis Malle. TriStar Pictures, 1985. Video, 1987.

Alexander, Caroline. "Across the River Styx." *New Yorker*, 25 October 2004, 44–51.

Alpert, Jane. *Growing Up Underground*. New York: William Morrow, 1981.

Alvarez, Everett, Jr., with Samuel A. Schreiner, Jr. *Code of Conduct*. New York: Donald I. Fine, 1991.

Amazon.com. Editorial Reviews. *The Things We Do to Make It Home: A Novel* (Ballantine Reader's Circle) (Paperback) by Beverly Gologorsky. 2000 (accessed 12 December 2005).

"An Unwelcome Visitor Center," Editorial, *New York Times on the Web*, 14 August 2006. http://nytimes.com/2006/08/14/opinion/14mon3.html?ex=1181188800&en=00eb1dc013c460d9&ei=5070 (accessed 5 June 2007).

Anderson, Terry H. *The Movement and the Sixties: Protest in America from Greensboro to Wounded Knee*. New York: Oxford University Press, 1995.

Appy, Christian G. *Patriots: The Vietnam War Remembered from All Sides*. New York: Penguin Books, 2003.

Ayers, Bill. *Fugitive Days: A Memoir*. 2001. Reprint. New York: Penguin Books, 2003.

Baez, Joan. *And a Voice to Sing With*. New York: Summit Books, 1987.

Baky, John. "Gendered War: Women's Fictive Viet Nam War." Paper presented at the annual meeting of the Popular Culture Association, New Orleans, La., April 2003.

Balaban, John. *Remembering Heaven's Face: A Conscientious Objector's Moving Memoir of the Vietnam War*. 1991. Reprint. New York: Touchstone, 1992.

Banks, Russell. *The Darling*. New York: HarperCollins, 2004.

Bass, Thomas A. *Vietnamerica: The War Comes Home*. New York: Soho Press, 1996.

Bates, Milton J. *The Wars We Took to Vietnam: Cultural Conflict and Storytelling*. Berkeley: University of California Press, 1996.

Bausch, Robert. *On the Way Home*. 1982. Reprint. New York: Avon-Bard, 1983.

Beattie, Ann. "A Clever-Kids Story." In *Secrets and Surprises: Short Stories*, 265–281. New York: Random House, 1978.

The Beautiful Country. Directed by Hans Petter Moland. Sony Pictures Classics, 2004. DVD, 2005.

Begley, Adam. "'Great Neck': To Know Which Way the Wind Blows." Review of *Great Neck* by Jay Cantor. *New York Times on the Web*, 2 February 2003. http://query .nytimes.com/gst/fullpage.html?res=9DO4E1D81E30F931A35751COA9659C8B63 &scp=2& (accessed 10 November 2004).

Be Good, Smile Pretty, Directed by Tracy Droz Tragos. New Video Group, 2003.

Beidler, Philip D. *American Literature and the Experience of Vietnam*. Athens: University of Georgia Press, 1982.

Beinart, Peter. *The Good Fight: Why Liberals—and Only Liberals—Can Win the War on Terror and Make America Great Again*. New York: HarperCollins, 2006.

Berkeley in the '60s. Directed by Mark Kitchell/Kitchell Films, 1990. DVD, First Run Features, 2002.

Berrigan, Daniel. *To Dwell in Peace*. San Francisco: Harper and Row, 1987.

Birkerts, Sven. "The Safe House." Review of *American Woman* by Susan Choi. *New York Times Book Review*, 5 October 2003, 9.

Bissell, Tom. *The Father of All Things: A Marine, His Son, and the Legacy of Vietnam*. New York: Pantheon, 2007.

Bittman, Mark. "Vietburgers: Hold the Bun." The Minimalist. *New York Times*, 23 July 2003, D3.

Blair, Sydney. *Buffalo*. New York: Viking, 1991.

Blakey, Scott. *Prisoner at War: The Survival of Commander Richard A. Stratton*. Garden City, N.Y.: Anchor Press/Doubleday, 1978.

Borton, Lady. *Sensing the Enemy*. Garden City, N.Y.: Dial Press/Doubleday, 1984.

Boyle, T. C. *Drop City*. New York: Viking, 2003.

Bradley, Jane. "What Happened to Wendell?" In *Power Lines and Other Stories*, 13–24. Fayetteville: University of Arkansas Press, 1989.

Brokaw, Tom. *Boom!: Voices of the Sixties*. New York: Random House, 2007.

Brown, Larry. *Dirty Work*. 1989. London: Penguin Books, 1990.

Broyles, William, Jr. "Why Men Love War." *Esquire*, November 1984, 55–65.

Bruck, Connie. "McCain's Party." *New Yorker*, 30 May 2005, 58–73.

Buckley, Christopher. "Rules of Engagement." Shouts & Murmurs. *New Yorker*, 4 October 2004, 51.

———. "Viet Guilt." *Esquire*, September 1983, 68–72.

Butler, Robert Olen. *The Alleys of Eden*. New York: Horizon Press, 1981.

———. "The American Couple." In *A Good Scent from a Strange Mountain*, 155–234. New York: Henry Holt, 1992.

———. "Crickets." In *A Good Scent from a Strange Mountain*, 59–64. New York: Henry Holt, 1992.

———. *The Deuce*. New York: Henry Holt, 1989.

———. "A Ghost Story." In *A Good Scent from a Strange Mountain*, 111–123. New York: Henry Holt, 1992.

———. "A Good Scent from a Strange Mountain." In *A Good Scent from a Strange Mountain*, 235–247. New York: Henry Holt, 1992.

———. "In the Clearing." In *A Good Scent from a Strange Mountain*, 103–110. New York: Henry Holt, 1992.

———. "Letters from My Father." In *A Good Scent from a Strange Mountain*, 65–72. New York: Henry Holt, 1992.

———. "Love." In *A Good Scent from a Strange Mountain*, 73–93. New York: Henry Holt, 1992.

———. "Mr. Green." In *A Good Scent from a Strange Mountain*, 17–28. New York: Henry Holt, 1992.

———. *On Distant Ground*. 1985. Reprint. New York: Ballantine Books, 1986.

———. "Open Arms." In *A Good Scent from a Strange Mountain*, 1–15. New York: Henry Holt, 1992.

———. "Relic." In *A Good Scent from a Strange Mountain*, 137–142. New York: Henry Holt, 1992.

———. "The Trip Back." In *A Good Scent from a Strange Mountain*, 29–43. New York: Henry Holt, 1992.

Byrd, Barthy. *Home Front: Women and Vietnam*. Berkeley, Ca.: Shameless Hussy Press, 1986.

Cantor, Jay. *Great Neck*. New York: Knopf, 2003.

Cao, Lan. *Monkey Bridge*. New York: Viking, 1997.

Caputo, Philip. *Indian Country*. 1987. Reprint. New York: Bantam Books, 1988.

———. "One Morning in October." Review of *They Marched into Sunlight: War and Peace Vietnam and America October 1967* by David Maraniss. *New York Times Book Review*, 5 October 2003, 10.

———. *A Rumor of War*. 1977. Reprint. New York: Ballantine Books, 1994.

Carroll, James. *An American Requiem: God, My Father, and the War That Came between Us*. Boston: Houghton Mifflin, 1996.

———. *Fault Lines*. New York: Dell, 1980.

———. *Prince of Peace*. New York: Signet, 1984.

Carter, Susanne. "Creating a Landscape That Never Was: Women's Fictional Interpretations of the Vietnam War Experience." *Midwest Quarterly* 33 (Spring 1992): 289–303.

———. "Variations on Vietnam: Women's Innovative Interpretations of the Vietnam War Experience." *Extrapolation* 32.2 (1991): 170–183.

Cawthorne, Nigel. *The Bamboo Cage: The Full Story of the American Servicemen Still Held Hostage in South-East Asia*. London: Leo Cooper, 1991.

Cease Fire. Directed by David Nutter. VHS. Double Helix Films/Cineworld, 1985.

Choi, Susan. *American Woman*. New York: HarperCollins, 2003.

Christopher, Renny. *The Viet Nam War/The American War: Images and Representations in Euro-American and Vietnamese Exile Narratives*. Amherst: University of Massachusetts Press, 1995.

Cofer, Judith Ortiz. "Nada." In *The Other Side of Heaven: Post-War Fiction by Vietnamese and American Writers*, edited by Wayne Karlin, Le Minh Khue, and Truong Vu,

25–32. Willimantic, Conn.: Curbstone Press, 1995. Originally published in Judith Ortiz Cofer, *The Latin Deli*. Athens: University of Georgia Press, 1993.

Colvin, Rod. *First Heroes: The POWs Left Behind in Vietnam*. New York: Irvington Publishers, 1987.

Coming Home. Directed by Hal Ashby. Jerome Hellman Productions, 1978. DVD, MGM/UA Home Entertainment,1978.

Currey, Richard. *Fatal Light*. 1988. New York: Penguin, 1989.

———. *Lost Highway*. Boston: Houghton Mifflin, 1997.

Daly, James A., and Lee Bergman. *Black Prisoner of War: A Conscientious Objector's Vietnam Memoir*. Lawrence: University of Kansas Press, 1975.

Daniels, Roger. "Asian American History's Overdue Emergence." *Chronicle of Higher Education*, 7 December 2002, B7–B9.

Darman, Jonathan. "1968: The Year That Changed Everything." *Newsweek*, 19 November 2007, 42–43.

Daughter from Danang. Directed by Gail Dolgin and Vicente Franco. Balcony Releasing, 2002. DVD, PBS Home Video, 2004.

Davidson, Sara. *Loose Change: Three Women of the Sixties*. Garden City, N.Y.: Doubleday, 1977.

Davis, Patti, with Maureen Strange Foster. *Home Front*. New York: Crown Publishers, 1986.

DeBenedetti, Charles. *An American Ordeal: The Antiwar Movement of the Vietnam Era*. Syracuse, N.Y.: Syracuse University Press, 1990.

The Deerhunter. Directed by Michael Cimino. Universal Pictures, 1978. DVD, MCA Universal Home Video, 2005.

Dell, Diana J. *A Saigon Party and Other Vietnam War Short Stories*. Lincoln, Neb.: Writers Club Press/iUniverse.com, 1998.

Dellinger, David. *From Yale to Jail*. New York: Pantheon Books, 1993.

Del Vecchio, John. *Carry Me Home*. New York: Bantam Books, 1995.

Denton, Jeremiah, with Ed Brandt. *When Hell Was in Session*. 1976. Reprint. Mobile, Ala.: Traditional Press, 1982.

Didion, Joan. "John Wayne: A Love Song," In *Slouching Towards Bethlehem*. New York: Farrar, Straus and Giroux, 1968.

———. "Where the Kissing Never Stops," In *Slouching Towards Bethlehem*. New York: Farrar, Straus and Giroux, 1968.

Dimock, Peter. *A Short Rhetoric for Leaving the Family*. Normal, Ill.: Dalkey Archive Press, 1998.

Dinh, Linh. "The Hippie Chick." In *Fake House: Stories*, 157–162. New York: Seven Stories Press, 2000.

Dodd, Susan. *No Earthly Notion*. New York: Penguin Books, 1986.

Dohrn, Bernadine. "From Revolutionary to Children's Rights Advocate." In *Sixties Radicals, Then and Now*, edited by Ron Chepesiuk, 223–239. Jefferson, N.C.: McFarland, 1995.

Douglas, Susan J. *Where the Girls Are: Growing Up Female with the Mass Media.* New York: Times Books, 1994.

Downs, Frederick, Jr. *Aftermath: A Soldier's Return from Vietnam.* New York: Norton, 1984.

Doyle, Robert C. "Unresolved Mysteries: The Myth of the Missing Warrior and the Government Deceit Theme in the Popular Captivity Narrative of the Vietnam War." *Journal of American Culture* 15 (Summer 1992): 1–18.

———. *Voices from Captivity: Interpreting the American POW Narrative.* Lawrence: University Press of Kansas, 1994.

Dramesi, John. *Code of Honor.* New York: Warner Books, 1975.

Duarte, Stella Pope. *Let Their Spirits Dance.* New York: Rayo, 2002.

Duong, Phan Huy. "The Billion Dollar Skeleton." In *The Other Side of Heaven: Post-War Fiction by Vietnamese and American Writers,* edited by Wayne Karlin, Le Minh Khue, and Truong Vu, 223–230. Willimantic, Conn.: Curbstone Press, 1995. Originally published in *Story* (Autumn 1994).

Dunn, Joe. "The POW Chronicles: A Bibliographic Review." *Armed Forces and Society* 9 (Spring 1983): 495–514.

Ebersole, Gary L. *Captured by Texts: Puritan to Post-Modern Images of Indian Captivity.* Charlottesville: University Press of Virginia, 1995.

Edgerton, Clyde. *The Floatplane Notebooks.* Chapel Hill, N.C.: Algonquin Books, 1988.

Egendorf, Arthur. *Healing from the War: Trauma and Transformation after Vietnam.* Boston: Houghton Mifflin, 1985.

Ehrhart, W.D. *Busted.* Amherst: University of Massachusetts Press, 1995.

———. *Marking Time.* New York: Avon Books, 1986.

———. *Passing Time: Memoir of a Vietnam Veteran Against the War.* Amherst: University of Massachusetts Press, 1986, 1995.

———. *Vietnam Perkasie.* New York: Zebra-Kensington, 1983, 1985.

Elshtain, Jean Bethke. *Women and War.* New York: Basic Books, 1987.

Ely, Scott. "The Child Soldier." *Pulpwood.* Livingston, Ala.: Livingston Press, 2003, 140–159.

Emerson, Gloria. *Winners and Losers.* New York: Random House, 1967.

Evans, Sara. *Personal Politics: The Roots of Women's Liberation in the Civil Rights Movement and the New Left.* New York: Vintage, 1980.

Fallows, James. "What Did You Do in the Class War, Daddy?" *Washington Monthly,* October 1975, 5–19.

Farber, David. "The 60's: Myth and Reality." *Chronicle of Higher Education,* 7 December 1994: B1–B2.

Farish, Terry. *Flower Shadows.* New York: William Morrow, 1992.

———. *A House in Earnest.* South Royalton, Vt.: Steerforth Press, 2000.

Farrington, Tim. *Lizzie's War.* New York: HarperCollins, 2005.

Faulkner, William. "Barn Burning." In *The Faulkner Reader,* 499–516. New York: Random House, 1954.

Fiedler, Leslie. "Come Back to the Raft Ag'in, Huck Honey!" In *American Literature, American Culture*, edited by Gordon Hunter. New York: Oxford University Press, 1999.

Figley, Charles R., and Seymour Leventman, eds. *Strangers at Home: Vietnam Veterans since the War*. 1980. Reprint. New York: Brunner/Mazel, 1990.

First Blood. Directed by Ted Kotcheff. Orion Pictures Corporation, 1982. DVD, Lions Gate Films Home Entertainment, 2003.

Fitzgerald, Frances. *Fire in the Lake: The Vietnamese and the Americans in Vietnam*. 1972. Reprint. New York: Vintage, 1973.

Fitzgerald, F. Scott. "Winter Dreams." In *Babylon Revisited and Other Stories*, 114–135. New York: Charles Scribner's Sons, 1960.

Fonda, Jane. *My Life So Far*. New York: Random House, 2005.

Ford, Elaine. *Life Designs*. Cambridge, Mass.: Zoland Books, 1997.

Franklin, H. Bruce. *M.I.A. or Mythmaking in America*. Brooklyn, N.Y.: Lawrence Hill Books, 1992.

———. *Vietnam and Other American Fantasies*. Amherst: University of Massachusetts Press, 2000.

Frazier, Sandie. *I Married Vietnam*. New York: George Braziller, 1992.

French, Albert. *Patches of Fire: A Story of War and Redemption*. New York: Anchor Books, 1997.

Freudenberger, Nell. "Letter from the Last Bastion." In *Lucky Girls: Stories*. New York: Ecco, 2003.

Gadbow, Kate. *Pushed to Shore: A Novel*. Louisville, Ky.: Sarabande Books, 2003.

Gardner, Mary. *Boat People: A Novel*. New York: Norton, 1995.

Garfinkle, Adam. *Telltale Hearts: The Origins and Impact of the Vietnam Antiwar Movement*. New York: St. Martin's Press, 1995.

Gilberg, Gail Hosking. *Snake's Daughter: The Roads In and Out of War*. Iowa City: University of Iowa Press, 1997.

Gitlin, Todd. Foreword to *The War Within: America's Battle over Vietnam* by Tom Wells, xi–xviii. Berkeley: University of California Press, 1994.

———. *The Sixties: Years of Hope, Days of Rage*. 1987. Reprint. New York: Bantam Books, 1993.

Gologorsky, Beverly. *The Things We Do to Make It Home*. New York: Random House, 1999.

Goodman, Walter. "Dark to Light in 1968." Review of *The Whole World Was Watching*, ABC documentary. *New York Times*, 12 December 1998, B5.

Gordon, Neil. *The Company You Keep*. New York: Viking, 2003.

Gosse, Van. "A Movement of Movements: The Definition and Periodization of the New Left." In *A Companion to Post–1945 America*, edited by Jean-Christophe Agnew and Roy Rosenzweig, 277–302. Malden, Mass.: Blackwell Publishing 2002, 2006.

———. *Rethinking the New Left: An Interpretive History*. New York: Palgrave Macmillan, 2005.

Gosse, Van, and Richard Moser, eds. *The World the Sixties Made: Politics and Culture in Recent America*. Philadelphia: Temple University Press, 2003.

Gourevitch, Philip. "The Boat People." *Granta* 50 (1995): 13–59.

Grant, Zalin. *Survivors*. New York: Norton, 1975.

Grigg, William Norman. "'Respectable Terrorists.'" *New American*, 19 November 2001. 5 pp. http://www.thenewamerican.com/ (accessed 16 July 2004).

Groom, Winston, and Duncan Spencer. *Conversations with the Enemy: The Story of PFC Robert Garwood*. New York: Putnam, 1983.

Gruhzit-Hoyt, Olga. *A Time Remembered: American Women in the Vietnam War*. Novato, Ca.: Presidio Press, 1999.

Gruner, Elliott. *Prisoners of Culture: Representing the Vietnam POW*. New Brunswick, N.J.: Rutgers University Press, 1993.

Guarino, Larry. *A POW's Story: 2801 Days in Hanoi*. New York: Ivy Books, 1990.

Guerilla: The Taking of Patty Hearst (also known as *Neverland: The Rise and Fall of the Symbionese Liberation Army*). Directed by Robert Stone. Robert Stone Productions, 2004. DVD, New Video Group, 2005.

Halberstam, David. *The Fifties*. New York: Villard Books, 1993.

Hall, George R., and Pat Hall, with Bob Pittman. *Commitment to Honor: A Prisoner of War Remembers Vietnam*. Jackson, Miss.: Franklin Printers, 2005.

Hanley, Lynne. *Writing War: Fiction, Gender, and Memory*. Amherst: University of Massachusetts Press, 1991.

The Hanoi Hilton. Directed by Lionel Chetwynd. Cannon Group, 1987. VHS, Warner Studios, 1993.

Harris, David. *Dreams Die Hard: Three Men's Journey through the Sixties*. 1982. San Francisco: Mercury House, 1993.

Hayden, Tom. *Reunion: A Memoir*. 1988. Reprint. New York: Collier Books, 1989.

Hayden, Tom, and Dick Flacks. "The Port Huron Statement at 40." *Nation*, 5 August 2002. http://www.thenation.com/doc/20020805/hayden (accessed 4 July 2006).

Hayslip, Le Ly, with James Hayslip. *Child of War, Woman of Peace*. New York: Doubleday, 1993.

———, with James Wurtz. *When Heaven and Earth Changed Places: A Vietnamese Woman's Journey from War to Peace*. 1989. Reprint. New York: Plume, 1990.

Heckler, Jonellen. *Safekeeping*. 1983. Reprint. New York: Fawcett Gold Medal Books, 1984.

Heinemann, Larry. *Paco's Story*. 1986. Reprint. New York: Penguin Books, 1987.

Hemingway, Ernest. *A Farewell to Arms*. 1929. Reprint. New York: Charles Scribner's Sons, 1957.

Henley, Patricia. *In the River Sweet*. New York: Pantheon Books, 2002.

Herr, Michael. *Dispatches*. 1977. Reprint. New York: Vintage Books, 1991.

Herzog, Tobey C. *Vietnam War Stories: Innocence Lost*. New York: Routledge, 1992.

Hirsch, James S. *Two Souls Indivisible: The Friendship That Saved Two POWs in Vietnam*. Boston: Houghton Mifflin, 2004.

Hoffman, Abbie. *The Autobiography of Abbie Hoffman*. 1980. New York: Four Walls Eight Windows, 2000.

Hollowell, John. *Fact and Fiction: The New Journalism and the Nonfiction Novel*. Chapel Hill: University of North Carolina Press, 1977.

Horowitz, David. *Radical Son: A Generational Odyssey*. 1997. New York: Touchstone, 1998.

Howes, Craig. *Voices of the Vietnam POWs: Witnesses to Their Fight*. New York: Oxford University Press, 1993.

Hubbell, John G. *P.O.W.: A Definitive History of the American Prisoner-of-War Experience in Vietnam, 1964–1973*. New York: Reader's Digest Press, 1976.

Hunter, Edna J. "The Vietnam POW Veteran: Immediate and Long-term Effects of Captivity." In *Stress Disorders among Vietnam Veterans*, edited by Charles R. Figley, 188–206. New York: Brunner/Mazel, 1978.

Huston, Nancy. "Tales of War and Tears of Women." *Women's Studies International Forum* 5.3/4 (1982): 271–282.

Isserman, Maurice. "How Old Is the New SDS?" *Chronicle of Higher Education*, 2 March 2007, B10–B11.

Jacknife. Directed by David Hugh Jones. Kings Road Entertainment, 1989. DVD, 2007.

Jaffe, Greg. "As Iraq War Rages, Army Re-Examines Lessons of Vietnam." *Wall Street Journal*, 20 March 2006, A1, A13.

Jason, Philip K. "Vietnamese in America: Literary Representations." *Journal of American Culture* 20.3 (1997): 43–50.

Jeffords, Susan. *The Remasculinization of America: Gender and the Vietnam War*. Bloomington: Indiana University Press, 1989.

———. "Reproducing Fathers: Gender and the Vietnam War in U.S. Culture." In *From Hanoi to Hollywood: The Vietnam War in American Film*, edited by Linda Dittmar and Gene Michaud. New Brunswick, N.J.: Rutgers University Press, 1990.

———. "Whose Point Is It Anyway?" *American Literary History* 3.1 (Spring 1991): 162–171.

Jenson-Stevenson, Monika. *Spite House: The Last Secret of the Vietnam War*. New York: Norton, 1997.

Jenson-Stevenson, Monika, and William Stevenson. *Kiss the Boys Goodbye: How the United States Betrayed Its Own POWs in Vietnam*. Toronto: McClelland and Stewart, 1990.

Just, Ward. *A Dangerous Friend*. Boston: Houghton Mifflin, 1999.

———. *The American Blues*. New York: Viking Press, 1984.

———. *To What End: Report from Vietnam*. 1968; New York: Public Affairs, 2000.

Kakutani, Michiko. "A Radical on the Run, Determined to Escape the Past." Review of *Eat the Document* by Dana Spiotta. *New York Times on the Web*, 3 February 2006. http://nytimes.com/2006/02/03/books/03kaku.html?ex=1140584400&en=bf147191 f1cf4dbe&ei=5070 (accessed 20 February 2006).

Kalpakian, Laura. "Veteran's Day." *Stand One*, edited by Michael Blackburn et al., 9–30. London: Victor Gollancz, 1984.

Karlin, Wayne. *Lost Armies*. New York: Henry Holt, 1988.

————. *Prisoners*. Willimantic, Conn.: Curbstone Press, 1998.

Keating, Susan Katz. *Prisoners of Hope: Exploiting the POW/MIA Myth in America*. New York: Random House, 1994.

Keenan, Barbara Mullen. *Every Effort: A True Story*. New York: St. Martin's Press, 1986.

Kidder, Tracy. *My Detachment: A Memoir*. New York: Random House, 2005.

King, Dave. *The Ha-Ha: A Novel*. New York: Little, Brown, 2005.

Kinney, Katherine. *Friendly Fire: American Images of the Vietnam War*. New York: Oxford University Press, 2000.

Kinzer, Stephen. "Hmong Hunter Charged with 6 Murders Is Said to Be a Shaman." *New York Times on the Web*. 1 December 2004. http://nytimes.com/2004/12/01/national/01hunter.html (accessed 3 December 2004).

————. "Hunter Tells Police He Was Threatened." *New York Times on the Web*. 24 November 2004. http://nytimes.com/2004/11/24/national/24hunters.html (accessed 3 December 2004).

Kinzer, Stephen, and Monica Davey. "A Hunt Turns Tragic, and Two Cultures Collide." *New York Times on the Web*. 28 November 2004. http://nytimes.com/2004/11/28/national/28hunter.html (accessed 3 December 2004).

Kirkwood, James. *Some Kind of Hero: A Novel*. 1975. Reprint. New York: Signet, 1976.

Kovic, Ron. *Born on the Fourth of July*. New York: Pocket Books, 1976, 1977.

Kuban, Karla. *Marchlands: A Novel*. New York: Scribner, 1998.

Lai, Thanhha. "The Walls, the House, the Sky." In *The Other Side of Heaven: Post-War Fiction by Vietnamese and American Writers*, edited by Wayne Karlin, Le Minh Khue, and Truong Vu, 258–265. Willimantic, Conn.: Curbstone Press, 1995. Originally published in *Threepenny Review* (Winter 1994).

Lahr, John. "Becoming the Hulk." Profiles. *New Yorker*, 30 June 2003.

————. "Sour Ball." The Theatre. *New Yorker*, 11 December 2006.

Lam, Andrew. *Perfume Dreams: Reflections on the Vietnamese Diaspora*. Berkeley, Calif.: Heyday Books, 2005.

Langness, David. "Them's Fightin' Words: A Tour of American War Fiction." *Paste* 18, (October–November 2005): 113–115.

La Rocco, Claudia. "Vietnam's Divide Endures for Native Dance Troupe." *New York Times on the Web*, 7 March 2007. http://nytimes.com/2007/03/07/arts/dance/07long.html ?ex=1179892800&en=5ff4adbe722b3223&ei=5070 (accessed 16 May 2007).

Leland, John. "Welcome Back, Starshine." *New York Times on the Web*. 20 May 2007. http://select.nytimes.com/preview/2007/05/20/arts/1154675732014.html?pagewanted=all (accessed 5 June 2007).

Lifton, Robert Jay. *Home from the War: Vietnam Veterans: Neither Victims nor Executioners*. New York: Basic Books, 1973.

Lim, Shirley Geok-Lin. "Assaying the Gold: Or, Contesting the Ground of Asian American Literature." *New Literary History* 24.1 (1993): 147–169.

"*Lizzie's War*." Review of *Lizzie's War* by Tim Farrington. Briefly Noted. *New Yorker*, 11 and 18 July 2005.

Lomperis, Timothy J. *"Reading the Wind": The Literature of the Vietnam War*. Durham, N.C.: Duke University Press, 1987.

Maag, Christopher. "Kent State Tape Is Said to Reveal Orders." *New York Times on the Web*, 2 May 2007. http://nytimes.com/2007/05/02/us/02kent.html?ex=1181188800& en=e371b56f86e787da&ei=5070 (accessed 5 June 2007).

MacPherson, Myra. *Long Time Passing: Vietnam and the Haunted Generation*. New York: Doubleday, 1985.

Mahoney, Tim. *Hollaran's World War*. New York: Delacorte, 1985.

Mailer, Norman. *The Armies of the Night: History as a Novel: The Novel as History*. New York: New American Library, 1968.

Mailer, Norris Church. *Windchill Summer: A Novel*. New York: Random House, 2000.

Marshall, Kathryn. *In the Combat Zone: An Oral History of American Women in Vietnam, 1966–1975*. New York: Penguin Books, 1987.

Martin, Andrew. *Receptions of War: Vietnam in American Culture*. Norman: University of Oklahoma Press, 1993.

Mason, Bobbie Ann. "Big Bertha Stories." In *Soldiers and Civilians: Americans at War and at Home*, edited by Tom Jenks, 202–216. New York: Bantam Books, 1986.

———. *In Country*. New York: Harper & Row, 1985.

Mason, Patience H. C. *Recovering from the War: A Woman's Guide to Helping Your Vietnam Vet, Your Family, and Yourself*. New York: Viking Penguin, 1990.

Massman, Patti, and Susan Rosser. *A Matter of Betrayal: A Novel Inspired by True Events*. Lincoln, Neb.: iUniverse.com, 1999.

McCain, John, with Mark Salter. *Faith of My Fathers*. 1999. Reprint. New York: Harper Perennial, 2000.

McConnell, Malcolm. *Inside Hanoi's Secret Archives: Solving the MIA Mystery*. New York: Simon & Schuster, 1995.

McDade, Charlie. *The Gulf*. New York: Harcourt Brace Jovanovich, 1968.

McDaniel, Dorothy Howard. *After the Hero's Welcome: A POW Wife's Story of the Battle against a New Enemy*. Chicago: Bonus Books, 1991.

McDaniel, Eugene B., with James L. Johnson. *Before Honor*. Philadelphia: A. J. Holman, 1975.

McDaniel, Norman A. *Yet Another Voice*. New York: Hawthorn Books, 1975.

McDougall, Walter A. "The Vietnamization of America." *Orbis* 39 (Fall 1995): 478–490.

Medved, Michael. "Nostalgic Baby Boomers Forget '60s Were Desperate Times." *USA Today*, 1 June 1998, 13A.

Michaels, Fern. *To Have and to Hold*. New York: Ballantine Books, 1994.

Miller, Arthur. *All My Sons*. In *Arthur Miller's Collected Plays*, 57–127. New York: Viking, 1957–1981.

Miller, Carolyn Paine. *Captured!* Chappaqua, N.Y.: Christian Herald Books, 1977.

Miller, James. *Democracy Is in the Streets: From Port Huron to the Siege of Chicago*. New York: Simon & Schuster, 1987.

Miller, John A. *Jackson Street and Other Soldier Stories*. 1995. Reprint. New York: Washington Square, 1997.

Missing in America. Directed by Gabrielle Savage Dockterman. Intrinsic Value Films, 2005. DVD, First Look Pictures, 2006.

Moniz, Dave. "Search for Vietnam MIAs Continues." *USA Today*, 29 April 2005, 1A.

Moore, Sandra Crockett. *Private Woods: A Novel*. San Diego: Harcourt Brace Jovanovich, 1988.

"More About the Film *Summer of Love*." *American Experience: Summer of Love*, 16 June 2007. http://www.pbs.org/wgbh/amex/love/filmmore/index.html (accessed 16 June 2007).

Moreau, Donna. *Waiting Wives: The Story of Schilling Manor, Home Front to the Vietnam War*. New York: Atria Books, 2005.

Morgan, Robin. "Goodbye to All That." In *The American Left: Radical Political Thought in the Twentieth Century*, edited by Loren Baritz. New York: Basic Books, 1971.

Morrell, David. *First Blood: A Novel*. New York: Warner Books, 1972.

Morris, Mary. *The Waiting Room*. New York: Doubleday, 1989.

Morrison, Toni. "Unspeakable Things Unspoken: The Afro-American Experience in American Literature." *Michigan Quarterly Review* 28.1 (1989): 1–34.

Mulligan, James. *The Hanoi Commitment*. Virginia Beach, Va.: RIF Marketing, 1981.

Mydans, Seth. "Former Refugees See Opportunity in Vietnam." *New York Times*, 5 December 1994, A1+.

———. "Diary of North Vietnam Doctor Killed in U.S. Attack Makes War Real." *New York Times on the Web*, 6 June 2006. http://www.nytimes.com/2006/06/06/world/asia/06vietnam.html?ex=1151294400&en=a362a93cfb5016b0&ei=5070 (accessed 6 June 2006).

———. "U.S. Combs Indochina for Clues to the Missing." *New York Times*, 20 July 2002. http://nytimes.com/2002/07/20/international/asia/20LAOS.html?ex=1028186473&ei=1&en=f8c9063670834af4 (accessed July 20, 2002).

Myers, Thomas. "Dispatches from Ghost Country: The Vietnam Veteran in Recent American Fiction." *Genre* 21 (Winter 1988): 409–428.

———. *Walking Point: American Narratives of Vietnam*. New York: Oxford University Press, 1988.

The National League of Families of American Prisoners and Missing in Southeast Asia, 24 July 2005. http://www.pow-miafamilies.org/index.html.

Niebuhr, Gustav. "More Than a Monument: The Spiritual Dimension of These Hallowed Walls." *New York Times on the Web*, 11 November 1994. http://select.nytimes.com/search/restricted/article?res=FB0C1FFF345A0C728DDDA80994DC494D81 (accessed 5 June 2007).

Nguyen, Kien. *The Unwanted: A Memoir*. Boston: Little Brown, 2001.

Nissen, Thisbe. *Osprey Island*. New York: Knopf, 2004.

Norman, Geoffrey. *Bouncing Back: How a Heroic Band of POWs Survived Vietnam*. Boston: Houghton Mifflin, 1990.

Novak, Marian Faye. *Lonely Girls with Burning Eyes: A Wife Recalls Her Husband's Journey Home from Vietnam*. Boston: Little, Brown, 1991.

Nunez, Sigrid. *For Rouenna.* New York: Farrar, Straus and Giroux, 2001.

———. *The Last of Her Kind.* New York: Farrar, Straus and Giroux, 2006.

Oates, Joyce Carol. *Black Girl/White Girl.* New York: Ecco, 2006.

Oates, Marylouise. *Making Peace.* New York: Warner Books, 1991.

Obama, Barack. *The Audacity of Hope: Thoughts on Reclaiming the American Dream.* New York: Crown Publishers, 2006.

O'Brien, Tim. "How to Tell a True War Story." In *The Things They Carried*, 73–91. New York: Penguin Books, 1990.

———. *In the Lake of the Woods.* New York: Houghton Mifflin, 1994.

———. *Northern Lights.* 1975. Reprint. New York: Broadway, 1999.

———. *The Nuclear Age.* New York: Penguin Books, 1985.

Olney, James. *Memory and Narrative: The Weave of Life-Writing.* Chicago: University of Chicago Press, 1998.

O'Nan, Stewart. *The Names of the Dead.* New York: Doubleday, 1996.

O'Neill, Susan. *Don't Mean Nothing: Short Stories of Vietnam.* New York: Ballantine Books, 2001.

Palmer, Laura. *Shrapnel in the Heart: Letters and Remembrances from the Vietnam Veterans Memorial.* New York: Random House, 1987.

Peacock, Nancy. *Life without Water: A Novel.* 1996. New York: Bantam Books, 1998.

Perlstein, Rick. "Who Owns the Sixties?: The Opening of a Scholarly Generation Gap." *Lingua Franca*, May–June 1996, 30–37.

Pfarrer, Donald. *The Fearless Man.* New York: Random House, 2004.

Pham, Andrew X. *Catfish and Mandala: A Two-Wheeled Journey Voyage through the Landscape and Memory of Vietnam.* New York: Farrar, Straus and Giroux, 1999.

Phan, Aimee. *We Should Never Meet: Stories.* New York: St Martin's Press, 2004.

Phien, Vo. "The Key." In *The Other Side of Heaven: Post-War Fiction by Vietnamese and American Writers*, edited by Wayne Karlin, Le Minh Khue, and Truong Vu, 252–257. Willimantic, Conn.: Curbstone Press, 1995.

Phillips, Jayne Anne. *Machine Dreams.* New York: Dutton/S. Lawrence, 1984.

Phong, Hoang Khoi. "Twilight." In *The Other Side of Heaven: Post-War Fiction by Vietnamese & American Writers*, edited by Wayne Karlin, Le Minh Khue, and Truong Vu. 266–274. Willimantic, Conn.: Curbstone Press, 1995.

Piercy, Marge. "The Grand Coolie Damn." In *Sisterhood Is Powerful: An Anthology of Writings from the Women's Liberation Movement*, edited by Robin Morgan, 421–438. New York: Random House, 1970.

———. *Vida.* New York: Summit Books, 1979.

Powell, Mary Reynolds. *Worlds of Hurt.* Chesterland, Ohio: Greenleaf Enterprises, 2000.

Proulx, Annie. "What Kind of Furniture Would Jesus Pick?" *New Yorker*, 18 and 23 August 2003, 127–137. Reprinted in *Bad Dirt: Wyoming Stories 2*, 59–86. New York: Scribner, 2004.

Puller, Lewis B., Jr. *Fortunate Son: The Autobiography of Louis B. Puller, Jr..* 1991. Reprint. New York: Bantam Books, 1993.

Pulley, John L. "Former Radicals, Now Professors, Draw Ire of Alumni at 2 Universities." *Chronicle of Higher Education*, 16 November 2001, A32.

Purcell, Ben, and Anne Purcell. *Love and Duty*. New York: St. Martin's Press, 1992.

Quindlen, Anna. "We've Been Here Before." Last Word. *Newsweek*, 31 October 2005, 70.

The Radical (also known as *Katherine*). Directed by Jeremy Paul Kagan. Jozak Company, 1975. DVD, Treeline Films, 2004.

Radosh, Ronald. "Don't Need a Weatherman: The Clouded Mind of Bill Ayers." *Weekly Standard*, 8 October 2001, 4 pp. http://weeklystandard.com/ (accessed 16 July 2004).

Rambo: First Blood Part II. Directed by George P. Cosmatos. TriStar Pictures, 1985. DVD, Artisan, 1998.

Rebels with a Cause. Directed by Helen Garvey. Shire Films, 2000. DVD, Zeitgeist Films, 2003.

Return with Honor. Directed by Freida Lee Mock and Terry Sanders. American Film Foundation, 1998. DVD, PBS Home Video, 2001.

Risner, Robinson. *The Passing of the Night: My Seven Years as a Prisoner of the North Vietnamese*. New York: Ballantine Books, 1973.

Rivers, Caryl. *Intimate Enemies*. New York: Dutton, 1987.

Rochester, Stuart I., and Frederick Kiley. *Honor Bound: American Prisoners of War in Southeast Asia, 1961–1973*. Annapolis, Md.: Naval Institute Press, 1998.

Rosen, Ruth. *The World Split Open: How the Modern Women's Movement Changed America*. Revised Edition. New York: Penguin Books, 2006.

Rosenblatt. Roger. *Coming Apart: A Memoir of the Harvard Wars of 1969*. Boston: Little, Brown, 1997.

Roth, Philip. *American Pastoral*. 1997. Reprint. New York: Vintage Books, 1998.

Rowan, Stephen A. *They Wouldn't Let Us Die: The Prisoners of War Tell Their Story*. Middle Village, N.Y.: Jonathan David, 1973.

Rowe, James N. *Five Years to Freedom*. 1971. Reprint. New York: Ballantine Books, 1984.

Running on Empty. Directed by Sidney Lumet. Double Play, 1988. DVD, Warner Home Video, 1999.

Rutledge, Howard, and Phyllis Rutledge, with Mel and Lyla White. *In the Presence of Mine Enemies, 1965–1973: A Prisoner of War*. Old Tappan, N.J.: Revell, 1973.

Rutledge, Paul James. *The Vietnamese Experience in America*. Bloomington: Indiana University Press, 1992.

Said, Edward W. *Orientalism*. 1978. Reprint. New York: Vintage Books, 1979.

Sayres, Sohnya, Anders Stephanson, Stanley Aronowitz, and Fredric Jameson. *The 60s without Apology*. Minneapolis: University of Minnesota Press/Social Text, 1984.

Scarborough, Elizabeth Ann. *The Healer's War*. New York: Doubleday, 1988.

Schaeffer, Susan Fromberg. *Buffalo Afternoon*. New York: Knopf, 1989.

Schappell, Elissa. "Roommates and Strangers." Review of *Black Girl/White Girl* by Joyce Carol Oates. *New York Times on the Web*, 15 October 2006. http://nytimes.com/2006/10/15/books/review/Schappell.t.html?ex=1174104000&en=eef5bb0fb38f352f&ei=5070 (accessed 15 March 2007).

Schell, Jonathan. *The Military Half: An Account of Destruction in Quang Ngai and Quang Tin*. New York: Knopf, 1968.

Schneider, Bart. *Secret Love*. 2001. Reprint. New York: Penguin Books, 2002.

Schroeder, Eric James, ed. *We've All Been There: Interviews with American Writers*. Westport, Conn.: Praeger, 1992.

Schuessler, Jennifer. "Passion at the Pickle Plant." Review of *Windchill Summer* by Norris Church Mailer. *New York Times Book Review*, 18 June 2000, 30.

Schwinn, Monika, and Bernhard Diehl. *We Came to Help*. New York: Harcourt Brace Jovanovich, 1973.

Scofield, Sandra. *Beyond Deserving*. New York: Plume Book, 1991.

Scott, A. O. "In Search of the Best." *New York Times on the Web*, 21 May 2006. http://nytimes.com/2006/05/21/books/review/scott-essay.html (accessed 13 May 2006).

Scott, Joanna C. *Charlie and the Children: A Novel*. Seattle: Black Heron Press, 1997.

Shea, Lisa. *Hula: A Novel*. New York: Norton, 1994.

Shepard, Benjamin. "Antiwar Movements, Then and Now." *Monthly Review: An Independent Socialist Magazine*. 53 (February 2002): 55–61.

Silver, Joan, and Linda Gottlieb. *Limbo*. New York: Viking Press, 1972.

Slotkin, Richard. "Dreams and Genocide: The American Myth of Regeneration through Violence." *Journal of Popular Culture* 5 (Summer 1971): 38–59.

———. *Regeneration through Violence: The Mythology of the American Frontier, 1600–1860*. 1973. Reprint. New York: HarperPerennial, 1996.

Small, Melvin. *Antiwarriors: The Vietnam War and the Battle for America's Hearts and Minds*. Wilmington, Del: Scholarly Resources, 2002.

Smith, Dinitia. "No Regrets for a Love of Explosives; In a Memoir of Sorts, a War Protester Talks of Life with the Weathermen." *New York Times*, 11 September 2001.

Smith, George Edward. *P.O.W: Two Years with the Vietcong*. Berkeley: Ramparts Press, 1971.

Smith, Michael P., and Bernadette Tarallo. "The Unsettling Resettlement of Vietnamese Boat People." *USA Today Magazine*, March 1993, 27–29.

Smith, Winnie. *American Daughter Gone to War: On the Front Lines with an Army Nurse in Vietnam*. 1992. Reprint. New York: Pocket Books Schuster, 1994.

Sorrentino, Christopher. *Trance*. New York: Farrar, Straus and Giroux, 2005.

Spencer, Elizabeth. *The Night Travellers*. New York: Viking, 1991.

Spiotta, Dana. *Eat the Document: A Novel*. New York: Scribner, 2006.

Staples, Brent. "The Oldest Rad." *New York Times Book Review*, 30 September 2001, 11.

Stanton, Maura. "Oz." In *The Country I Come From*, 25–35. Minneapolis: Milkweed Editions, 1988.

Steinhorn, Leonard. *The Greater Generation: In Defense of the Baby Boom Legacy*. New York: Thomas Dunne Books/St. Martin's Press, 2006.

Stockdale, James A. *A Vietnam Experience: Ten Years of Reflection*. Stanford, Calif.: Hoover Institution, 1984.

Stockdale, Jim, and Sybil Stockdale. *In Love and War: The Story of a Family's Ordeal and Sacrifice during the Vietnam Years*. 1984. Reprint. New York: Bantam Books, 1985.

Stolen Honor: Wounds That Never Heal. Directed by Carlton Sherwood. Red, White & Blue Productions, 2004.

Strom, Dao. *The Gentle Order of Girls and Boys: Four Stories.* New York: Counterpoint/ Perseus Books Group, 2006.

———. *Grass Roof, Tin Roof.* Boston: Houghton Mifflin, 2003.

Students for a Democratic Society. "Port Huron Statement." 1962. *The Sixties Project.* 1993. http://www.iath.virginia.edu/sixties/HTML_docs/Resources/Primary/Manifestos /SDS_Port_Huron.html (accessed 29 January 2006).

Summer of Love. Directed by Gail Dolgin and Vicente Franco. PBS. *American Experience*, 2007. http://www.pbs.org/wgbh/amex/love/.

Swift Vets and POWs for Truth. http://www.swiftvets.com/. (accessed 24 July 2005).

Tabin, John. "An Evening with Bill Ayers." *WSJ.com Opinion Journal*, 16 November 2001. http://opinionjournal.com/extra/?id=95001485 (accessed 28 June 2006).

Taylor, Laura. *Honorbound.* 1988. Reprint. New York: Jove Books, 1990.

Taylor, Pat Ellis. "A Call from Brotherland" and "Descent into Brotherland." In *Afoot in a Field of Men*, 99–106 and 107–112. New York: Atlantic Monthly Press, 1988.

Taxi Driver. Directed by Martin Scorsese. Columbia Pictures, 1976. DVD. Columbia TriStar Home Video, 2004.

Terry, Wallace. *Bloods: An Oral History of the Vietnam War by Black Veterans.* New York: Ballantine Books, 1984.

thúy, lê thi diem. *The Gangster We Are All Looking For.* New York: Knopf, 2003.

Timmons, Heather. "I Saw a Deadhead Sticker on a Bentley." *New York Times on the Web*, 9 June 2006. http://nytimes.com/2006/06/09/business/ 09hedge.html?ex=115 1985600&en=e3ab1c5f156cae2c&ei=5070 (accessed 2 July 2006).

Tram, Dang Thuy. *Last Night I Dreamed of Peace: The Diary of Dang Thuy Tram.* New York: Harmony Books, 2007.

Trussoni, Danielle. *Falling through the Earth: A Memoir.* New York: Henry Holt, 2006.

Turow, Scott. *The Laws of Our Fathers.* New York: Warner Books, 1996.

Ulee's Gold. Directed by Victor Nunez. Clinica Estetico Ltd., MGM Home Entertainment, 1997.

U.S. Senate Committee on Foreign Relations. *Legislative Proposals Relating to the War in Southeast Asia*, 22 April 1971. 32 pp. http://www.cwes01.com/13790/23910/ktpp 179-210.pdf (accessed 14 February 2007).

Van Devanter, Lynda, with Christopher Morgan. *Home before Morning: The Story of an Army Nurse in Vietnam.* 1983. Reprint. Amherst: University of Massachusetts Press, 2001.

Van Devanter, Lynda, and Joan A. Furey, eds. *Visions of War, Dreams of Peace: Writings of Women in the Vietnam War.* New York: Warner Books, 1991.

Vaughn, Stephanie. "Kid MacArthur." In *Sweet Talk*, 100–136. New York: Random House, 1990.

Vietnam Passage: Journeys from War to Peace. Directed by Sandy Northrop. Wind and Star Production Group, PBS, 2002.

Vu, Tran. "The Coral Reef." In *The Dragon Hunt*, 1–21. New York: Hyperion, 1999.

Walker, Keith. *A Piece of My Heart: The Stories of 26 American Women Who Served in Vietnam*. 1985. Reprint. Novanto, Calif. Presidio Press. 1997.

Walsh, Jeffrey. *American War Literature, 1914 to Vietnam*. New York: St. Martin's Press, 1982.

The War at Home. Directed by Emilio Estevez. Touchstone Pictures/Buena Vista Pictures, 1996.

The Weather Underground. Directed by Sam Green and Bill Siegel. Free History Project/Shadow Distribution, 2003.

Webb, Kate. *On the Other Side: 23 Days with the Viet Cong*. New York: Quadrangle Books, 1972.

Webb, James H. *A Country Such as This*. 1983. Reprint. New York: Bantam Books, 1985.

———. *Fields of Fire*. 1978. Reprint. New York: Bantam Books, 1979.

Wells, Tom. *The War Within: America's Battle over Vietnam*. Berkeley: University of California Press, 1994.

Wheeler, John. *Touched with Fire: The Future of the Vietnam Generation*. New York: Avon Books, 1984.

Wiest, Andrew A. *The Vietnam War, 1956–1975*. New York: Routledge, 2003.

Wills, Garry. *John Wayne's America: The Politics of Celebrity*. New York: Simon & Schuster, 1997.

Wilson, Edmund. *The Shores of Light: A Literary Chronicle of the Twenties and Thirties*. New York: Farrar, Straus and Young, 1952.

Wiltz, Teresa. "Joan Baez Unwelcome at Concert for Troops." Washingtonpost.com, 2 May 2007. http://www.washingtonpost.com/wp-dyn/content/article/2007/05/01/AR2007050101999.html (accessed 15 June 2007).

Winter Soldier Investigation. *What Are We Doing to Ourselves?* 31 January–2 February 1971. http://www3.iath.virginia.edu/sixties/HTML_docs/Resources/Primary/Winter_Soldier/WS_18_Ourselves.html (accessed 14 February 2007).

Wolfe, Alan. "The Left's Self-Destructive Extremism." *Chronicle of Higher Education*, 12 October 2001. http://chronicle.com/weekly/v48/i07/07b01301.htm (accessed 4 July 2006).

Wolfe, Tom, and E. W. Johnson, eds. *The New Journalism*. New York: Harper & Row, 1973.

Wolff, Tobias. *In Pharoah's Army: Memories of the Lost War*. New York: Knopf, 1994.

Wood, Robin. *Hollywood from Vietnam to Reagan*. New York: Columbia University Press, 1986.

Woolf, Virginia. *Three Guineas*. New York: Harvest/HBJ Books, 1938.

Wright, Stephen. *Meditations in Green*. 1983. Reprint. New York: Bantam Books, 1984.

[Wyatt, Barbara Powers, ed.] *We Came Home*. Toluca Lake, Ca.: P.O.W. Publications, 1977.

Yeats, William Butler. "The Second Coming." In *Selected Poems and Two Plays of William Butler Yeats*, edited by M. L. Rosenthal. New York: Collier Books, 1967.

Zacharias, Karen Spears. *Hero Mama: A Daughter Remembers the Father She Lost in Vietnam—and the Mother Who Held Her Family Together*. New York: William Morrow/HarperCollins, 2005.

Zaroulis, Nancy, and Gerald Sullivan. *Who Spoke Up? American Protest against the War in Vietnam, 1963–1975*. New York: Doubleday, 1984.

Zavarzadeh, Mas'ud. *The Mythopoeic Reality: The Postwar American Nonfiction Novel*. Urbana: University of Illinois Press, 1976.

Zhou, Min, and Carl L. Bankston III. *Growing Up American: How Vietnamese Children Adapt to Life in the United States*. New York: Russell Sage Foundation, 1998.

Index

Vietnamese in America (*continued*)
ties and, 274–77; bifurcation of, 269–74,
277–80; breaking connections and, 257–
63; diminution and, 263–65; language
acquisition by, 278, 280–83; parent-child
relationships and, 277–80; pilgrimages to
Vietnam by, 71–72, 290–93; shared bonds
and, 265–69; stereotypes of, 254–55
Vietnam Passage (film), 291
Vietnam-Persakie (Ehrhart), 29–30
Vietnam Veterans Memorial, 7–9, 15, 81, 97,
297, 304n8; pilgrimages to, 89–90, 222,
267, 286
Vietnam Women's Memorial Project, 8, 63
"Visitors" (Phan), 275
Vonnegut, Kurt, 68
Vu, Lan, 291
Vu, Tran, 310n1

Waiting Room, The (Morris), 66–67, 86–87,
94
Waiting Wives (Moreau), 74
Walker, Keith, 63
"Walls, the House, the Sky, The" (Lai), 264
Walsh, Jeffrey, 10
War at Home, The (film), 31–32, 49, 52–53, 56
Wayne, John. *See* "John Wayne syndrome"
Weather Underground, 155, 168–69, 217–18,
223–24, 230; fictionalized accounts of,
163, 166, 177, 181, 183–86, 196–97, 199;
members of, 207, 236; women in, 309n14
Weather Underground, The (film), 161
Webb, James, 203; *A Country Such as This*,
119–20, 131, 157–58; *Fields of Fire*, 30,
34, 75
Webb, Kate, 11, 103, 143, 144–45
We Came Home (Wyatt & Wyatt), 100
Wells, Tom, 209
We Should Never Meet (Phan), 289–90
We Were Soldiers (film), 74
"What Happened to Wendell?" (Bradley), 93
"What Kind of Furniture Would Jesus
Pick?" (Proulx), 25
Wheeler, John, 14
When Heaven and Earth Changed Places
(Hayslip), 291–92
When Hell Was in Session (Denton), 104,
105, 110

Wiest, Andrew, 250
Wills, Garry, 57
Windchill Summer (N.C. Mailer), 78–81
"Winter Dreams" (F.S. Fitzgerald), 26
wives, 44, 73–81, 97; adulterous, 136–38;
antiwar movement and, 134–36; asexual-
ity of, 133–34; empowerment of, 138–39;
gender roles and, 142; limbo for, 125–29;
of POWs/MIAs, 102, 124, 125–43; shared
bonds and, 127–28, 139–43; stereotypes of,
47–48; women's movement and, 128–29;
"you had to be there" and, 139, 141
Wolfe, Alan, 208
Wolff, Tobias, 24, 29
women, 26, 43–50, 60–69, 95–97, 295;
in antiwar movement, 173–76, 218,
238–45; in civil rights movement, 174; as
daughters, 70–73, 74–75, 97; metaphor,
use of, by, 92–95; as mothers, 49; post-
traumatic stress disorder and, 63, 75, 77;
as POWs/MIAs, 103, 144–45; in SDS,
241; as sisters, 81–92, 97; stereotypes of,
46–50; as veterans, 8, 63–65; Vietnamese, 50; as wives/lovers, 44, 73–81, 97,
102, 124, 125–43
women's movement, 7, 44, 61–62, 230, 241;
antiwar movement and, 174, 240–45;
POW/MIA wives and, 128–29
Wood, Robin, 28
Woodstock festival (1969), 190, 204, 219
Woolf, Virginia, 61
World War II, 5, 14, 16, 57, 142, 296
Wright, Stephen, 21
Wyatt, Frederic (Capt. and Mrs.), 100
Wyler, William, 16

Yet Another Voice (N. McDaniel), 116, 124
Yoshimura, Wendy, 177
"you had to be there," 296; antiwar movement and, 161, 306n6, 309n16; POWs/
MIAs and, 112; veterans and, 17–20, 23,
31, 54, 66–67, 69, 77; wives of POWs/
MIAs and, 139, 141

Zacharias, Karen Spears, 71–72
Zaroulis, Nancy, 165, 209
Zhou, Min, 278